ZEPPELIN ONSLAUGHT

*For Mum and Dad
This is what I do all day!*

ZEPPELIN ONSLAUGHT

The Forgotten Blitz 1914 – 1915

IAN CASTLE

FRONTLINE
BOOKS

ZEPPELIN ONSLAUGHT
The Forgotten Blitz 1914 – 1915

First published in 2018 by Frontline Books,
an imprint of Pen & Sword Books Ltd,
47 Church Street, Barnsley, S. Yorkshire, S70 2AS

Copyright © Ian Castle, 2018

The right of Ian Castle to be identified as the author of this work has been asserted by him in accordance with the Copyright, Designs and Patents Act 1988.

ISBN: 978-1-84832-433-6

All rights reserved. No part of this publication may be reproduced, stored in or introduced into a retrieval system, or transmitted, in any form, or by any means (electronic, mechanical, photocopying, recording or otherwise) without the prior written permission of the publisher. Any person who does any unauthorized act in relation to this publication may be liable to criminal prosecution and civil claims for damages.

CIP data records for this title are available from the British Library

Printed and bound by TJ International Ltd, Padstow, Cornwall
Typeset in 10.5/13 point Palatino

For more information on our books, please visit
www.frontline-books.com,
email info@frontline-books.com
or write to us at the above address.

Contents

Introduction		vii
Acknowledgements		ix
Chapter 1	'No Longer an Island'	1
Chapter 2	Something Out of Nothing	5
Chapter 3	Attack is the Best Form of Defence	16
Chapter 4	'Forcing England to Her Knees'	31
Chapter 5	'Oh, Good God, What is It?'	45
Chapter 6	'Discovering a New Country'	63
Chapter 7	'Only H.V.B. on Board'	79
Chapter 8	'The Devils Have Come!'	94
Chapter 9	A Glimmer of Hope	112
Chapter 10	London's Burning	124
Chapter 11	The 'Experiment' is Over	144
Chapter 12	The Guns Strike Back	160
Chapter 13	'Gazing With Horror and Dread'	178
Chapter 14	'An Absolute Feeling of Helplessness'	193
Chapter 15	'A Beautiful but Terrifying Sight'	213
Chapter 16	'What Are You Going to do About These Airship Raids?'	232
Chapter 17	London Surrounded	249
Chapter 18	'The Earth Shook and Trembled'	268
Chapter 19	The Home Front Line	288

CONTENTS

Appendices
    Appendix I   German Airship Numbering Systems   303

    Appendix II   Airship Raids 1915   305

    Appendix III   Individuals Killed in Air Raids – 1915   307

References and Notes   315

Bibliography   337

Index   343

LIST OF MAPS

Map 1	Zeppelins over East Anglia, January to April 1915	xi
Map 2	Aeroplane Raids December 1914 to September 1915	xii
Map 3	The Raids of Army Zeppelin LZ 38, 29 April to 31 May 1915	xiii
Map 4	Zeppelin Raids Around the Humber, June to August 1915; Zeppelin Raids Around the Tyne, April to June 1915	xiv
Map 5	Zeppelins Over London, August to September 1915	xv
Map 6	Zeppelins Over Essex and Suffolk, 11-14 September 1915	xvi
Map 7	London Surrounded – The Zeppelin Raid of 13-14 October 1915	xvii
Map 8	Zeppelin Raid Penetration 1915	xviii

Introduction

About fifteen years ago, while strolling around London one lunchtime, I stumbled across a plaque on a building in Farringdon Road. It showed that a Zeppelin bomb had destroyed the original building during an air raid in the First World War. As a military historian and a Londoner it occurred to me that period of London's history was one I knew very little of. I began to read what I could find, which was all very interesting but inevitably it did not go into the level of detail that I love. I started carrying out my own research, which in time resulted in two books on different phases of the London raids. In numerous conversations after this, people often commented they were unaware that Britain had been bombed prior to the Blitz of 1940. Those early twentieth century air raids had become almost a forgotten Blitz.

With the approach of the centenary of the First World War, I spread my research further afield and began to build a website detailing the air raids on all parts of the country, to reveal just how wide-ranging they were. I am therefore extremely grateful to Martin Mace of Frontline Books who saw the potential in my research and offered me the opportunity to expand it further into a series of books, which will eventually extend to three volumes, offering a level of detail not previously available. By bringing together stories from all corners of the country, from autobiographies, letters, diaries and newspapers, and weaving them together with official accounts, I believe I have been able to present a new and revealing insight into this first war on the Home Front.

While benefiting from these resources I have at the same time been frustrated and saddened by the absence of a national register listing those civilians killed in air raids. Their sacrifices deserve to be remembered as much as those of servicemen at the Front, at sea or in the air. During the process of writing this book I began building a list of my own and, perhaps surprisingly, the last two London raids have proved the most difficult to complete. I would therefore be delighted to hear from anyone who can help fill those gaps.

Acknowledgements

Although writing a book is naturally a solitary existence, through the magic of the internet help and assistance is always close at hand from people near and far. I owe a debt of gratitude to many. From Germany, Marton Szigeti provided me with excellent information on the raids on the Düsseldorf Zeppelin sheds, while in France, Benoit Dubus kindly granted me permission to quote from his great grandfather's diary on the same subject. Closer to home, I must thank Steve Smith for our numerous long discussions on the raids on Great Yarmouth and King's Lynn and for his enthusiasm in visiting the sites we discussed to photograph them for me. Rob Langham helped me with information regarding the North Eastern Railway and at the other end of the country, Andy White kindly made available a copy of *The History of Gravesend*. I met Christopher Langdon of the Southend Museum at a talk I gave in the town and he has subsequently answered a number of my questions regarding finer details of the two Zeppelin raids there. In London, Elizabeth Green at the Hackney Archives helped with copies of newspaper reports covering the first London raid. Then, while working on the details of the London raid on the night of 8–9 September 1915, I received helpful information from Helen MacDonald at the Carnegie Hero Fund Trust, and Sandra Gittins alerted me to the involvement of a group of men from the Great Western Railway. In other matters concerning that raid, I received a warm welcome at Wrotham Park from Charles Dace, the archivist there. For the final raid of the year, in October 1915, I received valuable assistance from Andrew Mussell, Archivist of the Honourable Society of Gray's Inn and from Rose Brown and Rachael Merrison, archivists at St Bartholomew's Hospital Archive. In addition, I would like to thank Aura Hargreaves for permission to quote from a letter on her website (www.ww1-letters.com) and Richard Dunning for some local insight into the raid on the Guildford area.

ACKNOWLEDGEMENTS

In Austria, as ever, I thank my friend Martin Worel, who is always available to help with German translations, and I offer special thanks to Alastair Reid. After a discussion, he translated the whole of Pitt Klein's 1934 book *'Achtung! Bomben Fallen!'* and has made it available in English for the first time, through Lulu.com, and from which I have quoted.

Throughout the course of writing this book I have been able to check Zeppelin facts with author Ray Rimell and always enjoy my exchanges with David Marks, another who, like me, caught 'Zeppelinitis' many moons ago and supplied many of the illustrations used in this book from his wonderful collection.

On this occasion though, my biggest debt of gratitude must go to Ian Campbell in Australia. Ian 'found' me through my website back in 2014 after seeing a Zeppelin documentary aired on television. His enthusiasm for the website project saw him using his editorial experience to run an eagle eye over each entry as I added it. With the start of the book he continued in this role, reading chapters as I completed them, coming back with advice or suggestions for greater clarity and readability. I cannot thank him enough for his help. Nor can my partner Nicola as it saved her the task!

Ian Castle,
February 2017,
www.IanCastleZeppelin.co.uk.

Map 1: Zeppelins over East Anglia, January to April 1915

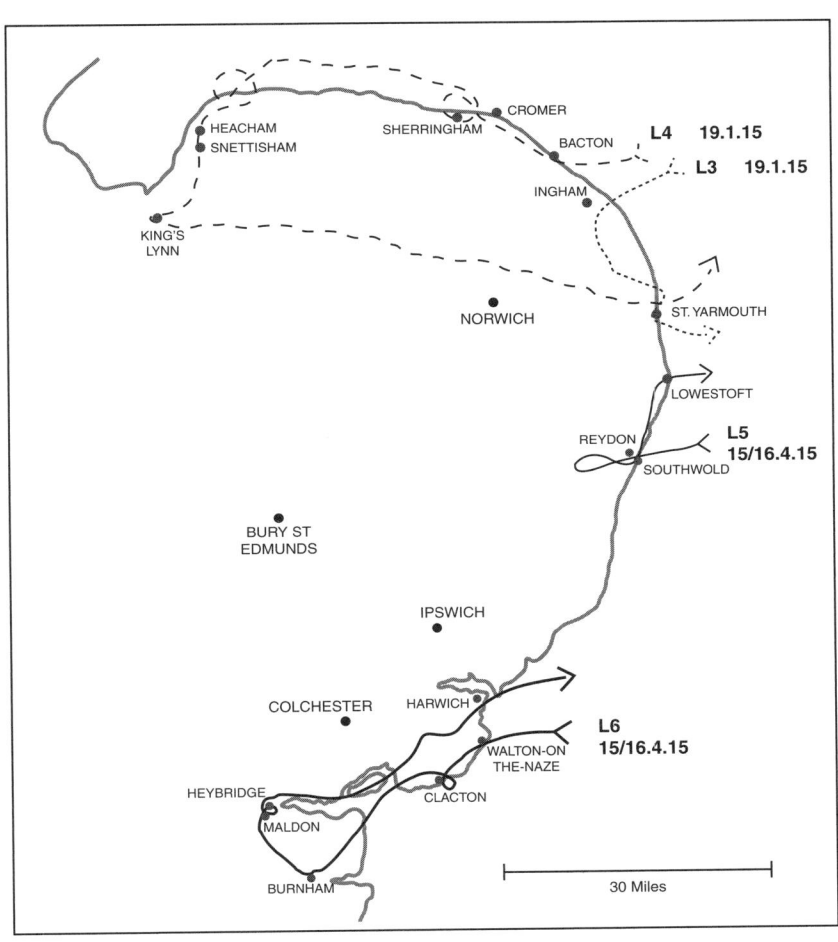

Map 2: Aeroplane Raids December 1914 to September 1915

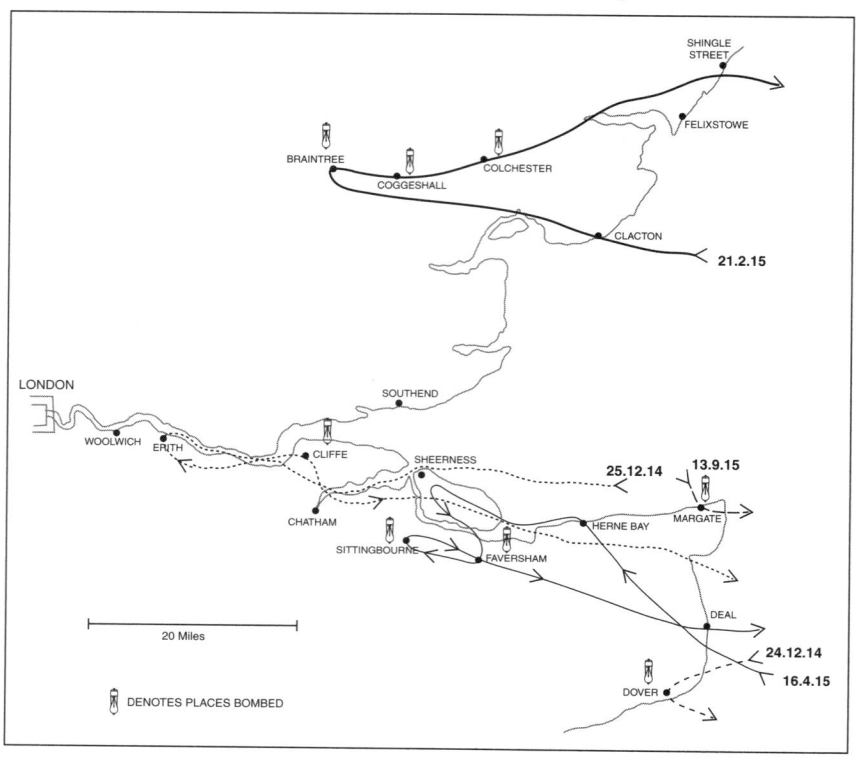

Map 3: The Raids of Army Zeppelin LZ 38, 29 April to 31 May 1915

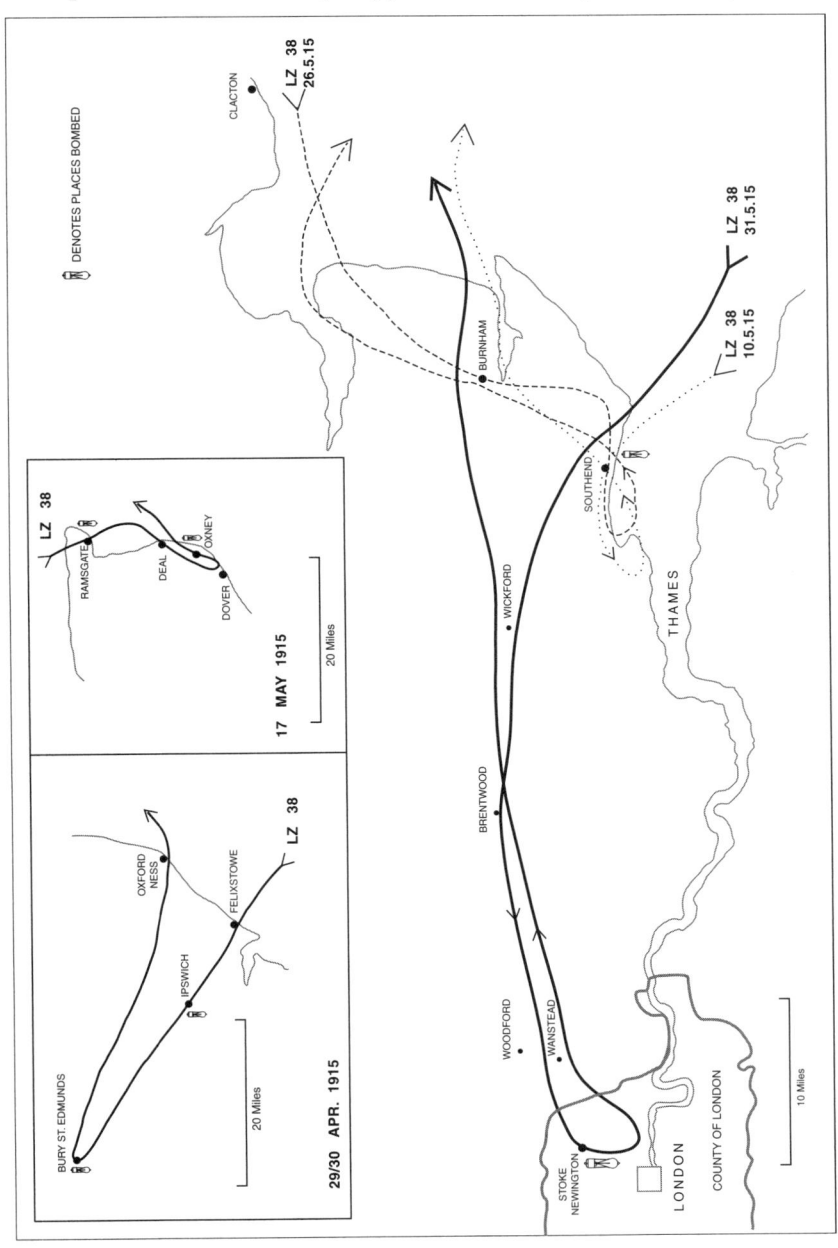

Map 4: Zeppelin Raids Around the Humber, June to August 1915 (top), and, bottom, Zeppelin Raids Around the Tyne, April to June 1915

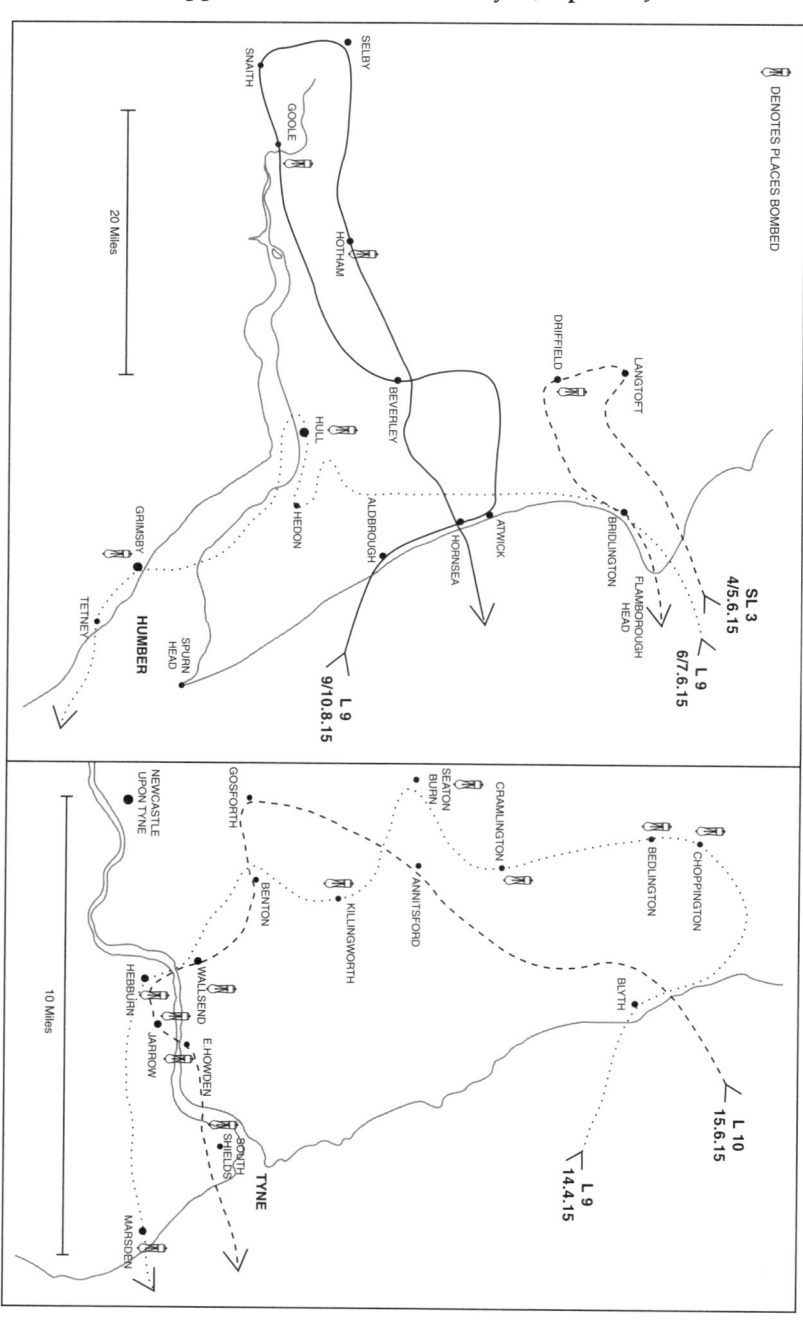

Map 5: Zeppelins Over London, August to September 1915

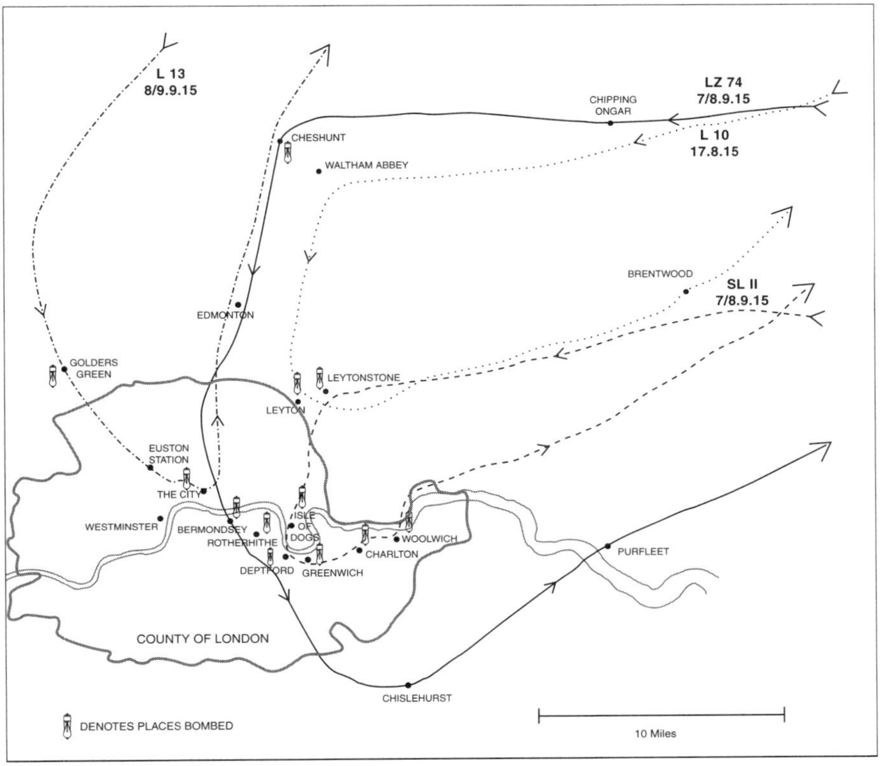

Map 6: Zeppelins Over Essex and Suffolk, 11-14 September 1915

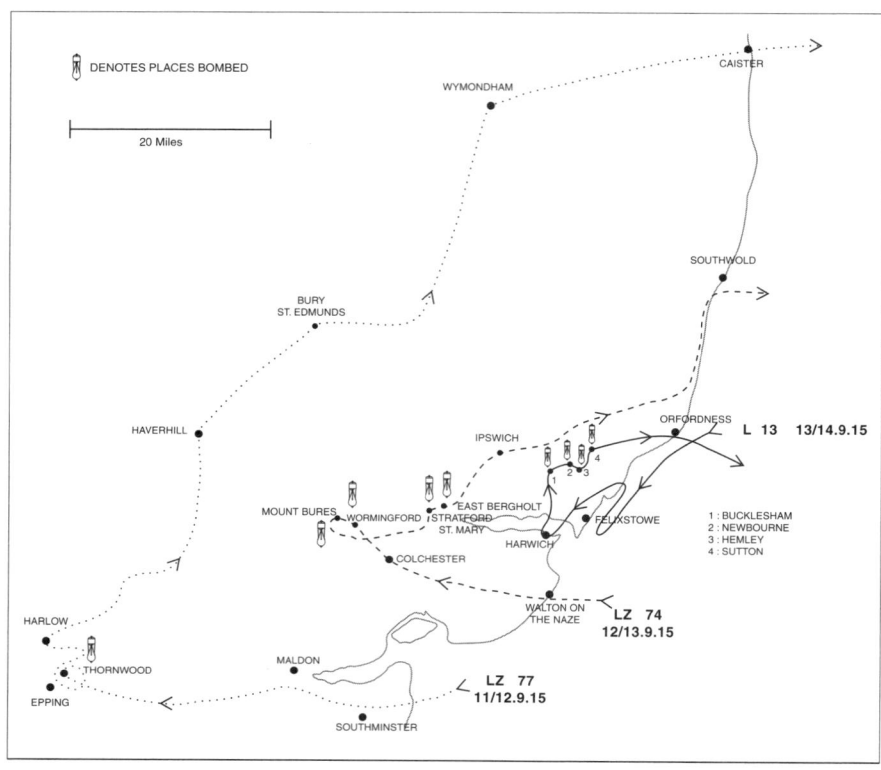

Map 7: London Surrounded – The Zeppelin Raid of 13-14 October 1915

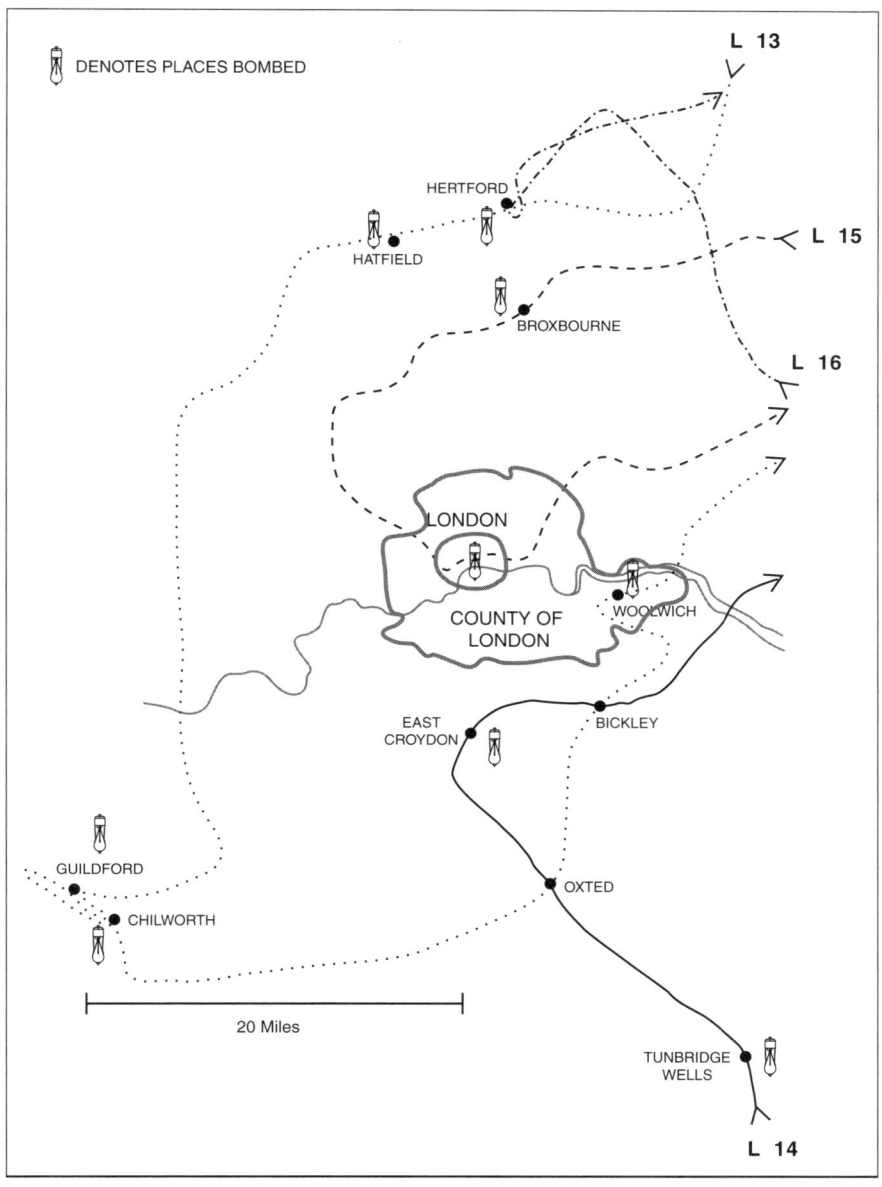

Map 8: Zeppelin Raid Penetration 1915

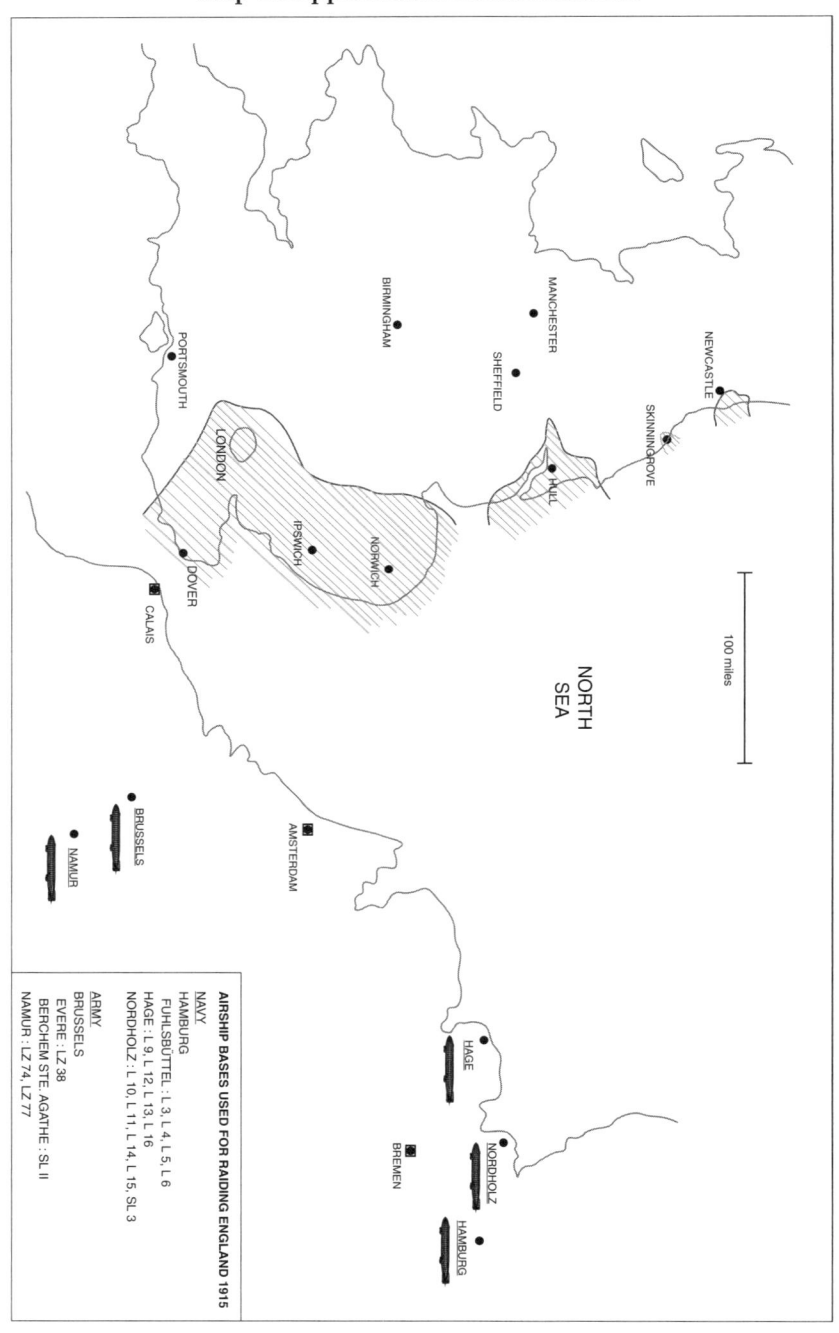

Chapter 1

'No Longer an Island'

Shortly after 4.00pm on a cold Monday in November 1906, a 33-year-old Brazilian aviation pioneer, Alberto Santos-Dumont, entered the record books for a second time. He already had a place there, having become a French celebrity five years earlier when he flew his own airship, *No. 6*, on a 7-mile course that took him around the Eiffel Tower and earned him prize money of 100,000 francs. In 1905 he had turned his considerable engineering talents to aeroplanes and now, a year later, from a field at the Château de Bagatelle outside Paris, a new flight record was about to become his.

Starting on the morning of 12 November 1906, before an audience estimated at a thousand enthusiastic onlookers, Santos-Dumont's first three attempted flights were disappointing, little more than exaggerated hops, but his fourth attempt in the autumnal twilight was different. His aircraft, *14-bis*, also known as *Oiseau de proie (Bird of Prey)*, reluctantly clawed its way up to a height of about five metres and, without touching the ground, flew in level flight for 21 seconds covering a distance calculated at 220 metres (722 feet). The *Fédération Aéronautique Internationale* recognized the achievement, handing him the world record for the first flight of 100 metres or more and allowing him to claim a prize of 1,500 francs. For many, this flight eclipsed the exploits of the Wright brothers three years earlier; Santos-Dumont's aircraft had an undercarriage and became airborne under its own power while the Wright brothers used a launch rail to get their *Wright Flyer* into the air.

Back in England, one man in particular kept a very close eye on this pioneering progress in aviation. That man was the newspaper baron, Lord Northcliffe, owner of *The Times*, *Daily Mail*, *Daily Mirror* and London's *Evening News*. Northcliffe, who sensed Britain falling behind countries such as France and Germany in the science of aeronautics, appointed a journalist at the *Daily Mail* as Air Correspondent, informing him: 'Make no mistake, the future lies in the air.'[1]

At 5.30am on 13 November 1906, just like any other day, Lord Northcliffe had the morning newspapers delivered to his bedroom. He opened a copy of his *Daily Mail* and found a brief matter-of-fact account of Santos-Dumont's record flight the previous afternoon. By the end of it he was fuming. His editor, as far as Northcliffe was concerned, had missed the significance of the story. He phoned him in a fury. The story, he impatiently explained to the editor, was not 'Santos-Dumont flies 722 feet', the story was 'England is no longer an island ... It means the aerial chariots of a foe descending on British soil when war comes'.[2]

Lord Northcliffe was right. And when those aerial chariots did appear just over eight years later, the air defences of Britain were still largely non-existent.

***

Britain lagged behind in the conquest of the air. The first recognized sustained powered flight in Britain only took place in October 1908, five years after the Wright Brothers, in an aeroplane designed, built and flown for the Army by an American, Samuel Franklin Cody. That flight across Farnborough Common in Hampshire lasted 27 seconds before Cody crashed having covered a distance of 1,390 feet.

Everywhere the skies were buzzing with new aircraft. Nine months later, in July 1909, the French aviation pioneer Louis Blériot made a rather more significant flight when he became the first man to pilot an aeroplane over the English Channel. He won the prize money of £1,000 offered by Lord Northcliffe's *Daily Mail*. Britain was indeed no longer an island.

Hard-earned records lasted but briefly as aviation development gripped the world and proceeded at a feverish pace, but not in Britain. As one writer put it:

> the heroic achievement of spring became the daily average performance of the ensuing autumn. The movement was fairly under way, and nothing could stop it ... In all these doings England bore but a small part ... To speak of England's share in these amazing years of progress is to tell the history of a backward parish, and to describe its small contribution to a great world-wide movement.[3]

The first steps in Britain to put matters on a more official footing came in 1911 when the Royal Engineers' Balloon Section evolved into the Air

Battalion. Previously the British government based its aviation policy on keeping abreast of developments rather than hastening them: 'It was felt that we stood to gain nothing by forcing a means of warfare which tended to reduce the value of our insular position and the protection of our sea power.'[4] By the autumn of 1911, however, attitudes began to change. The Committee of Imperial Defence (CID) appointed a technical sub-committee to study military aviation and the possibilities of expanding the Air Battalion into a more extensive organization. Their report passed through the various stages of approval with surprising alacrity and led to the creation of the Royal Flying Corps in April 1912, with both a military and naval wing.

Two months later the sub-committee sent two men, Captain Murray Sueter, Royal Navy, and Mervyn O'Gorman, the superintendent of the Royal Aircraft Factory, on a fact-finding mission.[5] The previous year Sueter had led the Navy's failed attempt to build and launch a British version of the Zeppelin airship and later in 1912 would become head of the Admiralty's newly created Air Department.[6] However, for now the two men were to travel to the continent and prepare a report on the state of aviation in Europe, paying particular attention to airship developments. They travelled extensively visiting airfields and factories in France, Germany and Austria. But while the German authorities granted quite generous access to their facilities, they drew the line at allowing their British visitors to board a Zeppelin. Zeppelin airships provided a very visible icon of German technical superiority in lighter-than-air flight and the German authorities were determined to keep its secrets from rival nations. Undeterred, Sueter and O'Gorman 'disguised themselves as Americans' – without detailing how this was achieved – and managed to travel as passengers on a six-hour flight on the *Viktoria Luise,* one of the commercial Zeppelins much-loved by the German people. They were impressed with what they saw and what they learnt in conversation with a German naval lieutenant attached to the airship for training. Their report detailed that current Zeppelins had the range to patrol the entire German coast; they could also fly to Britain and back without the need to refuel. They also learnt that Zeppelins had dropped bomb loads of up to 1,000lb in training exercises. When Sueter and O'Gorman delivered their report to the CID's technical sub-committee, chaired by Colonel J.E.B. Seely, the Under-Secretary of State for War, they concluded with disarming understatement: 'For any nation to have a ton of explosives dropped above their Admiralty, War Office, or Administrative buildings would, to say the least of it, be inconvenient'. When the sub-committee delivered the final report to the CID, it highlighted the threat German airships posed to Britain in a future war. Yet the government's response remained lukewarm while it considered the best course of action. And just two years later that war did come, on 4 August 1914, with the country still largely defenceless in the face of aerial attack.

Chapter 2

Something Out of Nothing

In the summer of 1914, after weeks of brinksmanship, the alliances that held Europe together now led the great nations of the continent on a rapid descent into war. On 4 August Britain placed the final piece in the jigsaw when it honoured its agreement to uphold Belgium's neutrality by declaring war on Germany as troops from that country poured across its border.

Just a month earlier, at this most tense of times, the military and naval wings of Britain's embryonic Royal Flying Corps separated. The two wings had differing agendas and right from the creation of the single body the naval wing had not always followed the prescribed course; now the Admiralty determined to take full control over her airmen.

The military wing had always had a clear understanding of its role in any coming war. For the Army flyers that role was reconnaissance. When any expeditionary force left Britain, the military wing would operate with it, conducting observation flights to watch and report on the movements of the enemy. For the naval men, their position was more complex. For centuries the Royal Navy had protected Britain's shores by its presence on the world's oceans. Due to the limited range of aircraft at this time, the initial role for naval aircraft was restricted to coastal defence. After setting up the first naval aeroplane station on an airfield at Eastchurch on the Isle of Sheppey, others for seaplanes appeared at Calshot, Felixstowe, Yarmouth and Cromarty. In time more stations joined the roster.

Much of the work undertaken by the naval wing prior to the outbreak of war had been of an experimental nature, particularly involved with developing the aeroplane as a fighting machine. Commander (Cdr)

Charles Samson led this work at Eastchurch. Experiments in bomb dropping began in 1912 when Samson first dropped a dummy 100lb bomb, and in the following year further experiments took place to determine the lowest height from which bombs of a certain weight could be dropped without endangering the pilot. Other experiments included looking at ways to destroy a Zeppelin and the use of machine guns on aircraft. This work by the naval wing received much encouragement from Captain (Capt) Murray Sueter, now in his role as Director of the Air Department at the Admiralty, which body also provided significant funding.

The War Office strongly maintained that responsibility for home defence lay with the Army and therefore its aerial defence should fall to the military wing of the Royal Flying Corps. In August 1912, following discussions concerned with coastal defence, the military wing was allotted responsibility to provide aircraft to be 'employed in conjunction with the fixed and mobile land defences of defended ports'. At the same time the naval wing would provide aircraft to support the fleet and for coastal patrol duties.[1] The War Office, however, failed to establish any concerted plans for home defence. Even so, at a conference in November 1913, it confirmed its responsibility, but agreed with the Admiralty that naval aircraft would defend significant naval establishments within reach of their coastal stations. This concern for potential attacks on British ports had existed since the Home Ports Defence Committee had, in 1910, considered airship progress in Europe and declared that air attacks on Britain 'should be regarded as *possible* operations of war'.[2] Despite the determination of the War Office to assert its role in home defence, in reality, it would lack the aircraft to fulfil its responsibility should war come

With the needs of the military wing and the naval wing following ever-divergent paths, they officially separated in July 1914, with the military wing absorbing the title Royal Flying Corps (RFC) and the naval wing becoming the Royal Naval Air Service (RNAS). This did little to solve the already uncoordinated attitudes to home defence.

At the outbreak of war the four completed squadrons of the RFC (Nos 2, 3, 4 and 5) flew out, arriving in France between 13–15 August to operate with the British Expeditionary Force. They had a mixed bag of aircraft: B.E.2, Blériot, Henri Farman, Avro 504 and B.E.8. What they left behind in Britain appears on paper to be a significant force, but numbers can be deceptive. Of these 116 aircraft, as one commentator put it: 'About 20 of them, more or less old fashioned, were in use at the Central Flying School for purposes of training; the rest were worn out or broken, and were fit only for the scrap heap.'[3] It was clear to the War Office that the RFC aircraft and men remaining behind could not effectively defend the skies over Britain and had to admit that it did not actually have a plan anyway. Fortunately the RNAS did have aircraft available, had air stations established on the coast and had given the subject of aerial defence some consideration. If the Zeppelins came it would fall to them to rise in opposition, but how effective they might be remained an unknown quantity.

British knowledge of the current German rigid airships was relatively well informed at the outbreak of war. Germany had 11 rigid airships at the time and although both the Army and the Navy were intent on building separate fleets, the German Army owned ten and the Navy just one in August 1914. There were two manufacturers building rigid airships, Zeppelin and Schütte–Lanz, which fundamentally looked similar but utilized different construction materials: Zeppelins initially had a framework of aluminium later replaced by duralumin – an aluminium alloy – while Schütte–Lanz employed laminated plywood. To those in Britain during the coming war, however, all German airships were simply known as 'Zeppelins'.

The German Army decommissioned the obsolete Zeppelin Z II (Ersatz) and Z III on 1 August 1914, leaving it with six Zeppelins (designated Z IV to Z IX), a single Schütte–Lanz, SL II, and three former civil Zeppelins, *Viktoria Luise*, *Hansa*, and *Sachsen*. The first two civil airships became training ships. *Sachsen* returned to the workshop for alterations to enable her to play an active role in the war, but she too soon 'retired' to the status of training ship. The Navy had a single airship, Zeppelin L 3, but with more on order. Of these 11 airships available to Germany in August 1914, Britain acknowledged that in suitable weather conditions five of them – the Army's Z VII, Z VIII, Z IX and SL II along with the Navy's L 3 – could potentially make a return flight to Britain carrying bombs.[4]

The steady progress of German airship development had received significant coverage in the British press over recent years. Each flight of its civil Zeppelins was carefully recorded and the interest shown by the German Army and Navy revealed, while in March 1913 newspapers reported that following successful trials, 'all Army and Navy Zeppelins airships built in the future will be fitted with machine guns'.[5] Clearly Germany was preparing her airships for war. When war did come, many in Britain, in both official and public circles, therefore anticipated an early aerial attack. The German Army, which possessed most of the nation's airships at the time, however, had other ideas. The Army anticipated her airships would provide her with great advantages as her troops launched their attacks into Belgium and France, and allocated four of their seven front-line airships for service with the armies in the west, with the remaining three supporting the Army operating in East Prussia against the Russians. Airships had never been flown in war before and mistakes made in the first few weeks quickly diminished any early threat to Britain from the air, even if it had been Germany's ultimate intention.

An experienced Zeppelin commander, Ernst Lehmann, at that time assigned to the former civilian airship *Sachsen,* was unimpressed with the Army higher command.

> We could see the lack of airship preparedness all about us. We had no bombs, neither explosive nor incendiary types, though everybody had taken it for granted that bombing would be one of the principal duties of the Zeppelins. The general staff evidently thought so, too, judging by its orders.[6]

In the west, on 6 August, Army airship Z VI took part in an attack on the Belgium city of Liège. There were no specialized aerial bombs available at the beginning of the war. Instead the crew carried five or six artillery shells (15cm howitzer grenades and a 21cm mortar grenade) which they planned to drop over the side, attaching blankets to them to give stability in flight. The airship successfully reached Liège, but cloud cover and the weight of the makeshift bombs kept her at a relatively low altitude such that she became a target for the guns in the forts defending the city and 'even made a fine target for the infantry behind the forts.'[7] Shrapnel and bullets cut into the gas cells of Z VI as she dropped her bombs, causing precious hydrogen to escape and forcing her even lower. She attempted to get back to her home base at Cologne about 85 miles away but the crew struggled to maintain control and she eventually made a bad landing in a forest near Bonn and was wrecked.

Keen to get maximum value from this new weapon, an officer of the general staff accompanied each of the Zeppelins on these early attacks to gain information on the enemy at first hand. It fell to him, whether he had any experience of airships or not, to select the route and targets to bomb. Lehmann noted the failings inherent in this system:

> Our pre-war [Zeppelin] types could not carry enough bombs, could not fly high enough, fast enough or far enough to accomplish the

missions which the general staff at first assigned them. But they tried it.[8]

Lehmann could have added, 'with disastrous results'.

On 21 August 1914 the German High Command ordered two Zeppelins, Z VII and Z VIII, on daylight reconnaissance flights to locate the retreating French First and Second Armies in Lorraine. Having negotiated her way with difficulty over the Vosges Mountains, Z VII dropped artillery shell 'bombs' on French encampments, then retreated to cloud cover. When she emerged, to the crew's horror, they discovered they were at a height of no more than 2,500 feet, directly over the French Army. Every French soldier who could open fire did so, as did the artillery. Z VII retreated out of range 'with her gas cells leaking like sieves'[9] and hit the ground near St Quirin in Lorraine. Significant damage inflicted on the structure resulted in her consignment to the scrapheap.

Her sister ship fared even worse. Zeppelin Z VIII fired a recognition signal as it crossed German lines but the troops below failed to recognize it, opening up an intense fusillade of 'friendly fire' that holed a number of gas cells. Undeterred, she continued on her mission and a few hours later discovered the French while at an altitude of only a few hundred feet. Rather than escaping with this important information, Z VIII attacked, dropping artillery shells, while some of her crew opened fire with rifles. The French immediately replied with 75mm artillery and firearms, peppering the gas cells of this massive target and shooting away her steering gear. Out of control, she drifted away until coming down in hilly, wooded terrain near Badonviller in the Lorraine region. With so little hydrogen remaining in the gas cells the crew were unable to burn their ship.

At this point a French cavalry squadron burst on to the scene and a sharp engagement developed among the trees. After a 'lively fight' with pistols and rifles four of the crew were captured. The rest managed to extricate themselves and traipsed eastwards for 11 hours until they found a detachment of German soldiers at a farm. With the news of the retreating French Army relayed to headquarters a rapid German advance followed. But Zeppelin Z VIII was lost.

On the Eastern Front, seven days later, Zeppelin Z V was engaged in bombing the railway at Mlawa during the Battle of Tannenberg. Damaged by Russian artillery, she came down too, allowing Russian cavalry to capture the crew as they attempted without success to burn their ship. It meant that by the end of the first month of the war the German Army had lost four of her seven pre-war front-line airships.

The Zeppelins did meet with some success though. On the night of 24–25 August Z IX, based at Düsseldorf, bombed Antwerp, the Belgium city bypassed by the German Army on its initial advance. Her bombs killed ten civilians. *Sachsen* made a second attack on the city, from Cologne, during the night of 1–2 September. The first raid in particular struck a chord in Britain, as an editorial in *The Times* explains:

> The visit of a Zeppelin airship to Antwerp on Monday night may prove the most significant episode which has so far occurred in the war. It marks the beginning of a new epoch in the conflicts of mankind. For the first time in history one of these huge and glittering structures has sailed over the housetops of a sleeping city, dropping death from the skies.[10]

By the end of August, losses sustained in action meant the Army airship service[11] had only two Zeppelins left for service with the western armies, Z IX and *Sachsen*. Any possible aerial threat to Britain from the Army had for now, evaporated. And the Navy's sole Zeppelin, L 3, offered no threat as she scoured the North Sea undertaking reconnaissance flights for the High Seas Fleet or fulfilled a training role for new crews joining the service. The Naval Airship Division (*Marine-Luftschiff-Abteilung*) did receive a welcome boost in September, however, with the arrival of its new airship, Zeppelin L 4. More new airships were on order for both the Army and Navy, and throughout the war a constant stream of improved models emerged from the factories producing fresh challenges for Britain's defences. For now though that initial Zeppelin threat to Britain would not become reality until the beginning of 1915.

In the meantime, in August 1914, the defence of Britain was – unofficially – in the hands of the RNAS. Discussions about guns for defence against airships had first taken place in May 1912 but progress was slow. While the Navy agreed to mount guns in an anti-aircraft role on some destroyers and small cruisers, it took the Army almost a year to provide four guns to defend two Navy magazines at Chattenden and Lodge Hill on the River Medway.[12] For aerial defence on the outbreak of war, other than 25 ineffective 1-pdr 'pom-poms', there were just five guns of any real value in position: a 4-inch gun at Portsmouth, the two 3-inch guns at both Chattenden and Lodge Hill, and 3-inch guns at Waltham Abbey and Purfleet. Four days after the declaration of war London received its first anti-aircraft guns – three of the 1-pdr 'pom-

poms' mounted on the roofs of buildings in Whitehall: Admiralty Arch, the Foreign Office and the Crown Agents Office. A report published after the war stated: 'The pom-poms were of very little value … the shell provided for them would not burst on aeroplane fabric but fell back to earth as solid projectiles.' Others recognized their limited value too. Winston Churchill, in office as First Lord of the Admiralty – the political head of the Navy – since October 1911, considered that the effect of the pom-poms 'will be to compel the airship either to expose itself to dangerous fire or to fly so high that accurate bomb-dropping would be impossible.'[13]

In fact Churchill's thoughts and opinions now became very influential. Although the War Office claimed responsibility for the aerial defence of Britain, with the imminent departure of the RFC to France, it was clear to all in authority that it could not fulfil this role. Fully aware of the situation, Churchill advised senior figures in the Admiralty of their role six days before the declaration of war. 'In the present state of aeronautics, the primary duty of British aircraft is to fight enemy aircraft, and thus afford protection against aerial attack … the naval aircraft are to regard defence against attack from the air as their first and main responsibility.'[14]

Even so, as the RNAS had to this point focused extensively on experimental work, it was not well equipped for war. It boasted an eclectic mix of around 50 serviceable aircraft – landplanes and seaplanes – and a somewhat limited arsenal of weapons spread around the naval air stations. There were only two machine gun armed aircraft and, although Eastchurch stored a maxim gun, 26 Hales bombs of 20lb, 42 rifle grenades and 150 hand grenades, the other stations had less. The civilian airfield at Hendon on the north-west edge of London, added to the RNAS roster on 7 August for the defence of the capital, could only boast an armament of 12 Hales hand-grenades, a similar number to those in store at Felixstowe. At the same time the Isle of Grain had just four grenades. Other than these weapons, the naval pilots took rifles with them on patrol.[15] It was not much with which to defend the realm.

On 8 August, on Admiralty orders, the RNAS commenced patrolling the whole east coast of Britain, from Fraserburgh, north of Aberdeen, to Dungeness in Kent on the English Channel coast. Due to the great distances involved, the Admiralty requested assistance from the War Office at the northern and southern extremes and these areas became the responsibility of the RFC squadrons that were waiting to be brought up to strength. This left the RNAS to cover what they considered the part of the coast most vulnerable to aerial attack, from North Berwick, east of Edinburgh, down to Clacton, north of the Thames estuary. Then, when German troops established themselves in Belgium, the focus of the RNAS effort concentrated further south, from Immingham on the Humber to Clacton.

Cdr Charles Samson and his Eastchurch squadron had relocated to Skegness for this purpose, but on 23 August, Churchill, who had maintained a keen interest in naval aviation developments and even taken flying lessons, instructed Murray Sueter to recall him. Churchill advised: 'Now that the Germans have overrun Belgium, the Thames and Medway are within easy striking distance not only of airships but of aeroplanes. The presence of Commander Samson with his mobile squadron is more necessary at Eastchurch than at Skegness.'[16]

Samson was a true pioneer of naval aviation and a genuine buccaneering figure. Sueter even likened him to Francis Drake![17] He was one of the first batch of naval pilots to gain their pilot's licences in 1911 and that same year he made the first flight from the deck of a static ship. In 1912 he followed this with the first flight from a moving ship and, with aircraft manufacturers Short Brothers, he designed the first seaplane. Then, in 1913, he developed the principal of folding wing seaplanes and became the first British pilot to fly at night without lights either on his aircraft or on the landing ground. Samson imbued his pioneering spirit in the men under his command and, aware of the high standards displayed by his squadron, the Admiralty now had other plans for him.

Two days after receiving the recall, Samson and his squadron were back at Eastchurch, from where they continued flying patrols along the east coast. The work was exhausting but tedious; there was no sign of the enemy. Shortly after his return to Eastchurch, Samson received a telegram ordering him to report to the Admiralty.

Samson arrived in Whitehall at 10.00pm on 25 August, upon which Murray Sueter informed him that a brigade of Royal Marines was sailing for Ostend on the Belgium coast the following day and that the Eastchurch squadron was to depart in the morning to support them. It was the news Samson had been waiting for, a chance for something rather more exciting than coastal patrols. Eager to get back to Eastchurch, he grabbed a quick meal at a coffee stall, phoned ahead to warn his squadron to have all aircraft ready for a morning departure, then set off back by car. In his enthusiasm to get back Samson admitted:

> I am afraid we exceeded the speed limit on many occasions; arriving [at Eastchurch] about 2 a.m. we found everybody collected in the Mess playing poker nobody was desirous of going to bed and all were as keen as mustard on setting out to War as soon as daylight appeared.[18]

Shortly after he reached Eastchurch, the phone rang and quelled the high spirits. The departure of the Royal Marines was put back a day to 27 August, likewise that of Samson's squadron. Samson observed that the news, 'depressed everybody, as we were all suffering from the fear of the War being over before we could get a chance to take part in it'. He need not have worried. There were, however, no more delays and after lunch on 27 August Samson led his squadron into the air.

The squadron comprised a mixed bag of nine aircraft of seven different types. 'The majority were,' as Samson conceded, 'old veteran servants of the Crown.' Dealing with the different aeroplane types and engines would prove challenging in the weeks ahead.

With the safety of his pilots in mind he considered the risks involved if any of his aircraft came down in the English Channel. With nothing else available he gathered a number of bicycle tyres from stores and issued each pilot with two to serve as lifebelts. Then, as aeroplanes carried no official distinguishing marks at the time, he arranged 'that each machine should fly a Union Jack lashed to one of its struts.' The flags, however, failed to have the desired effect.

After an unpleasant flight across the Channel through low cloud and thunderstorms, Samson followed the coastline from Calais, past Dunkirk to Ostend. There he selected a landing ground on a racecourse south of the town. Much to his surprise, as he came in to land he found himself subjected to rifle fire. The landing was tricky enough, forcing him to ignore the attempts to shoot him down, as he skimmed rooftops before eventually coming to rest against some railings. While he waited for the rest of the squadron to follow him down Samson discovered the identity of his assailants:

> I found I was being stalked by a couple of marines, who were very disappointed to find I was a British Naval Officer. They had come over to Belgium to shoot Germans and were simply aching to let off their rifles at the first opportunity.[19]

But those Marines were not alone and the next two pilots to land 'were received by a hot fusillade' which fortunately was not very accurate, before Samson finally managed to get word out that the incoming aircraft were British.

The following day, the squadron found a more suitable airfield on the northern side of Ostend harbour and were joined by their motor transport, stores and the ground crew who had come by sea. Reconnaissance flights then commenced over the area between Bruges, Ghent and Ypres but they saw nothing of the Germans. The Admiralty then experienced a change of heart, considering the Marine brigade rather exposed. Rather than risk losing them, the Admiralty recalled both the Marines and their supporting airmen on 30 August.

It was not the news Samson and his men wanted to hear. The squadron received orders to return along the coast to Dunkirk and then cross the English Channel from there. Keen to find a way out of returning to England, Samson 'started off with the fixed determination that at the slightest excuse I would stop at Dunkirk'. A slight haze over the town was enough of a pretext for Samson and he landed, followed by the rest of the squadron. One of the pilots made a bad landing and smashed his aeroplane. The pilot, Samson confided, 'failed to realise the extreme joy I displayed at his accident, which gave me a peg to build my plans around'.[20]

Matters fell into Samson's hands when General Bidon, the French officer commanding the Dunkirk garrison, arrived at the airfield. The squadron commander wasted no time pointing out to the general what valuable reconnaissance work his men could perform for him. The general began making phone calls to secure Samson's services. In the meantime Samson located Philip Sarell, the British vice-consul at Dunkirk. Having been won over too, Sarell contacted the Foreign Office, urging 'them to request the Admiralty to retain [the] squadron at Dunkirk pointing out how important it was both for our amicable relations with the French and for diplomatic reasons'. Then, to delay his departure while the wheels of diplomacy turned, Samson informed the Admiralty – mendaciously – that bad fog over the Channel prevented his immediate return and that the damaged aeroplane from his squadron was undergoing repairs and he could not leave it behind.

Unbeknown to Samson, some four months earlier, an Admiralty Committee set up to look into the value of camouflaging oil tanks and other vulnerable points, had defined its view on air defence. 'Whilst passive measures are useful as safeguards, the real key to the situation will be found to lie in a vigorous and offensive attack on the enemy's air-sheds, &c., and on his aircraft before they reach these shores.'[21]

Now, at the beginning of September 1914, Samson's machinations paid off. The Foreign Office contacted Churchill and Sarell spoke to Sueter. Together they recognized an opportunity to fulfil the committee's findings. On 1 September 1914 the Admiralty sent a request to the French Ministry of Marine at Bordeaux.

> The Admiralty considers it extremely important to deny the use of territory within 100 miles radius of Dunkirk to German Zeppelins, and to attack by aeroplane all airships found replenishing there. With your permission the Admiralty wish to take necessary measures to maintain aerial command of this region.[22]

The request indicated that a force of 30 to 40 naval aeroplanes was needed for this task along with a number of 'armed motor cars'. This force, it added, would operate in conformity with the wishes of the French, but hoped for a free rein to pursue targets of its own choosing. It concluded by stating: 'The immunity of Portsmouth, Chatham, and London from dangerous aerial attack is closely involved.'

The French authorities agreed at once. Cdr Samson had his war. And so did Churchill. Discussions between Churchill and his opposite number Lord Kitchener, the Secretary of State for War, reached an agreement that on 3 September the Admiralty would officially assume responsibility for aerial defence, its weapon the Royal Naval Air Service. On the outbreak of war Britain appeared largely unprepared for attack from the air, but a month later she now appeared at least to have a plan.

Chapter 3

Attack is the Best Form of Defence

Churchill's agreement to assume responsibility for Britain's aerial defence on 3 September 1914 led to a flurry of meetings in London. The following day the Third Sea Lord, Rear-Admiral Frederick Tudor, reported on the question of naval anti-aircraft resources. His report showed that a dozen 3-inch guns were available immediately and that the fleet reserve could, in time, find some 150 3-pdrs and 6-pdr Hotchkiss guns as well as another 38 'pom-poms'. Tudor went further, proposing the establishment of 12 double-gun positions with 18 double searchlight stations for the protection of London. Having read Tudor's report, Churchill dismissed his proposal. On 5 September he outlined his own policy regarding the guns:

> There can be no question of defending London by artillery against aerial attack. It is quite impossible to cover so vast an area; and if London, why not every city? Defence against aircraft by guns is limited absolutely to points of military value ... Far more important than London are the vulnerable points in the Medway, at Dover, and Portsmouth. Oil-tanks, power-houses, lock-gates, magazines, airship sheds – all require to have their aerial guns increased in number.[1]

In accordance with these sentiments, of the dozen 3-inch guns immediately available, half were sent to the fleet and of the rest, three went to Portsmouth, two to Chatham and one to Dover. As more guns became available they were to be distributed between the fleet and defended ports. For Churchill, however, the positioning of the guns was secondary to his primary defence initiative, as he now made clear: 'But, after all, the great defence against aerial menace is to attack the enemy's aircraft as near as possible to their point of departure.'[2] And for that purpose Churchill now looked to Dunkirk.

When Churchill had requested the redeployment of Cdr Samson from Skegness to Eastchurch in August, he also suggested a move for Major (Maj) Eugene Gerrard, Royal Marine Light Infantry. Another of the first batch of naval pilots, Gerrard was an instructor at the combined service Central Flying School[3] when Churchill commented that 'work of a more responsible character must be found for this officer'.[4] From his lofty position as political head of the Royal Navy, Churchill was not averse to a little micro-management. Gerrard received orders sending him to Dunkirk, where Samson handed him responsibility for leading an attack on the Zeppelin sheds at Cologne and Düsseldorf.[5] Having moved three of Samson's precious aircraft to Ostend, Gerrard headed to Antwerp to meet with senior Belgian officers and arrange the use of an airfield just to the south of the city on a racecourse at Wilryck. Gerrard then submitted his plans for the raid to the Admiralty and returned to Ostend to await approval. He waited but no reply came, and seven days later disaster struck. On 12 September a fierce storm struck Ostend. With no hangar to protect the aircraft they were pegged down in the lee of a sand dune but at 11.45pm a squall estimated at 70mph ripped out the pegs holding the aircraft down, sending them 'turning cartwheels' to their destruction. In less than a minute nothing remained of the aircraft but a jumble of broken spars, ripped canvas and tangled wires. Two days later, having collected up any serviceable components, Gerrard and his men returned disconsolately to Dunkirk.

September 1914: Antwerp, Belgium

Despite the setback, the importance of striking against the Zeppelin sheds had not diminished. While Samson now began to extend his influence in this area of France through wide-ranging motorized patrols using cars armour-plated in a Dunkirk shipyard, he also arranged more aircraft for Gerrard. Two days after the return from Ostend, Samson handed over his own aeroplane, a 70hp B.E.2b, to Gerrard and sent him and Lieutenant (Lt) Charles Collet, flying an 80hp Sopwith Tractor biplane, back to Antwerp to try again. Samson also dispatched three more aircraft and, although one was under repair when clear skies finally appeared over Antwerp on 22 September, Gerrard still had four serviceable aircraft to send against the Zeppelin sheds. Gerrard detailed two aircraft to attack each of the targets. Gerrard, flying the B.E.2b, and Collet in his Sopwith, set course for Düsseldorf, while two of the later arrivals, Lieutenant Commander (Lt Cdr) Spenser Grey (with Lt Edward Newton Clare as observer) and Lt Reginald 'Reggie' Marix headed for Cologne. Grey piloted a 100hp Sopwith Sociable (so called because the crew sat side-by-side rather than one in front of the other) and Marix flew Sopwith Tabloid No. 168.[6]

The direct line of flight from Antwerp was about 100 miles to Düsseldorf and about ten more to Cologne, the return journey a test for the endurance of all the aircraft, particularly if they encountered strong headwinds, which would increase fuel consumption. To solve this, Baron Pierre de Caters – a Belgian aviation pioneer and racing car driver – arranged an emergency fuel depot 50 miles east of Antwerp, protected by six armoured cars of the Belgian Army. As with the first attempt, the weather took a hand. The clear skies over Antwerp fused with a thick blanket of fog once the raiders crossed the Roer river, a tributary of the Meuse. Gerrard, Grey and Marix all found it impossible to locate anything in the murk and reluctantly abandoned the mission. Collet, however, pushed on.

22 September 1914, 8.45pm: Düsseldorf, Germany

When Collet reached a point that he considered must be close to Dusseldorf, having flown on a compass bearing without any ground reference points, he descended through the mist and finally emerged into clear air at just 400 feet. Whether by luck or incredible navigational skills, just a quarter of a mile ahead loomed the imposing Düsseldorf shed at Golzheim to the north of the city. With three 20lb bombs ready to drop, Collet pushed his aircraft to its maximum speed and headed straight for the shed. There were no anti-aircraft or machine guns to greet him, just soldiers armed with rifles. Those inadequately armed defenders had a huge responsibility because inside the Golzheim shed, hidden from Collet's view, lay Zeppelin Z IX, the Antwerp raider, and alongside it workmen had stacked wooden crates containing 15,000kg of bombs.

At 8.45am Collet released his first bomb. It exploded 100 feet short of the target. Seconds later the second bomb landed about 65 feet short of the shed but failed to explode, then the final one cleared it, landing on the ground beyond where it also failed to explode. Forced to release the bombs from very low level, they did not have enough time to arm properly as they dropped.[7] Disappointed, Collet turned back for Antwerp with bullets angrily whistling past him before the mist swallowed him up and he disappeared from view. All four pilots were back at Antwerp by 1.00pm. Collet had come close to success but it seems only broken windows resulted from his attack. Gerrard, however, remained determined to try again at the earliest possible opportunity.

The commander at Golzheim, Dr Karl Bamler, and the captain of Z IX, Hauptmann (Hptmn) Alfred Horn, recognized their lucky escape and demanded weapons to defend the facilities, but all they received were two machine guns. In the meantime a new, larger Zeppelin shed neared completion just over a mile to the north, at Lohausen. On 3 October Z IX transferred to this new shed, as did the machine guns.[8]

23 September to 7 October 1914: Antwerp, Belgium

Back in Antwerp two aircraft arrived the day after the raid to boost Gerrard's squadron to seven but accidents meant that on 28 September he could still only muster four serviceable aircraft. Now a dramatic change of circumstances meant that time was rapidly running out for Gerrard to mount a successful attack on the Zeppelin sheds.

After the German Army's advance stalled on the Marne on 5 September and its subsequent retreat to the Aisne, it became necessary to take Antwerp, which it had bypassed during the sweeping opening offensive. After taking time to manoeuvre its heavy guns into position, the Army began the bombardment of Antwerp's outer ring of forts, some ten miles outside the city, on 28 September. Outgunned, four of the forts were out of action three days later. The following day the Belgian Council of War shocked their British and French allies by announcing the government and the Army were preparing to move out of the city to Ostend. The allies urged the Belgians to delay. The British promised reinforcements and redirected Churchill, who was on his way to Dunkirk, to Antwerp where he arrived on 3 October.

That same day Samson ordered all available aircraft of the naval force to Antwerp. Samson followed with his armoured cars escorting an extraordinary convoy of 70 London buses rushed to the front as transport for a brigade of Royal Marines that had moved into the city on the night of 3 October. Samson arrived in Antwerp the next day and resumed command of all naval aircraft while that evening the remaining two brigades of the Royal Marine Division, partially trained, ill-equipped and rushed over from England, also reached the city. But it was all to no avail. On 6 October, German artillery began pounding Antwerp's inner ring of forts and the Belgian government announced it would delay no longer and they and the Army would evacuate the city.

Churchill left Antwerp that evening, ordering Samson to pack up and depart with his men at dawn the following day. His orders, however, permitted two pilots to remain behind until the last minute to try a final strike against the Zeppelin sheds if the opportunity arose. Reggie Marix, one of the two pilots detailed for this forlorn hope, wrote a personal account of the last few days in Antwerp. Marix claims that Lt Cdr Grey went to British headquarters at the Hotel St Antoine in the city to ask Churchill for permission to make this final attempt on the Zeppelin sheds.

> W.C. [Winston Churchill] replied that it was too late, Antwerp was to be evacuated that day, and the Germans might be in that night. We were all to get out of Wilryck as best we could, and that was that.
>
> W.C. then retired to the w.c., but S.G. [Spenser Grey] followed him, and through the closed door went on pleading, explaining that we would get back in time to get out. It seems that to get rid of him, W.C. gave his consent.[9]

Back at the airfield a mad scramble of packing continued through the night but at dawn on 7 October all was ready. All serviceable aircraft departed, leaving two Sopwith Tabloids with Spenser Grey and Reggie Marix awaiting their opportunity. Lt Sydney Sippe also stayed behind trying to revive a broken down B.E.2b, but two other aircraft undergoing major repair work had to be abandoned. Samson's brother, Flt Lt William Samson, also remained behind in command of a party of four mechanics who were to service the two Tabloids. During the day, the announcement that a German bombardment of the city would commence at midnight combined with the sight of their own Army marching away, broke the spirit of the population of Antwerp, who began to pour out of the city in a great sprawl of humanity. At Wilryck poor weather kept the two Sopwith Tabloids grounded.

8 October 1914: Cologne and Düsseldorf, Germany

That night shells began screaming over the airfield on their way to the city, but as morning dawned on 8 October an early mist conspired to prevent take-off. At 1.00pm conditions had not improved significantly but with the sound of fighting edging closer, Lt Cdr Grey, accepted that time had almost run out for them and gave the order. The raid was on.[10]

With the German Army occupying the territory east of Antwerp, there was no opportunity to establish an emergency fuel dump this time, so Belgian mechanics had built and fitted extra fuel tanks to both aircraft. At 1.20pm Grey took off in Sopwith Tabloid No. 167, his target the Zeppelin shed near Cologne. Marix climbed into the sky ten minutes later in Tabloid No. 168, aiming to strike against the Düsseldorf shed, without realising there were now two sheds, one at Golzheim and the new one close by at Lohausen. Both aircraft carried just two 20lb bombs; there was little room for error.

Grey reached the vicinity of Cologne without any problems but as he neared the city a thick mist limited visibility again. To complicate matters further he was unsure of the exact location of the Zeppelin shed – his map indicated two possible locations, one to the north-west and one to the south of the city. His search for both proved fruitless:

> I came down to 600 feet, but, after searching for 10 to 12 minutes under a heavy fire, I failed to locate them … I considered the best point to attack would be the main station in the middle of the town where I saw many trains drawn up, so let fall my two bombs on this.

There is some question as to whether Grey's bombs did hit the station. A Cologne newspaper reported that machine gun fire drove the aircraft away from the Zeppelin shed at Bickendorf, north-west of Cologne, before it dropped a bomb over the gasworks at Ehrenfeld on the way to the city. It was then tracked to the Rhine's Südbrücke (South Bridge) before turning away to the west.[11] The report does not mention where the second bomb fell, although a French POW at Düsseldorf wrote in his diary that he heard a bomb had broken windows at the station.[12] After his attack Grey touched down at Wilryck at 4.45pm, but of Marix, who had a slightly shorter distance to cover, there was no news. Grey, Sippe, Cdr Samson's brother William and the four mechanics looked to the sky and waited.

Marix had reached Düsseldorf without incident, but flying at 3,000 feet he could not find his target. In a personal account of the raid Marix explained that 'the shed was not where I expected to find it, and my map had been wrongly marked', adding nonchalantly, 'so I had to fly around a bit, which excited some interest'.[13]

The 'interest' Marix remarked on came from an anti-aircraft gun positioned at a munitions factory at Derendorf. Fortunately for Marix the shells fired by the gun were well off target before it jammed after just three rounds. In something of a bizarre twist, Marix, unaware Düsseldorf now had two Zeppelin sheds, saw the new one at Lohausen and headed for it, passing directly over the Golzheim shed apparently without realising. The guards at Golzheim immediately opened rifle fire on him, followed by a fusillade of bullets from an army rifle range nearby.

With bullets whistling past and some hitting his aircraft, Marix focused on the Zeppelin shed, even when the two machine guns on top burst into action 'with rapid points of flame'. As he approached the colossal structure the Tabloid dropped into a steep dive. Alerted by the firing, inmates at a warehouse serving as a POW camp 400 metres away pushed and shoved their way out into the yard to watch the attack. One of the French prisoners, Louis Cesar Duhaut, watched excitedly as 'suddenly [the aircraft] falls vertically, with its right wing lower. Intense emotion seizes us, we have tears, while the guards throw their hats in the air shouting "Hurrah, hurrah". It seemed that the aircraft was hit. But seconds later the mood changed. 'Now', Duhaut added, 'it is we who cry hurrah!'[14]

From a height of about 700 feet Marix released his bombs. The first fell short of the target, the explosion gouging a crater in the soil sending great clods of earth spinning into the air. The second proved lethal. The 20lb Hales bomb smashed through the roof of the shed and exploded. Sheltered within its soaring walls lay Zeppelin Z IX. Jagged shell fragments slashed through the outer envelope of the airship and into the gas cells, causing those vital organs to release hydrogen into the air, which the detonation ignited. Pulling the nose of his aircraft up, Marix glanced over his shoulder and saw 'enormous sheets of flame pouring out of the shed. It was a magnificent sight'.[15] But he had no time to dwell on his success. The fierce fusillade he had flown into had damaged the control wires leading to the rudder of his aircraft and this was now locked preventing him from turning – he was heading deeper into Germany. Fortunately, the Tabloid did not have ailerons for lateral control, but used wing-warping instead. Marix quickly appreciated that this method could also guide the aircraft into a slow turn, which enabled him to set a course back towards Antwerp.

At the Lohausen shed the flames shot 500 feet up through the hole made in the roof by the bomb and a great pall of thick black smoke hung over it. The flames prevented the machine gunners on the roof escaping by the internal stairway; instead they slid down the roof to ladders rushed forward for their rescue. But there was no hope of saving Zeppelin Z IX. After the hydrogen burnt off the metal framework screeched and crumpled under its own weight until all that remained was a tangled wreck of red hot girders. Four people died in the attack with ten others injured. Britain's war against the Zeppelin's had claimed its first victims.

Although Marix was no longer under fire he was not out of danger. Crosswinds had forced him some five to ten miles north of his course back to Antwerp and with fuel running low the thought of having to make an emergency landing later without rudder control convinced him to land early. He came down in a field and discovered he was about 20 miles from the city. Then began a memorable journey back to Antwerp, first on the footplate of a railway engine, then by bicycle that, according to an official report, Marix 'borrowed from a peasant'. In his more candid personal account, however, he relates how, 'with some difficulty I commandeered a bicycle and pedalled off'. It seems likely that the bemused Belgian never saw his bicycle again.

Once he reached the deserted streets of Antwerp Marix persuaded a couple of gendarmes to drive him out to the airfield in their car. It was close to 11.00pm when Marix arrived back at Wilryck, where he was almost shot. When the gendarmes, talking Flemish, approached the darkened mansion that had served as the naval pilots' headquarters, they sounded like Germans to Marix's comrades hiding inside. Fortunately Marix spoke in English just in time and averted disaster.[16] Time now was of the essence. The Germans had begun dropping shells on the airfield at 8.30pm. The shelling eventually caused serious damage to Grey's Tabloid and the B.E.2b Sippe had tried to repair. Now it appeared German soldiers were in the woods bordering the airfield and one had already taken a shot at the mechanics. Only 30 minutes after Marix returned, the whole party clambered into their motor transport and headed west, away from Antwerp, to safety. They had no choice but to leave the damaged aircraft to the mercy of the advancing Germans. There would be no chance of another strike against Cologne. German troops entered Antwerp the day after Marix's successful attack and six days later occupied Zeebrugge and Ostend. Cologne was now beyond the reach of Samson and his aircraft.

October 1914: London, England

October proved a busy month for the Admiralty. While naval aircraft made their strikes against the Zeppelin sheds there was much activity in London too. On 9 October, the day after the Düsseldorf raid, police Special Constables and civilians who had volunteered in September for part-time service manning searchlights in the capital became members of a new body, the Anti-Aircraft Corps. Now they took responsibility for London's guns too. Administered as a part of the Royal Naval Volunteer Reserve (RNVR), an organization of civilian volunteers who undertook naval training, they came directly under the control of Murray Sueter, the Admiralty's Director of the Air Department. Numerous employees of the Office of Works, who were erecting the searchlight and gun platforms, also volunteered for this new corps. These volunteers could choose either day or night duty and fulfilled this role every other day.[17] This work became ever more important because, despite Churchill's initial reluctance to allocate guns for London's defence, a deputation led by the Lord Mayor of the City of London resulted in ten more guns joining the original three 'pom-poms'. Green Park and Tower Bridge saw the installation of 3-inch guns, while positions created at Waterloo, Nine Elms and the Temple received 6-pdrs. In addition another five 'pom-poms' were positioned at St James's Street, Gresham College, the Cannon Street Hotel, St Helen's Court and Blackfriars. Additional searchlights to support them were installed at Cheapside, Finsbury Circus, King William Street, Waterloo and close to Tower Bridge.[18]

The passive defence of London also commenced in the form of a lighting reduction. The first general regulation issued by the Home Secretary on 17 September, particularly aimed at London, required the dimming of all 'abnormal lighting', such as illuminated advertising signs and shop windows. Attempts to disguise long, easily distinguished roads and the bridges over the Thames were made by switching off numbers of streetlights, but this was not a complete blackout. In the natural dark spaces of London's parks additional lights were installed in an effort to disguise their familiar unlit shapes. Efforts by the Commissioner of Police to press businesses to comply prior to any Zeppelin actually threatening the city had, however, proved generally ineffective. Therefore, on 1 October, at the Commissioner's request, these regulations became enforceable by law. From sunset to sundown the regulations specified amongst other things that,

> ... all powerful outside lights be extinguished; that street lamps be extinguished or shaded to break up conspicuous groups or rows of lights; that lighting on railway premises be reduced to a minimum; that lights inside shops or other premises be shaded; and that lights on omnibuses be no more than sufficed for the collection of fares.[19]

London had entered a new dark age. Birmingham also had official blackout regulations while less stringent lighting regulations spread to other towns and cities, particularly those close to the coast. A journalist summed up the feelings of many in London's vast population:

> For the first time Londoners knew what it was to be hampered a little by the darkness. They took it in the Londoners' way, good-humouredly, which is almost more than might have been expected, because the idea that his city might be in danger has scarcely yet penetrated the Londoner's easy going mind ... taking the whole thing as a not very good, but tolerable joke.

While these defensive preparations were under way, Murray Sueter at the Admiralty had also been looking at ways to build on the success of the attack on the Düsseldorf Zeppelin shed. He selected two targets. The first, the new Nordholz Zeppelin shed inland from Cuxhaven, and the second, a highly significant target, the Zeppelin works at Friedrichshafen on the northern shore of Lake Constance. Cuxhaven was out of range for land-based aircraft but Sueter planned it as seaplane raid with the aircraft taken out into the North Sea and launched from ships adapted as seaplane carriers. Friedrichshafen, on the other hand, was within range of land planes but because of the distances involved they needed to fly from a base in France close to the southern German border. Without wasting any time, Sueter planned an early attempt on the shed at Nordholz on 24 October but bad weather forced its abandonment. Despite plans to try again in November, it was not until December that the raid finally took place.

October/November 1914: Belfort, France

In the meantime, Sueter pushed ahead with plans to attack Friedrichshafen. Incredibly, he handed the complicated task of planning the operation to a civilian. Noel Pemberton Billing was an extraordinary individual who lived a varied and at times controversial life. From soldier to actor, to inventor, entrepreneur and adventure-seeker, he had done it all. His latest passion, aviation, led him to meet Sueter while trying to sell him his latest aircraft design. Sueter remained unconvinced by Pemberton Billing's aircraft but saw in this charismatic and patriotic man the qualities he felt were needed to plan the mission. He arranged temporary commissions in the RNVR for Pemberton Billing and a friend, Frank Brock, who, it is worth noting played a highly significant role in Britain's war against the Zeppelins some 18 months later. But for now the two men were destined for France. On 21 October they departed, their destination the town of Belfort just seven miles from the Swiss/German border. On arrival, Pemberton Billing wasted no time in negotiating the use of an airship station situated there before undertaking a dangerous clandestine mission from neutral Switzerland, across Lake Constance by fishing boat and into Germany to spy out the Zeppelin works at Friedrichshafen.[20] Seven days later, their mission accomplished, the two men were back in London, but the clock was already ticking – the French authorities' permission to use Belfort would expire on 23 November.

Meanwhile, Sueter had selected a team of four pilots to carry out the raid with a fifth as reserve. He handed command to Squadron Commander (Sqn Cdr) Philip Shepherd with an engineering specialist, Sqn Cdr Edward Briggs, as his deputy. The other places went to Flight Commander (Flt Cdr) John Babington, Flt Lt Sydney Sippe – one of recently returned Antwerp pilots – and in reserve, Flight sub-Lieutenant (Flt sub-Lt) Roland Cannon. The Admiralty selected the Avro 504 for the raid. It already possessed one and ordered three more from the manufacturer, A.V. Roe. To maintain secrecy Sueter had the aircraft delivered in crates for assembly in France. Briggs and Babington selected a team of ten riggers and fitters to assemble the aircraft and engines and then a final member joined the team, a young A.V. Roe designer, Roy Chadwick, with responsibility for the aircraft's bomb frames.[21]

The main body of the party departed from Southampton by freighter on 10 November and met Pemberton Billing at Le Havre, where Brock had arranged train transport to Belfort. Shepherd and Sippe travelled separately by road.[22]

The train pulled into Belfort at 9.30am on 13 November but to maintain secrecy, it remained in a siding until nightfall, when everyone transferred into the airship shed at the airfield. By working through the night the riggers and fitters had all aircraft ready by the morning, but delays on the road meant Shepherd and Sippe did not arrive until the following day, 15 November. The conditions then were perfect for the raid but due to the exhausted condition of the latecomers the mission was put back 24 hours, leaving everyone to settle down for another night in the draughty, damp and cold airship shed. When they awoke, however, the weather had taken a turn for the worse with temperatures plummeting to minus 7°C and strong headwinds blasting in from the east. To the intense frustration of the team, the weather showed little improvement over the next five days. Things worsened further when Sqn Cdr Shepherd became very ill, forcing him to give up his place on the mission roster. Briggs was now in command of the raid with reserve pilot Cannon taking Shepherd's place.

The French-imposed deadline of 23 November loomed ever nearer so it was a huge relief to the team to wake on the morning of 21 November and discover that the weather and wind direction had changed decidedly for the better. The daring raid, which involved a return flight of 250 miles mostly over Germany, was on.

21 November 1914: Friedrichshafen, Germany

The four pilots lined up their aircraft at the western end of the airfield, then at 9.45am took to the sky one after the other, all that is except Cannon. First, engine problems delayed him getting airborne, then a broken tail-skid ended his involvement entirely. He could only look on as the other three climbed to 3,500 feet and gradually disappeared into the distance.

The Zeppelin works at Friedrichshafen was a hive of activity with the Navy's latest airship, L 7, close to completion. Just the previous day workers had commenced filling the gas cells with hydrogen. A direct bomb strike on the shed would inevitably see a repeat of the Düsseldorf inferno.

Although Pemberton Billing had planned the raiders' approach to take them over the mountains of the Black Forest to avoid any incursion into Swiss territory, the pilots preferred to follow the more easily identifiable course of the Rhine. It meant all three breached Swiss neutrality as they passed over the enclave of Schaffhausen where the Swiss border juts like a bastion into Germany. By then the pilots had all lost sight of each other; each was on his own.

As the first aircraft passed the town of Constance at the west end of the lake, a warning advised Friedrichshafen of the presence of unidentified aircraft and gun crews dashed to man the three anti-aircraft guns and two machine guns defending the site.

Briggs was first to approach Friedrichshafen flying Avro 504 No. 874. From the lake he flew across the town towards the two great sheds that formed the Zeppelin works as the anti-aircraft guns opened on him. Briggs, like all the pilots, carried four 20lb Hales bombs, the same type used at Düsseldorf. He released his first bomb while still over the town at the same time that Werner Peterson, the nominated commander of the new Zeppelin in the shed, was walking towards the works. In a report he described how 'the plane flew over me and dropped the first bomb ... It hit a house and exploded about 60 metres from me and partly destroyed the upper storey'.[23] The bomb killed a 21-year-old Swiss tailor's assistant on his way back to work after lunch and seriously injured two women in the house.[24]

Approaching the sheds, Briggs now released two more bombs. Peterson continued to watch as the British pilot, 'skilfully dropped a bomb which, however, merely landed on the field, then another which was accurately aimed and hit between the two sheds [causing] minor damage to the doors of the new shed'. But Briggs was now in trouble. The determined defensive fire he had flown into had damaged his Avro – one bullet had critically punctured his petrol tank while another grazed his head above the right ear. With no chance of getting back, Briggs accepted the inevitable and brought his aircraft down, landing on the field right in front of the Zeppelin sheds. An angry mob of workers surrounded him and Briggs was struck but an officer appeared and threatened to shoot anyone who laid their hands on him. Guards led him away, first to hospital and then into captivity.

As Briggs had begun his attack, Sippe arrived at the west end of the lake and flew low, skimming the surface at just ten feet to lessen the chance of detection. Once beyond Constance he climbed to 1,200 feet over the north shore of the lake and headed towards Friedrichshafen. From the shells bursting over the town and aware that Briggs was ahead of him, he concluded correctly that his comrade had reached the target.

Rapidly approaching the works, Sippe dropped to 700 feet and noted the time as 11.55am as he began his attack. He dropped his first bomb close to the guns, hoping to put the gunners off their aim. Werner Peterson continued to look on and noted:

> Above the downed machine Sippe released two bombs which exploded in the field. Then he flew very fast above the sheds and dropped a bomb which caused damage to the workshops and damaged a window of the shed in which L 7 lay: 20 metres farther and the inflated ship would have been destroyed.

Sippe's final bomb caught up in his bomb frame and despite efforts to shake it loose over the lake it would not budge. Coming under fresh machine gun fire, Sippe gave up the attempt, flew back across the lake again at low level and set course for Belfort.

As Sippe streaked low across the lake the third raider, Babington, appeared high above flying at about 4,000 feet in Avro 504 No. 875. As he began to make his approach, the anti-aircraft gunners spotted him and opened fire but Babington happily recorded that all the shells burst below him. Then, with the sun behind him on this crisp autumnal day, he began 'a very steep descent in [a] slight curve over sheds', diving from 4,000 feet down to 950 feet, at which point he released two bombs. With the AA shells now exploding above him he continued to dive and, in his own words, 'at 450 feet released second two bombs, machine nearly vertical, continued dive over sheds and received shock of bomb explosion directly over shed'. Even as he struggled to regain control of his aircraft he managed a glance over his shoulder at the sheds before setting course back across the lake, convinced he had seen smoke emerging from one of them.

Sippe returned to Belfort without a hitch, landing at the airfield at 1.50pm. Babington lost his way over France and overshot, landing at Vesoul almost 50 miles away. Pemberton Billing debriefed both Sippe and Babington. Both reported damage to the Zeppelin works but neither could offer any information concerning Briggs. Everyone at Belfort feared the worst until a telegram the following day lifted the mood considerably. The Admiralty had learned through Dutch sources that Briggs was alive and in a German hospital.

On the morning of 23 November, the deadline set by the French authorities, preparations for the return to England were in full swing. Pemberton Billing explored all possible sources of information for the effects of the raid and reported back to the Admiralty:

> it may be confidently assumed that the damage caused by this raid includes complete destruction of one Zeppelin and serious damage to the larger hangar, and also demolition of the hydrogen producing plant.

On that same day Winston Churchill stood proudly in the House of Commons to report on the success of the raid – a Zeppelin apparently destroyed at its birthplace as a result of his strategy. He concluded:

> This flight of 250 miles, which penetrated 150 miles into Germany, across mountainous country, in difficult weather conditions, constitutes with the attack a fine feat of arms.

The British press delighted in trumpeting the news too, but they were all wrong. The damage inflicted on the Friedrichshafen works was limited and Zeppelin L 7 unaffected. On 23 November, while Churchill announced the success of the raid in the House of Commons, L 7 emerged from its construction shed and flew a trial flight over Lake Constance. Successfully concluded, Werner Peterson and his crew took her over the following day and set course for her new base at Leipzig.

Although the Friedrichshafen raid failed to deliver the desired result, the Admiralty's campaign against the Zeppelin sheds continued. On 22 November, the day after the raid, a naval force set out to lure the German High Seas Fleet into the Heligoland Bight with another seaplane attack planned on the Zeppelin shed at Nordholz, near Cuxhaven. But the following day orders recalled the seaplane carriers with their part in the plan cancelled.

The raid on Nordholz did eventually take place the following month, on Christmas Day 1914. The result of the raid would have far-reaching consequences but, even before it struck, German aerial bombs had exploded on British soil for the very first time. They were not, however, Zeppelin bombs.

Chapter 4

'Forcing England to Her Knees'

In Germany through the autumn months of 1914, a growing sense of frustration gripped the airship fleets of both the Army and the Navy. New airships had arrived, making good early losses. Between September and November the Navy received three new Zeppelins and the Army two. Each service took delivery of another in December. The wartime airship expansion programme was under way. In ideal weather conditions they were all capable of carrying the war to Britain. Yet any attempt to commence these raids remained blocked at the highest level – by the Kaiser. Wilhelm II, like so many at the time, believed the war would soon be over and, with his close family ties to the British Royal family, he demonstrated a marked reluctance to be held responsible for the destruction of any of London's important historical buildings and monuments, especially the palaces.

Autumn 1914: Berlin, Germany

That a rivalry existed between the Army and Navy regarding their airships is clear. Of the two, the Navy appeared more determined to open attacks on Britain in the early months of the war. Konteradmiral Paul Behncke, Deputy Chief of the Naval Staff, proved a vociferous advocate for opening air attacks on England. On 20 August he wrote to Admiral Hugo von Pohl, his ever-cautious superior, advising that the success of the Army's advance into France and Belgium created opportunities to establish forward airship bases from which all England could be reached, even as far north as Glasgow in Scotland. He also expressed his belief in the value of air attacks against the London docks and the Admiralty building in Whitehall. He expected these attacks, 'whether

31

they involve London or the neighbourhood of London, to cause panic in the population which may possibly render it doubtful that the war can be continued'.[1] Besides London, Behncke also highlighted the importance of striking against the Dover and Portsmouth naval bases and included among suggested targets the Humber and Tyne as well as Plymouth, Glasgow and the Firth of Forth. 'Air attacks ... particularly with airships,' he concluded, 'promise considerable material and moral results.' In response, von Pohl pointed out that the Navy's two airships were both required to fulfil an important scouting role for the High Seas Fleet, Germany's main battle fleet.[2]

Another advocate of aerial raids, the commander of Naval Air Forces, Konteradmiral Otto Philipp, contacted both the Navy Minister, Alfred von Tirpitz, and von Pohl on 2 October. That month the fleet of naval Zeppelins expanded to four, prompting Philipp to propose the release of Zeppelin L 3 from reconnaissance duties to commence attacks on England. Behncke wrote to von Pohl supporting this proposal, then penned a draft order, sending it to the commander of the High Seas Fleet, Vizeadmiral Friedrich von Ingenohl, for consideration. In it Behncke continued to stress the importance of attacks on London, where sites including some that were only of civil interest before the war now had a military significance too.

> Target area will be London and the Thames region from London to Woolwich-Bec[k]ton inclusive. Chief target within this is the Admiralty with its radio station. Further targets are: main telegraph office, gas works in London-Bec[k]ton, harbour works west and south of Woolwich, oil tanks at Greenwich and Woolwich and the Woolwich Arsenal.[3]

Of these, only bombs falling in the vicinity of the Admiralty building, about 1,000 yards from Buckingham Palace, had the potential to make the Kaiser nervous.

Behncke added that secondary targets could include Immingham, Dover, Portsmouth, Southampton, Liverpool and Manchester. But London was the chief goal and air attacks, he considered, offered a 'means of forcing England to her knees'. Behncke's proposals were not actioned and never reached the Kaiser. Now, however, the Army started to show an interest in air attacks.

On 10 October, two days after the successful raid on the Düsseldorf Zeppelin shed by the RNAS, the Chief of the Army General Staff, General Erich von Falkenhayn, rather surprisingly informed the

Navy that the Army planned to commence air raids on England on 1 November. Surprising because at that date the Army had only two Zeppelins in the west and one of those was the old *Sachsen*. Even so, the Army proposed cooperation with the Navy. It intended moving its airships from bases on the Rhine into France and Belgium, offering the use of these vacated bases to the naval airships. But again, nothing came of the proposal.[4]

At the same time the Army instigated a plan to commence aeroplane raids on London. The plan, proposed by Major Wilhelm Siegert, a great innovator and leader in German military aviation, called for the formation of a special squadron for raiding England. The plan received approval from the *Oberste Heeresleitung (OHL)* – the Army High Command – and, on 19 October, von Falkenhayn gave Siegert command of the squadron. The limited range and weight-carrying capacity of the available aircraft meant that a base close to Calais – the shortest route to London – was essential for the plan to succeed, and as the German Army pushed ahead, few doubted they would achieve that. In the meantime, Siegert recruited the very best pilots and observers for his special force, setting up a temporary base at Ghistelles in occupied Belgium about five miles south of Ostend. The new unit, *Fliegerkorps der OHL* (Air Corps of the Army High Command), operated under the rather unlikely code name of *Brieftauben Abteilung Ostende* – the Ostend Carrier Pigeon Detachment. But with each aircraft able to carry only four 10kg bombs it is hard to imagine these aircraft – B-type two-seaters designed for reconnaissance by the likes of Albatros and Aviatik – could have caused significant damage, but rapidly changing circumstances meant the opportunity to try would elude them. The first battle of Ypres halted the German IV Army's advance in November 1914, forcing each side to dig in. The rapid movement of the early months of the war was over, with Calais lying frustratingly out of reach. This stalemate meant London was now beyond the reach of Siegert's 'carrier pigeons', forcing them to refocus their attention on targets closer to home.[5]

Returning to the strategic use of airships, von Falkenhayn called a conference on 18 November to discuss a joint aerial operation against England, recommending a start date of 1 December. The naval officers who attended, Konteradmiral Philipp and Korvettenkapitän Peter Strasser, commander of the Naval Airship Division, were unimpressed with the command structure and organization of their opposite numbers in the Army and again nothing concrete arose from their discussions, which particularly rankled Strasser.

Peter Strasser was a man with an unswerving belief in the ability of airships to deliver a crushing blow against Britain. Born in 1876, Strasser joined the Imperial Navy aged 15, then progressed to the *Marineakademie*, the Naval Academy at Kiel. He became an expert in gunnery while serving on a number of ships, which led to a specialist naval posting. In 1911 he volunteered for aviation training and learned to fly airships on the *Sachsen*. Then, following the death of the Naval Airship Division's commander, Friedrich Metzing, in the crash of Zeppelin L 2 in September 1913, Strasser accepted the offer of command of the division. With the division moribund and in disarray following Metzing's death, Strasser displayed inspirational leadership, instilling confidence and pride in the men under his command. Totally committed to the job, Strasser proved a charismatic leader and a strict disciplinarian, but also took great care of his men, developing a fine *esprit de corps* in the ranks of the Naval Airship Division. He regularly flew on missions to experience at first-hand the difficulties his crews experienced in action and maintained his ultimately misguided faith in airships as an effective weapon of war right to the end.

The indecisive nature of the planning continued even after two raids by French aircraft on the German town of Freiburg in early December. Stung by this attack, demands for retaliation grew and the Army High Command put London on the back-burner and turned its attention to planning raids on Nancy, Dunkirk and Verdun, suggesting to von Pohl on Christmas Day that the Navy conduct simultaneous operations. Straining at the leash to take action, Strasser telegraphed von Pohl advising him that weather conditions were favourable for an attack on England. The vacillating von Pohl, swayed by these communications, recommended that the Navy's airships commence attacks on the east coast of England while those of the Army concentrated on targets in France. London, he felt, should remain free from attack until co-operation with the Army was possible. The Navy Minister, Tirpitz, however, advised caution, he preferred delaying all air attacks until both airship fleets could concentrate their efforts against the capital.[6]

Von Pohl wavered again, then his opposite number on the Army staff, von Falkenhayn, aired his concerns. How would the Kaiser react to future joint aerial operations against Britain if naval bombs caused damage to places over which he had already specifically raised concerns? Von Pohl, who feared the displeasure of the Kaiser keenly, changed his mind once more, sending a telegram direct to Strasser on 26 December cancelling the proposed raid. Then, the following day, he explained his change of heart to von Ingenohl stating, in reference to the Kaiser, 'with respect to an air attack on London, there prevail at this time in other circles very serious scruples which will first have to be resolved'.[7]

While indecision and prevarication hampered the highest echelons of the Army and Navy command structures, at the seaplane station at Zeebrugge the naval flyers were demonstrating an independent spirit and appeared unconcerned about awakening the wrath of imperial displeasure.

21–24 December 1914: Dover, Kent

German seaplane unit *Seeflieger Abteilung 1* (SFA 1) had set up its base at Zeebrugge in November 1914, becoming operational on 17 December. Commanding the seaplanes – or more correctly, floatplanes – was Oberleutnant-zur-See (Oblt-z-S) Friedrich von Arnauld de la Pérriere, with Oblt-z-S Stephen Prondzynski as second-in-command.

Four days after becoming operational, Prondzynski, with an observer, took off from Zeebrugge in a newly introduced 120hp floatplane, the Friedrichshafen FF 29, no. 203, and flew the 80 miles westward to the port of Dover. They carried on board two bombs. The FF 29 approached Dover unobserved and, as it closed on the harbour, released the weapons. They exploded in the sea 400 yards south-west of the Admiralty Pier. The boom of the explosions took Dover's defenders by surprise and those manning the gun defences contacted each other asking: 'What are you firing at?' A coastguard who caught a glimpse of the aircraft was able to settle matters, but it was too late to get any aircraft airborne. Many in the town remained convinced the sound had been that of guns firing and it was only five days later that newspapers reported that a German aircraft had dropped bombs over the harbour. It was the start of a long-running campaign of 'tip and run' attacks on Dover and other Kent coastal towns by German floatplanes based on the Belgium coast.[8]

Three days later, on Christmas Eve, SFA 1 launched another attack on Dover (see Map 2). This time the pilot was von Arnauld de la Pérriere himself, with Oblt-z-S Hermann Moll as observer, flying Friedrichshafen FF 29, no. 204. Concerned by the recent raid on the harbour, the RNAS decided to move two aircraft that day – Bristol T.B.8s – from Eastchurch to Dover as additional cover for the Christmas period.[9] However, for the residents of Dover, who were busy making their final preparations for Christmas, any thoughts of German aircraft attacking the town were far from their minds. Everyone was going about their business. Many were shopping in the town, elsewhere a gardener, John Banks, had clambered up into a tree in the garden of St James's Rectory to cut evergreen branches to decorate the church. The Reverend T.B. Watkins and his family, who lived at the rectory, were out but their cook was there, busy in the kitchen. Meanwhile, a short distance away on Taswell Hill, a couple of lads were chatting.[10]

The two aircraft intended to bolster Dover's defences left Eastchurch at about 10.15am on Christmas Eve, but just 15 minutes later the keen-eyed in Dover saw fleeting glimpses of an unidentified light-brown coloured aircraft through breaks in low cloud, approaching from the direction of Deal at about 5,000 feet. At about 10.45am, without warning, the raider dropped a single 10kg bomb. It seems likely his target was Dover Castle but the bomb fell 350 yards from the outer wall. One of the lads on Taswell Hill, the son of prominent Dover solicitor Martyn Mowll, heard a whirring sound, looked up and 'saw an object falling in the garden at the rear of St James's Rectory, with smoke following in its trail'. The eyewitness was standing about 25 yards away when the bomb hit the ground followed by what he described as a 'terrible explosion'; seconds later the bewildered friends were covered in a shower of earth but unhurt. In town, people stopped their shopping and looked up as they heard a muffled roar and saw a column of smoke and debris rise in the direction of the castle. Those of an inquisitive nature rushed off to see what had happened.

The bomb – the first dropped on British soil – landed in the kitchen garden of an auctioneer, Thomas A. Terson, gouging a five feet deep crater in the well-turned earth, blasting his cabbages asunder, wrecking a summerhouse and shattering the glass in his greenhouse. The concussion of the blast blew John Banks, the gardener, out of the tree but fortunately a bush broke his fall and he escaped serious injury. One of the many sharp metal fragments of the bomb case stuck into the tree close to where Banks had been moments before. Eager souvenir hunters recovered others up to a hundred yards away, although one piece found on the veranda of a house in Victoria Park must have travelled nearer 175 yards. One fragment of the bomb recovered by members of the Dover Anti-Aircraft Corps was mounted and sent as a gift to the King. All around the area windows were smashed, including those at the rectory. The Reverend Watkin's cook was showered in shattered glass but emerged unscathed.

As soon as the German aircraft had appeared, a Wight seaplane (Admiralty Type 840) took off from the East Promenade but the aircraft was a poor climber. At 11.10am, not having yet got above the clouds, the pilot gave up and returned to base. At about the same time the two aircraft from Eastchurch landed at the RNAS Dover aerodrome at Guston Road. Advised of the raid one of the pilots, Flt Lt Harold Buss, took off again but saw nothing of the long-departed raider.[11]

Britain had experienced its first air raid in history. It had not been made, as many anticipated, by a fleet of marauding Zeppelins loaded with a great cargo of bombs, rather it came from a lone floatplane dropping a single 10kg missile. After almost five months of waiting, this first raid raised little excitement in the press.

Christmas Day 1914: Thames Estuary, Kent

Buoyed by their achievement of being the first to bomb Britain, the pilots of SFA 1 were keen to keep up the pressure and on Christmas Day they planned a more daring attack (see Map 2). This time they would strike against the London docks. Again, a single aircraft made the raid, the same Friedrichshafen FF 29 that dropped the bombs in Dover harbour on 21 December, flown by Prondzynski and his observer Fähnrich-zur-See (Fähn-z-S) Ludwig von Frankenberg. In the meantime, anticipating another attack, the two Bristol T.B.8s that had arrived at Dover the day before flew alternate standing patrols northwards towards Deal and back. Unfortunately for Britain's defences, Prondzynski and von Frankenberg made their first appearance at 12.35pm about 30 miles to the north-west, off Sheerness on the Isle of Sheppey.[12] Although a number of AA guns blasted their shells into the misty sky, they found it difficult to estimate accurately the height of the FF 29, which was flying at about 7,000 feet. The raider then turned south-west, seeming to follow the River Medway towards Chatham but, having dropped to a height between 5,000 and 6,000 feet, then steered north-west across the Isle of Grain back to the Thames. Having regained the river, the FF 29 now followed the Thames upstream towards Gravesend and Tilbury.

As word of an enemy aircraft flying up the Thames spread, telephone calls alerted the RNAS airfields at Grain and Eastchurch, which both got an aircraft airborne. The RFC reacted too, with single aircraft taking off from Farnborough and Brooklands. More importantly, the RFC's Vickers F.B.5 'Gunbus', mounting a Maxim machine gun, took to the air from Joyce Green near Dartford. The 'Gunbus' was the first

British aircraft designed for combat in the air. It was a 'pusher' type, meaning that rather than having the engine and propeller mounted on the nose, they were positioned behind the crew 'pushing' the aircraft forward. This arrangement allowed the fitting of the machine gun to the observer's cockpit in the nose.[13]

The FF 29 was now flying at about 4,000 feet as it approached Erith where, at 1.15pm, it encountered the 'Gunbus' flown by 2nd Lieutenant Montagu Chidson with his observer/gunner, Corporal Martin. An eyewitness recognized the significance of the moment when he wrote:

> I heard from a westerly direction the heavy droning of a biplane, and looking up saw an aeroplane flying almost against the clouds, while some distance behind was a biplane which I immediately made out to be a British craft. While watching the flight of the two machines, which I thought was really that of two machines making their way from one base to another, I was startled to hear the boom of a gun, followed in quick succession by other reports. Going to the top room of my house I was able to see the first fight and pursuit between German and British aircraft and British gunnery in Great Britain … Although the pursued and pursuer were flying at a great height – the German must have been at least 4,000 feet up – the British craft seemed to be gaining. 'Boom, boom,' went the guns, and the hills around re-echoed the sounds of the first real warfare heard in the Thames estuary for centuries. [14]

Martin opened fire with his Maxim, at which point Prondzynski, perhaps only six miles from the first of the London docks, turned the FF 29 away with the 'Gunbus' in hot pursuit. Both aircraft came under anti-aircraft (AA) fire from Purfleet. Early reports indicated that the raider dropped a bomb on Dartford but later confirmation showed it was one of the shells fired from Purfleet. Martin continued firing short bursts at the FF 29 as they passed over Tilbury on the Essex side of the Thames, by which time the German aircraft had climbed back up to a height estimated at between 5,000 and 6,000ft.

Prondzynski now crossed back over the river to the south bank of the Thames near Shornemead Fort and, with his pursuers now struggling with a badly running engine, he gradually began to edge ahead. At 1.35pm, as the FF 29 passed back over the Hoo Peninsula towards the Isle of Grain, Prondzynski and von Frankenberg released their two bombs. Prondzynski reported they attacked oil storage tanks at Sheerness but the bombs exploded harmlessly almost 15 miles west of Sheerness, in open fields about 200 yards south of Cliffe station. At St Helen's church, Mr W. Wicker was attending a wedding service with his wife:

> While the clergyman was reading the service we heard a noise like someone banging carpets against the walls of the church. My wife said: 'Whoever's doing that hasn't much thought or sense.'
>
> But as we followed the bride and bridegroom to the door we realized that 'Fritz' had come to England with almost his first bombing aeroplane, and the happy couple and the guests made an undignified rush for the carriages and home. Bombs had been dropping: we could not partake of the wedding breakfast because some of the guests fainted.[15]

As the guests hastily dispersed, the pursuit continued down the Medway with the AA guns around Chatham joining the aerial battle, but the Maxim on the 'Gunbus' now jammed and Martin was unable to rectify the problem as he had forgotten to grab his gloves in the rush to get airborne, leaving his hands frozen by the cold. By the time the 'Gunbus' reached Sheerness at about 2.00pm it was now trailing about a mile behind the raider, so Chidson gave up the chase and landed at Eastchurch.

Over Herne Bay, one of Dover's Bristol T.B.8s, again piloted by Harold Buss, had taken up a position from where he hoped to intercept the raider on its return. Now spotting the FF 29 some way off, Buss gave chase back across Kent, but Prondzynski and von Frankenberg had a speed advantage and passed out to sea south of Ramsgate. Unable to close the gap, the disappointed British pilot returned to Dover. Before they reached Zeebrugge, however, the German crew landed on the sea off the coast of Flanders to verify their position and came under fire from an Allied position. Before they got airborne again von Frankenberg received a slight wound in his elbow.

When Chidson, Martin, Prondzynski and von Frankenberg checked over their aircraft at the end of their missions both crews discovered damage, whether caused by enemy bullets or AA shell fragments proved impossible to tell: the 'Gunbus' had a splintered landing skid while the FF 29 showed damage to its floats and fuselage. For their efforts the German crew received the Iron Cross, while their British opponents' reward came courtesy of the ever-enthusiastic gunners at Purfleet, who gave them another burst of AA fire on their flight back to Joyce Green. The gunner's enthusiasm far outweighed their aircraft recognition skills at this early stage in the air war. For Chidson and Martin it had been a Christmas Day to remember.

Christmas Day 1914: Nordholz (Cuxhaven), Germany

The excitement on Christmas Day extended beyond the Thames estuary. Far out in the North Sea, Churchill's determination to take the war to the Zeppelins before they could attack Britain continued. Previously aborted in November, the Navy again targeted the Naval Airship Division's Zeppelin sheds at Nordholz for the first ever carrier-borne seaplane attack. The location was hardly prepossessing. One airship commander based at Nordholz in 1914, Oblt-z-S Treusch von Buttlar Brandenfels (von Buttlar), bemoaned it as 'the most God-forsaken – one might almost say the most man-forsaken – hole on earth'. Perhaps, therefore, it should not come as a surprise that the attack is now better known as the Cuxhaven Raid, after the port about eight miles away at the mouth of the Elbe.[16]

On Christmas Eve three seaplane carriers, the converted cross-channel ferries, *Engadine, Riviera* and *Empress*, set sail from Harwich heading for the Heligoland Bight area of the North Sea. With them sailed two cruisers, HMS *Arethusa* and HMS *Undaunted*, with eight destroyers of the Harwich Force commanded by Commodore Reginald Tyrwhitt. The seaplane carriers were unlike modern aircraft carriers in that they did not launch aircraft from their decks. Their role was to carry three seaplanes each to the launch zone, then after the carriers had stopped, they lowered the seaplanes over the side on to the sea. At the end of a mission the seaplanes would, hopefully, manage to land close to the parent ship for recovery aboard. Tyrwhitt's force received support from HMS *Fearless*, eight destroyers and a submarine flotilla. As a back-up, in case Tyrwhitt's presence lured Germany's High Seas Fleet out to sea, Admiral John Jellicoe steered the Royal Navy's Grand Fleet to a position in the North Sea from where it could engage if the situation demanded.

The naval airship station at Nordholz, the seaplanes' target, had only recently become operational. Uniquely it featured a huge double shed constructed on a vast turntable. This gave it the significant advantage of being able to turn to the best angle to restrict the effects of potentially damaging crosswinds on Zeppelins when departing or returning. The shed was home to L 5 and L 6, two of the latest 'm-class'

Zeppelins, the same type as L 7 that had narrowly avoided destruction at Friedrichshafen, and the Army's Z IX incinerated at Düsseldorf.

Early on the morning of 25 December, Tyrwhitt's strike force reached its launch position north of the island of Heligoland. Although it was bitterly cold, the weather conditions seemed perfect for the raid with a calm sea and excellent visibility. The aerial strike force consisted of three different types of seaplane, all manufactured by Short Brothers: the Folder, the Type 74 and the Type 135. The carriers lowered all nine seaplanes to the water, three of each type completed checks and ran their engines. Just before 7.00am all was ready. While this process was under way Zeppelin L 6, commanded by Oblt-z-S von Buttlar, left the Nordholz shed at the start of a routine North Sea patrol. [17]

After a short delay seven of the nine raiders managed to take off, the other two returned to their carriers and the fleet steamed west to the area chosen for the rendezvous after the mission. The airborne raiders, each armed with three 20lb Hales bombs and following their own line, set course for Nordholz, but all kept to the east of Heligoland where the Germans had a seaplane station. Alerted to the presence of British ships, however, a number of seaplanes were out trying to locate them, and Zeppelin L 5, commanded by Kapitänleutnant (Kptlt) Klaus Hirsch, left Nordholz to join the search.

Two seaplanes were first to discover Tyrwhitt's ships. A Friedrichshafen FF 19 closed on the carrier *Empress*, which was struggling to keep up with the rest of the fleet. The commander of the *Empress*, Lieutenant Frederick Bowhill, began steering a zig-zag course hoping to put the attacker off his aim. It worked because all six of the FF 19's bombs landed some distance off. The second seaplane, believed to be a Friedrichshafen FF 29, then closed in to make its attack. It carried just two bombs and they landed much closer. Bowhill recorded one 'dropping 20 feet away on port beam and shaking the ship severely'. Having exhausted their supply of bombs the two seaplanes turned away but *Empress* had not escaped.

Zeppelin L 6, commanded by von Buttlar, had arrived and now prepared to attack.[18] Fortunately for *Empress*, as L 6 was on a reconnaissance flight she only carried three 50kg bombs. So began a cat-and-mouse pursuit of the struggling carrier as L 6 dropped its first bomb. It missed and von Buttlar had to retreat as the guns of *Arethusa* and *Undaunted* commenced firing at a range of about two miles. The two cruisers then turned away, at which point L 6 returned to attack *Empress* again. This time the bomb landed much closer to the target but von Buttlar had to seek cloud cover as the guns of *Arethusa* and *Undaunted* renewed their fire on him. And so it continued. L 6 attacked again, dropping its third and final bomb, which again missed the target, the cruisers engaged with their guns, then L 6 attacked *Empress* with machine gun fire, to which the carrier replied with her pair of 12-pdrs supported by rifle fire from the crew.

Without any bombs and under fire from the British ships, von Buttlar recognized that he was risking his airship and with little more to achieve he turned for Nordholz. He returned via the mouth of the Jade River. The flight home, however, became a struggle as the airship seemed heavy and only responded sluggishly to the controls. Following an inspection the next day, the crew discovered the reason why. The rifle bullets fired by the crew of the *Empress* had made around 600 tiny holes in the gas cells, causing a loss of hydrogen. In the meantime, as von Buttlar and L 6 had limped back after their encounter, the raid on Nordholz was already over.

Although the Nordholz shed was empty as the raiders closed in, its destruction would have still been a costly setback for the Naval Airship Division. It was not to be. Although all seven seaplanes crossed the coast, none managed to locate the great double shed. As they reached the coastline the clear skies over the sea disappeared, replaced by thick banks of fog blotting out the landscape below. The pilots described visibility of only 100 yards, while in other places they just caught fleeting glimpses of houses in occasional gaps in the swirling murk. The pilots flew backwards and forwards at low altitudes over the general location of the sheds but found nothing.

Eventually all pilots turned back over the coast, running the gauntlet of fire from ships anchored in the Jade, Weser and Elbe rivers. One of them, experiencing problems with the fuel supply, landed on the sea and had to out-run a German trawler before getting airborne again; two others also had close encounters with Zeppelin L 5. One of the returning seaplanes missed the rendezvous area completely and ran out of fuel, putting down on the sea where a Dutch trawler later found the forlorn pilot and took him back to Holland. Three of the raiders displayed excellent navigation skills and safely reached the rendezvous to be reunited with their carriers, but the crews of the remaining three were all rescued by submarine *E11* some miles south-east of the appointed area.

During this delicate retrieval operation Zeppelin L 5 spotted the submarine on the surface and tension rose as she closed rapidly. With the last of the rescued airman safely on board and the hatch slammed shut, the submarine submerged just as L 5 began her attack. She released two bombs but they exploded harmlessly above the submarine as it reached a depth of 40 feet.

While the raid was in progress the High Seas Fleet remained firmly in harbour, thus avoiding a great naval encounter in the North Sea. All the British ships returned safely to their home ports. The raid was over, another attempt to destroy the Zeppelins in their lair had failed, but with better weather conditions the outcome could have been very different. This aspect was not lost on the senior officers of the Naval Airship Division.

Late December 1914: London and Berlin

As 1914 drew to a close, Britain's aerial defences gradually showed signs of improvement. By the end of year many of the guns referred to in Rear-Admiral Tudor's report issued in September were in place. Of the Hotchkiss 6-pdrs, 63 were in position: 29 formed part of the Chatham and Medway defences, Portsmouth had 12, while Dover, Harwich, Woolwich, Erith, Waltham Abbey, Tyne, Humber and in Scotland, Rosyth, Ardeer and Invergordon, each received two guns. Single 6-pdrs took up positions at Portland and at Windsor Castle. Portsmouth also received seven 3-pdrs and Liverpool three. A number of 'pom-poms' were also distributed as were searchlights, all in anticipation of the long-awaited coming of the Zeppelins. Some of these guns had already been engaged in action, opposing the Christmas attacks on Dover and the Thames estuary.[19]

The progress of that lone German aircraft up the Thames also had a direct effect on London's defences. The Admiralty diverted three AA guns destined for the Fleet to form the beginning of a gun ring about six miles out from Charing Cross, supported by searchlights. One on Parliament Hill would serve to protect the north-western residential areas; another at the ground of Clapton Orient football club could oppose attacks from the northern Germany airship sheds; while the third, on One Tree Hill at Honor Oak, was in a position to oppose attacks on London from Belgium and northern France. It also led to an increase in the number of aircraft, both landplanes and seaplanes, allocated by the Admiralty to home defence.[20]

Back in Germany the indecision apparent in the corridors of power in the days leading up to Christmas contributed to a mounting frustration among those such as Behncke, Philipp and Strasser who wholeheartedly supported the commencement of Zeppelin raids against Britain. Following the latest attack on the Zeppelin sheds and von Pohl's decision on 26 December to cancel the latest plan to launch the naval Zeppelins against Britain, this frustration now came to a head. It was too much for Philipp, head of naval aviation. In an angry letter to von Pohl he wrote:

> Recently London, then the whole of England was forbidden to the naval airships for special operations because the Army is now using their airships in ground fighting in France and apparently does not want the Navy to go ahead by itself …
>
> If the Army uses ships in France indefinitely, and the Navy is forced to wait for a plan of common operations, the great fighting capacity of the Navy ships will remain completely unused for a long time. They will be destroyed without results by enemy plane attacks.[21]

He concluded by adding that he believed the Army lacked 'a determined and expertly trained leadership' and because of this he requested that the Navy airships be given a free hand to operate against London and the rest of Britain on its own terms. Pushed on by his subordinates, von Pohl, who had so far not presented any of the plans to commence aerial bombing of England to the Kaiser, met with him on 7 January 1915 and recommended that Navy airships begin an 'offensive employment' against Britain that month, adding that 'co-operation with the Army is not practical'. Three days later von Pohl was able to send a telegram to the commander of the High Seas Fleet, Vizeadmiral von Ingenohl. The message was music to the ears of men like Strasser. 'Air attacks on England approved by the Supreme War Lord [Kaiser Wilhelm]. Targets not to be attacked in London but rather docks and military establishments in the lower Thames and on the English coast.'[22]

Not a man to waste time, Strasser submitted his plans to von Ingenohl later that same day.

Chapter 5

'Oh, Good God, What is It?'

Strasser's plans submitted on 10 January to von Ingenohl, the commander of the High Seas Fleet, were straightforward. He listed his targets as the Tyne, the mouth of the Humber, Great Yarmouth, Lowestoft, Harwich and the mouth of the Thames, but excluded London. He also specified that of the five naval airships available in the west (L 3 to L 6 and L 8),[1] at least one should remain behind to be available for reconnaissance patrols.

Zeppelins would leave their bases during daylight hours and combine aerial scouting on the journey over the sea. Attacks would take place in the evening with the return flights made in the dark of night. Favouring the darkest nights, the attack period would roughly coincide with an eight-day window either side of the new moon, but be dependent on the weather. Individual commanders could abandon missions at their own discretion if weather became unfavourable when over the North Sea. The new moon was set for 15 January, giving a raiding window from 8 to 23 January. With his plans on the table, Strasser now just waited for a suitable opening in the weather. On 13 January it looked like that moment had arrived.[2]

January 1915: Germany

Although Strasser was away on an inspection, when he heard that the weather appeared suitable he gave his approval and four Zeppelins made ready. L 3 and L 4 departed from the Hamburg sheds at Fuhlsbüttel, with L 5 and L 6 taking off from the revolving shed at Nordholz. Kptlt Heinrich Mathy, destined to become one of Strasser's most trusted and effective commanders, was placed in command of the raid and flew in the control gondola of L 5. Mathy had been working as Strasser's deputy in an administrative role at Nordholz while awaiting the completion of the Navy's latest airship, Zeppelin L 9, which he finally took command of in March. No doubt the Zeppelin commanders set out in high spirits but the weather, as it did so often, thwarted the raid. By early afternoon heavy rain made further progress over the North Sea risky, forcing Mathy to give the order to turn back. Heavy rain soaking into the envelope (the linen outer covering of the airship) could add huge amounts of additional weight, which proved a significant problem for these early Zeppelins. All four airships returned safely to their home bases. The next opportunity came six days later.

19 January 1915: East Anglia

Tuesday, 19 January 1915 began like any other working day in the towns of Great Yarmouth and King's Lynn. The two towns shared little in common. Great Yarmouth, on the east coast of Norfolk, was a well-established seaside resort and home to a thriving fishing fleet. The RNAS had established a station just south of the town at South Denes in April 1913. Being so close to the town it ensured the residents became very familiar with the sight and sounds of aircraft; in many parts of the country, aircraft still exercised a novelty effect on those who saw them. Just under 60 miles away, King's Lynn stands on the Great Ouse river about five miles south of The Wash in west Norfolk, close to the county border with Lincolnshire. In medieval times King's Lynn could rightly claim to be the most important port in England due to the flourishing sea trade with Europe, but that importance had faded over the centuries. On 19 January the war must have seemed a long way away for the residents of both towns. And they had every reason to feel secure. Why would anyone want to attack them? Little did they know that Great Yarmouth featured as a target on Strasser's 'hit-list'. Later that day both towns would enter the history books, being subject to the first Zeppelin raid of the war on Britain.

19 January 1915: Fuhlsbüttel and Nordholz, Germany

At Fuhlsbüttel (now the site of Hamburg airport) on the morning of 19 January the thermometer hovered just below freezing as L 3 and L 4 lay cocooned in their great sheds. Outside, while the breeze hardly stirred the windsocks, all around was a storm of activity. The order had arrived, they were going to England. Just under 60 miles away to the west a similar scene played out at 'God-forsaken' Nordholz, where final preparations were under way prior to the launch of L 6. The moment had finally arrived. The weather, while not perfect, offered promise and it was good enough for Peter Strasser to give the go-ahead. With England apparently finally within reach, Strasser intended to share his crews' experience and assigned himself to L 6, which he ordered to strike targets close to London on the Thames estuary. The two Zeppelins from Fuhlsbüttel aimed for the north of England, heading for the docks and industrial sites close to the coast on the River Humber.

L 3 and L 4 both loaded 18 bombs, weighing about 500kg in total (eight high-explosive (HE) of 50kg and ten 11kg incendiary bombs), and carried crews of 16 men.[3] The commander of L 3, 30-year-old Kptlt Hans Fritz, had held command since the Navy commissioned her in May 1914, during which time he had undertaken many reconnaissance flights over the North Sea. Like Fritz, the magnificently monikered Kptlt Zdenko Magnus Karl Friedrich, Graf von Platen-Hallermund (von Platen), took command of L 4 immediately after commissioning in August 1914. Born in Vienna in 1880, Count von Platen had an interesting night ahead.

At Nordholz, the commander of Zeppelin L 6 – and vying with von Platen in the name stakes – Oblt-z-S Horst Julius Ludwig Otto, Freiherr Treusch von Buttlar-Brandenfels (von Buttlar), who had previously served as executive officer to Fritz on L 3, also made ready. He loaded a heavier weight of bombs – about 650kg – and carried more fuel, but a reduced crew of 11 men.[4] With Strasser on board, the excitement of the crew was palpable as they completed final checks before the colossal frame of their airship gently lifted into the sky at 9.38am (British time, 8.38am). Just over an hour later L 3 and L 4 were airborne from Fuhlsbüttel.

The excitement felt by the crew of L 6, however, soon evaporated. Five hours into the mission and averaging less than 30mph, L 6 was to the north-east of the Dutch island of Terschelling when the port engine's crankshaft broke. With the mouth of the Thames estuary still about 240 miles away and only two of the three engines working, to continue offered too great a risk in the freezing temperatures. After a short discussion, Strasser pondered for a moment then decided 'in agreement with the commander of L 6, but with heavy heart, to turn back.'[5] At the same time L 3 and L 4 were out over the vast expanse of the North Sea still heading for the Humber, but the wind, which had previously been blowing from the west and south-west, had now veered to the north and proceeded to push them south of their chosen course. For the crews of these 'm-class' Zeppelins, weather had a significant impact. The gondolas in which the crews worked, slung below the framework of the Zeppelin, were completely open to the elements except for a small windshield at the front. With cloud cover building and the onset of freezing rain, the already harsh conditions were becoming miserable. They made an average speed of 36mph across the North Sea, until, at about 7.40pm, a man at the village of Ingham in Norfolk, almost three miles south of Happisburgh, to his great surprise saw lights approaching from over the sea (see Map 1). He described them as 'like two bright stars'.[6]

19 January 1915, 8.20–8.35pm: Great Yarmouth, Norfolk

It appears that the lights separated shortly before they reached land. L 3 approached Happisburgh at about 7.55pm and dropped a magnesium parachute flare. These flares drifted slowly to the ground, giving off an intense bright light. As the flare burnt, officers studied the ground below and pored over maps hoping to pinpoint their whereabouts. Fritz managed to identify the Happisburgh lighthouse without too much delay, which suggests he already had an inkling when he consulted the maps that he had drifted far off course. The Humber was now out of reach, but Great Yarmouth had featured as a possible target on Strasser's list. Making his choice, Fritz came inland and proceeded towards the south-east. Keeping the coastline on his port side, he steered towards his new target.

At about 8.15pm, after enduring a flight of almost 11 hours in below-freezing conditions, Fritz dropped another parachute flare as he passed between Martham and the coast, and from its glare he identified the lighthouse at Winterton. He was now just eight miles north of Great Yarmouth.

High above, in the command gondola of L 3, Fritz ordered the release of an incendiary bomb. It became standard practice to release an incendiary before commencing the main bomb run. Observing the burning bomb allowed the commander to ascertain ground speed and sideways drift. This bomb fell in a waterlogged field on George Humphrey's farm at Ormesby St Michael (also known as Little Ormesby), where it ignited before sinking into the boggy ground.[7] It would appear, having watched the bomb, that Fritz felt the need to correct his course because at 8.22pm he passed south of Caister and out to sea, then turned immediately before heading directly over Great Yarmouth. Many residents in the town reported hearing a strange buzzing sound in the sky and came out into the streets to stare upwards. One newspaper reported that 'the night was dark and still, and it was difficult to distinguish the aircraft, but some people state that they saw the outlines of an airship'. Another reporter wrote: 'I could find no one in Yarmouth who actually saw the aircraft, although there are vague stories of "long black shapes" and things in the sky "like a big black cigar".' But a man at the quay was dismissive of such stories:

> Those who tell you they saw Zeppelins are telling a fairy tale. The night was as black as a ton of coal, and whatever it was gone before you could pull yourself together and feel if your legs and arms was still where they ought to be.[8]

Fritz brought L 3 over the town at a height of about 5,000 feet – about a mile high. His orders were to make his bombing run at 7,500 feet but the rain and ice had made his ship heavy and he was unable to climb higher. He released his first bomb over the town at 8.25pm. The incendiary landed on a lawn at the rear of fish dealer Norford Suffling's house at 6 Albemarle Road, which backed on to Norfolk Square, and buried itself a foot down in the soil. Although the bomb split open with 'a flash and a loud roar' it caused no damage other than splattering the walls of the house with mud.[9]

Because an incendiary bomb does not ignite with any great noise, most in the town remained unaware that anything was amiss. Then followed the sudden terrifying arrival of the first high-explosive (HE) bomb. It fell at the back of 78 Crown Road, the home of an elderly couple, Mr and Mrs Osborne. Mrs Osborne was in the backyard about to go through the gate on to Gordon Terrace 'to do a little shopping' when the bomb smashed into a concrete paving slab. Fortunately for Mrs Osborne it failed to explode. She fled back into the house and fainted in her husband's arms. Later, when she had recovered, she told a reporter from the *Yarmouth Mercury*: 'It was awful. If I had gone just a step or two further I must have been killed by it.'

There is some confusion at this point as to whether one or two bombs fell behind Crown Road. Certainly another bomb, or part of the same bomb, struck the gatepost of W.F. Miller's stable yard and buried itself in the ground. Either way it frightened the life out of Miller's sister-in-law and her daughter, Elsie, who were among those lured to their doors by strange sounds in the sky. There are no question marks, however, over the next bomb. It exploded in St Peter's Plain with deadly results.

That dark January night was misty and damp and, with the war now more than five months old without any sign of a Zeppelin attack, life carried on as normal. Samuel Smith, a 53-year-old shoemaker, had just finished work for the day at his shop in St Peter's Plain, while just opposite him, Edward Ellis, a fishworker, was at home alone with his wife and children away in Cornwall. Martha Mary Taylor, a 72-year-old spinster, was on her way back to Drake's Buildings, off St Peter's Plain, where she lived with her twin sister Jane Eliza. She had popped out to buy something for their supper. Mrs Scott, whose husband had joined the Army Service Corps the previous day, was getting her 2-year-old child ready for bed, while at St Peter's Church nearby, the Reverend W. McCarthy had just concluded a service.

The blast of the bomb sliced away the front of St Peter's Villa, the home of Edward Ellis. Fortunately, Mr Ellis had just gone to his kitchen and avoided the worst effects of the blast. Even so, the back door was blown off its hinges and landed on top of him, as did a shower of glass from the kitchen window. He received cuts to his head and legs, which required hospital treatment; but while he had been lucky others were not so fortunate.

Samuel Smith the cobbler was standing by the gate to his workshop and Martha Taylor, who had just reached the corner of St Peter's Plain and Lancaster Road, was walking up towards where he stood. Neither of them stood a chance. The blast flung Smith back down the dark passage to his workshop while Martha Taylor crumpled into a heap on the pavement, her body looking like a pile of carelessly discarded rags among the rubble, roof tiles and other debris cast about by the blast.[10]

The sound of the explosion alerted a company of the National Reserve based about 50 yards away at the Drill Hall. Sergeant Henry John Cox rushed to St Peter's Plain with some of the men. Private Alexander Brown reported at the inquest: 'I stumbled over a lot of refuse in St Peter's Plain, and saw what I thought was a bundle. On closer examination I found that it was the body of a woman.' Martha Taylor was dead. The post-mortem examination revealed the scale of her injuries:

> The left side, from shoulder to hip, was opened and the organs practically destroyed. The right shoulder joint and the right knee-joint bone were broken, the region of the right ankle was injured and the greater portion of the right arm was missing.[11]

A policeman found her severed arm in the street the following morning.

Shortly after the discovery of Martha Taylor's body, members of the public stumbled upon Samuel Smith lying in the passageway to his workshop. A policeman borrowed a candle to light the passage and then inspected the body. He found Smith 'lying on his left side. I could see he was badly knocked about and was dead ... He was lying in a pool of blood when I found him'. Dr Horace Potts, who performed the post-mortem, added more gruesome details. He noted that the top of Smith's 'skull had been nearly blown away, and the brain stripped from the base of the skull'. In addition he noted that the left thigh 'was very extensively lacerated, and almost divided from the body'. The post-mortems recorded that both victims were likely to have died instantly in the explosion, thus becoming the first recorded deaths in Britain due to aerial bombardment.[12]

The blast damaged neighbouring buildings too. At 17 St Peter's Plain the explosion rocked William Storey's house: the gas went out, plunging the house into darkness as windows smashed and doors flew off their hinges. There were five others in the house, including two babies, one aged two and the other just nine months old; all emerged covered in soot and dust, shocked but unscathed. Next door at No. 18, Mrs Scott was alone with her child. She heard engines in the sky and would have gone to the door to look if she had not been dressing the child. She told a reporter: 'I think the child saved my life,' adding, 'when the gas went out I dropped the babe on the floor in order to get light again. I had to leave it screaming while I did so'. Having found a candle, Mrs Scott surveyed the damage all around her, wiping the blood from her own face caused by flying glass, but her child was untouched.[13]

The blast shattered windows in all the surrounding streets. At St Peter's Church at the end of the road, the vicar, Reverend W. McCarthy, was in quiet conversation with a parishioner. Just before Christmas he had preached to his congregation on the need for fortitude in the face of German naval bombardment on east coast towns.

> The Admiralty tells us plainly that it cannot protect us against such raids at the cost of a change in the naval plans. It is better that we should be bombarded and suffer loss of life and property than that the issue of the war should be jeopardized by the endeavour to protect us ... No patriot will hesitate to admit that the destruction of the towns on the East Coast would be a small price to pay for the safety of England and the Empire ... It is our privilege, who live on the East Coast, to be in the firing line, and we should brace

ourselves to face the position with a brave heart … we shall now nerve ourselves to face possible loss of life and to have our own names inscribed on the roll of honour.[14]

His personal resolve was now about to be tested fully as the shock wave of the explosion in St Peter's Plain was felt at his church, bringing an abrupt end to his conversation as 'the glass in the windows came pouring in like a cascade'. He made a dash for the vicarage, noting on the way that the blast had ripped open the double-locked vestry door. As he approached the vicarage, much to his horror he saw only gaping holes where windows had previously been. But once inside, to his great relief, he found his two boys who had been sleeping in the nursery, and his mother who had been sitting in the window downstairs, had all escaped injury. He rushed his family down to the cellar that, with some foresight, he had prepared with sandbags for just such an occasion.[15]

The unfortunate Private Poulter, a Territorial soldier in the Essex Regiment, had emerged from a toilet just east of St Peter's Church when the bomb sent jagged metal fragments scything through the air. One struck him in the chest. Doctor Leonard Ley would successfully remove the fragment at the hospital, thus becoming the first doctor in Britain to operate on an air raid victim.

The horrors of the night did not end there. The next HE bomb smashed through the roof of stables in Garden Lane, off Friar's Lane, owned by butcher, William K. Mays. Incredibly, it landed on a pile of hay next to the butcher's pony and failed to explode. No one knew it was there until morning. When the butcher's assistant arrived to prepare the pony for work he noticed an unusual large grey object in the hay, telling a reporter:

> I wondered what it could be and started pulling it about… Suddenly I saw it was a bomb and ran out of the stable. He's a nervous pony, and there he was lying down quietly alongside the bomb … If you clap your hands that pony will jump out of it skin as a rule, and here he has been sleeping all night with a 100lb bomb as a bedfellow.[16]

A few seconds later an incendiary bomb landed on South Quay just yards from the door of the First and Last Tavern, cracking a granite sett in the roadway and smashing one of the pub's windows. The landlord, Arthur Smith, dashed out and grabbed some hot fragments of the bomb as souvenirs. He told a reporter that the bomb held 'some nasty, sticky, yellow stuff inside it'.[17]

'OH, GOOD GOD, WHAT IS IT?'

Two bombs quickly followed, both landing close to the River Yar. The first, an incendiary, struck the gates of Beeching Brothers' South Dock. It disappeared into the water but not before smashing two planks in the gate and flooding the dry dock where the pilot boat *Patrol* was under repair. The second, an HE, struck the edge of the quay at Trinity Wharf close to a sentry of the National Guard but luckily for him it failed to detonate and fell into the river. When a reporter asked him what he did next the soldier replied: 'Why I loosed off at it,' but admitted he could not see his attacker in the dark sky.

Fish Wharf was next on L 3's course over the town. An HE bomb exploded 'in a heap of empty basket nets' close to the base of a salt water tank built on a large brick tower. As it did so it blasted a crater through the granite setts 'in which you could stand up to your knees', bursting a water main below and bringing down an electric street light.

Norford Suffling must have felt like a marked man that night. The first bomb dropped by L 3 had fallen right behind his house in Albemarle Road; now a fragment from this bomb penetrated the wooden wall of his office on Fish Wharf, passing through his iron safe and embedding itself in the wall behind. The blast also shattered the wharf's glass roof and caused much damage to the sales offices. The water tower, which also suffered, having its door torn off and some bricks dislodged, stood between the bomb and a large building known as the Fish Wharf Refreshment Rooms. Even so, the blast lifted part of its roof and smashed all the windows. The owner, Joseph Steel, was out at the time but heard 'two loud reports in quick succession'. He lived with his children in rooms above the business and as he approached his home he must have done so with some trepidation for they were all inside. But fortunately all three children were physically unharmed:

> [My daughter] was seated in the front room of the house, and right in that portion where most of the shock was felt, playing the piano at the time, and the force of the explosion lifted her completely from the piano stool and planted her a distance away against the door of the drawing room. She escaped miraculously without injury. Then my two boys were fortunate in escaping injury. Had they been in bed ... they would have been sleeping in a room where glass was strewn all over the bed and floor after the explosion ... As luck would have it, on this occasion they were rather late, and were playing with Meccano downstairs instead of being in bed.[18]

At night the wharf was largely deserted and from this chaos and destruction only one casualty emerged – Captain Smith, the fish wharf master, with a cut hand.

Moments later another HE bomb exploded by the quayside, peppering and piercing Harry Eastick's steam drifter *Piscatorial* with bomb fragments. 'Looks as if she'd been taking on the German navy all by herself,' remarked a fisherman who viewed the damage later. Then the last bomb dropped. It landed behind the grandstand of the racecourse on South Denes and not far from the Crossley Auxiliary Red Cross Hospital, which had opened just two months previously. Besides gouging a great crater reported to be two feet deep and six feet across and destroying some fencing, it also killed a large black dog.

Kptlt Fritz and the crew of the L 3 passed back out to sea at about 8.35pm. The raid, which lasted only ten minutes, was over. Just as the good people of Great Yarmouth were attempting to make sense of what had just happened, the town authorities belatedly reacted to the attack and switched off the electric supply, plunging the town into darkness in case the raider should decide to return.

Once over the sea, L 3 turned back on to a north-west course and followed the Norfolk coast until, off Cromer at about 10.00pm, Fritz set a new course across the North Sea and headed for what appears to be a pre-arranged rendezvous with L 4 off the Dutch island of Vlieland. But while L 3 had brought terror and death to the streets of Great Yarmouth, what had happened to Kptlt von Platen and L 4?

19 January 1915, 8.30-10.55pm: North Norfolk coast

Von Platen first came inland at Bacton, a little further north than L 3 (see Map 1). Unlike Fritz, the commander of L 4 believed he was close to his target of the Humber. Studying the curve of the coastline he calculated that he was off Lincolnshire somewhere south of Grimsby. He was in fact 80 miles off course.

L 4 passed over the town of Cromer, which was in darkness, but a few moments later, having passed Sheringham, something attracted von Platen's attention causing him to turn back over the town. Many heard it getting closer, L 4's 'approach being heralded by the loud hum of its engines'. At about 8.35pm von Platen released a parachute flare followed by an incendiary bomb.[19] The bomb crashed down through a house occupied by Robert Smith, a bricklayer, and his family in Whitehall Yard off Wyndham Street. Having smashed through the roof and bedroom it came to rest near the fireplace in a ground floor room doubling as a kitchen and living room where Mr and Mrs Smith, their daughter May and her friend were all gathered. Mrs Smith told a reporter: 'I never had such a fright in my life', while her husband added, 'It all came so suddenly ... it is a wonder how we escaped serious injury'. May's friend 'received an injury to her wrist and her hair was singed' while the stool May had been sitting on was damaged.[20] But the incendiary did not fully ignite. How different it could have been. These German incendiary bombs contained benzol (petrol) and thermite, a pyrotechnic composition that burns at incredibly high temperatures. Once ignited by an inertia fuse on contact, the thermite rapidly heats up and burns with an intense heat while spreading burning petrol across the room. Tarred rope wrapped around the bomb keeps it burning after the chemical reaction has died down. The bombs are sometimes called Goldschmidt bombs after the German chemist, Hans Goldschmidt, who patented the thermite chemical reaction in 1895 and which was used extensively in welding.

A second incendiary dropped about 300 yards further on, landing on a building plot between The Avenue and Priory Road, where it burnt itself out.

Von Platen now took L 4 back out over the sea. Still convinced he was approaching the Humber, he reported: 'I turned off north, in order to get behind the sea front and to reach and attack the Humber industrial area from the land side. Against expectations, I did not find the north bank of the Humber on a north-west course.'[21] In fact he next came inland over Thornham (between Hunstanton and Brancaster) on the north Norfolk coast, where he dropped an incendiary harmlessly on The Green. L 4 then flew back eastwards to Brancaster, where it 'twice circled round and over the village' making a noise 'like about ten or a dozen traction engines at work'. Then a witness saw 'a bright flash go up'. L 4 had dropped another incendiary, which had landed in a roadway about 50 yards from Dormy House on Butcher's Lane.

Von Platen now continued his confused thrusts along the Norfolk coast. At about 10.15pm, although the town was in darkness, he circled around Hunstanton before dropping a single HE bomb. It landed in a field close to the road about 300 yards inland from the lighthouse and wireless station but failed to explode. Continuing on a southerly course, he now released two more bombs as he passed over Heacham. An incendiary struck a glancing blow on a cottage in Lord's Lane. It hit the sill of a bedroom window, broke off some bricks, and damaged a washhouse attached to the cottage before falling into a water butt. The bomb shattered the butt but the water quickly extinguished the bomb's fury. Although the cottage was unoccupied, the adjoining one was not and one of those inside had a close shave. Mr T. Allen was looking out of his own bedroom window when the bomb struck the adjacent sill, just six feet away. The second bomb, an HE, failed to detonate, being discovered two days later in a field owned by Mr Brasnett between the council school and the chalk pit. The 50kg bomb enjoyed brief fame as a 'must see' relic of the raid.[22]

The next quiet English village to feel Germany's wrath was Snettisham. Again, L 4 appeared uncertain and circled before eventually releasing an HE bomb. The Reverend Charlton, vicar of the late fourteenth century St Mary's Church, was in the vicarage garden with his wife and a friend looking for the source of the approaching noise caused, he presumed, by an aeroplane. But at 10.40pm, as the noise got louder, he saw:

> ... exactly overhead, the outline of a Zeppelin, hovering over the church and Vicarage at a great height ... No sooner had we identified it as probably a German airship, than suddenly all doubt was dispelled by a long, loud hissing sound; a confused streak of light; a tremendous crash.[23]

The bomb exploded in a field owned by Mr Coleridge just yards from the Sedgeford Road on the south side of St Mary's. The vicarage stood on the north side of the church, which protected Reverend Charlton's party from the full wrath of the bomb. A hedge and wall running along the road between the bomb and the church, however, could not completely protect the ancient building. Holcombe Ingleby, MP for King's Lynn, wrote to *The Times* describing how:

> ... the force of the explosion was so great that most of the windows on the south and east sides of the church were blown in, together with some of the stonework of the mullions. Tablets in this part of the church were knocked down and other damage done.[24]

From Snettisham, von Platen continued southwards, passing over Dersingham and close to the Royal Estate at Sandringham, from which the King and Queen had left only that morning. Now, still believing he was somewhere north of the Humber, the commander of L 4 saw the lights of an unidentified city on the southern horizon. Perhaps in an attempt to impress Strasser, in his post-raid report von Platen claimed that heavy artillery and infantry opened fire on L 4 as he prepared to attack but this was not true. The 'big city' in his report was the undefended town of King's Lynn.

19 January 1915, 11.00pm: King's Lynn, Norfolk

Word had reached King's Lynn about 10.00pm of earlier Zeppelin activity over Great Yarmouth and Sheringham, prompting Charles Hunt, the chief constable, to order the extinguishing of the streetlights, which had to be done individually as they were on the same circuit as those in the houses. This was still in progress when Hunt received a phone call from Dersingham advising him of the approach of a Zeppelin. He then heard the first bomb fall on the outskirts of the town and ordered the borough electrical engineer to throw the master switch and all across the town the lights faded. But by then it was too late.[25]

Steering towards the lights and following the Hunstanton to King's Lynn railway line, L 4 approached the town from the east a few minutes before 11.00pm. She announced her arrival with an HE bomb that exploded in a field next to the railway line at the back of Tennyson Avenue, breaking many windows there and in Park Avenue too. Moments later another HE bomb detonated on allotments to the south of the railway; the bomb dug a crater and 'some of the splinters flew through the coachhouse in which the [Great Eastern Railway] keep the Royal carriages'.

Meanwhile, in Bentinck Street – a very narrow road with poor quality terraced houses either side – at No. 12, John Goate, a fitter's mate at R & W Paul's Mill, had retired upstairs for the evening. He was in one room with his wife, Mary, while their children, Percy (aged 14) and Ethel (4), were asleep in another. Mrs Goate heard buzzing and thought it might be an aeroplane but her husband reassured her that it was just a motor car. Then they heard the first bomb explode at Tennyson Avenue. Mary rushed to put out the light in the children's bedroom while her husband got up, and searched for his trousers in the dark. Then the bomb struck.

John Goate reached out and grabbed the bed but he and the bed crashed down through the house. He came to rest partly buried under the rubble and pinned down by the bedstead. When rescuers arrived he told them to help his wife and children first. But while he lay there, he became dismayed: 'I could hear my wife and baby calling for help and I could do nothing … but I heard nothing of the boy, and I think I should have done had he been alive.'

Mrs Goate had entered the children's room and looked on horrified as the HE bomb smashed through a skylight and glanced off Percy's pillow. In the split second before the bomb exploded downstairs she remembered trying to wake him to no avail, for he was dead, then the house collapsed. While Mr and Mrs Goate and Ethel, blown by the blast across the room and into the fireplace, went to hospital for treatment, rescuers recovered Percy's body about midnight. His injuries appeared superficial, the doctor who examined him recorded a one-inch lacerated wound across the front of his nose and a bruise on the chest, concluding that Percy died of shock.

Next door at No. 11, Mr and Mrs Fayers had spent part of the evening with 26-year-old recently widowed Alice Gazley who lived a few doors away at Rose Cottage. Alice's husband, Rifleman Percy George Gazley, had died less than three months earlier, killed in action on the Western Front. Like others nearby they heard the buzzing noise of L 4's engines. According to Mrs Fayers: 'They had just had supper together, when Mrs Gazley remarked, "There's a dreadful noise!"' Then they heard a bomb explode and Alice exclaimed: 'Oh, good God, what is it?' She then dashed out just as the bomb exploded in Bentinck Street and buried her out of sight below the flying rubble. After the raid Alice Gazley's father, Henry Rowe, searched for her through the night. In the meantime rescuers had dragged Mr and Mrs Fayers from the wreckage of their home and took them to hospital for treatment to their surprisingly minor injuries.

Houses up and down Bentinck Street and Melbourne Street, which backed on to it, suffered damage from the blast and many residents recounted tales of their own narrow escapes. One reporter who visited Bentinck Street described the confronting scene:

> There is not one house in the street whose windows or doors have not been shattered. The street was littered with glass and broken slates and tiles. Furniture was upset, window frames were shaken out of their sockets, and doors thrown off their hinges. It was like a rubbish yard in places.

It was not until about 8.00am the following morning that Henry Rowe, assisted by a policeman and neighbours, found the body of his daughter, Alice Gazley, among the rubble and debris. Like Percy Goate, her injuries did not appear serious. Doctor G.R. Chadwick reported bruises to her face and abrasions but concluded, as he had in the case of Percy Goate, that Alice Gazley died from shock. At the inquest the coroner recorded death occurred in both cases 'from the effects of the acts of the King's enemies'.

After dropping the bomb on Bentinck Street, von Platen continued on a westerly course before turning over the river and heading north across the town. His next bomb fell on East Street, a turning off Albert Street. It fell at the back of a house occupied by T.H. Walden, a vet and blacksmith:

> Mr Walden heard a roar, which startled him and he got out of bed and began to dress. Before he had time to get half his clothes on the bomb fell with a terrific noise. Mr Walden fell over blinded with the smoke and dust, which almost smothered him. The place was in total darkness.

The blast sent a chest of drawers flying across the bedroom occupied by Walden and his wife, and filled the room with shattered glass, but the couple were untouched. Gladys and May, their daughters, were sleeping in another bedroom when the explosion wrenched off the door to their room and brought down part of a wall, but they too escaped injury. Mr Walden went to the rear of the building overlooking the yard where the bomb had exploded. The sight that greeted him was shocking. The explosion had obliterated his shoeing shop, and the back part of the house where his son Tom's bedroom was had collapsed: 'He could just hear his boy's voice calling out for help, and he was able to dig the lad out from underneath the pile of masonry.' Incredibly, like the rest of the family, Tom escaped virtually uninjured.

The bomb also caused serious damage to the house next door. Three of the four occupants sustained injuries but only one required treatment at hospital, Miss G. Partlett, a visitor from Hungerford, who received a cut to her forehead and an injury to the back of her head. Damage to roofs, doors and windows extended over a wide area.

Continuing on its northerly course, L 4 crossed a railway line just to the east of the docks and dropped an incendiary bomb. It smashed through the roof of 63 Cresswell Street, the home of widower John Charles Savage and his daughters Alice and Ellen. The bomb passed through an empty bedroom causing a small fire and down to the kitchen, where it had a soft landing in a linen basket. No one was hurt and, although the fire brigade received a call, neighbours had rushed to help and extinguished the flames before they arrived. A newspaper report suggests another bomb in Cresswell Street failed to detonate.

Moments later an HE bomb landed on an allotment owned by Mr Wyatt at the north end of Sir Lewis Street, which runs parallel to Cresswell Street. It dug a large crater, causing some minor damage nearby, and smashed a number of windows in houses at the north end of Cresswell Street.

Von Platen, who must have observed the docks on his northward course, now circled around and headed back towards them. An HE bomb landed short of the target, in the garden of a house occupied by Mr Kerner-Greenwood in St Ann's Street. The bomb, most likely an incendiary, buried itself in the soil without causing any damage.

The commander of L 4 now had just one HE bomb left. He was on a direct course for the docks and released the bomb with excellent timing. It landed directly on the power station located on the southern quay of Alexandra Dock. The explosion caused 'considerable damage' to the engine room, destroying its two boilers and the hydraulic gear that operated the dock gates, while also damaging surrounding buildings. 'Fortunately,' a newspaper concluded, 'there was no one in the engine-house when that was struck, the last man at work there having left about ten minutes before.'

The raid, like that on Great Yarmouth, had lasted no more than ten minutes before L 4 turned eastwards, flew back across the town and disappeared into the enveloping darkness of the night sky. She was heading home.

King's Lynn had no anti-aircraft defence, its response to the attack just a few desultory rifle shots fired by the dock guard. People had rushed into the streets after the first bomb exploded but about 500 soldiers of the National Guard and Yeomanry stationed in the town turned out to ensure order. It was effective. 'The people behaved calmly and there was no sign of panic or disorder, but many went through terrifying moments and were badly shaken.' Besides the two deaths in the town, estimates suggest between 30 and 40 people suffered injury but of these only 13 required hospital treatment.[26]

Having crossed Norfolk, L 4 departed just north of Great Yarmouth sometime after midnight, the noise of her engines causing a scare in the town still recovering from L 3's raid earlier in the evening. Although largely unaware of where he had been, before he left English skies, von Platen sent a fallacious radio message: 'Successfully bombed fortified places between the Tyne and Humber.'[27]

After making a rendezvous with L 3 off the Dutch coast near Vlieland, the pair returned to Fuhlsbüttel together at about 9.45am (local time) after a mission that lasted just a short of 23 hours. They returned to a hero's welcome, each man receiving the Iron Cross, while the German press revelled in what the *Hamburger Fremdenblatt* described as 'the mad joy and untiring satisfaction at the news of the deeds of German airships'.[28]

A few days after the raid, German–American journalist Karl von Wiegand grabbed an interview with Count von Zeppelin in Berlin. Asked how he felt about the killing of non-combatants during the raid, the count displayed a distance from the practicalities Zeppelin crews encountered when raiding over England:

> No one regrets that more than I do. But have not non-combatants been killed by other engines of war? Why then, this outcry? Simply because England fears that the Zeppelins will destroy her splendid isolation, because, failing in her efforts to build something similar, she hopes to arouse the world and bring pressure to bear against Germany's use of a weapon which to her is unavailable.
>
> The crews of Zeppelins are exposed to far greater dangers than fighters in any other branch of the military service, but they are just as humane. They have no more desire or intention to kill women and children than have the officers and gunners of the artillery. So far as in their power they always try to avoid this.[29]

17 February 1915: The Danish coast

For the crews of L 3 and L 4 the celebration they encountered on their return did not last long. Less than a month later, on 17 February 1915, while patrolling over the North Sea towards Norway a fierce storm struck. One of L 3's engines failed early in the mission then, after she had turned back, the second of her three engines failed too. With no alternative, Kptlt Hans Fritz brought L 3 down on the Danish island of Fanø. She hit the ground hard and her framework crumpled on impact, but all the 16-man crew got off safely. After setting fire to the wreckage the crew were interned in neutral Denmark. However, the crew of L 4 fared worse.

Von Platen and L 4 encountered the gales too, also suffering failure of two engines. Unable to progress into the battering headwind, von Platen tried to land on the Danish coast at Blåvands Huk, but a strong downdraft forced her into the sea. Of the 15-man crew, 11 swiftly leapt overboard and got ashore through the freezing waters. But this sudden lightening of the airship meant L 4 shot back up into the air. There the fierce winds swept her out to sea with four men still aboard. Somewhere out in the icy North Sea the battered hulk of L 4 sank below the waves and those four desperate men were lost without trace. The rest of the crew surrendered to Danish police and entered internment like their comrades from L 3.[30]

Britain's limited aerial defences had offered no opposition to this first Zeppelin raid. The appearance of Zeppelins over England for the first time caught the defences off guard. The RNAS station at Great Yarmouth did not receive notification until after L 3 had departed and, although two RFC pilots from Joyce Green were airborne shortly after 9.00pm, their duty was to protect London. Both experienced engine problems and had to make forced landings. When all else failed though, Britain could still rely on one implacable ally in the aerial war – the weather. The losses of L 3 and L 4 in the storm off the coast of Denmark had reduced the Naval Airship Division's available force in the west to four airships and removed two of the most experienced crews from the war.

Chapter 6

'Discovering a New Country'

The Zeppelin raid on East Anglia in January 1915 caused a headache for those charged with Britain's air defence. The limited fixed gun positions in the region protected military and naval establishments only, allowing the raiders to wander largely unmolested over the British countryside. The Director of the Admiralty's Air Department, Murray Sueter, therefore proposed the formation of a motorized anti-aircraft force.

January–February 1915: England

The scheme received quick approval, leading to the creation of the Eastern Mobile Section of the RNAS. No one expected the force to chase Zeppelins along the country lanes of East Anglia but with a headquarters at Newmarket, these mobile units could move to positions on their anticipated path on receipt of information detailing approaching raiders. As this force was required to cover the whole of East Anglia, substations were established across the region, at King's Lynn, Chelmsford, Lowestoft, Ipswich and at the hamlet of Shingle Street. Their armament was limited: a number of 1-pdr 'pom-poms', maxim machine guns and searchlights all mounted on motor vehicles. Although these weapons offered little real threat to raiding Zeppelins due to their limited range, they went some way to reassuring the civilian population of the region that they were defended. In addition, although the rounds fired were unlikely to reach their target, Zeppelin commanders did not know that. Evidence shows that on occasions they would climb to avoid the attack and with increased height came a reduction in bombing accuracy.[1]

Another direct result of this first raid was an implementation of lighting restrictions across the country. Ten municipal authorities applied under the Defence of the Realm Act (DORA) for compulsory powers to control the lighting in their areas. By 8 April 1915 the Home Office exerted overall control of lighting and gradually extended restrictions over a very wide area inland and around the coast. Exceptions, however, were granted for certain lights considered essential, such as those at docks, on the railway system and at certain naval and military defence establishments – in fact the very places Zeppelins sought to bomb.[2]

Many had believed the raid of 19 January heralded the start of the long-anticipated Zeppelin offensive against Britain, but it did not materialize. In Germany both the Army and Navy were taking delivery of new airships, making good their losses and building their strength. At the same time, an extended period of bad weather generally proved unsuitable for these early 'm-class' Zeppelins to venture across the North Sea. One Army Zeppelin commander, Ernst Lehmann, remained critical of the timing of that first raid by the Navy airships:

> Looking at that first raid from the German point of view, I have always maintained that this premature isolated raid was a most foolish mistake. It served no reasonable purpose and since it could not be followed up for more than three months, it simply betrayed our hand. The enemy had time to prepare a sort of defence, thus making it more difficult for later attacks.[3]

Lehmann was correct that three months passed before a Zeppelin again appeared over Britain, but the country did not remain free from attack. The seaplane pilots at Zeebrugge saw to that.

21 February 1915, 8.30pm: Braintree, Essex

The weather over south-east England on Sunday, 21 February had been cold but fine with just a slight wind. Late in the afternoon Oblt-z-S Stephen Prondzynski, the same man who had made the attack on Dover and flown up the Thames estuary in December, clambered back into his familiar aircraft, Friedrichshafen FF 29, no. 203. This time he took 20-year-old Fähnrich-zur-See (Fähnrich-z-S) Thomas Heym as his observer and a cargo of just two HE and two incendiary bombs.[4] Their flight over the North Sea was uninterrupted but keen ears picked up the sound of their engine at Clacton on the Essex coast at 7.45pm (see Map 2). From there they followed a westward course inland, passing Brightlingsea and on towards Inworth. It is unclear if they had a specific target in mind. As the aircraft passed between Kelvedon and Coggeshall, Cyril Webb of the latter town told a reporter: 'I saw an aeroplane in the sky ... it was up against the moon so high as to look no bigger than a pigeon. It went towards Braintree.'[5]

At Braintree railway station, Signalman Reeve was on duty and witnessed what happened next:

> I heard the buzz of an aeroplane, and, looking up, I saw the machine clearly visible between me and the moon ... In a moment I saw a streak of fire shoot out of the aeroplane. It was just like a shooting star, but it fell straight to earth.

Prondzynski in fact circled around Braintree and dropped his first bomb, an incendiary, on the south side of the town. The bomb seen by Signalman Reeve fell in the grounds of Lynton House, between London Road and Notley Road, about 100 yards from the railway line and 'fairly near' to St Michael's Church. A group of soldiers from the transport department of the 5th Notts and Derby Regiment (The Sherwood Foresters) was walking along the Notley Road at about 8.30pm when they too heard the sound of an engine. Running up a hill the men saw an aircraft 'at a tremendous height in the sky, looking just like a bat against the moon' and watched as a bomb dropped and began blazing before it hit the ground with a distinct thud. Corporal A.E. Large and Private J. Goodall dashed forward and found the bomb partly buried in the ground from where it had set both a fence and a nearby tree alight. Goodall began throwing soil on the blazing bomb and attempted to smother the flames with an old sack. The two men then pulled a rail from the fence and pushed it through the handle of the bomb to lift it. The bomb, however, re-ignited. Without stopping, the two men ran with it to the River Brain where they held the fizzing, spitting bomb under the water until it finally stopped burning. Then, like safari porters of old carrying the hunter's prize, Large and Goodall slung the bomb suspended from the rail on their shoulders and, surrounded by their excited comrades, proudly bore it back to their headquarters, where they delivered it up to a somewhat surprised officer of the guard. In a statement Corporal Large concluded: 'Neither Pt. Goodall nor myself was hurt by the flaring bomb, although it proved a bit hot.' The gallantry of the two soldiers impressed the town council, who demonstrated their appreciation by presenting Corporal Large with an inscribed silver cigarette case and Private Goodall with a silver wristwatch the following evening.

After releasing their first bomb, Prondzynski and Heym headed across Braintree and dropped a second on the eastern edge of the town, which landed in a field at Great Bradfords Farm on the Coggeshall Road. A domestic servant who worked at the farm was on her way home at about 8.30pm 'when a flash of light fell from the sky'. Staring into the darkness she 'saw a sheet of fire shoot up in a field on the farm ... I at once told my master, Mr Garrod, that there was something burning in a field on the farm, and he went out to see'. Together they found the bomb burning in a hole it had dug in the ground. Later a soldier arrived and took the burnt out remains to the Sherwood Foresters' guardroom before Superintendent W. Cowell of Braintree Police Station took possession. The following day, two of the new mobile AA gun teams arrived from Newmarket and took the bombs away for examination.

21 February 1915, 8.35pm: Coggeshall, Essex

Prondzynski and Heym had not waited to see the effects of their attack on Braintree and headed east, following the straight line of the Coggeshall Road, the former Roman thoroughfare of Stane Street. Ten minutes after Cyril Webb had caught a glimpse of the aircraft heading towards Braintree, he saw it return to Coggeshall and, although he was a mile away when it dropped, he felt the explosion of the next bomb. Bertie Clark and Police Constable Tyrell were standing near the church at about 8.35pm when they heard the 'whizz of an engine'. PC Tyrell climbed on a wall to get a better view. He thought it was an aeroplane but could not locate the source of the noise. Then Clark saw a bright red light appearing briefly in the sky among the clouds:

> We could not see the aeroplane, but we could hear the ever-increasing buzz of the bomb as it dropped from the aeroplane and approached the earth. We knew we were nearly beneath the red light which had appeared in the sky – we were standing near the churchyard wall – and at once thought the church was the target of the bomb; so we lay down quickly on the path to avoid being hit. The next instant there was a terrific explosion in the Starling Leeze field, 100 yards from where we stood.

Bert Raven, a dairyman, was standing with a friend not far from the point of impact. 'There was cloud of smoke and a flicker like lightning,' he explained, 'and clods of earth were thrown up high in the air.' His friend then brushed a hand over him and said comfortingly: 'You're alright, Bert!' Only then did the dairyman realize a piece of debris had started burning his jacket.

According to a newspaper reporter, the bomb fell in a paddock adjoining Starling Leeze. It landed about 50 yards from Abbey View (57–59 East Street), the home of Mr J.S. Surridge, who was ill in bed at the time, and 'much upset by the occurrence'. The following morning William Williams, his gardener, showed a reporter around. The crater in the paddock caused by the bomb measured 18 inches deep and about eight feet across. The reporter then described more of the bomb's effects:

> Pieces of shrapnel thrown from the bomb damaged the carpenter's shop and greenhouse at Abbey View. One missile went through the cowhouse and smashed a window in Mr Surridge's house, just missing in its flight a cow. The glass in the greenhouse was shattered … The bullets from the bomb were so powerful that they cut through two or three wooden walls in succession, and some penetrated even an iron roof.

The unexpected explosion of the bomb in Coggeshall had a wide-ranging effect on the small rural community. The blast caused a horse pulling a wagon loaded with soldiers along Church Street to bolt. As the horse careered along the road, other soldiers gave chase. Unfortunately some of these men collided with Mrs Andrew Eady, who was in the street, knocking her down and leaving her with a broken right thigh. The horse eventually came to a sudden halt when it crashed into the doorpost of Stead and Simpson's boot and shoe shop at Market End, catapulting one of the soldiers into the air and causing him serious injuries. The horse broke a leg and had to be slaughtered. And there was still one more deadly repercussion. The wife of agricultural labourer Thomas Parker, who lived on the Surrex Road, 'sustained such a shock on Sunday evening on the occasion of the air raid that she never recovered'. She died the following evening, leaving a husband and two young children.

Prondzynski and Heym continued to follow the old Roman Road towards Colchester. A couple of minutes after dropping the bomb at Coggeshall they passed over the village of Marks Tey. There is some confusion as to whether a bomb dropped here or not. Some, but not all, reports state a bomb fell in a back garden 'causing some damage to cottages' but that is the extent of the information.[6] The German raiders now had just one more bomb to drop; they released it as they approached the artillery barracks in Colchester.

21 February 1915, 8.40pm: Colchester, Essex

It was a fine clear evening at Colchester and at 8.40pm many people were in the streets returning home from church when this last bomb dropped. A 'violent explosion' sounded over a wide area and many believed it caused by a boiler or gas explosion, or maybe a railway or tram collision. But word soon spread that it was a bomb. It landed in the small back garden of a house at 41 Butt Road, the home of Quartermaster-Sergeant Rabjohn, 20th Hussars, his wife and their 22-month-old baby son. As Rabjohn explained, they 'had a marvellous escape':

> My wife was standing at the table preparing supper. Before we could realize what was happening there was a horrible thud, which seemed to shake the house. At the same time there was an immense cloud of brick and dust, which covered and blinded me. I at once tumbled to the state of affairs. I rushed to the corner and turned the gas off. My wife meanwhile had turned dizzy. I seized her and rapidly brought her round. She said, 'Go up for the baby,' and, going up to the bedroom, we were overjoyed to find the child still sleeping as if nothing at all had occurred. Only then did we realize fully that our home was wrecked. The bullets came clean through the door and windows, breaking all our pictures, smashing our furniture, and even in two places going clean through the plaster and a nine-inch brick wall across the room where my wife and I were seated, to bury themselves in the further wall ... It is the dickens of a job for us, but we had a wonderful delivery.

Outside the house 'scores of holes were punched in the thick walls by flying shrapnel' and the blast of the bomb destroyed a corrugated iron shed that housed the baby's perambulator, now lying mangled amongst the debris. The blast also smashed all the windows in the house and blew the kitchen door into the living room. Mrs Rabjohn's cloak, which was hanging on the door, had two shrapnel holes through it. Outside a small tree attracted much attention. It had been, 'shredded and partially severed by shrapnel, but it still stood upright'. The neighbouring houses had their back window frames blown in and broken windowpanes in another 50 houses close by served as a reminder to the occupiers that this brutal war had now extended its battle lines to the streets of Britain.

At a small shop nearby a Mrs Dicker found herself suddenly buried under a pile of groceries, and at another house a woman sitting at a table writing a letter had the unnerving experience of seeing a large piece of glass scything across the room just above her head.

The largest fragment of the bomb landed in ivy growing over the house at 35 Butt Road. Inside, Mary Starling was writing a letter to her son, a sailor in the Royal Navy. The rush of air from the blast blew out the light on her table and the fragment of the bomb struck the wall so heavily that it dislodged a brick. 'I thought the side of the house was coming in,' said Mary, who admitted that the experience had left her 'in a tremble'. In West Street, about 120 yards away from the explosion, a Mrs Griggs was blown from her bed on to a chest of drawers, hitting her head badly, while another piece of shrapnel travelled some 200 yards, being later picked up in Crouch Road.

Prondzynski and Heym were over Colchester for no more than two or three minutes before they headed back towards the coast, passing out to sea near Shingle Street at 9.42pm. Back in Colchester there appears to have been no undue panic or alarm and perhaps rather oddly, about 30 minutes after the bomb, 'a gang of lads marched through the streets singing, "The Germans are coming, they are, they are!" to the tune of "The Campbells are coming". There was also some good news for Mr and Mrs Rabjohn. Smarts Brothers, 'The largest all-British firm of Credit House Furnishers', offered to replace all their damaged furniture free of charge, and Lady Colebrook, wife of Lord Colebrook, Captain of the King's Gentlemen-at-Arms, made them a gift of a new perambulator.

In contrast, all was not well for Prondzynski and Heym. Somewhere out over the North Sea on the homeward flight their engine failed and their seaplane dropped into the sea. As they hit the waves the impact threw Heym overboard but after a few anxious moments Prondzynski managed to haul him back on to the aircraft. The crash, however, damaged a wing and one of the floats, preventing them from getting airborne again. Soaked to the skin by the freezing water, Heym suffered badly as the pair clung on as best they could. Desperately they sent up rockets periodically but no response came. With Monday morning came snow and it remained bitterly cold. Hanging on with difficulty to their partly submerged aircraft, the two men began to fear that the end was approaching. At about 4.00am on Tuesday morning, and more than 30 hours after crashing into the sea, the exhausted pair half-heartedly sent up another rocket. Out in the darkness William Dunnett, the skipper of the British fishing smack *New Boy*, saw it burst in the sky. Dunnett, 'thinking something was the matter', hoisted his sails to investigate but as there was virtually no wind it took him another five hours to reach the shattered aircraft. As they neared the wreckage, Dunnett sent a small boat across 'and took off the two men, who were in a shocking state of exposure', and noted that Heym was 'half dead with cold'. Once the two men were down inside the warm cabin the crew gave them food and dry clothes and the airmen began to recover from their ordeal. And they had plenty of time for that. After docking at Lowestoft the two men became POWs and were eventually incarcerated at Dorchester.[7] Heym actually escaped in September 1915 and reached West Hartlepool with a fellow prisoner before they were both arrested when trying to board a Swedish ship.

While Prondzynski and Heym were floundering at sea, the British Fire Prevention Committee, with government approval, made a timely release of a poster advising householders of precautions they should take during an air raid. At the first warning or sign of a raid people were advised to seek refuge in their cellar, basement or lower floor of their house, closing all doors and windows on the way and turning off gaslights, stoves and switching off at the meter. The same applied to any electric lights. Any fires burning in the hearth above basement level were to be put out and oil lamps extinguished and removed to the cellar. The instructions also recommended that householders fill buckets three-quarters full of water and distribute them around the house, and buckets of sand too if they had appliances using oil or spirit. The government was clearly in no doubt that more raids were on the way.[8]

February–March 1915: Germany and Belgium

Nine days before the seaplane raid on Essex, on 12 February, the Kaiser had issued an Imperial Order. It expressed his hopes that the Army and Navy carry out an air war against England with 'the greatest energy'. As targets he highlighted, 'war material of every kind, military establishments, barracks, and also oil and petroleum tanks and the London docks'. But he added, 'No attack is to be made on the residential areas of London, or above all on the royal palaces'. The fact that row upon row of dockworkers houses crowded around the London docks seems to have escaped the attention of the Kaiser.[9] By an interesting and free interpretation of this Order, the Army General Staff remarkably concluded they were free to bomb targets east of a line drawn through

Charing Cross Station and began to make plans. Hearing of this on 18 February, the new Naval Chief of Staff, Vizeadmiral Gustav Bachmann, who had replaced Von Pohl at the beginning of February, recommended a similar approach for the Navy airships.[10]

The German Army had begun establishing airship bases in Belgium in the late autumn of 1914, with sheds constructed at Gontrode, outside Ghent, and at Evere, Berchem St Agathe and Etterbeek surrounding Brussels, all well positioned for raiding England. Keen to steal a march on the Army, the Navy had based its latest Zeppelin, L 8, at Düsseldorf since its commissioning on 22 December 1914. Now, following the Kaiser's Order of 12 February, the commander of L 8, Kptlt Helmut Beelitz received instructions to attack London at the earliest opportunity. He made an attempt on 26 February but abandoned it and sought shelter at the Army's Gontrode shed having encountered strong winds. He remained there for a few days but on 1 March the Army advised him that they needed the shed for one of their own Zeppelins. L 8 departed on 4 March with Beelitz deciding to try for London again prior to returning to Düsseldorf.

It was not a good move. Low cloud made navigation difficult and forced Beelitz to descend to check his position. The second time he did this he was flying west of Ostend, over the Allied line. Flying at no more than 1,000 feet over Nieuport, the Belgium troops below opened up a heavy rifle and machine gun fire. Beelitz immediately released his bombs, excess fuel and water ballast to gain height and climb away from his assailants. But the damage was already done. The now wounded Zeppelin, with its gas cells heavily punctured, turned back towards Düsseldorf but at about 1.00am on the morning of 5 March she came down near Tirlemont in Belgium. With two of her three engines out of action, strong winds forced her down into some trees, the winds continuing to batter her until all that remained was a useless tangle of wreckage.[11] Ten days later, however, the Navy took delivery of a new Zeppelin, L 9 of the interim 'o-class', with command given to 31-year-old Kptlt Heinrich Mathy.

Meanwhile, the Army prepared to begin raiding England. On 11 March an Army order instructed her crews to commence bombing raids 'whenever possible, on military objects in England, preferably London'.[12] On 17 March, Zeppelin Z XII, commanded by Ernst Lehmann, set out from Maubeuge with the intention of attacking London. The attempt, however, ran into an impenetrable bank of fog that rose at the English coast and extended far inland, forcing Lehmann to abort and attack

Calais instead. On the return flight Z XII made a bad landing, which kept her out of action for two weeks.[13] However, by now the Kaiser had become aware of the military's interpretation of his Order and forbade any further attempts on London beyond the docks.

14 April 1915: Northumberland

As the winter months melted into spring, the German Navy planned a mine-laying expedition to the Swarte Bank, an offshore sandbank lying a little under 50 miles off the north-east Norfolk coast. Four days before the mission, on 14 April, Zeppelin L 9 flew a reconnaissance patrol to the area from its base at Hage on the north German coast, to observe British naval activity in the area. It seems clear, however, that Heinrich Mathy, the commander of L 9, had more extensive plans in mind. On naval reconnaissance flights Zeppelins normally carried just a handful of HE bombs, but Mathy loaded ten 50kg HE bombs and 40 incendiaries. Incendiary bombs had little value on a maritime reconnaissance. In bright and sunny weather Mathy reached Swarte Bank without observing any British warships. Now he made his move. With the British coast within reach, Mathy requested permission by radio to carry out an attack, and received the go ahead. He did not choose to strike at the nearest point of the coast, instead he planned to attack the shipyards on the Tyne, some 190 miles away, for in his opinion, 'effective use of incendiaries in this industrial area would cause more disturbance in the already restless mass of British workers'.[14]

Two North Shields trawlers, fishing about 45 miles off the mouth of the Tyne, made the first sighting of L 9, but without radios they could not report it until the next morning, by when it was old news. The Zeppelin was flying low enough for them to read its number, although they thought it was Z 9 instead of L 9. This left the honour of being the first to report the approach of the raider to the pilot cutter *Protector*. She was lying about a mile and a half off the mouth of the Tyne and reported the Zeppelin flying a NNW course towards Blyth (see Map 4).[15]

Mathy, in his report, stated that he flew directly to the mouth of the Tyne from where he dropped his first bombs on timber yards at South Shields, before following a winding course along the river and dropping more bombs on Jarrow, Hebburn, Carville, Walker and Newcastle. Mathy noted the land below was generally dark, which he put down to the darkening of this heavily industrialized area in response to the attack. But he was wrong.[16]

Approaching the north-east coast, L 9 actually flew past Tynemouth and appeared off the harbour mouth at Blyth, about eight miles to the north, at around 7.45pm. At that moment a large crowd had gathered in the town's Market Place, where the Reverend J.W. Ogden was addressing a recruiting meeting.[17]

> Whilst Mr. Ogden was vigorously condemning the atrocities perpetrated by the Germans in Belgium, and pointing out that even the shores of England were not yet safe, there was the 'purring' of engines overhead, and the Zeppelin came into view. Seizing the dramatic moment, the speaker pointed to the huge airship, and said: 'See, there is a visitor for you.'

The police superintendent of Blyth, James Irving, immediately ordered the electric and gas supplies cut off and, unable to get a telephone connection, sent officers to Whitley Bay and Bedlington 'to warn all concerned'. All those who watched L 9 over Blyth concluded that her commander appeared indecisive, unsure of his position. After about ten minutes Mathy continued up the coast a short way before turning inland and following the River Wansbeck. At Cambois, riflemen of C Company, 1st Northern Cyclist Battalion opened fire, then, as L 9 passed over West Sleekburn, Mathy released his first bomb on English soil. The incendiary landed in a field, gouging a hole about two feet deep but without causing any damage. According to a local report, the bomb fell within a couple of yards of a soldier, momentarily stunning him but he quickly recovered his wits and went for help.

After that first bomb at West Sleekburn, two more incendiaries quickly followed, both also landing harmlessly in fields, one to the east of Bomarsund Colliery and the other on the west side. Another incendiary dropped in a brickfield near Barrington Colliery. The next bombs landed around Choppington.

A commercial traveller, Mr James G. Henderson, was at Bedlington at the time of the raid and the following day gave an interview to a local newspaper:

> At about 8.18 p.m., I heard someone shout out there was a Zeppelin. I was talking to Dr Lee whose surgery is next to the King's Head, and we rushed into the yard and could hear the engine going. How high the Zeppelin was flying I could not say, but you could easily make it out against the sky. There were no lights showing from the Zeppelin. I stood watching the airship perhaps a couple of minutes,

and then I had to rush away to catch my train for Newcastle, which was due to leave Choppington Station at 8.27. It was a good seven minutes' walk to the station, and I started to trot. The Zeppelin was going in the same direction as I was – towards the station. At 8.22 there was a flash, and lightning was not in it! I kept on running towards the station ... fifteen seconds after I had seen the flash there was a tremendous crash. By the time I got to the station, at 8.27, there had been eight such cracks, and whilst I was waiting at the station for my train, which was about ten minutes overdue, I heard two more cracks, making ten in all. The last one I heard was at 8.29.

According to the police records, a group of five bombs landed around Choppington. Two were incendiaries – one landed in a brickfield just south of Choppington Station, on the east side of the road. It must have thrown up some debris when it landed as it smashed a window at the neighbouring Railway Hotel. The other incendiary landed in a hedge opposite a large house near the station known locally as the 'Jarmin Hoose' (German House) which in 1901 had become the Barrington and Choppington Workmen's Club, but it failed to ignite. The other three were HE bombs. They fell in a field to the west of Mr Huntley's Glebe Farm, between Choppington and Bedlington. Each dug a large crater but caused no damage. Bedlington, where the lights had been extinguished and special constables patrolled the streets, was next to experience the German war machine at first hand. An HE bomb exploded in a field west of the village, excavating a crater some 12 feet in diameter and three feet deep, but the only damage were three smashed windows in Catholic Row. Another HE Bomb and an incendiary then landed in a field just south of Land House Farm, breaking four small panes of glass. A local miner named Muldoon claimed a splinter from one of the bombs had struck his hand and ripped his trousers. The local police were dismissive, commenting, 'no credence is placed on his story, other people in the same neighbourhood allege that his injury was caused by a barbed wire fence'.[18]

As L 9 headed south towards Cramlington, two policemen, Sergeant Marshall and PC Middlemiss, were walking along the road when they heard the throb of the Zeppelin's engines and then saw it coming directly towards them. Running into a field at Crowhall Farm, they lay flat on the ground, but as they did so Mathy released an HE bomb. It exploded just 30 feet from where they lay, covering them with clay and debris, but they were unharmed. Three more bombs dropped around Cramlington. The first, an HE bomb, exploded in a field at West Farm. Just a short distance away in the Wesleyan Chapel, choir practice was taking place. A member of the choir, Mr Sims, reported that everyone rushed out into the street and clearly saw L 9 pass over the chapel. He described it as 'a big black cigar-shaped vessel – a horrible thing to look at'. Mathy then released an incendiary bomb. It fell through the roof of a barn at Village Farm used by the council as a warehouse, setting fire to the interior, but council workers turned a hose on the fire and quickly extinguished it. The last of these three bombs, an incendiary, fell in a field to the south of the village, at West Cramlington.

From there L 9 continued southwards for about two miles. An eyewitness living in Wansbeck Road, Dudley, was looking out of a window at the time. 'I noticed,' he told a newspaper, 'the sudden flare of three lights in a field about 200 yards to the south. I rushed downstairs, and in the back street I heard a humming sound of engines overhead.' The witness later went to the field on the west side of the railway line with PC Cockburn and two postmen, F. Hardiman and G. Winder, where they found three incendiary bombs still burning, all within a radius of 50 yards and close to the railway.

Mathy now changed direction, heading west towards Seaton Burn. Before he reached the village an incendiary dropped in the garden of Seaton Burn House without causing damage. L 9 then turned south again over the village, dropping another incendiary, which again landed harmlessly. An HE bomb then dropped as the raider headed towards Dinnington Colliery but it exploded in a field near Hazlerigg without effect, like so many others that night. Moments later, another HE bomb landed in Gosforth Park. One of the workers at the YMCA building there explained to a reporter what a narrow escape it had been:

> I heard a report that I – well I'd never heard anything like it: it shook the ground and the hut and the [racecourse] grandstand like an earthquake. The building was full of soldiers. We rushed out and saw the cigar-shape of the Zeppelin moving away.
>
> We found the bomb had fallen in the middle of one of the Park fields and it must have been a bomb! There was a big hole 15 feet each way across and 4 feet deep: and there it had fallen and done no harm. What harm it would have done if it had caught us I can't imagine.[19]

From Gosforth Park, L 9 followed a south-east course and, as it passed over Benton, an incendiary bomb ignited in a field where soldiers had been digging practice trenches. The field lay just north-west of Benton station on the North Eastern Railway. Reports state that the bomb damaged a bicycle. An eyewitness recalled that L 9 then seemed to head in the direction of Wallsend, where Mathy would finally reach the River Tyne, but the blackness of the night soon swallowed up the raider and the drone of its engines subsided. The same eyewitness, however, quickly confirmed that Wallsend was indeed next to be targeted, 'for from the direction in which it had disappeared a bright flash, spreading out like a fan from the earth, lit up the lower sky'.[20]

14 April 1915: Wallsend, Northumberland

Mathy released two incendiary bombs as he approached Wallsend. They both landed in fields at Westmorland Cottage Farm. One burnt itself out while the other appears to have failed to ignite. The next landed in the roadway at the north end of Station Road, which Mathy must now have followed because his next incendiary bomb struck 238 Station Road. The upper floor and attic of the house were a self-contained home. The tenants were George Robinson, a shipyard worker, who was not at home at the time, his wife and their two children, Eddie their seven-year-old son and a daughter aged three.

As Mathy and L 9 approached, Mrs Robinson was bathing her daughter in the kitchen with young Eddie standing by her side. May Taylor, a friend of the family, was also there. Suddenly there came a crash from the attic. An incendiary bomb smashed through the roof tiles, damaged the floorboards and ignited in the children's attic bedroom, while burning liquid from the bomb dripped down to the room below, from where Mrs Robinson then takes up the story:

> It was as if a sheet of flame dropped from the ceiling to the floor and shot back again. We guessed what it was. Even Eddie knew. He has had a dread of Zeppelins from the time the war started, and every night he has asked me to draw the blind for fear the Zeppelins should come. Well, I snatched up the baby out of the bath and my friend picked up Eddie, and we ran out of the room. The ceiling was already alight and there was a blaze in the attic. My hair was singed and so was Eddie's, and our arms are spotted with black where the oil touched us. We took the children to a neighbour's house, and we came back to put out the fire. A man helped us, and we had it almost out before the fire brigade came.[21]

A later inspection of the blackened attic revealed that the bomb just missed Eddie's bed – a few minutes later and he would have been in it. The flames had burnt the floorboards and charred the supporting beams but the smoke effect was great. The Robinsons had recently whitewashed and repapered the ceiling and walls, now they were 'thickly begrimed with fast-sticking soot'.

About a third of a mile further on, while Mrs Robinson and May Taylor were carrying the children to safety, Mathy released two more incendiary bombs. They fell on the railway track between 200 and 300 yards east of Wallsend station as a train from Tynemouth was approaching. Thomas Carr, a foreman fitter at Swan Hunter shipyard, was making his way from work to the station when he noticed a 'curious sound'. The next thing he heard 'was a crack, and instantly a flame about 20 yards long sprang up'. The driver of the electric train, which had all its lights on, slammed on the brakes and managed to stop before it reached the burning bomb.[22] A newspaper reported: 'There were a fair number of passengers, including women, to whom the terrifying experience was a trying ordeal.' One woman on the train became hysterical and received medical assistance, 'but the fortitude of the passengers generally was most praiseworthy'. Two wooden sleepers were burnt as a result of the bombs but after the fire brigade doused them with water the train made its way into the station and then, eventually on to Newcastle where the city had earlier been darkened on news of the presence of L 9.[23]

Now, after his long and meandering course over the mining villages of Northumberland, Mathy finally arrived over the Tyne as he neared the end of his raid. Approaching the river, he passed between the Neptune Bank Power Station and the chemical works of the Castner Kellner Alkali Company and dropped an HE bomb but it fell in the water, although the blast smashed windows in both premises. Mathy dropped one more bomb, an incendiary, on the south bank of the Tyne. It landed harmlessly at Hebburn on the floor of the dry dock at Palmers Shipyard. Official sources recorded the time of this last bomb at 8.48pm. Mathy then followed an easterly course towards the coast, causing great excitement in South Shields, where the electric lights had been switched off at about 8.30 pm:

> Large crowds of people assembled in the main thoroughfares of South Shields and a considerable number proceeded to the sea front where the sounds which appeared to resemble distant firing were heard.
>
> Shortly before nine o'clock a buzzing noise indicating the passage overhead of some aircraft attracted attention, and the vessel was apparently proceeding along the coast.[24]

Over in Newcastle people appeared in the streets in large numbers in anticipation of an attack. 'For several hours, crowds good-humouredly patrolled the city streets, but as nothing of a sensational character transpired up to 11 o'clock, the citizens gradually wended their way home.'

While the residents of South Shields strained their eyes trying to pick out the shape of the departing raider in the night sky, an RNAS Bristol T.B.8 took off from the air station at Whitley Bay and patrolled towards Newcastle in an attempt to intercept it. The pilot, Flt sub-Lt Peter Leigh, was making his first night flight, having only qualified as a pilot a month earlier. His observer, an Australian flight mechanic, Bert Hinkler, carried only a military carbine for armament, firing Martini–Henry incendiary bullets, which were officially deemed ineffective the following month. While they searched blindly in the night sky, Mathy steered out to sea over Marsden and set his course for home. Although he returned to Germany claiming a successful raid along the industrial banks of the Tyne, he revealed in an interview later in September 1915 that the raid was merely the start of a steep learning curve:

> The first time I took my Zeppelin to England it was something akin to discovering a new country, and my impressions were much more vivid than now. It and some of the following [raids] were more or less experimental. We had much to learn, despite all our practice and training. It was a new sort of warfare, in which we had, more or less, to feel our way and study aerial strategy, aerial tactics, and to learn to locate in darkness the military points and objects we desired to attack.[25]

Despite all the 'practice and training', in reality most of Mathy's bombs had landed in fields, leaving the British government to estimate the cost of the damage inflicted by the raid at a trifling £55.

However, with no anti-aircraft guns positioned on the Tyne and the minimal impact of the Home Defence aircraft, the region had escaped lightly. Switching off the power seemed to be reasonably effective and the newspapers reported that the civilian population had reacted well in the face of a much-feared Zeppelin attack, much as they had done in East Anglia three months earlier. Even so, a 3-inch gun was quickly dispatched from Whale Island, Portsmouth, to defend the Tyne.[26]

With improving weather, three more air raids reached England in April 1915, but the North-east would not be among the targets this time.

Chapter 7

'Only H.V.B. on board'

No sooner had Heinrich Mathy returned Zeppelin L 9 safely back to its shed at Hage than he informed Strasser of the apparent success of his supposed foray along the Tyne. Keen to build on this, Strasser announced he would send three of his Zeppelins out later that day to raid the Humber. And he would go along too, accompanying Oblt-z-S Werner Peterson on board L 7 – the Zeppelin that so narrowly avoided destruction during the Friedrichshafen Raid in November 1914. As L 9 needed to refit after her raid on Northumberland, Strasser ordered his only other Zeppelins, L 5 and L 6, to make ready.

15–16 April 1915: East Anglia coast

The commander of L 5, Kapitänleutnant der Reserve (Kptlt-d-R) Alois Böcker, a former captain of the *Hamburg-Amerika* shipping line, had only taken command of the airship the previous day, so no doubt felt nervous as he left the shed at Fuhlsbüttel and lifted gently into the air. Although with a moonless night ahead and promising weather conditions all boded well for the mission. As the raiders progressed, however, the sky became cloudy and misty while an increasing wind blowing from the west hindered movement. Weather forecasting remained a headache for Germany throughout the air war. While the Germans were able to predict weather patterns over the North Sea, they were not able to anticipate weather approaching from the west of Britain.

Böcker first sighted England at about 9.40pm but he was not off the Humber. The prevailing wind had forced him way off course to a position off Southwold on the coast of Suffolk, about 110 miles south-east of the target (see Map 1). British reports suggest L 5 remained off the coast for two hours, presumably while Böcker and his officers tried to work out where they were. After fruitless searching, Böcker made his mind up and came inland. Feeling his way, he passed over Reydon heading westwards as he followed what became a great circular route, being seen at Wenhaston, and then from Bramfield at about 12.10am, where four soldiers defiantly opened fire with their rifles. Having reached Halesworth and still with no clearer idea of his position, Böcker turned back to the east.[1] Standing just north of the village of Blythburgh was Henham Hall, the home of the Earl and Countess Stradbroke. The Earl had given over the Hall to the Red Cross, which had established an auxiliary military hospital there. With the Earl away serving in the Army, the Countess remained at the hall as matron.

The hospital was full of patients as L 5 approached over the dark Suffolk countryside. Reports suggest the Zeppelin circled menacingly over Henham Hall at 12.25am before releasing an HE and 23 incendiary bombs. Fortunately for the patients, Böcker's aim was poor. Not one bomb hit the house and 'the majority were not within 100 or 200 yards of the hospital and the furthest quite 400 yards from it though within the grounds'. There was, however, almost a tragic conclusion to the incident. After the Zeppelin departed, gamekeepers and staff went out to investigate the damage. As they moved stealthily through the grounds they noticed they were not alone; another shadowy group of figures appeared in the gloom. They feared that the Zeppelin had landed a desperate band of German soldiers. It must have been a tense moment or two before they realized that the 'Germans' were actually the Countess and some of her nurses out in the grounds on a similar mission to themselves.[2]

From Henham Hall it was just a short distance back to Reydon. At 12.27am Böcker released an HE bomb that landed 'in the marshes' there. The bomb detonated a short distance from Cave Cottage, the home of Benjamin Snowling, ripping the doors from their hinges, blowing in the windows and damaging the roof. Although asleep at the time, Snowling was able to bring his wife and two daughters out, shaken but uninjured by the blast. Three incendiary bombs quickly followed without causing any damage: one at Old Hall Farm, another near the water pumping station in Quay Lane and the last one at Laurel Farm.[3]

Continuing on his uncertain course, Böcker turned south-east to Southwold, where an incendiary bomb landed in a railway truck at the station, damaging both the truck and a small shed. Another incendiary dropped on the seashore close to the pier before L 5 turned and flew across the town back to Reydon. Here Böcker released two more bombs, HE and incendiary. The incendiary landed harmlessly near a gamekeeper's house at Mere Farm Corner while the HE bomb detonated in a meadow at Mere Farm. It landed about 100 yards from the farmhouse owned by W.F. Self, and 80 yards from farm buildings 'making a hole 8 feet deep and 20 yards in circumference'. The explosion lifted some of the farmhouse's roof tiles and blew in a window of a separate dwelling on the farm occupied by W. Fairhead.[4] Turning north Böcker passed over the hamlet of Easton Bavents from where soldiers of 6th Battalion Sussex Cyclists opened a steady rifle fire and L 5 dropped two incendiaries on fields at Easton Farm.

Still trying to confirm his location, Böcker released a parachute flare when north of Easton Bavents, which eventually landed on Richard Nirling's farm near Wrentham, between Southwold and Lowestoft. In fact, as many as six of Böcker's bombs, initially identified as incendiaries, were later reclassified as parachute flares, an indicator of how difficult he found it to determine his position.[5]

15–16 April 1915, 1.05am: Lowestoft, Suffolk

The town of Lowestoft now lay about seven miles away. As L 5 approached the town a police superintendent observed her progress and reported that she passed over the Herring Market on the Outer Harbour at about 1.05am:

> She then became stationary, and her engines stopped. She had been in that position about a minute or two when the 'Syren' at the Electric Light Station commenced to be sounded and she remained there for about another minute and then slowly moved off taking a slight turn to the south and went towards the Great Eastern Railway (GER) Central Station and the Inner Harbour.[6]

The crew of L 5 clearly heard the sound of the siren below too and Böcker began to climb from 2,000 feet up to about 5,200 feet before moving off to the south-west and circling over Lowestoft. Three very loud explosions followed, which shook the town. The first HE bomb landed with shattering effect in the garden at the back of 48 Denmark Road, close to the railway station, making a hole 'large enough to bury half a dozen people'. The Pratt family living at No. 48 had a narrow escape:

81

Mr and Mrs Platt were asleep when the bomb exploded. They state that they were literally lifted out of bed to the floor. Glass flew about, furniture was thrown over and broken, and the bedroom was reduced to chaos.

Mr Percy Pratt, son of the occupier, had a similar experience. He got up on hearing the throbbing of the Zeppelin engine, and had just risen from bed when the whole place, as he put it, seemed to rock. He was thrown to the floor, broken glass and plaster raining on him. The door was blown to the centre of the room, just missing him by inches.[7]

The Pratt family had two lodgers living with them. One, Mr Bloomfield, who shared the room with Percy received cuts from the flying glass and the other in the adjoining room received similar injuries.[8]

Later a neighbour, Mr Merrington Smith, took a look inside the Pratt's shattered house:

The beds were covered in broken glass and woodwork from blown-in windows, this debris having fallen on people where they lay asleep.[9]

Nearly every house as far as Trafalgar Street, about 200 yards away, suffered smashed windows while others lost the window frames too and had their doors blown in. Some walls were reduced to rubble and:

Greenhouses and outbuildings were shattered, corrugated iron sheets were twisted as though they were cardboard, and the scene was one of utmost confusion.[10]

At a neighbouring house occupied by Mr Fitte, the ceiling came down and the blast hurled doors across rooms. And at 52 Denmark Road, George Mobbs, awakened by the sound of the Zeppelin's engines, had just climbed out of bed when the bomb exploded. As he reeled from the blast, fragments of shattered glass slashed at him, leaving his face a bloody mess. A few yards away a barber's shop had its whole front blown in.[11]

Then, while the residents were trying to make sense of what had just happened, an incendiary bomb landed on the tramlines in Denmark Road: 'A big pool of greenish liquid was left. This blazed up for a time, and then died down. It speedily turned solid.'[12]

Having crossed Denmark Road, L 5 dropped a second HE bomb that landed close to stables in the GER yard. In the demolished building, rescuers found two dead horses and two or three others with injuries, while outside stood the shattered wreckage of five lorries and a parcel cart. The blast also damaged sheds belonging to the railway and smashed windows in a signal box.[13]

Crossing over the railway, L 5 released an incendiary as it approached the Inner Harbour. Fortuitously for Böcker it fell among stacks of timber piled in Latten's Timber Yard on Commercial Road. The blaze soon took hold, setting fire to the timber and buildings while illuminating the surrounding district. Large numbers of people, awoken by the explosive bombs, now headed towards the scene of the great conflagration. Sailors from minesweepers and a gunboat moored close by rushed to help before the fire brigade arrived and took control. Some naval personal grabbed rifles and opened fire on L 5 while other servicemen helped hold back the crowds. Within an hour the blaze was contained and half an hour later largely extinguished. Another horse, however, died in the fire.

Now south of the Inner Harbour, Böcker released an HE and incendiary bomb together. They landed in a field close to houses in Kimberley Road and, according to a police report, caused 'a deal of damage to the brick & wood work; nearly all the windows were either blown out or broken'. Turning over Oulton Broad, Böcker dropped four more incendiary bombs that failed to cause any damage, before he passed back over Lowestoft and out to sea at about 1.25am.

This sudden awakening in the night by enemy attack does not seem to have caused any panic among the population of Lowestoft. Although a great many people were in the streets after the first explosions, a newspaper reported they remained calm: 'The demeanour of the people,' it explained, 'was one of curiosity, and there was nothing in the shape of excitement.' As those same people took stock of what had happened and a gossiping countryside was alive with tales of German bombs, one uncomprehending resident of Lowestoft was left to survey the damage that surrounded him: 'I've lived in this house nigh 19 years and nobody has ever played me such a trick before.'[14]

About 15 minutes after Böcker took L 5 back out over the North Sea, Zeppelin L 7, with Strasser on board, appeared off Brancaster, on the north-east coast of Norfolk, and about forty miles south-east of the mouth of the Humber. The commander, Peterson, had encountered a fierce 34mph headwind over the North Sea, which prevented further progress, and at Brancaster he gave up and turned with the wind, following the Norfolk coast. British reports placed him near Cromer at

2.05am and at Happisburgh ten minutes later. He continued hurtling along the coast to Gorleston, south of Great Yarmouth, where he went out to sea at 2.35am, having averaged a wind-assisted speed from Brancaster of about 65mph. The lighting restrictions on the coast proved effective because Peterson reported that he never saw land and therefore dropped no bombs on England.[15]

15–16 April 1915, 12.20am: Maldon, Essex

The third of the raiders that night, von Buttlar, commanding L 6, also encountered serious navigation problems (see Map 1).

L 6 made the coast of Essex at Walton-on-the-Naze at about 11.30pm, although von Buttlar was unaware he had reached England. Reports trace him circling over Clacton 15 minutes later. At the same time, von Buttlar grew concerned because he had expected to sight land by that time. Having checked his fuel reserves, he determined to keep searching for the English coast until 1.00am (midnight, British time) at which point he accepted he must turn back to Germany. While von Buttlar continued to search for any sign of land, observers plotted him crossing the mouth of the River Blackwater and on towards Burnham-on-Crouch, while a newspaper carried a report that two bombs dropped harmlessly as L 6 passed over Tillingham. These may have actually been parachute flares because at Burnham von Buttlar changed course to the north-west. But time was moving on: 'It was 1am and still no land was in sight! Should I turn back after all? It was very hard to make up my mind. I allowed myself another quarter of an hour's grace.' Finally he saw some faint lights below.[16] British reports state that L 6 circled over the town of Maldon at 12.20am before dumping its entire load of four HE bombs and 30 incendiaries on the town and neighbouring Heybridge.

Henry Foreman, a widower, was in bed at Rose Cottage (23 Spital Road) when he heard the sound of engine noise in the air. Also in the house were his three sons, Reginald (aged 15), Arthur (12) and Leslie (10), as well as the housekeeper, Annie Hinton. As he got out of bed to investigate, he heard a 'terrific explosion, and tiles rattled off the roof and plaster tumbled down inside'. Henry rushed to his sons' bedroom and was shocked to find 'them covered with fallen lumps of ceiling'. The boys could not speak, their mouths 'choked with plaster'. Much to Mr Foreman's relief the eldest and youngest sons were unharmed, while Arthur merely suffered a scratched nose. Mr Foreman ordered them under their bed for protection.[17]

The bomb had actually landed next door to Mr Foreman's cottage, on a large timber and iron workshop owned by a builder, Arthur Smith, situated opposite the Union Workhouse. It demolished the workshop, hurling timber and sheets of corrugated iron over a wide area and into the grounds of the workhouse, while 'tools were scattered about like apples from an overturned cart'.

The cottage on the other side of Smith's workshop suffered badly too. Walter Mott, the supervisor at Maldon post office, lived there with his 63-year-old mother, Eliza, but again the occupants escaped without injury. 'Mr Mott's house had the end bespattered by shrapnel, and one or two of the bullets pierced the wall, passed through a picture, over the bed in which he was asleep, and made their exit by the front of the house.'

The explosion also destroyed or damaged a number of outbuildings nearby. In one, a chicken coop owned by Harry Hutson, a hen died from a broken neck and another emerged with an injured leg!

Across Spital Road at the workhouse, the Master, W.H. White, had also heard the sound of engines and got out of bed. He thought he could see something up in the sky and guessed it was a Zeppelin: 'I heard the first bomb explode with a terrific report, and there was a great cracking noise of glass, then panes fell in all directions.' A reporter who visited the building the following day described the effect of the bomb:

> ... wholesale destruction of windows, scarcely a frame being undamaged, while the woodwork in some cases was forced inwards ... In one room the gas globes were shattered and in another the blinds were torn down and the gas brackets twisted awry, while a large quantity of plaster was shaken down.

Despite the damage, Mr White was able to report that the inmates remained calm, although many were understandably 'very much upset with the shock' and moved into the corridors for safety. In the grounds the blast destroyed a greenhouse while two incendiaries badly scorched some trees, but soldiers were quickly on the scene to extinguish the fires.

A second HE bomb landed about 100 yards away on a meadow near Mount Pleasant, where it excavated a crater described by a local reporter as 'some 20 feet across and nearly six feet deep'. Shrapnel bullets pierced a wooden fence in several places and a young girl suffered a minor flesh wound.

Incendiaries also dropped on Maldon, bombs that von Buttlar explained 'had to be thrown out by hand' from these early Zeppelins. He describes how 'a pin had to be taken out of them to make them 'live', after which they were flung in a gentle curve overboard, to crash and burst below a moment later and burn merrily'.[18] There are mentions of incendiaries falling in a garden adjoining the workhouse, a couple in Fambridge Road and one in Beeleigh Chase. One also fell in London Road, at William South's house, where it set fire to the weatherboards of a lean-to scullery, but a few buckets of water sufficed to extinguish the flames. Others fell near East Maldon Station and in the River Chelmer close to Fullbridge. Generally the incendiaries did very little damage and became much sought after as souvenirs: '… at six o'clock this morning, the inhabitants of Maldon and district … were in their back gardens carefully wrapping up the remains either to forward them to the police or to treasure them as "tokens of frightfulness" for the benefit of posterity.'[19] Elsewhere that morning great crowds gathered at the craters left by the two bombs to witness Maldon's entry into the war for themselves.

Von Buttlar's course next took him over the River Chelmer to Heybridge, where his bombs caused only limited damage. As he lay in bed at his billet in Heybridge Hall, 2nd Lt Stanley Booker of the 2/7th Worcestershire Regiment heard the approach of the Zeppelin:

> I heard it come closer and heard it dropping bombs and it was an anxious moment wondering where they would fall. I heard one or two drop in front of the house and the others behind it. One I heard come down especially loudly and that one exploded with a heavy report and a white flash in the back garden.[20]

A local newspaper explained a little more: 'A third [HE] bomb fell in a field near the Hall … making a big pit, in which a horse and cart could easily be hidden, while huge lumps of earth were hurled yards away into the river. In this quarter, along Heybridge Hall Road, dozens of windows were smashed, and one old building was almost unroofed.'

A woman living in the road heard a noise that she described as like a car pulling up outside her house: 'I got out of bed,' she explained, 'and then came a terrific explosion … Although it woke me my children did not awaken till I called to them the Germans were here, and they laughed and would not believe me.' An incendiary also landed close to this bomb, which a local resident later dug up, while the witness in Hall Road reported seeing five more incendiaries land near the river.

Another HE bomb followed, landing the other side of the hall where 'it tore a great hole in a field'. And more 'flaming bombs' were recorded dropping between the hall and Heybridge Basin. As an eyewitness put it: 'It seemed to be raining fire.'

Now, having released all his bombs, von Buttlar followed an erratic course back to the coast. Soldiers at a Royal Engineers camp at Brightlingsea opened up with rifles as L 5 flew over them at about 12.35am before she passed over the ports of Harwich and Felixstowe about 25 minutes later. The officer commanding the defences from Landguard Fort at Felixstowe, Lieutenant Colonel (Lt Col) W. Howel Jones, Royal Garrison Artillery, received news of the Zeppelin's approach at 12.30am.[21] Fifteen minutes later the sound of its engines became audible. Rather than give his position away, he chose not to open his two searchlights. Having estimated the height of L 6 at about 5,000 feet, he considered that it was beyond the range of his two 1-pdr 'pom-pom' guns at the fort and refrained from opening with the AA guns at Parkeston, on the Harwich side of the harbour, as any shells that missed the target would likely come down in Felixstowe. He did however permit the 'pom-pom' positioned near the oil tanks to fire three rounds, which followed an almost vertical trajectory. None hit the target and all three burst when they hit the ground on Landguard Common, not far from the fort. A number of soldiers at the fort opened a fierce rifle fire on L 6 too. Von Buttlar recalled how 'little red spots of fire appeared below'. That rifle fire, combined with that from Brightlingsea, however, proved quite effective. When L 6 got back to Fuhlsbüttel one gas cell had 'two large and six smaller holes from two to ten centimetres in diameter made by gunfire' and had lost most of its hydrogen. There was also evidence of 17 bullet strikes and damage to two other gas cells.[22]

16 April 1915: Hamburg, Germany

Von Buttlar almost ran out of fuel on his return journey, so was relieved to get back to Fuhlsbüttel, but then the questions started. Everyone wanted to know where he had bombed, but he had no idea. Strasser then telephoned from Nordholz to ask that same question:

> Heavens! How inquisitive everybody was! With the best will in the world I could not answer his question. I stammered and stuttered into the telephone, and declared that opinions were still divided as to the precise spot, but that it must have been one of two places. He asked me what they were.
>
> I thought there was something wrong with the line. I could hardly hear what he was saying – at least so I declared.
>
> Well, the long and short of it was that he did not catch the two names which I mumbled into the telephone, and I told him I would telegraph them to him.[23]

Relieved that he had gained himself some time, von Buttlar wrote out a long report, leaving a blank for the name of the target and handed it to a typist. He then washed, changed and headed to Deeke's Bierhaus in Hamburg. As he discussed the raid with his second-in-command, a newspaper seller entered with the evening edition and announced, 'Airship raid on England'.

> I read the Admiralty's official report, which stated that an airship had attacked certain fortified places in England. But as far as I was concerned the most important piece of news came at the end. Below the heavy type of the official announcement there was a short paragraph giving an extract from the *Nieuwe Rotterdamsche Courant*. It ran as follows:
>
> We learn from our London correspondent that a German airship carried out a bombing raid at 1.15am to-day over the English town of Maldon.

Wasting no more time, von Buttlar telephoned the typist, telling her to type the name Maldon into the gaps he had left in his report, then no doubt he smiled and breathed a great sigh of relief. And the smile on his face was to grow even wider, for the punchline was still to come.

> About a fortnight later I received through the usual official channels a communication from the authorities with regard to L 6's raid. In it they declared that 'the accurate navigation of the airship and location of the place raided were worthy of the highest praise'.[24]

Von Buttlar survived the war and wrote a number of fulsome reports of his raids but he proved one of the less determined airship captains.

Beyond the false praise von Buttlar had enjoyed, both he and Böcker were now aware of just how difficult accurate navigation over England was going to be. Strasser's own experiences that night had made him very aware of the problems too. It became clear that the 'm-class' Zeppelins, with their limited range and weight-carrying ability, were not up to the task required. And the whole experience was extremely testing for the crews, exposed as they were to the worst that nature could throw at them in their open gondolas. But an improved Zeppelin – the 'p-class' – was under construction and would soon be ready for service.

April 1915: London

The analysis of the material damage caused by the raid reflected the limited effect obtainable from a few HE bombs. During the raid, L 5 and L 6 dropped just ten HE bombs between them and around 60 incendiaries, but the incendiary bombs often failed to ignite or landed harmlessly on open ground. When they did manage to find a suitable target, however, they were effective. For instance, the fire at the Lowestoft timber yard caused damage estimated at the time at £2,300. The official estimate of total damage for the raid stood at £6,498, with £5,953 of that inflicted by L 5 on Lowestoft.

Once again defence aircraft had been unable to oppose the raiders. The RNAS station at Great Yarmouth received news of a Zeppelin at Southwold at about 12.40am and prepared a Sopwith Seaplane Type 880 for patrol. Taking off at 12.55am it remained airborne for nearly an hour and although L 5 was attacking Lowestoft only seven miles away, Flt Cdr de Courcy Wynder Plunkett Ireland and his observer, Leading Mechanic C. Notley, could not find her in the dark. Earlier in the evening, at about 6.15pm, Great Yarmouth had sent up a Sopwith Two-seater Scout. Although the crew saw no Zeppelins, that moment marked a significant step forward for Britain's air defence because she had taken off in response to an advanced warning of a Zeppelin attack.[25]

At the beginning of the war Britain established a number of wireless intercept and direction-finding stations along the coast to pick up German U-boat signals. These also received Zeppelin signals. On 19 January and again on 14 April these stations intercepted signals that included the Zeppelin's identification number and the decoded words 'only H.V.B. on board'. Operators received these same words again on 15 April. The British naval intelligence team at the Admiralty's Room 40 quickly recognized that raids followed these signals. Even as the raid of

15–16 April was developing, naval intelligence passed an alert to RNAS Great Yarmouth in advance of the arrival of the raiders. The letters H.V.B. were an abbreviation of *Handelsschiffsverkehrsbuch*, the German codebook used by the Navy to communicate with merchant ships. The Royal Australian Navy had captured a copy of the H.V.B. codebook when it seized a merchant ship of the German–Australian shipping line near Melbourne in August 1914. The Admiralty in London had received a copy in October. Rather than risk losing other codebooks, should something go wrong on a mission, the commanders of Navy Zeppelins about to set out on raids against England were instructed to send the 'H.V.B.' signal as confirmation they had no other codebooks on board.[26]

Having the ability to intercept and understand the implicit meaning of the 'H.V.B.' signal gave British naval intelligence a significant advantage in knowing when Navy airships were about to strike against Britain. Where they would strike, however, remained a mystery. Given the difficulty Zeppelin commanders were experiencing with navigation, it often remained a mystery for them too!

As it was, the Naval Airship Division would not trouble Britain's defences again until June while it awaited its new 'p-class- Zeppelins. The Army, however, was happy to pick up the baton. The first to enter the arena was a single aeroplane and its determined two-man crew.

16 April 1915, 12.15pm: Sittingbourne, Kent

During the morning of 16 April, before von Buttlar had even discovered that his bombs had landed on Maldon, a lone Albatros BII of *Feldflieger Abteilung Nr. 41* took off from its airfield near Gits in Belgium, 18 miles south-east of Ostend, and headed across the English Channel towards Kent (see Map 2).[27] On board were Oblt Freiherr Dietrich von Kanne and his pilot, Offizierstellvertreter Karl Ritter. They came inland near Kingsdown at about 11.40am before flying across the county and out to sea again near Herne Bay on the north Kent coast. The aircraft then disappeared until a sergeant of the Royal Engineers at Harty Ferry reported it turning inland over the eastern mouth of the Swale. Second Lt E. Browne, commanding the 3-inch AA gun at Faversham, protecting the explosive works at the Cotton Powder Company, found himself in a quandary. The RNAS had purchased a German Albatros before the war and had informed local gun batteries that it would be flying from Eastchurch that day. So when, at about 12.10pm, through breaks in the cloud Browne saw an aircraft approaching at great height, he could not tell if it was friend or foe.

Only when he finally focused on black crosses on the wings through the telescopic sight was he sure: 'By the time we had definitely identified it, the machine was practically over the gun and we traversed right round and opened fire at 2,000 yards – firing seven rounds after which target was obscured.' Browne believed the third round came close.[28]

Having passed over Faversham, Ritter approached Sittingbourne, skirting around the north side of the town. The first bomb fell at the village of Borden, south-west of the town. It landed in a brickfield pit on Cryalls Farm just north of the village. Then two more dropped on the south side of Sittingbourne. One landed about 200 yards from a camp of the Royal Dublin Fusiliers at Gore Court and the other, following a few seconds later, landed at Glover's Farm. It is possible that this bomb was the one that claimed the only victim of the raid. The press made much of the fact that a bomb landed in an orchard, where it uprooted an apple tree and killed a blackbird. A drawing of the unfortunate bird even featured on a postcard issued shortly afterwards to commemorate the raid.[29]

Ritter and von Kanne continued to circle Sittingbourne, climbing to a height reported as 8,000 feet, and dropped a fourth bomb, which fell in a brickfield at Grovehurst, before releasing a fifth as they approached the Kingsferry Bridge. It missed the bridge, which carried the road over the Swale, and buried itself some five feet deep in farmland just to the south-west of the structure. Turning eastwards, the Albatros then flew across Sheppey before returning to Faversham at about 12.30pm. As the aircraft approached from the west the AA gunners again strained their eyes looking for the telltale black crosses on the wings before daring to open fire. As soon as they got a positive identification the gun roared into action, opening at a range of 3,000 yards from its position north of the town. This time Browne and his crew got off 22 rounds, the range gradually extending to 5,800 yards, while the aircraft dropped five bombs on the south side of the town.

The 30 patients at The Mount military hospital escaped further injury when the first bomb of this second salvo landed in the grounds and within yards of the main London–Dover railway line, narrowly missing a signal box. The second bomb, believed to be an incendiary, landed on the Ashford Road, close to the junction with the London Road, and set fire to the wooden boundary fence of a sports field. Three people, the Reverend F.H. Barnett, Police Constable Hopper and Mrs Philip Heath, the wife of a factory inspector, were within 100 yards of the bomb when it struck the ground but were unharmed.

Two five-year-old children, Sydney Clark and Myra Higgins, were crossing the long bridge over the railway at Faversham as they walked home from school for lunch when they saw the aeroplane. In his later years Sydney recalled the moment:

> The sight of a single aeroplane was interesting, for they were still new and rare, but we felt no reason to be afraid, although we'd already learned that the strange cigar-shaped Zeppelins were dangerous. When things began to fall from the 'plane' it was even more interesting, and we stopped and put our heads through the ironwork for a better view.
>
> Then our anti-aircraft guns began to fire, and we thought better of it, hurrying home into the welcoming arms of anxious mothers who talked about the dangers from falling shrapnel.[30]

As little Sydney and his neighbour Myra scuttled home to Preston Avenue, a third bomb landed at Preston village, in Mr Ratcliff's field behind cottages and some engine sheds belonging to the council, followed by a fourth that buried itself about four feet deep in the ground at a fruit plantation on Macknade Farm. A boy who was in a shed not far from the where the bomb landed was lucky to escape unharmed. A final bomb fell south-east of the town near the railway at Colkins hop gardens, burning some fences and hop poles.

As in other towns visited by German raiders, a reporter in Faversham told how there was little sign of alarm on the streets. However, contrary to advice, the people did not seek safety in cellars and basements: 'Indeed the sense of danger was exceeded by curiosity, and the people flocked into the streets.' Those people found it hard to see the raider, 'but when it executed a circling movement its wings glittered in the sunlight'.

Having released all ten of their bombs, von Kanne and Ritter continued on their course taking them towards Canterbury, which they reached at about 12.45pm. By now thirteen British aircraft from Dover, Eastchurch and Westgate, had taken to the sky, but gathering cloud made location of the small but fast-moving enemy aircraft a difficult task. Once in the air they had no radios to guide them, they were on their own.

Eluding its pursuers the German aircraft reached the coast again near Deal. Onlookers at Kingsdown described it as 'a mere speck in the sky' when it emerged from the clouds at a great height and disappeared out over the English Channel heading towards Dunkirk.

Safely back at Gits, von Kanne filed his report on the raid and shortly afterwards both he and Ritter received the Iron Cross 1st Class. Perhaps von Kanne's imaginative claim that they had reached Greenwich on the outskirts of London helped. The raid by this lone aircraft was the first successful attempt by any German Army aircraft to reach Britain. Airships of the German Army had failed to make any impact on Britain so far. Of their three active airships in the west, Z X was lost on 21 March while returning from a raid on Paris, and just over three weeks later AA guns damaged LZ 35 after a raid on the Western Front. She made a forced landing among trees near Aeltre in Belgium, where a storm wrecked her. And the Army had withdrawn its 'b-type' Schütte–Lanz airship, SL. II,[31] for reconstruction to increase her hydrogen capacity.

And so the Army, like the Navy, awaited delivery of the new 'p-class' Zeppelins before striking against Britain again. In all, the Zeppelin Company (Luftschiffbau Zeppelin GmbH) would build 22 airships of this new type. While both services lobbied to receive the first, that prize was delivered to the Army in the opening week of April 1915; the Navy would have to wait another forty days before receiving its first. In that time the Army opened its campaign against Britain in earnest.

Chapter 8

'The Devils Have Come!'

The new Zeppelin type – the 'p-class' – showed a marked improvement on current models. The overall length increased to 536 feet 5 inches, an extension of a little over 18 feet, with the diameter increasing by 13 feet to 61 feet 4 inches. As a result, the hydrogen capacity grew around 42% from 794,500 cubic feet to 1,126,400 cubic feet.[1] That increase in hydrogen dramatically increased its performance. Whereas the 'm-type' had a ceiling in the region of 9,000 feet, the new type could climb to a maximum of 12,000 feet and its load-carrying ability almost doubled, allowing for more fuel and a bomb load of up to two imperial tons, and these bombs could now be released at the flick of an electric switch.[2] Three 210hp Maybach engines provided the power for the first airship of this class, but those that followed mounted four – and the crew had the added bonus of enclosed gondolas. There was still no heating to combat the sub-zero temperatures encountered at altitude, but at least they now had some protection from the direct blast of the icy winds. Working as part of a Zeppelin crew was never a pleasant experience.

Having received the first of this new Zeppelin class, the Army handed command of LZ 38 to Hptmn Erich Linnarz. Aged 35, Linnarz had served in *Infanterie Regiment Nr. 50* before the war, becoming regimental adjutant in 1905. After a year's unpaid leave in 1908–09, he attended the Military Technical Academy for almost two years before transferring to *Luftschiffer Bataillon Nr. 1* (Airship Battalion No. 1) in 1912, where he became an instructor the following year. Prior to taking command of LZ 38, it appears that Linnarz served as an officer on the Army's Zeppelin Z IV. Now, for a month, Linnarz had the skies over Britain all to himself. In that time he carried out five headline-grabbing raids on south-east England.

29 April 1915, 11.55pm: Essex Coast

Linnarz set out on his first raid on the evening of 29 April. Unlike the Navy's preference for dark nights, he chose the night of the full moon. Departing from the Army's airship shed at Evere, on the north-east periphery of Brussels, he followed a direct north-westerly course. Encountering only light winds, LZ 38 made good progress and the first notice the British defences received of an approaching Zeppelin came at about 11.00pm from the Galloper Lightship moored about 30 miles ESE of Harwich because as an Army Zeppelin it did not transmit the Navy's 'H.V.B.' code. Word had not yet reached those manning the coastal defences when at 11.55pm both police and the military at Felixstowe reported the sound of her engines coming inland near the mouth of the River Debden (see Map 3). Although they heard her engines, thick coastal fog meant she remained invisible to those scanning the sky. This same fog prevented any defence aircraft getting airborne to intercept LZ 38 until 4.30am. Then four aircraft from RNAS Yarmouth took off hoping that LZ 38 might still be lurking in the area, but she was long gone.

The fog blanket spread far inland, but as Linnarz felt his way forward, LZ 38 crossed the River Orwell and he became aware of a town ahead. For his first raid over England Linnarz chose a load of ten HE bombs and more than 60 incendiaries. He dropped the first of these firebombs on the village of Belstead, where it failed to cause any damage, then flew on towards the unidentified town that lay about three miles distant.[3]

30 April 1915, 12.10am: Ipswich, Suffolk

In Gaye Street, Ipswich, Walter Mullet, a nightwatchman, was warming himself by his fire when he heard a strange sound:

> It was just ten minutes past twelve o'clock when the rumbling noise of something like a huge motor car met my ears. A few minutes later I heard four loud bangs. I wondered what was the matter and then a bright light lit the whole place up ... Looking in the direction of the noise I saw a blaze on the sky-line. I knew it must have been a Zeppelin.

Mullet was about 200 yards from where the first of three bombs landed, perhaps a little over 400 yards from the second and half a mile from the third. That first bomb crashed down about 100 yards from the

Artillery Barracks, and close to the wall of the Presbyterian Church at 'Barrack Corner', causing a slight indentation in the ground but failing to ignite. Seconds later the next fell in the roadway in Waterloo Street 'with a big whizzing noise', where it 'scattered burning fragments in all directions', but did no damage other than making a small dent in the road. However, it was the third of the bombs that nightwatchman Mullet heard that left a lasting impression on Ipswich.

Richard Ellwood, a tramway inspector, of Springfield Lane, had not been home long when he heard the ominous hum of engines:

> I had just come in from my work and was finishing my daily report in the little sitting room. My wife at about a quarter after twelve went out into the back yard to gather coals. Almost before I knew it she burst open the back door, shouting to me, 'Come out, Dick, into the garden and hear this awful noise'... and then almost before we knew it we heard an explosion ... and immediately afterwards there was a huge blaze at the back of the houses in Brookshall [Brooks Hall] Road.

A policeman standing in the road saw 'a spark fall from the clouds'. The spark was an incendiary bomb and it struck the roof of 60 Brooks Hall Road, a terraced house in a section of the road called Roseberry Villas. The house was home to Harry Goodwin, his wife and 12-year-old Elsie.[4] Goodwin's wife, hearing the engines, had just awoken her husband when the bomb fell. It smashed through the roof into the back bedroom where Elsie was sleeping and struck a chest of drawers just a few feet from her bed. Burning furiously now, the bomb continued on its path, through the floorboards and down to the kitchen. Mr Goodwin made a dash for Elsie's bedroom which was a 'mass of flames', but he found the girl 'unharmed, although naturally she was terribly frightened'. All three escaped the house and sought refuge with a neighbour.

The flames had quickly taken hold and spread easily to No. 58 next door, the home of W.T. Easey, his wife and son, Alfred[5]. Mr Easey heard the engines too and then the crash as the bomb hit the roof next door. The shock left his windows shattered and, as the house filled with the smell of burning wood, he rushed out into the street to see what had happened. A quick glance was all he needed before running back inside and leading his wife and son to safety. Mr and Mrs Farnham at No. 56 had a little more time and, seeing the flames heading in their direction, with great presence of mind began removing furniture from their house with the help of neighbours. Although the fire brigade was quickly on the scene, by 12.45am all three houses were blazing fiercely and an hour after the bomb dropped all that remained were the blackened empty shells of what had so recently been three peaceful homes. It was proof that if the incendiary bombs actually hit a target, rather than landing in fields, gardens or on roads, they were able to inflict unprecedented levels of indiscriminate destruction on the civilian population of Britain. As the flames leapt up into the night sky, illuminating the scene for some distance, LZ 38 turned away from Ipswich, dropping a fifth and final incendiary that landed harmlessly at Whitton, a village on the north-western outskirts of the town.

From Whitton, LZ 38 turned to the west and, when over the village of Bramford, dropped five incendiary bombs on fields at Grove Farm, but no one discovered these until the following day. Now returning to a north-west course, Linnarz may have seen some lights in the small villages below, although there was still much fog here, or alternatively he decided to lighten his ship. Whatever the reason, at 12.20am five HE and 11 incendiary bombs landed between Nettlestead and Willisham about seven miles north-east of Ipswich. The HE bombs caused some damage to crops, digging craters between 14 and 17 feet in diameter and five feet deep. Continuing on the same bearing, Linnarz bypassed Stowmarket, home to the New Explosives Company's works, and now defended by two 6-pdr guns. Beyond Stowmarket, Linnarz dropped an HE bomb on the village of Bradfield St George without causing any damage of note, but by then Linnarz had the town of Bury St Edmunds in his sights. Although the town had dimmed its lighting, the fog had not penetrated that far inland, leaving it a clear target: 'The moon was at the full, and shone with a brilliance which showed up everything as though by light of day.'

30 April 1915, 12.50am: Bury St Edmunds

The police reported a Zeppelin approaching at 12.50am and, as in other towns, many residents awoke to the unexpected sound of engine noise. One of those residents was a tailor, W.C.H. Cullen, who had his business and home in Butter Market:[6]

> Just at one o'clock – I cannot tell the exact time it was – I was lying awake when I heard the whirl of an airship. Going to the window I saw a policeman, whom I asked if there were any aircraft about, and he said 'yes.' I immediately dressed, went down the street and

saw the machine coming as if it were from over Moyse's Hall ...
In the sky over the Railway Station I noticed a peculiarly brilliant
light.

Arriving over the town, Linnarz took LZ 38 to the northern edge before heading in towards the centre. Without any fear of coming under attack he circled over Bury St Edmunds two or three times raining down about 40 incendiaries and three HE bombs on the sleeping market town. The first of the HE bombs dropped in a field in Northgate Avenue, described as a 'select residential district'. It tore up a tree by the roots, followed by a 'great rain of earth and stones' which smashed windows in local houses and demolished wooden fencing along the side of the road. Mr J.W. Searle, who lived close to the spot where the bomb exploded, described the sound as 'like the large guns he had heard discharged at Shoeburyness'. Moments later, as LZ 38 approached the railway station, two incendiary bombs landed close by. A goods train had just arrived at the station and the three-man crew were taking on water; they heard the Northgate Avenue explosion but did not think anything of it. Then someone shouted and the crew saw the Zeppelin coming towards them. Diving for cover, they watched as LZ 38 continued dropping bombs. Driver F. Gynn later told a reporter: 'It was anything but a pleasant feeling.'

The other two HE bombs also fell outside the centre of the town. One exploded in a field about 60 yards south of the Newmarket Road, narrowly missing some buildings on Sexton's Hall Farm and landing just a short distance from the Suffolk Regiment's Gibraltar Barracks. The other fell in a field at Westley, west of the town. The incendiary bombs, however, made a lasting impression, with two serious fires breaking out just 150 yards apart. A soldier thought it looked like 'a cartload of bombs were being poured down'.[7]

One firebomb smashed through the roof of 32 Butter Market, where Jeremiah Day made boots and shoes. The eyewitness, Mr Cullen, who had rushed out into Butter Market when the Zeppelin first appeared, 'heard a bomb drop on Messrs. Day's, and immediately saw a big light on the ground floor of their boot premises'. He realized the burning bomb had passed right through the building from top to bottom. Five other businesses were now in danger from the fire. On one side of Day's shop was a ladies' outfitters owned by Ellen Wise (No. 33) and T.H. Nice and Co., motor and cycle agents (No. 33a). On the other side, at No. 31, stood Miss Alice Clark's tobacconist, with the Johnson Brothers dyer's business at No. 31a and a photographer, George Cousins, at No. 30. Only at No. 33 and No. 31 did the owners live on the premises. Knowing this, as the flames quickly took hold, Cullen 'immediately ran across to rouse Mrs Wise, but could make no one hear'. Undaunted he grabbed a ladder, intending to smash a window to awaken her but another neighbour shouted to him: 'She is not at home.' The would-be rescuers, however, were unaware that her collie dog remained trapped inside. Searchers later discovered its charred body in the smoking ruins of the shop. Meanwhile, Cullen had turned his attention to Miss Clark's shop but found she was already alert. Miss Clark gave an account of her experience to a newspaper reporter:

> I was awakened by a sound like the report of a gun, and I at once awoke my assistant (Miss Manning), and said 'The Germans are here.' Just then a terrific explosion occurred outside the side window in the bedroom, followed by the smashing of the glass roof over the kitchen and lavatory. I jumped out of bed, slipped on my coat, and seizing my cash box, left the bedroom and went downstairs as quickly as I could, followed by Miss Manning.

They found a policeman at the door trying to alert them and he would not let them go back to collect more clothes. Miss Clark did not immediately realize the danger they were in: 'When we got outside my shop and looked up to see what was the matter, the place was one huge blaze.' Neighbours took the women in, gave them extra clothes and generally looked after them.

The following day Miss Clark and Miss Manning, accompanied by a reporter, returned to the ruins of the building:

> The bed was burnt to ashes, and the washstand and dressing table had all been entirely consumed in the flames, as also all clothing, boots, linen, articles of jewellery and everything else. 'I have not even so much as a brooch left,' Miss Clark plaintively remarked.

As soon as the fire brigade arrived it quickly got to work to limit the spread of the flames, assisted by the military, while members of the public helped drag stock from Nice's shop at No. 33a, where the workshop had started to burn. At one point an onlooker feared that flames would envelop the whole of one side of Butter Market but, 'the firemen worked zealously, and despite the great tongues of flame, they soon succeeded in becoming masters of the situation'. Within two hours the firemen had the blaze under control but continued to damp down the remains of the burnt out shops into the daylight hours. The quick responses of the town's special constables and the members of the Voluntary Aid Detachment (VAD) also earned high praise. The town's emergency planning was working well. But by now another incendiary bomb had started a second serious fire at the corner of St Andrew's Street and King's Road.

Having been busy unloading wounded soldiers, three members of the VAD were walking home from Suffolk General Hospital in Hospital Road as the raid began. One of them, Frank White, explained how they heard a strange noise. At first they could not work it out:

> Looking up, and catching sight of an object in the air, I said: 'It is an airship. Look, there it is, it is right over us.' Just as we got to the bottom of Mill Road and into King's Road, I saw a bomb drop from the Zeppelin at the bottom of King's Road. That was the one that fell on Mr. Pettitt's premises.

James Pettitt was a local entrepreneur. He ran his motor engineer business from 43 St Andrew's Street South, but a few doors away, at the junction with King's Road, he owned St Andrew's Hall, which he used as a warehouse and an auction house, adjoining which were his livery stables with an entrance in King's Road. Besides the motor business he also had various horse-drawn vehicles for hire, including landaus, an omnibus and a funeral car.

The bomb that Frank White saw fall may have actually have been one of three bombs, as it appears one smashed into St Andrew's Hall, while Private P.O. Bass, 4th Essex Regiment, believed two crashed into the stables next door. Only that morning Pettitt had moved a quantity of household furniture, the effects of Major and Mrs J.Y. Potter, into the hall for auction, but now those possessions just added fuel to the fire that began to engulf both premises. Private Bass was one of the first on the scene. From his billet a few yards away at the Everard's Tap Inn in Woolhall Street, Bass heard the bomb drop and rushed out into the street to discover the buildings well ablaze. He ran to the stable door hoping to release the horses but found the door locked. A newspaper described what he did next:

> Pvt. Bass then tried to smash the door open, and in the first attempt was successful; he was almost pitched into the stable head first, and one of the horses 'let out' at him. The soldier managed to get

the horses – they were four Army animals – out in less than five minutes, and took them down to the White Lion [in Brentgovel Street]. There were three storeys to the premises, and he says that when he went there first the roof had fallen in, and other parts of the roof were blazing.

Eager crowds now gathered to watch, mesmerized by the flames as they consumed the buildings in Butter Market and at the corner of King's Road. In describing the scene, a newspaper wrote poetically: 'Overhead shone the pale cold moon, while at the two points in the town named, flames were bursting forth from the bomb stricken buildings and showers of sparks whirled hither and thither like clouds of golden-winged insects.'

Other incendiary bombs rained down all over the town, issuing a blue smoke before they burst into flames and giving off a foul smell, but did little or no damage as they burnt out or residents bravely attacked them with buckets of water. As well as in the streets mentioned, other bombs fell in Etna Road, the southern end of Northgate Street, Angel Hill, Lower Baxter Street, Crown Street, Southgate Street, Hospital Road and York Road, as well as in fields and gardens.

Despite this shocking impact on the life of the town and its inhabitants, those tradesmen and women who had become early victims of aerial warfare faced up to their situation stoically and did not sit about moping over their losses. In an edition of the local newspaper dated 1 May, just hours after the raid, Jeremiah Day, the bootmaker, took out an advert advising his customers that he would be trading again 'on Monday next' from temporary premises in Cornhill, while Mr Cousins the photographer announced 'business will be resumed in a day or two'. While a week later a report informed readers Mr Nice had set up at St John's Street and that Miss Clark had resumed trading from premises in Whiting Street. They made them tough in Bury St Edmunds.

Some 45 minutes after LZ 38 had departed, some of the RNAS mobile AA guns roared into the town but they were too late. As in other towns already visited by the dreaded Zeppelins there was no sign of panic. It was not, however, something the residents were keen to repeat. Mr Suckley, who had been walking from the hospital with Frank White, considered it 'an exciting experience, but rather too exciting to be pleasant'. While on Southgate Street, Mrs Whiting, who ran a bakehouse with her husband, had a bomb land in an allotment just ten yards behind their premises. She expressed the opinion of many: 'We have thought a good deal about the war, but never thought it would come so near as this.'

Having set a course back to the coast, Linnarz still had a few bombs left on board and dropped them at regular intervals. The first of these, his last HE bomb, fell on open ground at Woolpit at about 1.05am, then, disappearing back into the fog, Linnarz dropped five more incendiaries to complete the raid but none caused any damage. They landed at Green Lane Farm in Creeting St Mary at 1.15am, at Pear Tree Farm in Otley, then at 1.27am at Bredfield, followed by one at Melton three minutes later before the final bomb dropped at Bromeswell, just north-east of Woodbridge. Linnarz crossed back over the coast near Orfordness at about 1.50am.[8]

The shattered buildings and charred timbers, the tangible results of the raid, now proved an irresistible draw for the curious:

> The week-end drew crowds of visitors to Bury St Edmunds to view the damage to property wrought by bombs in the Zeppelin raid on the town early last Friday morning. By motor, cycle, horse vehicle, and on foot they came from all quarters throughout Friday, Saturday, and Sunday, and the handiwork of the invaders was viewed with wonder and interest.[9]

When officers of the fire brigade completed their assessments they estimated the material damage at Ipswich and Bury St Edmunds amounted to £9,010. With LZ 38 safely back at Evere, Linnarz filed his report. Although his bombs landed at Ipswich, Bury St Edmunds and various Suffolk villages, the communiqué issued by the German authorities claimed, 'Coast fortifications at Harwich were bombarded last night'.

Linnarz no doubt looked back on his first foray over England with satisfaction. He had taken a new ship from Belgium to England, the crew had the opportunity to familiarize themselves with its handling in war conditions, they had found and bombed targets, then returned safely without any interference from the British defences.

Eight days later Linnarz and LZ 38 tried again, excited by the apparent news that the Kaiser had opened up London as a target. On 5 May, in response to further pressure on him, the Kaiser issued a notice: 'London east of the longitude of the Tower [of London] permitted for air attacks; within this area military installations, barracks, oil tanks may be attacked, particularly the docks.'[10] Initially some took this as the long-awaited approval for general attacks on London, but then the Army High Command started to have reservations about the insistence on very specific targets. Rather than risk Imperial displeasure, the Army instructed Linnarz to avoid London. But it was clear that an attack on the capital was not too far off. Linnarz could sense that too and his next bombing raid served as a useful reconnaissance mission.

10 May 1915, 2.45am: Southend-on-Sea, Essex

LZ 38 left its Evere shed in the late evening of Sunday, 9 May. She eluded all observation until appearing over the long pier at Southend-on-Sea and above the moored *Royal Edward* (see Map 3). Unknown to Linnarz, the former passenger liner now served as a floating internment camp for German nationals. From his lofty platform the ship seemed a worthy target and at 2.45am he dropped an incendiary bomb, which narrowly missed, landing close to the port side of the ship, where flames reached up ten to twelve feet before the waves doused them. Two more bombs landed in the sea, then LZ 38 was over the town. As at Bury St Edmunds, LZ 38 followed a meandering zig-zag course, but unlike his previous raid, Linnarz carried a bomb load made up primarily of incendiaries, with just four HE bombs recorded falling on Southend. And it was the first of these that shattered the peace and woke the citizens of the town from their slumbers.[11]

Earlier, it had been a beautiful sunny Sunday but with a strong easterly wind; even so many had enjoyed a bracing stroll along the seafront or out along the pier. Others had enjoyed the day with their families while some, like George and Agnes Whitwell, keen members of the Salvation Army, focused more on the spiritual aspects of Sunday. For Agnes it was to be her last.

When evening fell the sky became less clear: 'The night was dark, and in the early morning the sky was streaked with small clouds, with a haziness that made it difficult to detect anything moving in the sky above.' As LZ 38 appeared over the town in the grey chill of morning, the very first faint glimmer of dawn appeared, hinting at warmth to come during the day.

Eyewitnesses, shocked by the appearance of the enemy at such a time of day, produced a number of contradictory reports of what happened that night. It seems clear that LZ 38 generally followed an irregular course across Southend as she progressed from east to west dropping her bombs. She continued on her course over Westcliff and on to Leigh-on-Sea, where around 12 incendiary bombs landed close to the gas works and at least another 28 fell in the mud of the estuary. But it may well be that these bombs were not aimed at the gas works, instead they may have been dropped to allow LZ 38 to climb rapidly because she was now under AA fire from the guns at Thames Haven and those at Curtis & Harvey's explosive works at Cliffe across the Thames estuary. From Thames Haven a 6-pdr fired off 22 rounds, while a 'pom-pom' optimistically fired 49 rounds. The 3-inch gun at Cliffe shot ten rounds and a 6-pdr got off eight, but both batteries later complained that they had difficulty setting the fuses as they lacked suitable lanterns to provide light for this delicate task.

In response to this gunfire, LZ 38 turned away from its westerly course over Canvey Island and, heading north, released about six bombs as she approached Thundersley, some falling at Combe Wood. Turning back towards Leigh and Southend now, Linnarz dropped more bombs over the town before steering north-east and heading back out to sea near the mouth of the River Crouch.

Those bombs dropped by Linnarz as he progressed to the west and back again made a significant impact on Southend, Westcliff and Leigh. Having released his first bombs near Southend's famous pier, Linnarz dropped an HE bomb as he approached the landmark of St Erkenwald's Church on the corner of York Road and Southchurch Avenue. It exploded in the garden at the back of 192 York Road East, the home of Mr and Mrs S.J.C. Warr and their two little girls. At the time the house also served as a billet for Corporal Hannay of the Border Regiment, whose wife and child had come to visit him. Although the bomb missed the house, it tore up a section of concrete paving, digging a crater over six feet across while throwing the soil high into the air. Mr Warr found it impossible to describe the noise of the explosion but the sudden detonation shook him awake and he leapt from his bed shouting: 'Oh my God, the devils have come!' There was hardly a pane of glass left unbroken in the house, but Mr Warr managed to get his family safely outside. For Corporal Hannay, sleeping with his family in the back bedroom, the awakening was even more shocking. Their room took the full blast. Hannay raised himself in bed as the bomb exploded but plaster falling from the ceiling knocked him back down. The walls cracked dramatically and glass shards scythed across the room. Mrs Hannay described how the bed lifted up before crashing down again as her baby started to scream, adding: 'It seemed as though the house was falling around us.'

Miraculously, Mrs Hannay and the child were unhurt, while her husband escaped with just a few cuts to his head. A reporter from *The*

Times, who saw the family later that day, commented that their child looked as though 'she had never passed a more comfortable night in her short life'.[12]

The second explosive bomb landed nearby, descending on vacant land near the corner of Ambleside Drive and Southchurch Avenue with a noise as of a rushing train, according to an eyewitness. It dug a three-foot deep crater, threw up a great cloud of smoke and dirt, and smashed the windows of scores of neighbouring houses. It appears another HE landed in the playground of Westborough Road School but failed to detonate before LZ 38 appeared to hover over the junction of Victoria Avenue, High Street, London Road and Southchurch Road, known locally at the time as Cobweb Corner. Here LZ 38 released a fourth spherical HE bomb.[13] A group of special constables standing at the junction heard her engines then saw her coming towards them. One of them, William Ledicott, saw a bomb drop.

> It fell within five yards of the special constables in front of the tramway centre, but fortunately it did not burst. It fell with terrific force and buried itself under the wooden paving. Mr Anderson of the Special Police, who was on duty for the first time, was knocked over on to the pavement by the force of the concussion, but I did not feel anything.

Ledicott then watched helplessly as LZ 38 started to move away westwards.

LZ 38 dropped a great number of incendiary bombs as it flew over Southend. Many fell in gardens or on roads with little effect, but others made a destructive impact on the town. Two incendiaries that landed in a builder's yard on Southchurch Road, owned by J.C. Flaxman, caused the most material damage of the raid. Stacked high with timber and fanned by a breeze, the yard soon became a raging inferno. Mr Flaxman, whose house was at the front of the yard, only escaped the flames with his family by climbing out through the windows. The noise of those first explosive bombs had brought many people out into the streets. They now looked on mesmerized as the fire brigade, assisted by men of the Border Regiment, tackled the blaze. It took five hours to subdue the conflagration completely.

The first alarm received by the fire brigade was to 45 Ashburnham Road. The owner, Thomas May, his wife and their baby daughter, were asleep in a room on the first floor. Mr May described hearing a loud buzzing sound and a crash as the bomb smashed through the roof, then on through an unoccupied bedroom and down through the floor and into the room below. The family's black Pomeranian dog was sleeping there and it died in the flames. It was a shocking awakening for Mr May: 'I leapt out of bed to find the place filled with suffocating smoke and flames leaping up from the end room. I roused my wife and we picked up the child and got out into the street as quickly as we could. Having got my wife and child into safety I went back and helped put the fire out.' While Mr May helped the fire brigade deal with the fire more and more people emerged from their houses into the streets to discover what was happening.

At 65 London Road, on the corner of Ashburnham Road, an incendiary bomb fell on the home of a naval surgeon, Henry Woolcott Hull. The bomb passed between two bedrooms, one occupied by Dr Hull and the other by his maid – within a yard of the maid's bed – then down through the floorboards before burying itself in the kitchen floor. Dr Hull described how the flames rapidly spread as the rooms flooded with a petrol-like liquid. The fire gutted two bedrooms and a storeroom, while downstairs the flames burnt out the kitchen and sitting room.

Also in London Road, an incendiary struck a boarding house, the Cromwell Board Residence, run by Mrs Sammé. Awoken by the sound of bombs, she got up and woke her daughter. As they looked out of a window, an incendiary crashed through the roof and all the way down through the house to a room at the front, having passed within a few feet of where Mrs Sammé stood. Benzol from the bomb spread rapidly over the floor and, within moments, the house became a blazing inferno. All eight occupants dashed out to the safety of the street but flames scorched two of the guests, Mr and Mrs Mills of Walton-on-the-Naze, when the bomb passed close to their bed. The fire brigade was on the scene but a journalist felt there was little they could do:

> The fire had got a tremendous hold in the top of the building, and it was soon apparent that the premises were doomed. The conflagration raged for about three hours, and the front upper storey was reduced to a mass of wreckage, while the front sitting room was also considerably damaged. The whole of the furniture in these rooms was destroyed, and the place presented a desolate appearance.

Two bombs in West Road added to the night's terror. An incendiary smashed through the roof at 165 West Road, the home of a London accountant, Herbert Pensam, his wife, three daughters and a maid.

As the bomb struck, one of the daughters cried out and Mrs Pensam shouted to her husband: 'There's a bomb, wake the girls.' But as he opened the bedroom door his youngest daughter, 17-year-old Evelyn, burst in with her hair singed. Behind her the stairs were already burning fiercely and flames had taken hold on the landing. Trapped in their room by the flames, Mr and Mrs Pensam and Evelyn leapt from the front bedroom window. Mrs Pensam sustained minor injuries in the jump. The two other daughters, Gladys, aged 20, and Irene, 18, in another front bedroom also jumped. Mr Pensam then dashed around to the back of the house to rescue their maid, who had been sharing a room with Evelyn. Heroically, he caught her as she threw herself from her window. Men of the St John's Ambulance then arrived and tended their injuries.

The following morning a newspaper reporter visited the scene:

> The house was completely gutted and only the four outside walls and one skeleton wall in the centre were left standing. Every stick in the house was utterly destroyed and a cat perished in the flames … Mr Pensam, however, succeeded in rescuing some puppies but got badly burnt about the hands and face.

Directly on the other side of the road, at 146 West Road, lived Mr and Mrs Jay, with their 4-year-old son Arthur and maid, Alice Butcher. The boy and Alice slept in the same room and when a bomb crashed into it, it passed between the two beds just inches from the occupants before embedding itself in a wall. Alice awoke, bewildered, to the sound of crackling and then the room burst into flames. Mr Jay then takes up the story:

> The first thing I heard was the noise of something crashing through the roof. A slight explosion followed, and I went at once to a bedroom at the back of the house, where my little boy was asleep … The floor was one mass of flames. Even the hangings of the cot were on fire. I caught up the boy and shouted to the maid to follow. She scrambled out of bed and we all got out of the house as fast as we could. Three special constables and some neighbours then went in, put the fire out with buckets of water, and saved the house. I never imagined for a moment that it would be possible to do so.

Elsewhere, an incendiary struck an empty house at 105 Baxter Avenue. The most recent occupant, Mr Freeman, had moved out only a week earlier. While fighting the flames a fireman, W. Sawkins, fell through the roof but fortunately only suffered a twisted ankle. Mr Fuller, an eyewitness living in Boston Avenue, took in the bewildering spectacle.

> I was awakened ... by loud explosions, and looking out of the window I saw three houses burning within a radius of 500 yards, and what appeared to be bonfires on the ground in several places. There were two between the electric light station and the Girls High School, and one on the allotments, all in Boston Avenue. A house, fortunately empty, was ablaze in Baxter Avenue and at 44 Harcourt Avenue a bomb had gone through the roof.

Mr Fuller did not just sit back and watch though. He had an exciting night, volunteering to assist the fire brigade in dealing with a number of fires. After a sleepless but exhilarating night he still caught the train to work as normal in the morning. He got talking to another passenger, a man from Shoeburyness, only about three miles away. Much to his surprise he discovered the man was completely oblivious to the air raid.

Despite the great number of bombs dropped in the raid only one person died. Whereas in a number of other cases bombs had narrowly missed the occupants of houses, at 120 North Road the result was tragically different. An incendiary crashed into the house, home to George and Agnes Whitwell, devoted members of the Salvation Army. The bomb penetrated the roof and dropped into the front bedroom, where it landed directly on 60-year-old Agnes as she lay asleep in bed. Her husband, George, a carpenter, received a heavy blow to his head at the same time and serious burns to his neck and shoulders. In his shocked and bewildered state he tried to feel for his wife in the fiercely burning, smoke-filled room, but could not find her.

Their adult son, Crispin, awoke to the sound of rattling slates on the roof. He emerged from his room to find the house filling with smoke and his dazed father, now on the landing, calling out 'Oh mother!' Crispin also shouted for his mother as flames leapt up all around, but when no reply came he led his father out to a neighbour's house. There Mr Whitwell was treated by members of the St John's Ambulance Brigade before later being admitted to Victoria Hospital, but he was distraught: 'When rescued [Mr Whitwell] was in a pitiable condition, exhausted and burnt, and moaning, "My poor wife; my poor wife."'

Rescuers, under the impression that the house was clear, concentrated on saving what furniture they could. It was only later, when a special constable checked through the blackened front bedroom, that he found what was left of Agnes Whitwell. In her final agonising moments she must have summoned her last ounces of energy to try to escape the searing flames because her body was discovered lying in the corner about four feet from the bed, covered in debris. A doctor who later viewed her remains described them as 'nothing more than a charred mutilated mummy', adding that the flames had practically destroyed the trunk beyond recognition.

It is interesting to note that Southend had an air raid siren. Unlike in the Second World War there was in fact no universal siren. Instead the government left it to local authorities to decide what was best for their town. Southend had installed a steam whistle at the electricity station for this purpose. To warn of a raid it would give a sustained blast then, when danger had passed, three short blasts followed at 15-second intervals. Perhaps due to the novelty of the night, no one remembered to employ the whistle until after the raid was over.

Despite the horror of the night, the streets of Southend began to fill with the curious as the sun rose:

> It can safely be said that never before had people dressed so quickly. The same impulse stirred all, young and old, to be out seeing. The authorities' warning to remain quietly indoors was as if it had never been given. We Britishers are not going to sit mum at home whenever there is a sight to be seen out of mere considerations of safety; so Southend in its thousands crowded the streets.[14]

While local residents jostled with day-trippers from London for the best view of the bomb damage, there was one unexpected souvenir left by the crew of LZ 38. The owner of 11 Rayleigh Avenue noticed what appeared to be a piece of rubbish in his garden. On closer inspection, however, he discovered a piece of cardboard with writing in blue pencil: 'You English. We have come, and we'll come again soon. Kill or cure.' It was signed, bluntly, 'German'. And Linnarz did return.

8–12 May 1915: Liverpool, London and Southend

Before he did so a new trend appeared – anti-German riots. On 7 May 1915, two days before Linnarz attacked Southend, a German U-boat had torpedoed and sunk the Cunard liner *Lusitania*, with the loss of almost 1,200 passengers and crew. Over the weekend of 8–9 May serious anti-German riots broke out in the liner's home port, Liverpool, in Birkenhead and to a lesser extent in Salford. Many bakers and pork butchers of German origin who had traded happily for years in

Britain now became easy targets for hatred. On 11 May, the day after the Southend Zeppelin raid, the rioting spread to London, where it erupted into a frenzy of brutality, theft and destruction. One newspaper summed it up: '[London] has managed to compress into the space of 24 hours as much destruction and violence as were spread over four or five days in Lancashire.' And it was not necessary to be German to suffer at the hands of the mob. Many Russians suffered too, and in Leytonstone the unfortunate landlord of the Thatch House public house had all his windows smashed and had to seek police protection. It seems that his name sounded German to some among the mob, but he was a Scotsman named Strachan![15] Then on 12 May the residents of Southend lashed out against the Germans in their midst in retaliation for the Zeppelin raid on their town and the sinking of the *Lusitania*. The mob attacked a number of shops and it proved necessary to put troops on the streets to restore order.[16]

12 May 1915: Nordholz, Germany

That same day, 12 May, at the headquarters of the Naval Airship Division, Strasser made a move. Perhaps frustrated by the wait for the delivery of his first 'p-class' Zeppelin, and hearing about the two successful bombing raids completed by the Army's LZ 38, Strasser ordered the old L 5 to prepare for a flight to England. Strasser informed her commander, Alois Böcker, that he would join them on the mission. They were lucky to get home in one piece.

L 5 encountered storms of rain and snow as it crossed the North Sea, which resulted in a heavy coating of ice forming, adding a considerable weight to a ship already operating at the extreme of its range. When they approached the Norfolk coast at about 8.00pm, the sky had not yet fully darkened so L 5 turned for the Humber. About 20 minutes later problems with the oil supply made it necessary to shut down the forward engine, followed an hour later by the temporary loss of the rear port engine.

With only one engine now functioning and carrying the heavy ice coating, L 5 began to drop alarmingly. Böcker reacted by using his bombs as ballast, dropping the entire load (six 50kg HE and 30 incendiary) into the sea. He then aborted the mission and turned for home. His mechanics managed to coax some life back into the port engine, but it was unable to attain full power. Battling against a strong headwind the mechanics also managed to get the forward engine running again at half speed in the early hours of the morning. Due to the negative effects of the wind and the lack of engine power, Böcker and Strasser recognized that L 5 could not make it back to Germany so steered for Belgium, crossing neutral Holland above the clouds to avoid detection. They finally landed at Namur exactly 24 hours after they set out on their mission, but another week would pass before they were able to return to Nordholz.[17]

This mission was the third time Strasser had accompanied a Zeppelin on a raid against England. All three had failed to reach their target, defeated by adverse weather or mechanical failure. Naval men were a superstitious breed and there were those amongst them who began to consider Strasser, the commander of the Naval Airship Division, a 'Jonah'. But it was not all doom and gloom. The day Strasser landed safely at Namur, his first 'p-class' Zeppelin, L 10, made her maiden flight at Friedrichshafen. Kptlt Klaus Hirsch took command of her four days later, on 17 May, and flew her to Nordholz to begin a period of familiarisation for her crew.

That same day Erich Linnarz and Army Zeppelin LZ 38 struck against England for a third time.

Chapter 9

A Glimmer of Hope

17 May 1915, 1.50am: Ramsgate, Kent

On 16 May, a week after his raid on Southend, Linnarz and LZ 38 set out for England again, while two other Army Zeppelins headed for Calais. At about midnight, observers at the North Foreland, the most north-easterly point on the Kent coastline, became aware of the sound of engines in the sky. Then, at 12.15am, an anti-aircraft observer positioned on Ramsgate's East Pier reported bombs being dropped in the sea towards Deal,[1] from where a newspaper reported: 'The force of the explosions was so great that houses were shaken, and windows rattled in an alarming manner.'[2] After releasing those bombs, LZ 38 proceeded towards Ramsgate. As she approached the town a number of armed drifters opened fire, causing Linnarz to turn away and follow a circular route to attack the town from the landward side. Observers on the Tongue Lightship north of Margate, saw LZ 38 at about 1.00am and then about 35 minutes later she crossed the coast over Margate, at a height estimated at only 1,500 to 2,000 feet (see Map 3). From there she flew across the corner of Kent to Ramsgate, arriving just before 1.50am. At that time of night the majority of the residents and visitors to this popular seaside town were fast asleep in their beds.[3]

At the Bull and George Hotel at 77 High Street there were 12 guests and staff. One of the staff, Miss Pilkington, awoke to an unusual noise and went to the window. As she opened it the throbbing sound of LZ 38's engines filled her room. She ran to her friend's room and pulled barmaid Kate Moffatt from her bed, and not a moment too soon. Seconds later two bombs smashed through the roof of the hotel, with one crashing through the ceiling above Kate's bed. Miss Moffatt received scratches, bruises and singed eyebrows but had a lucky escape. She was taken to the General Hospital in West Cliff Road for treatment. Others did not fare so well.

The bombs crashed through the roof and passed through the building, apparently bursting on reaching the ground floor and then leaving a gaping hole to the cellar. The contents of the upper floors tumbled down to this lower level, piling up in a plaster and debris covered mass of destruction.

John Herbert Smith, a restaurateur and publican from Sutton in Surrey, had arrived at the hotel with his wife Fanny two days earlier. They had been married for 18 years and had a 14-year-old daughter called Vera. Another guest at the hotel, Florence Lamont, married to Albert Charles Lamont, a clerk at the War Office, had come down to the coast for the weekend from Thornton Heath. They had been married for 19 years.[4]

According to newspaper reports, Mr and Mrs Smith, occupied a room on the first floor but were discovered groaning among the debris in the cellar by the police and firemen. Such was their condition that a newspaper described Mr Smith as 'an old gentleman', even though he was only 42. He sustained flesh wounds to both legs and was suffering from shock but did not seem too seriously injured. He was admitted to the General Hospital while his wife, whose injuries were considered more serious, went to the VAD Hospital situated at the former British and Foreign Sailor's Rest on Harbour Parade. Later that day, expressing great concern for his wife, the matron allowed him to visit her. He went in a cab and had to be lifted from it. But the following afternoon, Mr Smith 'was suddenly taken ill ... and died within an hour'.[5] There is no further mention of his wife, Fanny Smith, so we must presume she recovered, but Florence Lamont was not so fortunate. On 20 May, suffering from broken ribs, flesh wounds and shock, Florence died. The jury at her inquest returned the verdict of 'death from injuries received through an illegitimate and dastardly act of war'.[6]

The damage to the hotel proved so extensive that the building was later demolished, although not all mourned its passing. The removal of the hotel opened up the area, which a local publication approved of: 'In this way, the widening of a very narrow main street, good came out of evil and the marauding Germans, bent on destruction, brought about a much-needed improvement which had for long been beyond the power of the local authority to accomplish.'

The narrow nature of the street meant numerous neighbouring shops and businesses suffered broken windows and doors from the blast, particularly the David Greig's grocers shop opposite. The manager, Mr Banell, lived on the premises with his wife and three very young children. The blast smashed the shop's plate glass windows and later a shrapnel bullet was discovered in the children's bed. Undaunted by the destruction, however, traders just got on with it: 'Typical of the attitude of the inhabitants was the action of one enterprising trader whose premises had been damaged but who announced, "The glass is gone, but the goods are here."'

In all, Linnarz dropped a string of four HE and 16 incendiary bombs across Ramsgate. Most did little damage. The first probably landed on open land at Nethercourt, followed by bombs on Bell Cottages, then Chapel Road and others near St Lawrence's Church, on the playground at Ellington school and then the bomb on the Bull and George. From there LZ 38 continued towards the sea, roughly following the line of the High Street to the harbour. Bombs fell on Ellington Park and in the grounds of St Catherine's Hospital at 142–146 High Street, with others landing near St George's Church. An incendiary caused a fire in Chapel Place, which residents extinguished with buckets of water, while another glanced off the roof of the Star Cinema at 2 George Street and on to a chicken house in an adjoining garden: 'There was a burst of flame, but no serious damage was done.' In Queen Street, Mr Brackenbury, owner of a draper's shop, was awoken by the sound of the first HE bomb and looked out from a side window to see what was happening. As he did so another bomb exploded and blew out the bedroom windows but no one was hurt. He went to another window overlooking the street and saw an incendiary burning in the roadway within four yards of a butcher's shop owned by Mr Britton: 'It seemed to leap into a large flame, which spread up the road immediately it hit the ground.'[7] But the incendiary was not responsible for smashing his windows. That was caused by an HE bomb that exploded a few streets away in Albion Hill.

Mr F. France was asleep in a room on the first floor above his shop in Albion Hill, the Imperial Bazaar, as LZ 38 loomed out of the darkness. An HE bomb dropped at the back of the building, exploding in the cellar and excavating a hole 'eight feet deep by 20 feet square'. Mr France, who had been just five yards from where the bomb exploded, had a lucky escape. Against his bedroom window he had stored some of his shop's stock, a large number of children's buckets and spades. When the bomb exploded, the buckets and spades flew into the room, burying him where he lay in bed, but in doing so absorbing much of the blast's fury and deflecting the razor sharp shards of window glass, allowing Mr France to emerge shaken but relatively unscathed. Linnarz then ended his attack on Ramsgate by dropping two or three bombs in the harbour, causing minor damage to some fishing smacks moored there. As LZ 38 departed, soldiers from a unit billeted in the town continued firing until she melted into the dark night sky and the protective clouds that had begun to form.

When LZ 38 first crossed the coast into Kent at about 1.35am, the RNAS station at Westgate received immediate warning. Five minutes later, Flt sub-Lt Redford Henry Mulock, a 28-year-old Canadian pilot from Winnipeg, took to the air in an Avro 504B in pursuit of the raider. 'Red' Mulock had been an electrical engineer before enlisting in the Canadian Army in September 1914, then transferring to the RNAS in January 1915. Now, four months later, he was flying alone in the dark over England in pursuit of a Zeppelin. To tackle the 536 feet long aerial monster, bristling with lethal machine guns, he carried just two incendiary bombs, two hand grenades and a revolver.[8]

Mulock first caught sight of LZ 38 about five miles ahead, when he had reached 500 feet, noting that the Zeppelin was about 1,500 feet higher than him and heading south-east. Having passed over Ramsgate and out to sea, LZ 38 began to climb steadily as she headed south, following the Kent coast until she came inland again at Deal at about 2.10am. She then continued across country towards Dover. As she did so the coastguard station at St Margaret's heard her engines and alerted the Dover Anti-Aircraft Corps, which switched on the searchlight at the Langdon Battery. Flicking across the sky, the light quickly found LZ 38 – the first instance of a searchlight in Britain locating a Zeppelin – but the gun at Langdon was out of action.[9] The guns at Drop Redoubt, however, reacted to the searchlight activity and fired five rounds from a 6-pdr and 28 rounds of 1-pdr ammunition. They all fell short, but for Linnarz and his crew the searchlight activity and AA fire was a new and unpleasant experience. Unwilling to risk his ship, Linnarz turned away from Dover, releasing a great quantity of water ballast and bombs that allowed him to climb rapidly out of danger. The bombs fell in woods and on farmland at Oxney, just over three miles north-east of Dover.

Shaken awake by the sound of bombs dropping, Mr Bennett, of the Station Hotel at Martin Mill, looked outside and saw the searchlights but not LZ 38. He went out to the east side of the hotel: 'Looking towards

Oxney Court Farm, I saw thirteen bombs alight in the meadow close to the Round House, the flames rising to a height above the trees and they burnt for about three-quarters of an hour. Meanwhile, we went up to the meadow, and then we found that some ten other bombs had been dropped in the wood and the meadow beyond.' Bennett found an unexploded bomb, which he handed over to Special Constable Smith, but others were keen on keeping a memento of the night: '... a number of the exploded bombs were lying about, which were quickly snatched up by souvenir hunters, a large number of people having now arrived on the scene.' From the recovered bombs and from the burnt holes others had left in the ground, the authorities estimated LZ 38 dropped 33 incendiaries, none causing any damage.[10]

When LZ 38 climbed rapidly and turned away, 'Red' Mulock was still in pursuit, trying to get above her to release his bombs. Reports that LZ 38 was close to the North Goodwin Lightship at around 3.00am resulted in two aircraft from Dover and two more from Westgate joining the hunt, but they saw nothing. Mulock, however, continued to trail LZ 38 as she set a course back to Evere, climbing to 7,000 feet, but he gradually fell further behind and eventually gave up the chase as he neared the Belgian coast.

17 May 1915, 2.45am: Dunkirk, France

While LZ 38 attacked Ramsgate, the Admiralty followed the now standard procedure of informing No. 1 Squadron, RNAS, based at St Pol, Dunkirk, to be on the alert for the returning Zeppelin. They also received information that Calais had been bombed. At 2.45am Flt sub-Lt B.D. Kilner took off from Dunkirk in a Voisin with orders to patrol along the coast to Zeebrugge and engage any returning Zeppelins he encountered. Thirty-five minutes later a Nieuport crewed by Flt sub-Lt Reginald Warneford and Leading Mechanic G.E. Meddis received similar orders. As Warneford left the ground, observers reported a Zeppelin about ten to 15 miles off the coast at De Panne, which lay about 12 miles east of Dunkirk. Five more aircraft ascended from Dunkirk and two from Furnes. The Zeppelin – LZ 39 commanded by Hptmn Hans Masius – was returning from an aborted raid on Calais.[11]

At 3.35am Kilner was on his way back along the coast flying at 5,000 feet, having turned over Zeebrugge, when he saw the Zeppelin over the sea between Ostend and Middelkerke. However, with a misfiring engine he was unable to close with her. Kilner later reported that LZ 39 sighted him, turned inland towards Ostend and began to climb. Warneford and Meddis spotted LZ 39 about five minutes after they got airborne and set off in pursuit. They had attained about 5,000 feet when they reached Ostend, 1,000 feet below the climbing Zeppelin. Meddis grabbed a rifle and fired five 'flaming bullets' (incendiary ammunition), reporting that two of them ignited and hit the target but had no effect. LZ 39 continued to climb and was soon out of reach for Warneford's heavily laden aircraft, weighed down with Meddis, a Lewis gun and ammunition, a number of hand grenades and the .45 rifle. Warneford continued towards Zeebrugge hoping to gain height but was unsuccessful. He was a wild individual when in the cockpit, so in frustration he looked around for another target. He found it in the form of a U-boat and steamer just leaving Zeebrugge harbour. Warneford zoomed down to 2,000 feet and began hurling hand grenades at the departing ships. He failed to inflict any damage this time but three weeks later his time would come.

Sqn Cdr Spenser Grey made the next attack.[12] Grey had reached about 9,600 feet in his Nieuport when he came up close to LZ 39, but as she was still climbing he abandoned the idea of dropping hand grenades on her and attacked with his Lewis gun from a position just 50 to 100 feet below. He aimed at the rear gondola and it seems possible that he injured some of the crew, however, four machine guns opened a heavy return fire and, as LZ 39 continued to climb, he turned back to Dunkirk. Four other pilots, including Flt Cdr John Babington[13], failed to gain the necessary height to make their attacks, but one, Flt Cdr Arthur Wellesley Bigsworth, had more luck.

Bigsworth took off from Dunkirk in Avro 504B No. 1009 at 3.30am and quickly located LZ 39 out to sea. He headed along the coast, climbing all the time and when he reached Nieuport he was at 8,000 feet. As LZ 39 was still out at sea he circled, climbing to 10,000 feet over the town before continuing to Ostend, near to where he intercepted her shortly after Grey's attack. At 4.05am, from a position 200 feet above, Bigsworth flew along the length of the beleaguered LZ 39 from stern to bow and dropped his four 20lb Hales bombs. At the same time, despite his closeness to the Zeppelin, an intense AA fire opened up from Ostend. As he completed his run over LZ 39 he turned to starboard and flew back alongside her in the opposite direction. He reported 'very heavy black pungent smoke coming out of the Airship about 100 feet from her tail'. Having released all his bombs, Bigsworth flew out to sea to avoid the heavy shelling and returned to Dunkirk.

Masius and the crew of LZ 39 were lucky to be in the air. All four of Bigsworth's bombs hit the target, although it seems unlikely all exploded, because if they had, the hydrogen would have ignited and turned LZ 39 into a blazing inferno. It appears that three of the bombs passed right through the outer envelope, tearing open five of LZ 39's 15 gas cells, while another bomb blew off the starboard aft propeller. It is hard to explain the 'heavy black pungent smoke' observed by Bigsworth, but perhaps an oil tank caught fire only to be extinguished by the crew. The damaged gas cells were at the front and rear and this balance may have helped keep her in the air, while Bigsworth noted that she was now steering with difficulty, 'yawing considerably above 5 points on either side'. About an hour later observers saw her approaching Ghent with her tail down and she made a bad landing at Evere where, according to British intelligence, waiting ambulances took off the body of a dead officer and some wounded crew. It would be a few days before LZ 39 could return to her shed at Bercham St Agathe.

The British defences could finally take something positive from their night's work, offering a glimmer of hope for the future. A searchlight had held a Zeppelin in its beam, a home defence pilot had seen a raider and pursued it, while Churchill's plan of September 1914 to engage Zeppelins returning to their sheds in Belgium had met with some success. Yet the fact that bombs dropped on LZ 39 had not ignited the hydrogen was puzzling. On 29 May, after some consideration, Murray Sueter, the Director of the Admiralty Air Department, issued a report on the action over Ostend. He concluded that a layer of inert gas protected the gas cells:

> It was very disappointing to then not to be able to fire the airship with the incendiary ammunition and bombs provided. Probably the exhaust gases from the motors are turned into the ring space. If this is so, the matter of igniting the hydrogen of a Zeppelin is one of great difficulty.[14]

Sueter was wrong, but the theory affected anti-Zeppelin tactics right into 1916. Then, even while Sueter was deliberating, the untiring Erich Linnarz raided England for a fourth time. Living up to the promise made on the piece of cardboard dropped during his raid of 10 May, LZ 38 returned to the Essex coastal town of Southend-on-Sea on the night of 26 May.

The night he raided Ramsgate, Linnarz had mentioned in his report a tantalising glimpse of London in the far distance. Now, during this raid he appeared to be checking his preferred route to the capital, as it was clear to all that it was only a matter of time before the Kaiser finally gave his approval to open the campaign against London.

26 May 1915, 11.13pm: Southend-on-Sea, Essex

With the moon in its first quarter and a clear sky, Linnarz's approach was first observed at Clacton, from where special constables reported her heading west at 10.30pm (see Map 3). Crossing the mouth of the Blackwater she passed over Bradwell-on-Sea 20 minutes later, then Dengie, where the noise of her engines 'caused the streets to become alive with people', and on to Southminster, from where a 1-pdr 'pom-pom' fired the first of 57 rounds into the sky. She was climbing as she passed Burnham-on-Crouch just before 11.00pm, then five minutes later as she passed Shoeburyness, a 3-inch gun opened fire. Undeterred, Linnarz steered LZ 38 over Southend and at 11.13pm shattered the peace of the town:[15]

> It was a clear moonlight night, and the Zeppelin flew at a great height, so high up that it appeared to be no larger than a cigar ... Crowds of people watched its flight in the moonlight, which sometimes was so bright that the body of the airship could be seen glistening, although no lights were shown on the craft itself.
>
> The arrival of the great ship over Southend was made known by a loud and continuous noise, and then the dropping and bursting and flaring of the many bombs.

The Reverend Thomas J. Watson, of the United Methodist Church, saw the Zeppelin high up against some clouds that appeared white in the moonlight. He thought it looked like a 'straight black caterpillar'. Convinced it was travelling towards his house in Victoria Road, he ran home and told his wife and daughter to get under the kitchen table while he stood in the doorway to watch.

One of the first bombs appears to have landed in Hamstel Road as LZ 38 followed a westward path across the town. Two fires then broke out in Sutton Road, one in a house and the other at All Saints schoolroom. Leonard Stokes was walking down Ilfracombe Avenue when he heard a loud bang. On looking up he saw the dim outline of the Zeppelin. He ran towards the High Street and, just as he reached the corner of Sutton Road, bombs fell in a field and on a house owned by a Mr Ansell. In Sutton Road a soldier on leave, Signalman Letton of the 11th Battalion, Essex Regiment, also heard the explosion and with great presence of mind quickly wrapped his jacket around one arm and an overcoat around the other, before joining Mr Stokes as the two men smashed their way into Mr Ansell's burning house. The smell from the bomb was overpowering, forcing them to cover their mouths as they fought their way in. With his arms protected Letton managed to tip the burning incendiary into a bucket and together they removed it outside, but both men suffered burns to their hands while extinguishing the flames. Undeterred by their experience, however, the two men then ran to the All Saints schoolroom, where they put out the flames – there too aided by some special constables and a bath full of water.

Another incendiary bomb fell on 3 Broadway Market, the home of a boot repairer, John Pateman. It crashed through the roof, igniting in the bedroom of his 7-year-old daughter Marion, known to everyone as 'Queenie'. Fiercely burning liquid quickly soaked into her bedding as the terrified child screamed. The little girl's mother and her 16-year-old sister, Minnie, were standing at the front door watching the raid when the bomb struck. Horrified, they bounded upstairs: 'Mrs Pateman ... found the child's clothing well alight. She endeavoured to put the flames out, but without avail. Minnie then gallantly clutched the flaming bundle and literally squeezed the flames out.' One newspaper optimistically told its readers that they expected Queenie to make a good recovery, but they were wrong. Two days later she died in hospital from terrible burns to her head, back and legs.

The fire brigade dealt with three more serious fires. One destroyed a bedroom in a house occupied by Charles Waller at 2 Dowsett Avenue, while three bombs fell in St Helen's Road. At No. 25 an incendiary smashed through the roof, setting fire to a bedroom in which two children were asleep, but they had a narrow escape. Two other children in the same road were also fortunate to escape injury when another incendiary hit the house where they were sleeping. The third fire had broken out in a bedroom at 45 Anerley Road. In all cases the fire brigade prevented the fire spreading beyond the room where it started. There were other fires across the town but residents and neighbours worked together to extinguish them. Many had heeded the warning of the first raid and kept buckets of water at the ready.

Linnarz dropped fewer bombs on this second Southend raid. Official figures record 47 incendiaries and 23 small HE bombs, described as grenades. A newspaper, in accounting for 60 of these bombs, listed 31 falling on Southend and Westcliff with another 29 at neighbouring Leigh-on-Sea.[16] Of those that dropped on Leigh, most fell in gardens or on roadways without causing any damage and only two struck houses. One caused a fire in Lord Roberts' Avenue and the other in Oakleigh Park Drive, where a boy received burns as he ran downstairs to escape the flames and his father suffered cuts to his hands when he smashed a window to drop another child into a waiting policeman's arms.

The whole time LZ 38 was over Southend, the AA gun at Shoeburyness continued to fire at her, getting off 37 rounds, but with tragic results.

May Fairs, the 35-year-old daughter of a London dental surgeon, was in Westcliff staying at the family's villa 'Fairdene' in Southbourne Grove for Whitsun week with her mother and sister-in-law. Her father, William Fairs, was coming home from work on a late train. The rest of the family had gone to the station to meet him, but their tram ride back to the house coincided with LZ 38's flight over Southend. When they reached their stop, LZ 38 appeared to be directly overhead and, as they hurried to reach shelter, a fragment from a shell fired by the Shoeburyness gun struck May on the head. Her family carried her into a nearby house from where she was taken to hospital, but it was too late, May was dead.

Just a few roads away a similar tragedy occurred. Florence Smith, who had only been married to her husband Frank for two years, was watching the raid from the door of their house, 'Farndon' in Westminster Drive. A piece of AA shell landed no more than ten yards from her, sending fragments slicing through the air and slashing her head and breast open. An ambulance took her to hospital and, fearing the worst, her husband sent a telegram to her family in Newark: 'Self and baby safe. Flo seriously injured. Come at once.'[17] Florence lay in hospital for almost three weeks but never recovered from her injuries. She died on 15 June.

After releasing the bombs on Leigh, LZ 38 made off to the northeast, passing Wakering at 11.25pm. At Burnham, 'A' company, 2/8th Battalion, Essex Regiment, made a final defiant gesture, firing off 200 rifle rounds to send Linnarz and his men on their way. She went out to sea over the mouth of the River Blackwater at 11.45pm, untroubled by any British aircraft. Word had reached the RNAS late and it was not until 11.20pm that the first of five aircraft took off from the air stations at Eastchurch and Grain. By the time they had clawed their way up to LZ 38's altitude she was long gone.

As with previous raids, the newspapers remarked on the lack of panic shown by the public in the face of aerial attack. Of the residents of Ramsgate earlier in the month, the Press Association's local correspondent wrote: '... practically during the whole of the night people paraded the streets and inspected the damage caused by the bombs.' He then added: 'Indeed, the residents appeared to treat the raid as a huge joke.'[18] The situation was similar in Southend. There a journalist wrote: '... the great anxiety of one and all seemed to be to catch a glimpse of one of the German terrors rather than seek a place of safety.'[19] It is obvious, however, that not everyone felt quite so calm in the face of aerial bombardment. However, while the raids continued to cause few deaths and little significant destruction, for those who were not directly targeted by the German bombs the whole experience could be thrilling and fascinating.[20] Right from the first Zeppelin raid in January 1915, enterprising local photographers, keen to cash in on this fascination, had toured the damaged streets and houses with their cameras, reproducing their photographs as postcards for sale to the public. These proved extremely popular, as were the white porcelain models of the bombs dropped on Maldon and Bury St Edmunds manufactured by the crested china souvenir industry, which also produced model Zeppelins for the eager market in mementos. It was, perhaps, not quite the reaction the German authorities had anticipated or hoped for.

May 1915: London

Meanwhile, all was not well in Whitehall's corridors of power. On 5 May the government had issued D. Notice 206 through the Press Bureau. A D. Notice – or Defence Notice – was an official request to editors not to publish articles on specified subjects, in this case to prevent the publication of news 'likely to cause needless alarm or distress among the civil population'. D.206 informed editors that unofficial reports were not to be published prior to the printing of the official account of a raid, and that no mention was to be made of the route of enemy aircraft or the amount of damage inflicted. While a D. Notice was not legally enforceable, the government expected editors to follow its advice. All reporting up to that time had given accounts of the raids in significant detail, and it was through information in the British press, later confirmed in a Dutch newspaper, that von Buttlar had discovered that he dropped his bombs on Maldon in Essex during an earlier raid. The newspaper coverage of the first raid after issuing D.206 (Southend, 10 May), however, was still revealing. A senior intelligence officer at the

War Office, General George Cockerill, closely monitored the coverage the following day and expressed particular concern over one revelation, some newspapers stating: '… bombs were dropped on Canvey Island, where there is a large explosives depot'. In his report on 12 May he wrote:

> It seems that the morning newspapers on the whole were very careful to comply with the notice. *The Times*, so far as I know, was the only leading morning paper in which the Canvey Island rumour was repeated. The evening papers, however, published sufficient data between them to enable the enemy to plot the route followed … with considerable accuracy, and generally to prepare for himself a very satisfactory reconnaissance report.[21]

It can only be wondered, therefore, how General Cockerill reacted the day after he submitted his report when a local newspaper, the *Southend Standard*, printed a special 18-page air raid supplement crammed with detail and photographs.

The Press Bureau continued to issue general reporting guidelines, but then on June 1 everything changed with the issue of D.217 shortly after midnight. It informed editors that they could now only publish official press communiqués. The timing of this press blackout in the early hours of the morning was not a routine matter, it came as a direct result of what had just happened. At around 11.00pm on 31 May, for the first time, Zeppelin bombs had fallen on London.

Chapter 10

London's Burning

After a month of meticulous preparation, Erich Linnarz was ready to strike against London. Following his latest raid against Southend he had his route planned, and now, finally, the Kaiser gave his approval. In fact he had signed an order granting permission to attack the capital on 5 May but only issued it towards the end of the month.

31 May 1915: Evere, Belgium

The order stated: 'London east of the longitude of the Tower [of London] permitted for air attacks; within this area military installations, barracks, oil tanks may be attacked, particularly the docks.'[1] As far as Linnarz was concerned, however, that meant he had approval to drop bombs anywhere east of a line drawn through one of the city's world famous historical landmarks. On the morning of 31 May Linnarz received orders from Berlin to make ready to raid that night. The ground crew at Evere, as Linnarz described, followed their well-rehearsed pre-flight checks:

> Engines were tested, ballast tanks examined, the radio apparatus thoroughly overhauled …
>
> Then the bomb-racks were loaded … A ton and a half of death …
>
> My crew, clad in their leather jackets and fur helmets, were standing in groups on the landing ground. A siren sounded shrilly and they moved to the shed, entered the gondola and took up their posts.
>
> Gently guided by ropes the ship slid smoothly forward. The sounding of a second siren indicated that the ship was clear of the shed.

'Hands off, ease the guides,' I shouted. The men at the ropes let go.

Great eddies of dust swept through the air as the final test to the mammoth propellers was given. An officer approached and told me all was ready, I stepped in, gave a signal, and mysteriously the ship soared upwards. We were on our way to London.[2]

As LZ 38 headed towards England, Linnarz reflected on the task ahead:

On, on we sped. It was a beautiful night – a night of star-spangled skies and gentle breezes, a night hard to reconcile with a purpose as grim as ours.

Linnarz cut across the north-east corner of Kent, passing over Margate at 9.42pm from where a maxim gun of the short-lived RNAS southern section mobile AA force opened fire, followed eight minutes later by another of the mobile section's maxim guns at Reculver, near Herne Bay. LZ 38 flew on, crossing the mouth of the Thames estuary to the Essex coast. At 10.12pm the 3-inch gun at Shoeburyness opened fire, getting off 12 rounds at LZ 38, estimating her height at 7,500 feet.[3] From the control gondola Linnarz reported: 'We crossed the black ridge of the coast. Immediately from below anti-aircraft guns spat viciously. We could hear the shells screaming past us. We increased our altitude and speed.'

Linnarz skirted to the north of Southend, passing between Rochford and Rayleigh at 10.25pm and, continuing on a westerly course, his engines were heard from Woodford and Brentwood. London was visible in the distance (see Map 3).

31 May 1915, Evening: London

In London, 31 May had been like any other ordinary Monday. In Stoke Newington, Albert Lovell, a 39-year-old clerk, had spent a pleasant evening at home in Alkham Road with his wife, Eleanor, and two friends, a woman and her daughter, who had come to stay. The guests retired to bed at 10.30pm, sleeping in an attic room at the top of the house. Shortly afterwards Albert Lovell popped out to post a letter. The moon was rising, the weather fine, and just a light wind rustled the leaves.

Less than a mile to the south, Samuel Leggett, a 38-year-old deliveryman for a mineral water company, was at home in Cowper

Road. He and his wife occupied rooms on the first floor of No. 33. At 10.45pm, Samuel was sitting in the armchair reading a newspaper and chatting to his wife, Elizabeth, who was in bed in the same room. Their five children were asleep in the adjoining room.

Another half a mile on, Henry Good, a 49-year-old former pepper grinder, now working as a labourer, was at home with his wife Caroline. They rented three of the four rooms on the first floor of a three-storied house at 187 Balls Pond Road. At the front of the house, Sarah Coningsby, a 53-year-old widowed charwoman, occupied the fourth room. The owner, Thomas Sharpling, a builder, lived on the ground floor with his family. Mr and Mrs Good's recently married son, also called Henry, had visited his parents earlier in the evening, but now they were preparing for bed. For all three families the war was about to become very real.

31 May 1915, 11.00pm: Stoke Newington, London

Police stations all across north and east London had their routines broken at 10.55pm when the shrill ring of the telephone brought the long-feared news: 'Aircraft raid impending.' But no air raid warning followed for the public – it would be another two years before London had one.

Five minutes later, Sub Inspector Locking of the Special Constabulary could not believe his eyes when the unmistakeable cigar shape of a Zeppelin appeared high in the sky over Stoke Newington station. Linnarz and Zeppelin LZ 38 had arrived over the capital:

> The quivering altimeter showed our height was 10,000 feet. The air was keen, and we buttoned our jackets as we prepared to deal the first blow against the heart of your great and powerful nation …
>
> I mounted the bombing platform. My finger hovered on the button that electrically operated the bombing apparatus.
>
> Then I pressed it. We waited. Minutes seemed to pass before, above the humming song of the engines, there rose a shattering roar …
>
> I pressed again. A cascade of orange sparks shot upwards, and a billow of incandescent smoke drifted slowly away to reveal a red gash of raging fire on the face of the wounded city.[4]

The first bomb to fall on London was an incendiary. It struck a chimney before smashing through the roof of Albert Lovell's house at 16 Alkham Road in Stoke Newington, on the borough border with Hackney. Lovell had just returned from posting his letter when screams echoed down from his guests at the top of the house. The bomb had ignited in their bedroom. He bounded up the stairs, but their door was locked and the key fallen to the floor in the confusion, smoke and fumes that now filled the room. After some frantic fumbling his guests recovered the key and Lovell led his guests, coughing and spluttering, from the building. Then Mr and Mrs Lovell roused their children and led them to safety at a neighbour's house.

With his family safe, Lovell turned his attention to saving his home. With no telephone, he grabbed his son's bicycle from the hallway and cycled hard, yelling 'fire' all the way to the fire station in Brooke Road. The fire brigade responded quickly, limiting the damage to the top floor of the house, although that damage was severe.[5]

With his first incendiary bomb burning, Linnarz dropped another on Northwold Road, then directed LZ 38 across Stoke Newington High Street, before releasing his first HE bomb.[6] It landed in the back garden of 15 Lavers Road, but failed to detonate. Seconds later an HE bomb exploded at the rear of houses in Dynevor Road, where the gardens backed on to those of Lavers Road. The blast tore off the backs of Nos. 43 and 45 and damaged No. 41, the home of recently retired police inspector Herbert Wells. Falling debris at No. 45 fractured the right arm of 24-year-old Amy Grant, inducing shock. Her brother Percy rescued her and carried her to a doctor. In Nevill Road an incendiary bomb landed on a former coach house at the back of the Nevill Arms public house, but proved to be another dud, causing only minor damage. Two doors away, however, an incendiary struck No. 27, occupied by nightwatchman George West and his family. The bomb had smashed through the roof before passing down through the first floor and setting the house ablaze. From the fire gutted rooms, West's 26-year-old son, Alfred, emerged with burns to his face as did 62-year-old Anne Booty who also lived in the house. The police managed to deal with the blaze before the fire brigade arrived.

At 55 Allen Road, on the corner of Shakespeare Road, an HE bomb buried itself eight feet down in the garden, while a few yards away another HE bomb, possibly one of the small type described by the British authorities as a grenade and weighing about 2kg, struck a house at 102 Shakespeare Road. The bomb glanced off the coping then fell into the front area, carrying away the steps and causing severe damage inside. The bomb also damaged the steps and basement of No. 104, where flying debris caused minor facial injuries to both the occupier, Charles Pollington, and his 6-year-old daughter Violet.

Although about ten bombs had fallen so far, injuries had been light. That was about to change as LZ 38 passed along Cowper Road. On the first floor of No. 33, Samuel Leggett was still reading his newspaper. He had been chatting to his wife but she had now dropped off to sleep, while their five children were all asleep in the back bedroom. Moments after 11.00pm, Samuel heard something hit the slate roof, he woke his wife, who told an inquest what happened next: 'He at once rushed to the children's room. As he rushed in another bomb crashed through the ceiling and fell on to the bed as he opened the door.' The bomb had passed through the room above on the second floor occupied by Rose Clark and her little niece, known to everyone as 'Curly'. Smoke and flames quickly filled the room as Mr Leggett bravely battled to save his children, while Mrs Leggett ran out into the street wearing just her nightdress, screaming for help. A neighbour, Mr C. Smith, had just got into bed when he heard what he described as 'a terrible rushing of wind' followed by shouts of 'fire' and, even more chillingly, 'The Germans are here'.[7]

Battling the flames and suffering serious burns to his hands and face, Samuel Leggett dragged his children, all also suffering burns, from their bedroom inferno, which moments before had been a peaceful haven. Then he dashed up to the top of the house and rescued young Curly too. Amidst the confusion neighbours crowded around to help. For a moment, Mr and Mrs Leggett looked around for their youngest daughter, 3-year-old Elsie, but someone meaning well said they thought a neighbour had taken her to safety. Traumatised by the whole experience, the Leggetts took themselves to the Metropolitan Hospital in Kingsland Road, while a neighbour, Bernard Holland, carried 11-year-old Elizabeth May, whose burns were serious.

Sadly for the Leggett family the trauma of that night had only just begun. At about 4.00am, Police Constable Churchill and Mr Smith, the neighbour, entered the Leggetts' burnt out home to look for the policeman's cape. While searching they discovered that neighbours had not carried infant Elsie to safety after all. In the smoke-blackened bedroom they found her little charred body buried beneath the still smouldering debris. And yet there was still more dreadful news to come for the distraught family. A few days later their eldest daughter, Elizabeth May, died in hospital, her death attributed to 'shock from burns as the result of a bomb flung from a hostile airship'.[8]

Distanced from the personal horrors his bombs were causing, Linnarz continued southwards, dropping more across the Mildmay Park area of Dalston, where they caused a few minor injuries and slight damage to property, but the fire brigade was quickly in attendance dealing with the fires that broke out. The next tragedy, however, was just seconds away.

31 May 1915: Dalston, London

Henry Good junior set out from his parents' house at 187 Balls Pond Road at about 9.30pm to walk the short distance to his own home. About 90 minutes later and now asleep in his own bed, 22-year-old Henry junior awoke to the shocking sound of explosions. He jumped up and, from his front door, saw flames in the night sky from the direction of Balls Pond Road. He quickly dressed and ran back to his parents' home.

Two incendiary bombs had crashed down through the house to the basement, setting fire to the staircase, which now burnt furiously. On the ground floor, Thomas Sharpling, heard a bang, saw smoke and quickly roused his wife, son and daughters, Nellie (aged 22), Ada (20) and Ethel (14), and got them out of the house, although the girls all suffered superficial injuries. Unable to fight his way up the burning stairs, Thomas ran to the side of the house and shouted up to Mr Good. Getting no answer, he grabbed a brick and threw it through the window. As there was still no response, Sharpling concluded that Mr and Mrs Good must be out.

Henry junior now reached his parents' house. He pushed his way through the crowd that had gathered and into the garden next door, from where he could see his parents' broken window. A fireman assured him that the occupants of the house were safe, as indeed the Sharplings were. Henry then went to his grandparents' house to see if his mother and father had sought refuge there. There was no sign of them.

Police Constable Barnett was standing nearby when the bombs struck the house on Balls Pond Road. He reported hearing the sound of the Zeppelin's engines, saw a bomb drop, and then the house burst into flames. As he approached, a woman appeared at a front window pleading for help. It was Sarah Coningsby, who had a room on the same floor as the Goods. The policeman grabbed a ladder but was unable to reach her due to the intense heat. Instead, he secured a blanket and, with the help of others, held it out so she could jump to safety; she suffered only slight injuries in the process. Two fires burning in Mildmay Road had delayed the arrival of the local fire brigade.

Only around midnight was the whereabouts of Henry and Caroline Good finally revealed. With the flames extinguished, Constable Barnett placed a ladder against the house again and peered into the blackened smoking room at the back. There, kneeling by the bed as if in prayer, were two figures. But they were not in prayer, they were dead.

Henry and Caroline Good were naked, their clothes burnt from their bodies. All that remained was a small band of woollen jersey on Henry's arm. That arm was tenderly around his wife's waist. The flames had burnt all the hair from Henry's body, while Caroline gripped a large piece of her own hair in her hand. The doctor who attended the scene gave evidence at the inquest and agreed that she had probably snatched at her own hair in agony. He pronounced death due to suffocation and burns. How tragic their last moments must have been. Unable to effect an escape from the fiercely burning building, the couple, married for 27 years, knelt down together by the bed and died in each other's arms.[9]

Linnarz and LZ 38 now followed a southerly course along the line of Southgate Road on a direct route towards the Tower of London, which lay about two miles away. Eight or nine bombs fell in Southgate Road, mainly in the street, where they caused only minor damage. The shock, however, was great. One resident, Mr A.B. Cook, recalled:

> Terrific explosions startled us … as bombs fell just outside my house. People flung up their windows and saw an astonishing sight, the roadway a mass of flames from the incendiary bombs. Flames reached a height of 20 feet. A policeman ran up, his helmet in his hand, 'Get inside!' he shouted, 'They're here!' Then people realized what was happening.[10]

The shock that people were experiencing had tragic results nearby. In Southgate Grove, the sound of exploding bombs reached a terrified Eleanor Willis, a fragile 67-year-old spinster living at No. 8. She became seriously ill; three days later she fell from her couch and died. At her inquest, the jury returned the verdict, 'Death was due to shock following bombs dropped from hostile aircraft'.[11]

31 May 1915: Hoxton and Shoreditch, London

Steering over Hoxton now, Linnarz, described his view:

> One by one … the bombs moaned and burst. Flames sprung up like serpents goaded to attack. Taking one of the biggest fires, I was able by it to estimate my speed and my drift. Beside me my second in command carefully watched the result of every bomb and made rapid calculations at the navigation chart.[12]

That biggest fire may well have been one that engulfed and gutted the premises of cabinetmakers Messrs Beresford and Hicks located at 31 Ivy Street. Or maybe it was the fire at 5 Bacchus Walk, where flames consumed the workshops of the British Toy Aeroplane Company and those of cabinetmakers Enlayde Limited. Between those two major fires another incendiary bomb smashed through the roof of a house at 49 Ivy Lane, occupied by a Jewish tailor, Herman Morris, and his family. Fire broke out in a room where his two young daughters, Hilda, aged 4, and 18-month-old Dora, were asleep. A neighbour, Henry Barrett, cut his hand while breaking a window to rescue the two little girls. Hilda suffered slight burns but the family was safe.

Fires were burning all over Hoxton now. At 329 Hoxton Street, a great number of boxes in the yard of Braun & Francis, bamboo furniture manufacturers, were ablaze. Peter Begovich, a 44-year-old nightwatchman, fled in terror from the burning premises. Unfortunately for him, he ran straight into an angry crowd who, although he was Russian, accused him of being a German and of starting the fire, then attacked him. He received treatment from a police surgeon for eight cuts to his head. Although Linnarz still had many more bombs to drop, for Hoxton, the worst was over.

South-east of Hoxton, Shoreditch was busy that Monday night and its music halls were doing a good trade. Linnarz's next batch of bombs descended around Shoreditch High Road. Three incendiaries landed on the roof of the Shoreditch Empire Music Hall, where a performance was still in progress. They made a large hole in the roof and damaged the ceilings above the stage and a dressing room. As plaster rained down only the swift actions of the manager, who calmly addressed the audience from the stage, prevented a panic. Then, according to a police report: 'The band played lively airs while the audience left the house in an orderly manner.'

Other bombs fell close by, then three smashed through the glass roof of the main shed at the GER's Bishopsgate goods yard, but caused only minor damage.

Positioned over Shoreditch it would have been simple for LZ 38 to strike at the heart of the City of London. Linnarz, who had spent several months in London in 1910, described his view from almost two miles high in the sky: 'There were the old familiar landmarks – St Paul's, the Houses of Parliament, and Buckingham Palace, dreaming in the light of the moon which had now risen.' But the Kaiser's orders were specific, restricting bombing to the east of the Tower of London and Linnarz's navigation had been spot on that night. So LZ 38 steered away from the City, and headed instead over Spitalfields, dropping a number of bombs that caused little damage, and on towards Whitechapel.

31 May 1915: Whitechapel, London

In Whitechapel, Greenberg's Pavilion, a popular picture house, would soon be emptying its customers into the Commercial Road. Nearby, Isaac Lehrman, a Russian Jewish tailor, and his wife, Rachel, were waiting for the return of their 16-year-old daughter, Leah, who had gone to Greenberg's with a girlfriend. A street away another tailor, Louis Reuben, and his wife, Sarah, were growing increasingly concerned by the late return home of their 8-year-old son, Samuel, who had also gone to Greenberg's.

At about 11.15pm, the audience emerged on to the Commercial Road and began to disperse, but as they did so the night sky filled with an extraordinary sound – exploding bombs. Looking back towards Shoreditch, the sky glowed an eerie red. Then bombs began to fall in Commercial Road and the reality of the moment sank in. The audience and others in the street ran in every direction desperately attempting to seek shelter. Leah Lehrman lost her friend in the panic and turned down Christian Street, just two doors down from Greenberg's. Others did the same, including Samuel Reuben. As they did so, a bomb exploded in the street. A policeman who had been standing about 200 yards away ran to the spot where a colleague joined him. There they found Samuel slumped in a doorway, a pool of blood seeping across the pathway; he was dead. They found Leah too, her body ravaged by grievous injuries – a fractured skull, wounds to her face, a deep lacerated wound to her right breast and injuries to her elbow and thigh – but she was alive, just. Ten others, including sisters Sarah and Yetta Seigler, lay in the street, bewildered, shocked and bearing painful injuries.

After a desperate search, Samuel's father finally found his dead son lying on a stretcher in the London Hospital. At the inquest, the coroner recorded the cause of death as haemorrhage from wounds to his abdomen, and others to his shoulder, legs and hands. A separate police report concluded that the bomb had disembowelled young Samuel.

Leah's parents were also searching for their daughter. They eventually found her in the hospital in the early hours of the morning. Her mother described her as 'unconscious and hurt all over'. Leah died a few hours later.[13]

After dropping an HE bomb on the roadway at Burslem Street, LZ 38 steered back across the Commercial Road, taking a north-east course, having come within 500 yards of the London Docks. The next six bombs fell across Stepney but none of these caused any personal injury or serious damage.

31 May 1915: Stratford and Leytonstone

Linnarz was now on his way home. He had still not come under attack over London by AA gun, searchlight or aeroplane, but did not wish to tempt fate. As he steered out towards Leytonstone, he readied his last seven bombs. The first two fell in Stratford, one in Wingfield Road and the other on a house in Colegrave Road. Herbert Osborne told the police: 'I heard the droning of an aeroplane but I could not see anything. According to the noise it came lower and then I saw the bomb drop, it was simply a dark object and I saw it drop through the roof of number 26.'

The bomb, an incendiary, crashed through the roof of 26 Colegrave Road and passed within five feet of 60-year-old Peter Gillies and his wife Emma, as they lay in bed on the first floor of the house. It smashed right through a wooden chair in the room, through the floorboards and down to the hallway on the ground floor, home to John Stacey, his wife Mary, and their two sons. The now burning bomb dug a hole about 12 inches deep as smoke and fumes filled the hallway and flames caught the floor and wallpaper. Stacey and a neighbour managed to throw the burning bomb out into the street, where Police Constable Cosway managed to get it into a bucket of water and carried it, angrily hissing and spitting, a mile and a half to West Ham Police Station.

Linnarz dropped his final salvo on Leytonstone. Bombs fell on Florence Road, Park Grove Road, Granleigh Road, and Dyers Hall Road, but most of the damage was minor and only three people suffered slight injuries: Rebecca Green, Thomas Gilbert and Frederick Foreman. The very last bomb landed on 46 Fillebrook Road, the home of Albert Fisher. It damaged the roof, ceiling and the front and back bedrooms. By the time Mr Fisher realized what was happening, LZ 38 had gone. The first London air raid, which started in Stoke Newington and ended in Leytonstone, and which had lasted less than 30 minutes, was over.

The London anti-aircraft guns remained silent throughout the raid. An official report explained: 'The reason given for this inaction is that the ship was so high that she was neither seen or heard: "There is no authentic case of anyone having been able to see it during its passage over London ... it was faintly heard by the gun-station at Clapton."

Britain's ground defences still had a final ineffective but defiant gesture to make. A mobile AA gun at Burnham fired off 179 rounds of 1-pdr ammunition, and the gun at Southminster sent up 20 rounds, both without success. Hptmn Linnarz's account shows this caused some concern:

> We could see ahead of us the sea, through which the moon had laid a silver path to guide us home. As we crossed the black ridge of the shore we were met with a further attack from the anti-aircraft guns at Burnham and Southminster.
>
> ... Shell after shell whizzed past ... Some burst dangerously near. On, on we flew, and at last we were out of range and the firing died down.[14]

31 May 1915: RNAS Hendon, London

The aircraft defending London that night fared little better. In all 15 took off, flying from the RNAS stations at Chingford, Dover, Eastchurch, Hendon, Rochford and Westgate, but at least three of these only got airborne after LZ 38 had departed. Just one, a Blériot Parasol flown by Flt sub-Lt A.W. Robertson out of Rochford, actually saw the raider on her return flight, but his engine failed, forcing him to crash land in the mud at Leigh-on-Sea. He survived without injury. Two other aircraft suffered damage in landing accidents but their pilots walked away. Another was not so fortunate.[15]

A telephone message arrived at Hendon airfield advising Flt Lt Douglas Barnes of a possible Zeppelin raid and instructing him to stand by and await orders. As the only serviceable aircraft available there that night was the two-seater Sopwith Gunbus, No. 802, Flt sub-Lt Ben Travers, despite his professed dislike of guns, volunteered to fly as Barnes observer/gunner. Travers, who claimed to have joined the RNAS because he disliked marching, then takes up the story:

> I waited with Auntie (Barnes' nickname) and eyed the silent telephone, conscious of a gradual evaporation of my urgent lust for battle ... At length Auntie made bold to go to the telephone and prompt the hesitant Admiralty. 'What?' came the reply. 'Haven't you gone up yet? Go up forthwith.' I later ascertained that by this

time the Zeppelin was well on its homeward journey somewhere over the North Sea.[16]

Once in the air, Travers recalled he had no idea how long they were up for or what height they reached, although he guessed at 'a ceiling of a sulky 5,000 feet', as they peered blindly 'in conscientious ineptitude through the mist'. Now disoriented, Barnes decided to make an emergency landing. Their chosen ground was a field at Theobalds Park in Hertfordshire. Something told Travers to go against correct procedure and he unfastened his safety harness as they descended into a low ground-fog. The Sopwith hit the ground hard at high speed, bounced twice then turned over on its back. The first impact shot Travers clear of the aircraft 'like a stone from a catapult', but Douglas Barnes died in the wreckage. Ben Travers eventually recovered from his injuries, returned to flying and later went on to become an extremely successful playwright and novelist.

1 June 1915: East London

Back in London, the police reported positively on their night's work and on the generally calm response from the public and a lack of disorder. This lack of disorder, however, may have been in part due to the sheer numbers of police (both regulars and specials) on the streets. 'H' Division in the East End had called out 475 officers, while at 'K' Division, centred on West Ham Police Station where only two bombs dropped, an immense army of 955 police officers assembled, ready to react to the slightest trouble. The following day, when the police presence was less evident, the mood of the crowd changed.[17]

Sylvia Pankhurst, working for women's welfare in the East End at the time, had been close to the bombing. In the morning after the raid vast numbers of sightseers descended on the stricken areas, keen to see the damage for themselves. Of those who appeared in Hoxton, she wrote:

> Streams of people led the way to the damaged buildings ... Crowds mostly made up of women gathered before each ruined home. One, where a child had been killed, was still inhabited. A soldier in khaki stood at the door striving in vain to keep back the press of human bodies surging against it ... In the ashes left by the fires which had ravaged [homes] nothing save the twisted ironwork of the bedsteads could be identified.[18]

According to a local newspaper, one of those great streams of people congregated outside the Leggetts' home in Cowper Road, where they were eventually allowed in to view the burnt out rooms. The congestion became so great that the next door garden and house were used as an exit: 'Practical help was afforded the distressed family by every person passing through being asked for a voluntary "copper", and it was understood at the time that a sum running well into three figures was raised.'[19]

In this environment rumours and unrest spread quickly. It was time to make the Germans in their midst pay – those that remained after the riots earlier in the month anyway. *The Times* newspaper gave a brief report on damage to property, but Sylvia Pankhurst, who witnessed some of this disorder at close hand, gave a far more personal view of this terror on the London streets:

> Down the street … a babel of shouting, tremendous outcry. A crowd was advancing at a run, a couple of lads on bicycles leading, a swarm of children on the fringes screaming like gulls. Missiles were flying. In the centre of the turmoil men dragged a big, stout man, stumbling and resisting in their grasp, his clothes whitened by flour, his mouth dripping blood. They rushed him on. New throngs closed around him.
>
> From another direction arose more shouting. A woman's scream. The tail of the crowd dashed off towards the sound. Crowds raced to it from all directions … fierce, angry shouts and yells …
>
> A woman was in the midst of a struggling mob; her blouse half-torn off, her fair hair fallen, her face contorted with pain and terror, blood running down her bare white arm. A big, drunken man flung her to the ground. She was lost to sight … "Oh my God! Oh! They are kicking her!" a woman screamed.[20]

Pankhurst pleaded with a soldier standing nearby to intervene but he just replied, 'Why should I?' When a military car drew up she asked the officer inside if he would take the woman away. 'I don't think we can,' he answered, 'we are on military business.'

Then, the mood of the mob changed, its anger seemingly satiated. Pitying hands picked up the woman, who had now fainted and supported her, while someone attempted to tidy her hair. Those people, who moments before had been shrieking their anger, were now standing silent and awed. Finally, the police arrived and heavy-handedly dispersed both crowd and victim.

A calm gradually settled over the city. Subjected to assault from the air for the very first time, the fears of uncontrollable fires, mass death and panic on the streets had not materialized. London emerged from the raid unbowed.

The London Fire Brigade reported 41 fires. Only one of these was considered serious and required a district call out, the majority being dealt with by local appliances, policemen and the public. LZ 38's raid had caused seven civilian deaths and that of a RNAS pilot, and injured 35, of whom two were soldiers. When the fire brigade concluded its investigations it estimated material damage at a little under £19,000, which was in fact just less than the cost of the damage caused in the London anti-German riots almost three weeks earlier. In response to the raid London received three more AA guns to fill gaps in the outer line, at Blackheath, Finsbury Park and West Ham. Originally destined for Royal Navy ships, the guns were in place at the beginning of July.[21]

Back in Germany, Linnarz and the crew of LZ 38 returned as conquering heroes. Newspapers extracted every ounce of bombastic rhetoric they could muster to celebrate this occasion. One in particular captured this mood:

> At last the long yearned for punishment has fallen on England, this people of liars and hypocrites – the punishment for the overflowing measure of sins past. It is neither blind hatred nor raging anger that inspires our airship heroes, but a solemn and religious awe at being the chosen instruments of the Divine wrath. In that moment when they saw London breaking up in smoke and fire they lived a thousand lives of immeasurable joy, which all who remain at home must envy them.[22]

In Britain the term 'baby killers', coined by Churchill in reaction to the German Navy's bombardment of Scarborough in December 1914, began to be applied increasingly to the hated aerial raiders. Meanwhile in Belgium, after five successful raids on England, Erich Linnarz's LZ 38 was about to run out of luck.

7 June 1915, 2.20am: Evere, Belgium

Six days after the raid on London, three Belgium-based Army Zeppelins – LZ 37, LZ 38 and the recently repaired LZ 39 – received orders to attack England again. Shortly after getting airborne from her shed at Evere, engine trouble forced Linnarz and LZ 38 to abandon the mission and return to base. Later, LZ 37 and LZ 39 aborted their missions after encountering heavy fog out over the English Channel. Word of their approach had reached the Admiralty in London, who advised Arthur Longmore, commanding No. 1 Squadron RNAS at St Pol near Dunkirk that the raiders were heading back to Belgium. Longmore immediately issued orders to four of his pilots. At Furnes, Flt sub-Lt Reginald Warneford and Flt sub-Lieutenant John Rose, both flying Morane–Saulnier monoplanes, received orders to intercept the returning Zeppelins over Ghent or, if unsuccessful, to bomb the Zeppelin shed at Berchem St Agathe near Brussels. Two other pilots, Flt Lt John Wilson and Flt sub-Lt John Mills, in Henri Farman HF27 pusher aircraft, received instructions to fly direct from St Pol to Brussels and bomb the Zeppelin shed at Evere. Longmore hoped that even if his pilots failed to intercept the returning Zeppelins, a successful attack on the sheds would deny them safe harbour.[23] Unbeknown to Longmore, Wilson and Mills, LZ 38 was already back inside the Evere shed.

After a flight lasting about 90 minutes, and having benefitted from a strong tailwind, Wilson reached the Brussels area just after 2.00am, but the sky was very dark and he struggled to identify the target. Then a searchlight reached up and began flashing signals to him. With nothing to lose he took out a torch from his pocket and made some random flashes in return, which appeared to satisfy those on the ground. Wilson continued circling the area at 2,000 feet for about 15 minutes before the sky brightened a little and he was finally able to make out the Zeppelin shed below in the gloom.

Wilson released the first of his three 65lb bombs but it missed the target. Alerted now by the explosion, German gunners rushed to man their weapons as Wilson turned to make a second attack:

> Approached again from the same direction and dropped the second bomb, and, though I did not actually see the explosion, the flash appeared to come from the centre or side of the shed, and the third pitched outside the north west corner.
>
> The explosions shook the machine considerably and the second explosion was extremely bright.[24]

Wilson then steered away. As he looked back at the Zeppelin shed he observed a large column of black smoke above it, but disappointingly no flames.

By now, Flt sub-Lt Mills had arrived over the Evere shed, where the now alert defenders commenced a heavy fire. Loaded with 12 bombs, Mills takes up the story:

> I then decided to get more height, and, reaching 5,000 feet, I got on a line heading about N.W., and, going straight for the shed, dropped all my bombs, one after the other, when I thought I was in position.[25]

Despite the distracting angry fire aimed at him, Mills was in the correct position, as he quickly discovered:

> On looking back, some seconds afterwards, I saw the shed burning furiously; flames coming from almost every part, reaching to a considerable height and with much black smoke pouring out of the top of the shed.

At Evere, the ground crew made a desperate attempt to haul LZ 38 from the shed but her nose had only emerged a few yards when the bombs struck. With her gas cells fully inflated, flames swiftly engulfed the once proud raider of Ipswich, Bury St Edmunds, Southend, Ramsgate and London. As the hydrogen burnt off, LZ 38 screeched in agony in its death throes as the now unsupported framework collapsed under its own weight until all that remained was a twisted jumble of smouldering red hot metal girders.

The brief but dramatic career of LZ 38 was over – it had lasted just sixty-six days. Erich Linnarz and the crew were not caught up in the destruction of their airship. Together they went on to serve on LZ 86 on the Eastern Front before they returned to the west as the crew of LZ 97 in April 1916. The tangled wreckage of LZ 38's forlorn skeleton was bundled on to seven large railway trucks and unceremoniously transported back to Germany. For their gallant actions that night both Wilson and Mills received the Distinguished Flying Cross. But for the Army airship service the night had another crushing blow in store.

7 June 1915, 2.25am: Ghent, Belgium

The other pilots Longmore despatched, Flt sub-Lt Reginald Warneford and Flt sub-Lt John Rose, both flying Morane–Saulnier monoplanes, took off from Furnes at about 1.00am. After climbing through the mist, Rose quickly became disoriented and had to return, leaving Warneford to pursue his mission alone. It was perhaps when alone that Warneford was happiest.

Reginald 'Rex' Warneford joined the Army in December 1914 after almost ten years at sea as a merchant seaman. He immediately regretted his decision and transferred to the RNAS, joining as a probationary pilot in February 1915. He quickly passed through both a civilian flying school and the military Central Flying School, and it was obvious to those who taught him that he was a natural, but his fearlessness and over-confidence raised concerns.[26] He was not popular with the other pilots and seems to have effected an American accent. Ben Travers, who trained with Warneford at Hendon, described him as: 'a brash character, half, or perhaps wholly, American by birth. His cocksure and boastful nature annoyed us all.'[27] It would appear Warneford went out of his way to keep people at a distance. On his first posting, to RNAS Eastchurch on the Isle of Sheppey, he strode into the officers' mess, twirled his gun around his finger and fired it into the roof, shouting in an American drawl, 'Hi suckers! What about this?' His entrance did not go down well. One instructor noted: 'It would be difficult to find a wilder or more untameable individual than Rex Warneford.'[28]

Warneford's discipline issues hindered him at Eastchurch, but his squadron commander decided to send him to France before his problems at home became insurmountable, believing he had the personality and skill to make an excellent front-line pilot. Thus Rex, now aged 23, joined No. 1 Squadron RNAS, where the squadron commander, Arthur Longmore, noted that he arrived 'with a very indifferent "chit" to the effect that he lacked discipline and was as wild as a hawk'.[29]

After a spell flying two-seater aircraft, Longmore recognized that Warneford's aggressive instincts were ideally suited to fast single-seaters. He allocated him a French-built Morane–Saulnier L monoplane armed with a Lewis gun and six 20lb bombs. Thus armed, Longmore gave Warneford his head. The lone airman hunted up and down the front line for targets, attacking German aircraft and observation balloons wherever he found them. Undeterred by enemy fire, he rarely returned from his sorties without damage to his aircraft. So frequently did this occur, but so effective his work, that Longmore allocated him a second Morane for times when his first was under repair. Warneford was in his element.[30]

So it was in the early hours of 7 June 1915 that Warneford, in his second Morane, armed with six 20lb bombs and flying alone, headed for Ghent. Once clear of the mist, he scanned the horizon and there, some

13 miles away, he spied the unmistakable outline of a lone Zeppelin. He turned towards the distant airship and began the long chase. The 'Wild Hawk' was hunting once more.[31]

Oberleutnant (Oblt) Otto van der Haegen, the commander of Zeppelin LZ 37, had set course for home after the aborted raid on England and was a few miles beyond Bruges when Warneford caught up with him. Van der Haegen's machine guns opened fire on Warneford's tiny aircraft, then he released ballast to enable the Zeppelin to climb away easily from its hunter.

Convinced he had shaken off the lone attacker, the Zeppelin commander returned to his previous course and prepared to commence descent towards Brussels. Warneford, however, was not a man to be deterred by a few bursts of enemy fire. He kept well astern of LZ 37, waiting for another chance to pounce. At 2.25am Warneford was flying at 11,000 feet when he saw LZ 37 commence her descent.

Unnoticed above his quarry, Warneford switched off his engine and began a silent, curving descent. By the time he was ready to make his attack, LZ 37 had descended to 7,000 feet and Warneford had swooped down until he was just 150 feet above her. As he flew along the length of the great aerial raider, he smartly pulled on the toggles that released his bombs. The first two were unsuccessful, but he recalled that, 'the third definitely did the trick'.[32] The full force of the hydrogen blast tossed his fragile aircraft up into the air like a discarded toy and somersaulted it out of control. After a few moments the Morane righted itself but the engine would not restart, leaving Warneford to glide the aircraft down as best he could. Below him he saw the flaming mass of LZ 37 plummeting to earth. 'I looked down and watched it burning. I had a strangest feeling of detached curiosity, almost as though its death agonies had nothing to do with me.'

While Warneford looked on, the worst fears of the crew of LZ 37 were about to be realized. As the airship began to burn the helmsman, Alfred Mühler, looked around in bewilderment and recalled hauntingly:

> … we were encompassed by an increasing and terrible heat. I saw dark shapes of men silhouetted against a ruddy glow as their flailing arms tried to protect their faces. Some of them climbed over the sides of the car and flung themselves into space.[33]

The burning, plummeting airship smashed into a convent in Ghent. The now unconscious Mühler fell clear just before impact and, crashing through a skylight, landed miraculously on a recently vacated nun's bed. Although badly burnt and with injuries to his elbow, Mühler was the only member of the crew to survive. Two nuns, a man and a child also died in the fire, and another man fell and broke both his legs while attempting to rescue a child.

Warneford now had his own problems. He managed to glide his aircraft down behind enemy lines and landed on the side of a small hill near a wood. Dismissing the idea of destroying his aircraft, he started to cobble together a repair to his fuel pipe, which he had identified as the cause of his engine problem. Then Warneford froze. A German cavalry patrol had entered the wood, his discovery seemed certain, but a fortuitous swirling mist concealed him and the patrol moved off. He now needed to start his engine, normally a two-man task. Summoning all his strength he:

> ... pulled and pushed and bounced [the aircraft] along until I got her nose pointing downhill, which was luckily pretty steep. Then I swung the prop. I kept on hauling and pushing her until ... she started to move, slowly at first, and then as she gathered speed ... I made a leap for the cockpit ... The old girl responded magnificently as I opened the throttle and managed to climb out of range.[34]

He was climbing out of range of the carbines of the cavalry patrol that had now returned. In spite of the danger he could not resist a parting gesture, shouting back, 'Give my regards to the Kaiser'. After his hair-raising escape Warneford eventually landed back in France near Cape Griz Nez and finally returned to St Pol at 10.30am. Having filed his report, the exhausted Warneford went to bed.

His report caused a sensation. The following morning the newspapers in England heralded his actions as 'one of the most brilliant exploits of the war'.[35] This was just what the government needed, a story to excite the nation: for the first time a brave British pilot had destroyed one of the hated Zeppelins in the air. And while the nation thrilled to his exploits over the breakfast table, a telegram from the King winged its way to No. 1 Squadron. Warneford was to receive the Victoria Cross. Before that, however, the French called him to Paris to receive the *Légion d'honneur*. But ten days later Warneford was dead. In Paris to receive his French award and to ferry a new aircraft back to Dunkirk, the French authorities annoyed him by granting an American journalist, Henry Beach Needham, a flight with him.

Count Ferdinand von Zeppelin (1838-1917). Count Zeppelin launched his first airship in 1900, three years before the Wright brothers made their first manned, controlled and powered flight by a heavier-than air machine – an aeroplane. Just fifteen years later airship and aeroplane were at war in the skies above Britain. (Author's Collection)

Peter Strasser (1876-1918). An inspirational and charismatic leader, Strasser had command of the Naval Airship Division from 1913 and maintained an unshakeable belief in the ability of Zeppelins to take the war effectively to Britain right to the end. (David Marks Collection)

The *Viktoria Luise*, one of Count Zeppelin's former commercial airships, carried 10,000 civilian passengers prior to the outbreak of WW1, while also serving as a training ship for both Army and Navy crews. In August 1914, she switched exclusively to the role of training ship. (Author's Collection)

An historic photograph taken on 21 November 1914 showing the three RNAS Avro 504 aircraft about to take off prior to attacking the Zeppelin factory at Friedrichshafen in Germany. From left to right they are those flown by Flight Lieutenant Sydney Vincent Sippe (No.873), Flight Commander John Tremayne Babington (No.875) and Squadron Commander Edward Featherstone Briggs (No.874). (Author's Collection)

Bomb damage in St. Peter's Plain, Great Yarmouth, after the first Zeppelin raid on Britain on 19 January 1915. The bomb dropped by *L 3* killed Samuel Smith as he stood at the entrance to his workshop (dark brick building on right), and Martha Taylor, who was walking from right to left, to Drake's Buildings (a passageway between the light and dark brick buildings). They were the first deaths in the country caused by a bomb dropped from the air. (David Marks Collection)

Local people gather in Mr Brasnett's field at Heacham, Norfolk, for a photograph with an unexploded 50kg Carbonit high-explosive bomb dropped by Zeppelin *L 4* on 19 January 1915. The Navy Zeppelins favoured this type of High Explosive (HE) bomb, while the Army used the spherical A.P.K. (Artillerie-Prüfungs-Kommission or Artillery Test Commission) type HE bombs. (David Marks Collection)

Soldiers sift through the shattered remains of 11 and 12 Bentinck Street, King's Lynn, destroyed by a bomb dropped from Zeppelin *L 4* on 19 January 1915. The bomb killed 12-year-old Percy Goate as he lay asleep in his bed, and Alice Gazley who had run out into the street. (Author's Collection)

The bomb crater and damage at the back of a house at 41 Butt Road, Colchester, home to Quartermaster-Sergeant Rabjohn, 20th Hussars, his wife and their young son. A single floatplane of See Flieger Abteilung 1 carried out the raid. (David Marks Collection)

A crater at Bedlington, Northumberland, caused by a bomb dropped from Zeppelin *L 9* on 14 April 1915. Wherever bombs left craters local people would gather to have their photographs taken. (David Marks Collection)

The room at 238 Station Road, Wallsend, where Mrs Robinson was bathing her three-year-old daughter when an incendiary bomb dropped by Zeppelin *L 9* smashed through the roof on the evening of 15 April 1915. The bomb set fire to the attic bedroom from where burning liquid poured down into the room below. (Author's Collection)

Damage to the rear of 48 Denmark Road, Lowestoft, and neighbouring properties, caused by a bomb dropped from Zeppelin *L 5* just after 1.00am on 16 April 1915. The occupiers of No.48, the Pratt family and their two lodgers, all escaped with just minor injuries. (Author's Collection)

Crater formed in front of Cave Cottage, Reydon, by a bomb dropped from Zeppelin *L 5* shortly after midnight on the night of 15/16 April 1915. The occupier of the cottage, farmworker Benjamin Snowling, stands in the crater holding the hand of his daughter, 4-year-old Marjorie, while his wife, Laura, is carrying their other daughter. (David Marks Collection)

GERMAN INCENDIARY BOMB: WEIGHT ABOUT 16 LBS.
DROPPED AT MALDON DURING AIR RAID. APRIL 16/15. F.H.

The damage caused at Maldon, Essex, when a bomb dropped by Zeppelin *L 6* shortly after midnight on the night of 15/16 April 1915 demolished a workshop and shed owned by builder Arthur Smith. The cottage to the right of the photo is that occupied by Henry Foreman, his three sons and their housekeeper, Annie Hinton. It would seem likely that the five people in the centre of the photo are they. (David Marks Collection)

An incendiary bomb dropped on Maldon, Essex, by Zeppelin *L 6* on the night of 15/16 April 1915. This cylindrical type, favoured by the Navy Zeppelins, contained thermite and benzol with the outside wrapped in tarred rope, which prolonged burning after initial ignition. Army Zeppelins favoured bell-shaped incendiary bombs. (David Marks Collection)

The scene in Brooks Hall Road, Ipswich, after an incendiary bomb dropped by Zeppelin *LZ 38* had caused a fire destroying the upper floors of Nos. 60 (on the left), 58 and 56, shortly after midnight on 30 April 1915. The bomb struck No.60, home to the Harry Goodwin, his wife and 12-year-old daughter (some sources say niece), igniting in her bedroom. (David Marks Collection)

Damage caused by incendiary bombs in Butter Market, Bury St. Edmunds, dropped by Zeppelin *LZ 38* in the early hours of 30 April 1915. The two damaged premises on the left are Clark's tobacconists and Johnson Brothers, dyers. The gap in the middle had been Day's bootmaker, then came Wise's ladies' outfitters. (Author's Collection)

After a five-minute test flight of the new aircraft, Warneford called Needham over to join him. Keen to get it over, Warneford intended a short, simple flight; neither man strapped into their safety harness. Then disaster struck. It all happened very quickly. The subsequent enquiry surmised that Warneford came in too high when preparing to land:

> To lose height he dived the machine too steeply, and pulled up too hard. Under the strain the right wing went back and broke. With the propeller smashed by part of the tail, and the engine still running, it was impossible to prevent disaster.[36]

Both Warneford and Needham slipped from their seats and fell as the aircraft rolled over. Needham was already dead when they found him. Warneford was unconscious but still breathing, although he suffered terrible injuries: a fractured skull, both arms broken and multiple fractures to his right leg. He died shortly after arrival at hospital.

The government decided on a public funeral in London. At Victoria Station, eight seaman placed his flag-draped coffin on a gun carriage and 20 sailors of the Royal Navy drew it past the thousands who lined the route to Brompton Cemetery, intent on paying their respects to the dead hero. His body lay overnight in a chapel and then the following day, 22 June 1915, they finally laid him to rest. The 'Wild Hawk' who sought to soar the skies in solitude, was committed to the ground amidst a throng of thousands.

The loss of two Zeppelins in the early hours of 7 June proved a serious setback for the Army airship service. They did not return to raid again for three months. For Strasser and the Naval Airship Division, frustrated that the Army had beaten them to London, the stage was now clear for them to renew their attacks on Britain.

Chapter 11

The 'Experiment' is Over

The press blackout in Britain made itself felt immediately after that first London raid on the night of 31 May 1915. The following day the only news printed was the official bulletin released by the Admiralty. This first bulletin merely referred to bombs in 'certain outlying districts of London', then added, a little disingenuously: 'Many fires are reported, but these cannot be absolutely connected with the visit of the airships.' A second bulletin, issued at 5.00pm on 1 June, confirmed it was a Zeppelin attack, stated that four deaths were known at that time, that all fires were quickly dealt with and no public buildings were damaged.

There was no clue as to which areas of London had been struck. So different from the blanket coverage of earlier raids. This must have been particularly galling for the local newspapers in the areas where the bombs fell. Here was probably the biggest local story ever, but they could say nothing. Not until the lifting of press restrictions after the end of the war could the *Hackney & Stoke Newington Recorder* tell its readers the story of that shocking night in full.[1] The restrictions also gave the German press free rein to make claims for a successful raid on the capital: 'We last night threw numerous bombs on the wharves and docks of London.'[2]

From then on reports released to the press only gave vague descriptions of where attacks had taken place, such as the Eastern Counties, the east coast, or on a northern town, with the addition of casualty figures. Newspapers could report the findings of inquests on the victims of air raids but without reference to where the deaths had occurred. This sudden lack of information was frustrating for some but they understood its purpose. If it kept the British public in the dark, it also had the same effect on the Zeppelin commanders. They could no longer extract valuable information as to where their bombs had dropped from press reports that reached Germany via neutral countries.

While the Army airships had raided Britain regularly through May, Strasser's Navy airships were engaged in scouting operations over the North Sea for the German fleet. But two days after the first raid on London, the Navy gave permission for their latest Zeppelins, L 9 and the new 'p-class' L 10, to recommence the air campaign against England. Two more of the new type – L 11 and L 12 – would join them as the month of June progressed. On the afternoon of 4 June the commander of L 10, Kptlt Klaus Hirsch, received his orders, 'to attack the English south-east coast, target London'. In addition, one of the Navy's wooden-framed Schütte–Lanz airships, SL 3, commanded by Kptlt Fritz Boemack, received orders to carry out a scouting mission over the North Sea but, if weather appeared favourable, she could attack sites located on the River Humber.[3]

5 June 1915, 1.05am: Driffield, East Yorkshire

The British radio trackers picked up the departure signals of both airships and SL 3 was later observed about 85 miles east of the Humber at 7.30pm, heading slowly towards Britain's east coast. She eventually appeared about 30 miles south of the Humber at 10.55pm, at Ulrome, between Bridlington and Hornsea. Boemack then appears to have flown up and down the coast until 12.30am looking for a recognisable feature from which to plot his course, when he discovered the promontory of Flamborough Head (see Map 4). A quick consultation with his maps told him he could reach Hull overland and so he turned towards the city. He dropped an incendiary bomb between the villages of Kilham and Langtoft,[4] from which he realized he was making only slow progress into a headwind, a fact confirmed over the town of Driffield when Boemack saw the lights of a southbound train begin to outdistance him.[5] SL 3 aimed two HE bombs at the railway junction at Driffield at about 1.05am, which landed just north of the station in the Beckside area of the town. One exploded in an orchard and the other in a field: '… tearing up and splitting the fruit trees in all directions, and slicing the vegetable crops as if they had been cut with a scythe.' The explosions also smashed the windows in almost every cottage within a hundred yards but there were no casualties.[6]

Boemack tried to continue on his southward course towards Hull but had to admit defeat in the face of the strong headwind. He turned back to the coast, retaining the rest of his bomb load, and eventually went back out to sea at Flamborough Head at about 1.25am, the coastguard there opening up with rifles as he set course back to Nordholz.[7]

Hirsch, commanding L 10, also encountered problems with navigation. He believed he was off the coast of Lowestoft, where he thought he recognized the lighthouse. From that position and with a rising headwind, Hirsch now considered London unobtainable so selected Harwich as his secondary target. Hirsch would later write in his report: 'The City of Ipswich, off to the west, was brightly lit and offered an excellent aid to navigation.'[8] But he was way out in his calculations. His bombs fell on Gravesend and Sittingbourne in Kent, some fifty miles south-west of Harwich, while the lights he saw so 'brightly lit' were actually those of London.

4 June 1915, 11.20pm: Sittingbourne, Kent

L 10 was first sighted south of the Sunk Lightship by armed trawlers between 9.35 and 9.55pm, just over 12 miles south-east of Harwich. She followed a course to the south-west, crossing the mouth of the Thames estuary and passing over Sheerness on the Isle of Sheppey at 11.00pm. From there L 10 followed what some observers described as a figure of eight course, first eastwards towards Whitstable then back to Faversham, before she reached Sittingbourne at about 11.20pm. Local records suggest 24 incendiaries dropped across Sittingbourne and neighbouring Milton Regis, although the official report records only eight. Either way, both state that the incendiaries did little damage, although it appears some fires did break out. L 10 also dropped four HE bombs. These left their mark on a wheat field at Chilton Farm on the south-east edge of Sittingbourne, in Jackson's Field between Charlotte Street and Chalkwell Road and another in St Paul's Street near Pear Tree Alley.[9] The only bomb that caused significant damage was one that landed on a garden wall at the back of a house occupied by Mr W.H. Harvey in Park Road. The explosion blasted the fronts of properties in Unity Street, which faced on to the back gardens of Park Road. The houses at Nos. 58 and 60 took the main force of the blast but lesser damage extended along the road and two people, a man and woman, sustained injuries.

From Sittingbourne, L 10 approached Chatham, coming under fire from an AA gun. Hirsch dropped an HE bomb in retaliation. It landed on Twydell Farm near Rainham where it killed a horse.[10] L 10 must then have flown across Chatham before approaching Gravesend where she received a few shots from an AA gun across the Thames at Tilbury. Reports suggest that Hirsch circled over Gravesend for up to 30 minutes before dropping five HE bombs and three incendiaries, although it appears likely there were more.

5 June 1915, 12.25am: Gravesend, Kent

The sound of L 10's four Maybach engines woke the people of Gravesend from their sleep at about 12.25am:

> ... those who went to their windows and gazed out saw beneath the starry heavens, at a great height, what looked like a silver cigar, hovering over Windmill Hill. Immediately there was a terrific crash, followed by a flare which lit up the surrounding property. Afterwards it was discovered that three incendiary bombs had been dropped on the hill, making deep holes in the ground.'[11]

The next bombs caused varying amounts of damage. A bomb in Windmill Street struck a house called 'Feldon', the home of Mr J. Dyce, 'slicing away one side of it as if it had been cut clean with a giant's axe' and caused extensive damage as well to a house at 100 Windmill Street. The blast from the bomb smashed a great number of windows in Windmill Street, including those at the Tivoli School, and in Wingfield Road. An incendiary in Peppercroft Street set fire to a house occupied by Mr and Mrs Dodd and their five children. All got out safely but the fire destroyed a bed and other furniture. The next two bombs fell in Wrotham Road and Arthur Street. In Wrotham Road the explosion demolished two houses, Nos. 48 and 50, burying five people in the wreckage but rescuers brought them all out alive from the chaos of bricks and timber. In Arthur Street road works were under way and a nightwatchman was on duty by a coke brazier. When the bombs fell he explained how he 'armoured himself' by holding a large shovel over his head. Bombs landed at the back of Woodville Terrace then another landed on stables in Brandon Street owned by the Tilbury Laundry Company.[12] Mrs G.A. Pratt's husband was on duty as a special constable that night and she was in her house in Brandon Street with her two sons, a daughter and a maid. Mrs Pratt was in bed when she realized that the noise that she originally thought came from the railway station was in fact overhead. She got up:

> Just as I reached my boys' room a bomb dropped in a yard next to our garden, destroyed a large brick stable, and blew four horses to pieces.
>
> As I stood, half-dazed, at the door a piece of bomb came through the boys' room window frame, across the bed, through the door post, grazing my face, and embedded itself in the brick wall behind me.[13]

Hearing the bomb, Mrs Pratt's elder son reacted quickly and threw himself on to his younger brother to hold him down. In her daughter's bedroom a large mahogany mirror shattered and crashed down onto the bed, but the 11-year-old girl was unharmed. Mrs Pratt recalled: 'Every ceiling in the house was down, every window broken, and every door off its hinges: in the kitchen every article of crockery on the dresser was broken.'

L 10 then approached the railway station, where Hirsch released a bomb that landed on 2 Cobham Street, penetrating right through the house occupied by Mr J. Russell but failing to detonate: '... it shot through a room in which a young lady was sleeping, it just missed her bed, and she had a marvellously narrow escape.' Having passed over the station, the next bomb set fire to a garden fence at 34 Bath Street, followed immediately by another that struck the night nurses' quarters at the general hospital, causing a serious fire. Fortunately all the nurses were on duty at the time and damage was limited to a burnt out box room and damaged furniture. The penultimate bomb exploded outside the south-west corner of the VAD Hospital, located in the former Yacht Club building on Clifton Marine Parade.[14] The blast damaged the façade and brought down all the ceilings, forcing the hospital to vacate the building and move to Chatham while repairs were made. Although none of the patients suffered injury, at least one had a narrow escape. A soldier recovering from an operation recalled: 'I ... was coming round when I heard a rushing noise, and was just able to pull the sheet over my face. There was a shattering explosion, the window was blown out, and big pieces of plaster covered my bed and me. The iron cradle over my body saved my life, the doctor said.'[15] The only casualty at the hospital was a nurse, Miss R. Herring, who suffered a dislocated shoulder.

L 10's next bomb buried itself in the river's sludge near the Imperial Paper Mills jetty before the final one fell in the Thames, perilously close to a loaded ammunition ship, before being sucked down into the muddy depths as peace returned to Gravesend. L 10 followed a north-east course away across Essex and Suffolk, eventually going out to sea just south of Southwold at 1.35am. Estimates of material damage caused by the bombs came in at £8,740 and casualties amounted to eight people injured: three men, four women and a child.

Once again the aerial response had been poor and it appears that was due to fog. Although L 10 had flown over RNAS Eastchurch on the Isle of Sheppey at 11.00pm, the first aircraft to take off from that airfield only did so an hour later. Other sorties from Eastchurch and RNAS Grain took off even later, and although the RFC flew sorties from Joyce Green and Northolt, the pilots saw nothing.[16]

6 June 1915, 11.35pm: Hull, East Yorkshire

The Naval Airship Division was back in action two days later on 6 June. The same night that RNAS pilots destroyed LZ 37 and LZ 38 in Belgium, the Navy sent out Zeppelin L 9 to 'attack London if possible, otherwise a coastal town according to choice'.[17] From Germany's viewpoint, the raid by Heinrich Mathy proved the most effective to date.

First sighted at 8.15pm about 12 miles off the Norfolk seaboard, north-east of Mundesley, L 9 seemed uncertain of her position as she moved off the coast for the next 45 minutes. Then, with concerns over making a long overland flight to the capital on a short summer night, Mathy abandoned the idea of attacking London and redirected his attention to Hull. He approached Lincolnshire but coastal fog hampered his navigation. Continuing north, he crossed the mouth of the Humber, and finally managed to fix his position when he identified the outline of Flamborough Head at 11.10pm (see Map 4). From there he set a course inland towards Hull. He dropped two incendiary bombs east of Hull, at Wyton, then approached Sutton-on-Hull on the eastern edge of the city at about 11.35pm, but fog extending out from the Humber made it hard for Mathy to pinpoint his target. As the frustrated commander peered through the gloom, the fog suddenly began to clear, revealing the streets and docks of Hull below.[18] Mathy approached the city at a height estimated between 8,000 and 10,000 feet, but with no anti-aircraft fire opposing him he descended to around 5,000 feet and commenced the first of two lethal bombing runs. However, when AA shells did belatedly appear in the sky, a surprised Mathy climbed back up to 6,500 feet to avoid what he described as a 'light battery without searchlights'.[19] This 'battery' was in fact the 4-inch guns of the scout cruiser HMS *Adventure* under repairs in Earle's Yard dry dock.

Mathy dropped the first of his total of 13 HE and 48 incendiaries in and around Alexandra Dock, with a least two falling in the water while another damaged a pile of pit props, caused minor damage to a railway track and cut a telegraph pole half through. The exact route then taken by L 9 over the city is confused because different sequences are given by the Chief Constable of Hull and by Thomas Charles Turner, a local photographer. Turner, who watched the raid from his home and then toured the streets the next morning, spoke to a number of those who witnessed events and later photographed many of the sites where bombs fell.[20]

An HE bomb that landed in Walters Terrace off Waller Street exploded with devastating effect.[21] Turner annotated his photograph: '14 houses demolished or at least made unsafe, 4 of which collapsed.' Rescuers were unable to save the lives of five of the residents: Florence White, a dockworker's wife, and her 3-year-old son, George Isaac who lived at No. 3; Eliza Slade, a widow living at No. 4; and 50-year-old boilermaker Alfred Matthews, who occupied No. 11. Although in shock as a result of the blast, neighbours in Ella's Terrace, which backed on to the stricken street, rallied to extinguish a fire in a house in their street caused by an incendiary. Bombs that landed in Dansom Lane completely destroyed Hewetson's Saw Mill and timber yard, while an incendiary burnt out a stable in the same street. In East Street, running between Clarence and Church streets, an explosive bomb destroyed Nos. 11 and 12, killing a married couple, George and Jane Hill, and a 10-year-old boy, Edward Jordan, who 'was literally blown to pieces'.[22] Both his parents were seriously injured and taken to hospital. In the High Street, a bomb blasted surrounding buildings, digging a hole six-feet deep in the street and fracturing water and gas pipes, which in turn started a fire. Only the swift action of G. Penrose, a pipe-layer for Hull Corporation, prevented the situation getting worse when he sealed the fracture with wet clay.

Close to the Humber Dock, an incendiary smashed through the roof of 39 Blanket Row, the home of the Mullins family and the site of their grocer's shop. The bomb ignited in a bedroom where the Mullins boys slept: George, aged 15, Norman, 10, and Horace, just seven. His father battled to rescue the boys but he was too late to save Norman. George and Horace were pulled out alive but George, in a state of shock, ran off. At the Monument Bridge, about 500 yards away, he collapsed. People in the street picked him up and carried him to the infirmary but he died there later.

For the population of Hull, perhaps the most dramatic incident took place in South Church Side alongside the landmark of Holy Trinity Church. Separated from the church by the width of the road stood the well-established draper's store of Edwin Davis & Co. When bombs fell on the store and the neighbouring Fleece Inn an uncontrollable fire broke out that completely obliterated both businesses. A newspaper reported:

> There was no use in pouring water upon the burning shops. They were a red-hot mass, and every wall and pillar was gradually falling, bringing storey after storey to the ground.[23]

The heat from the fire was so intense that the lead in some of Holy Trinity's stained glass windows began to melt, but fortunately the wind was blowing from the north-west and kept the flames away from the church. The landlord of the Fleece Inn, Demetrious Franks and his family, took shelter in their cellar and later emerged unharmed into the hellish vision of destruction above ground. The fire continued to burn at the store into the next day, when all that remained was a mountain of bricks and charred timbers. Some ten days later a woman's body was recovered, buried beneath the debris, but sadly it seems she was never identified or reported missing. The photographs of Holy Trinity Church looming above the smouldering ruins of the draper's store just yards away have come to define the raid.

At 50 South Parade an incendiary bomb smashed through the roof of the house occupied by the family of Maurice Richardson, who was away serving in the Army. Richardson's wife was sleeping in the same room as their two children, but when the bomb burst through the ceiling, bewildered and shocked she panicked and ran from the house screaming. Fire engulfed the bedroom, killing their 11-year-old son, also called Maurice, and daughter, Violet, aged eight.[24] Then, at 2 St Thomas' Terrace, Campbell Street, which ran parallel with South Parade, an HE bomb landed directly on the house, completely demolishing the upper storey and seriously damaging the houses either side. The bomb claimed the lives of William Walker, a 62-year-old tanner's labourer, and his daughters Alice, 30, and 17-year-old Millicent. The force of the blast ripped off both of Millicent's feet and deposited her body twenty feet away in the yard. It also physically lifted Alice on her mattress and threw her 30 feet across a pathway to land on the roof over the aisle of St Thomas' Church from where her lifeless body rolled off and fell to the ground.[25]

More bombs dropped in the narrow confines of Edwin's Place and Sarah and Ann's Place, both off Porter Street, and proved extremely destructive. At the latter address a 68-year-old widow, Emma Pickering, was asleep in bed when an incendiary crashed into her room. Suffering badly from rheumatism, she was unable to get out of bed as the flames took hold and she burnt to death. At Edwin's Place, on the other side of Porter Street, an explosive bomb caused extensive damage, wrecking four houses and damaging several more. The couple living at No. 21 stood no chance as their house collapsed around them. Both William Watson, a 67-year-old tram painter for Hull Corporation, and his wife Annie, aged 58, died in the wreckage, 'their bodies so badly mutilated that identification was extremely difficult'.[26] And next door at No. 22 rescuers recovered the lifeless body of 27-year-old Georgina Cunningham from the rubble.

Hull had a number of steam whistles known locally as 'buzzers' installed on important buildings to serve as a warning of possible air raids to allow for a rapid extinguishing of the lights and for the assembling of special constables and ambulance workers. After this first raid on Hull, however, whenever it sounded it had another significant effect, as the Chief Constable of Hull stated later that year:

> The result of it also is that when it sounds great numbers of people leave their houses and troop out with their children into the country, and in some cases stay there for hours in the fields ... They are perfectly orderly and show no signs of panic, but it must be a very harassing thing for the women and children, and as a matter of fact the schools do not open the morning after.[27]

7 June 1915, 12.25am: Grimsby, Lincolnshire

Mathy left Hull by following the northern shore of the Humber. Although now flying at a height estimated at 10,000 feet, maxim guns positioned at Sunk Island and Stallinborough, on either side of the Humber, opened an ineffective fire and a 1-pdr 'pom-pom' at Immingham also joined in, but none offered any real threat. Mathy then took L 9 across the Humber at 12.25am, approaching Grimsby, where he dropped his seven remaining incendiary bombs near the docks, one of which failed to ignite. One bomb dropped on a dockyard railway siding, setting fire to two or three empty goods trucks, and two fell in the Royal Dock. Others followed in Fish Dock Road, then one near a railway crossing and one in Freeman Street near the junction with Church Street. Riflemen at

New Clee fired a few shots as L 9 headed away to the south-east and a 'pom-pom' at Waltham managed to get off 12 rounds before Mathy finally headed out over the coast at Tetney Haven at about 12.35am. Although the RNAS had a station at Killingholme between Hull and Grimsby, fog prevented any aircraft from taking off to engage L 9. The official report on the raid includes a wry comment from the head of the Army's Northern Command, who pointed out that 'Killingholme, a place whose normal condition is one of fog, is hardly a good position for a seaplane station'.[28]

Jeanne Berman, living in Grimsby, wrote in her diary that although she heard the noise of the Zeppelin, she did not believe at first that it really was an enemy airship. But that soon changed:

> At last we heard the shooting, so all doubt was removed ... We got up & roused the children. We all dressed. We felt faint ... I felt my teeth chattering a little, but soon became calm. Mother came in and took the few shillings out of the drawer & the silver. We peeped out of the window & saw a red glow in the sky, & guessed that buildings were burning somewhere ... All the time we could hear the engines throbbing, the noise of the bombs, & the shooting.[29]

When the firing died down, Jeanne and her family tentatively went outside and heard that some buildings at the docks had been set on fire. It seemed calm outside: 'It was a most lovely night, the sky clear, lit with stars & the air scented ... Who would imagine that amongst so much beauty & peace there had been death and destruction.'

And death and destruction there had been. The bombs dropped on Hull had killed 24 people and injured another 40, with an estimate of 40 houses, shops and places of business demolished or wrecked and countless others damaged to a lesser extent. Official estimates evaluate this damage at £44,795.[30] These figures demonstrate the greatest death toll and recorded damages for any air raid so far. Therefore, when the official press communiqué appeared in the papers the following morning it created much ill will in Hull. The announcement, issued at 1.15am, was brief and inaccurate: 'During last night hostile airships visited the East and South-East coasts of England. Bombs were dropped at various places, but little material damage was done. The casualties so far reported are very few.[31] Then the newspapers filled with stories of the exploits of Warneford, Mills and Wilson in destroying Zeppelins LZ 37 and LZ 38, and only ten days later did a further announcement gave a more accurate summary of the Hull raid:

> It is now possible to state more exactly the casualties resulting from the airship raid on another portion of the North-East coast on the night of June 6.
>
> The number of deaths is 24 – namely, five men (all civilians), 13 women, and six children. There were also 40 cases of more or less serious injury. The principal fires were in a drapery establishment, a timber yard, and a terrace of small houses.[32]

The people of Hull had, however, wasted no time in demonstrating their anger by turning against Germans in their midst. Large crowds formed in the streets in the early hours of the morning and serious anti-German riots broke out, with attacks on businesses owned by, or perceived to be owned by, Germans. As in other towns and cities, numbers of pork butchers and bakers of German origin had lived and traded in Hull for years and their premises now suffered under the mob's anger. The police finally brought these outbreaks of violence under control with Army support but sporadic outbursts continued to flare up for the next two days.[33]

Then, in an attempt to convince the population of Hull that moves were in hand to protect them in the case of further air raids, a gun appeared on the roof of Rose, Downs & Thompson's foundry in the appropriately named Cannon Street on 5 July. But it was all a ruse, the 'gun' was a wooden dummy and it was removed in early 1916.[34]

15 June 1915, 11.40pm: Tyneside, Northumberland

Pleased with the reports of Mathy's raid, Strasser followed it up nine days later, sending two of his Zeppelin fleet to attack the mouth of the River Tyne. The former commander of L 6, Oblt-z-S von Buttlar, had recently been appointed to command L 11 but his new ship had to turn back early after damage to the forward engine's crankshaft. This left Klaus Hirsch and L 10 to attack alone, just as he had done earlier in the month over Sittingbourne and Gravesend.

The commander of the Tyne Garrison, Brigadier General H.G. Fitton, wrote in his report that he received notification at 7.00pm of Zeppelin activity half an hour earlier about 100 miles off Flamborough Head. Warnings were passed on to all police authorities in the north-east and principal industrial sites by 8.30pm, but at this point no further action was required as no one knew where the Zeppelin was heading.[35] It could have easily been Hull again, or anywhere along the north-east coast. At 8.41pm he received another message advising that a Zeppelin was approaching Flamborough Head, just over 80 miles south-east of the Tyne. In fact, Hirsch had made a fast crossing over the North Sea and when he arrived off the British coast he found it still in bright daylight, the raid taking place just a week before the summer's longest day. He kept out at sea accordingly, cruising up the coast for almost three hours before finally coming inland just north of Blyth at 11.23pm (see Map 4). Telephone warnings were sent to airfields and anti-aircraft guns but the pre-arranged system to alert police authorities and important industrial sites through the North Shields Telephone Exchange proved ineffective due to delays in transmitting the code word 'Extinguish', which warned to switch all lights off. It meant that after L 10 had made a rapid wind-assisted southward flight from Blyth, the lights of many of the shipyards and works along the Tyne were still blazing when she arrived over Wallsend flying at about 6,000 feet. Another prearranged warning signal, the sounding of a siren from the scout cruiser HMS *Patrol* on the Tyne, began at 11.35pm but it appears few recognized its significance and the lights continued to burn.

Hirsch, from his position in the command gondola of L 10, realized he was approaching a target of some relevance: 'I noticed on the portside a great number of lights and the glare of blast furnaces. Approaching closer, the course of a river could be distinguished, on the banks of which were a great number of industrial works.'[36] Yet he was unsure where he was. Nevertheless, Hirsch recognized that he had a valid target below, his conclusion confirmed moments later when the 3-inch AA gun at Carville let loose three rounds, joined by the 13-pdr at Pelaw (three rounds) and a 6-pdr at Low Walker, which fired off six.[37] Hirsch reported:

> L 10 was suddenly subjected to heavy fire from various ground batteries. We were glad to note that shrapnel and not incendiary shells were being fired. The shrapnel all burst below the airship. On account of the gunfire I decided to bomb the locality below as the many factories and blast furnaces afforded good targets.

He dropped his first seven bombs around 11.40pm on Wallsend, a place previously bombed by Mathy and L 9 in April.[38] One incendiary and two HE bombs fell just to the south of the Infectious Diseases Hospital, followed by two HE, one close to Holy Cross Church and the other at Burn Closes, and two incendiaries that fell near the Secondary School at Church Bank. None caused any significant damage. Seconds later, bombs fell close to the railway line, damaging a boiler shed at Wallsend Colliery and causing damage estimated at £400 to McCarthy's Cafe and lesser damage to houses in Jubilee Street, Dene View and South Terrace. Then, as L 10 neared the Tyne, six HE and three incendiaries rained down on the works of the North Eastern Engineering Company. The bombs caused serious damage to the pattern, machine and crane shops, while also setting fire to a large timber stack. When firemen eventually brought the blaze under control assessors estimated the cost of the damage at £30,000, significantly more than the entire losses inflicted on London in the first raid on the capital six weeks earlier. There were, however, no casualties.

Crossing the Tyne, Hirsch turned to the east and headed directly towards the lights blazing from Palmers Shipbuilding Yard and Ironworks at Jarrow. Before he reached Palmers he dropped a few bombs over Hebburn. An HE bomb landed at Hebburn Colliery on The Square followed by two incendiaries on the Ordnance Works football field, then another HE bomb that dropped in Blackett Street caused damage to windows and roofs in 65 houses at a cost estimated at £70. An incendiary then dropped in Back Berkley Street as L 10 loomed over Palmers and commenced dropping seven HE and five incendiary bombs on the works, where the night shift was hard at work. The explosion of the HE bombs destroyed the glass roof over the Engine Works department, sending lethal razor-sharp shards of glass arrowing down among the men of the night shift. Another bomb 'fell through a turbine and exploded, casting bits of metal around'.[39] The explosions also cut down others outside the building and more bombs landed close to the ships under construction between the Engine Works and the river, damaging the monitor *Marshal Ney* just nearing completion.

At the inquest Ralph Errington told how he first heard, 'two reports, not heavy ones at 11.40 on Tuesday night'. These first sounds were probably from the bombs at Wallsend. He continued:

> and these were followed by other reports, some of which were heavier than others, and the time which elapsed was six or seven minutes. The sound of the reports and the breaking of glass caused much commotion. Some men were injured and others were killed outright.[40]

It is hard to imagine the horror of the scene in the Works moments after the 400-foot-long glass roof shattered. Among the glistening carpet of glass and blood that now stretched right across the workshop floor lay the majority of the casualties: 16 killed and 72 injured. The ages of those who died ran from 16 to 67. One of the 16-year-olds killed, William Young, had gone to Palmers to deliver food to his father who worked there. The bombs smashed windows and damaged roofs in 328 houses in streets near Palmers, and in one of them a 62-year-old woman, Ann Isabella Laughlin, died of shock.

Although soldiers at Jarrow and East Bolden opened fire at L 10 with their rifles, they offered no real threat. Hirsch now crossed back to the north bank of the Tyne, flying over Wilmington Quay and East Howdon. Two incendiaries and one HE bomb fell between the river and Stephenson Street, on Cookson's Antimony Works, where they destroyed a crane, a shed and damaged machinery. Another incendiary landed in Pochin's Chemical works, next to Cookson's, and one in Stephenson Street close to the chemical works. Then an HE bomb fell in Coach Open, at the junction with Bewicke Street and Church Street, where the explosion fatally injured Police Constable Robert Telford, aged 22, who was out on patrol. He had recently signed on for the Army and was awaiting his call-up. The blast also smashed many windows in the neighbouring streets and caused other minor house damage. Hirsch then released four more incendiary bombs as he headed east over Tyne View Terrace, parallel with the river. One landed in the Tyne Commissioners' Yard, two more in Tyne View Terrace and the last one in Dock Street, on the approach to the Northumberland Dock.

Hirsch dropped no bombs on Northumberland Dock or Albert Edward Dock, where he crossed back over the Tyne again as he made for the coast. Once across the river, he resumed bombing. He dropped an HE that landed in the river close to the Harton Colliery staithes (coal jetties), destroying two cabins on the staithes, then, as he came over South Shields, he released another HE bomb with considerable effect. It detonated in a fairground on Ferry Street owned by Thomas Murphy. The fire brigade had extinguished the ensuing blaze by 2.10am but by then the flames had consumed an orchestral organ, a scenic railway, damaged a locomotive, and also destroyed numerous sideshows including 'shooting saloons, hoop-la, dolly shies [and] coconut shies'. The impact of the bomb extended over a wide area. The Chief Constable of South Shields reported: 'This latter bomb caused considerable air disturbance which resulted in the whole of the windows in Ferry Street being damaged, also some in Church Row, Coronation Street, Market Place, King Street, East Holborn, Mill Dam, Spring Lane and Thrift Street.'

A 1-pdr gun at South Shields fired off 25 rounds with no effect as L 10 headed towards the sea and a 4.7-inch gun at Cleadon joined in with five rounds. The penultimate bomb fell on Bents Ground, only recently opened as a public park. The HE bomb landed about 25 yards from the northern perimeter of the park, where the explosion dug a crater some 14 feet wide by 4 feet deep and damaged the park railings. Then, at 11.52pm, as L 10 crossed the coastline and set a course for Germany, she dropped her last bomb, an incendiary, which landed on the beach, from where the military authorities dug it up and took it away to add to their growing collection. Hirsch believed he had bombed either Sunderland or Blyth and reported that the glow of the fires he had started were still visible when he was 30 nautical miles (35 miles) out to sea.[41]

As L 10 dropped its first bombs at 11.40pm, a B.E.2c aircraft took off from the RNAS station at Whitley Bay. With no other information available to the crew, Flt Cdr C.E. Robinson and Leading Mechanic Hinkler, headed towards Newcastle searching for the raider in their heavily laden aircraft, but by the time they had laboured up to a useful height, L 10 was on her way home. Giving up the search the crew turned for home, expecting danger. During take-off they had damaged the undercarriage and this gave way as they touched down. Although the aircraft was destroyed in the landing, Robinson and Hinkler were able to walk away from the crumpled wreck. A second B.E.2c took off ten minutes after the first and also headed towards Newcastle while L 10 was over South Shields and flying in the opposite direction.[42] There were no searchlights along the Tyne to aid the airmen, which left them flying blind; their only hope being to stumble across a Zeppelin in their path.

Summer 1915: Nordholz, Germany

Hirsch's thorough report on his night's work had an effect on future raid planning. Being just a week before midsummer's night, Hirsch noted that the sky never really became completely dark, and he felt that in those circumstances British aircraft could remain aloft throughout the night searching for Zeppelins. Strasser listened and no more airship raids took place until August. Hirsch had also attempted to use the Navy's new system for gauging location by radio bearings from two direction-finding stations located on the German coast. Unfortunately the two stations, at Borkum and Nordholz, were only 80 miles apart and almost in line with the Northumberland coast, giving only a narrow angle of detection that led to inaccurate positioning. This resulted later in the introduction of two more stations over a wider area to improve triangulation.[43] The weakness in this method of location was that British listening stations could intercept the radio signals and locate the incoming Zeppelins. Zeppelin commanders soon learned to keep these requests to a bare minimum.

Klaus Hirsch, however, would not trouble the British defences again. He had handed over L 10 in July 1915, but a month later he resumed command and on the afternoon of 3 September 1915, the 30-year-old officer, was returning to Nordholz at the end of a reconnaissance flight over the North Sea when L 10 flew into a considerable storm of thunder and lightning. At 3.20pm (local time) observers at Nordholz saw 'a large flash of flame like that of an explosion' in the sky in the direction of Cuxhaven. Then news arrived at the airship base that L 10 had crashed in flames at Neuwerk Island just off the coast with the loss of Hirsch and all 18 men of his crew. The cause of the crash was attributed to the release of hydrogen. Hydrogen expands when atmospheric pressure decreases, as it does when an airship climbs. Once an airship gets above a certain height – the pressure height – automatic valves release excess hydrogen that can no longer be contained in the gas cells. According to Strasser, L 10 had suddenly climbed just before the fire: 'Shortly before the crash the ship – whether on purpose or not cannot be ascertained – went over pressure height ... The ship was thus valving gas at the time. This could have led to her being set on fire by lightning.'[44] Because of the loss of L 10 in this way, Strasser passed orders to his Airship Division: Commanders should always attempt to go around thunderstorms; if they could not they should fly through the storm at as low a height as possible below pressure height and they should reel in their radio antenna, which could act as a lightning conductor.

The official account of damages inflicted on the Tyne by Hirsch's last raid amounted to £41,760, a similar amount to that recorded at Hull nine days earlier.[45] The disjointed raids of the first half of 1915 now reached a hiatus while the long summer evenings settled over Britain. In many ways these early raids were experimental, as airship crews learned the skills needed to fly to Britain, locate targets, drop bombs and return safely. Now, however, the time for experimentation was over. Strasser was determined, once the skies began to darken again, to launch his airships against Germany's prime target, London.

Chapter 12

The Guns Strike Back

Although there were no air raids on Britain during the second half of June and the whole of July 1915, there was much going on behind the scenes. The first one-million cubic feet hydrogen capacity 'p-class' Zeppelins had made their appearance and Germany was already planning the next development that would see the launch of the 'r-class' with double the hydrogen capacity in the following summer. Work also began on the construction of a new airship base with four sheds at Ahlhorn, about 25 miles south-west of Bremen, due for completion in September 1916. Meanwhile, both Zeppelin and Schütte–Lanz began construction of new factories near Berlin, at Staaken and Zeesen respectively. The targeting of London received more attention too.

June–July 1915: Berlin

The Kaiser's restriction on only bombing to the east of the Tower of London still limited air raids. However, following a French air raid on the German city of Karlsruhe, the Chief of the Naval Staff, Admiral Gustav Bachmann, believed the time was right to give German airships free rein to attack London. His opposite number in the Army, Erich von Falkenhayn, agreed but recommended waiting until both services had built up their airship fleets. The Army, however, had recently transferred its only two Zeppelins in the west to the Eastern Front, while the Navy had four of the new 'p-class' Zeppelins – L 10 to L 13 – plus the older L 9 ready for action by the end of July. Earlier that month, Bachmann had received support from the German Chancellor, Theobald von Bethmann-Hollweg, but it came with the proviso that raids on the City of London, the financial heart of the capital, should only take place at weekends when most of the workers were absent and that historical monuments should not be targeted. With raids being dependent on suitable weather, Bachmann knew this was impossible. Undeterred, he appealed directly to the Kaiser, pointing out that as the City emptied of workers each night the result would be the same as attacking at weekends. Bachmann concluded: 'Therefore I request Your Majesty to withdraw this prohibition and to authorize the Commander-in-Chief of the Fleet and the Chief of Flanders Naval Forces to designate the City of London as a target; monuments like St Paul's Cathedral and the Tower will be spared as far as possible.' On 20 July the Kaiser finally gave his approval: unrestricted bombing of London could begin.[1]

9 August 1915, 11.15pm: Goole, East Yorkshire

On 9 August, on the dark night of the new moon, Peter Strasser ordered all five of his Navy Zeppelins to raid England; L 9 was to attack the Humber while the other four had orders to strike London.

Out over the North Sea the armada diverged. Commanding a Zeppelin over England for the first time, Kptlt Odo Loewe in L 9, appeared off the Yorkshire coast between Bridlington and Hornsea at 8.15pm. As there was still daylight, Loewe headed south along the coast at a height estimated to be just 3,000 feet. From Skipsea, soldiers fired a couple of rounds at L 9 before she flew past the RNAS station at Atwick.[2] Five minutes later two aircraft, a Bristol T.B.8 and a Blériot XI, gave chase. Loewe easily evaded them by climbing to 10,000 feet and heading out to sea, where he disappeared into the fog. Both aircraft returned to Atwick but the pilot of the Blériot, Flt sub-Lt R.G. Mack, crashed on landing due to poor visibility. Meanwhile, Loewe had turned north and reappeared off the coast at Fraisthorpe, a few miles south of Bridlington, but then went back out to sea and, flying south again down the coast, appeared off Hornsea at 9.10pm (see Map 4). Alerted to the return of the Zeppelin, the T.B.8 from Atwick took off again in the thickening mist and her pilot, Flt Cdr Chris Draper, pursued L 9 out to sea for 35 minutes before he lost her again.[3] Loewe returned to the coast for a third time at 10.05pm, near Aldbrough, south of Hornsea, and although he again passed close to Atwick, the heavy mist prevented any further take-offs.

Ten minutes after coming inland, although struggling to identify his position because of the ground mist, Loewe was able to pick up the main railway line at Hutton Cranswick, south of Driffield, and began to follow it south towards Hull. At 10.30pm, as L 9 reached Leconfield, near Beverley, she hit a problem. A broken rudder cable forced her to fly in circles for 20 minutes while the crew made the necessary repairs.[4] This disruption seems to have confused Loewe's navigation for, instead of resuming his southerly direction towards Hull, he veered off to the south-west. He reached the Humber near South Cave at 11.10pm, from where he followed the river westwards to its junction with the River Ouse, which led him on towards the lights shining at Goole. Steam 'buzzers' were to warn the town of the approach of enemy aircraft but that night the system failed and no warning sounded until after the raid was over.[5]

An empty goods train from Hull was also traveling towards Goole at the same time as L 9. In accordance with a recent experimental arrangement with the North Eastern Railway, trains heading in the same direction as a Zeppelin were to stop. The driver brought his train to a halt before the bridge over the Ouse, giving Loewe, who carried about a ton of bombs, the opportunity to try to hit it.[6] Three incendiary bombs landed harmlessly just east of the bridge at about 11.15pm, and two more fell in the river. Unsuccessful with the train, Loewe continued to release bombs between the river and the town but these landed in saturated fields. The first bomb to strike Goole, an incendiary, smashed through the roof of a house in Axholme Street in the Shuffleton district, where it burnt fiercely:

> Suddenly, just after 11p.m., residents were startled by a tremendous explosion, which was followed by others equally loud, and for the next few minutes there was an indescribable pandemonium. Those who were in the streets or looked out from their house-windows saw the rays of a brilliant searchlight thrown on the town from the sky, and many observers thought they could observe the shape of the Zeppelin itself as it travelled rapidly through the air over the town from east to west, dropping its deadly missiles in rapid succession.[7]

At 2 Sotheron Street, at the corner of Victoria Street, an incendiary bomb landed with tragic consequences. Sarah Acaster, a 65-year-old widow, ran a small shop selling toys and sweets with her two daughters, Sarah Ann (34) and Kezia (32). They were all in the kitchen enjoying a late supper with Alice Smith (17), a visitor from London, when the bomb struck. Rescuers found the bodies 'fearfully scorched'; Kezia was dead while Sarah and Sarah Ann died shortly afterwards and Alice Smith died a few days later. The family were well-known in the town and their deaths evoked much indignation and sympathy. Another incendiary crashed down on a house on the other side of Victoria Street but rescuers managed to pull the elderly couple who lived there out through their bedroom window. In a house at Belle Vue Terrace an incendiary burnt and killed two young children, Beatrice Alice Harrison (aged 6) and her sister Florence (4). Other bombs struck in the close-packed streets nearby.

A HE bomb caused devastation in North Street and Bromley's Yard, shattering ten small houses and burying a number of people in the wreckage, compounded seconds later when another HE and an incendiary dropped in neighbouring George Street. Describing this latter explosion in a letter written to his daughter on 12 August, Mr West, a shipping clerk for the Lancashire & Yorkshire Railway, wrote: '3 houses had wall blown out into the lane, and beds, bairns, bolsters and pictures after them.' The blast killed four members of the Carrol family: James, aged 31, his wife, May (30) and their children, Alice (4) and Gladys May (3). West's letter continues: 'Mr Gunnee carried girl out, all flesh of one leg torn away – next he fetched a young baby, but the sight finished him; he was done … sick … he went away … to vomit.'[8]

While Wells does not name the child, it may have been 9-month old Margaret Pratt, the youngest victim, who died with her mother Agnes, aged 36. Also recovered from the wreckage were the bodies of Grace Woodall, aged 31 and her 3-year-old daughter Annie Elizabeth, along with widow Hannah Goodall (74) and her granddaughter Violet Stainton (18). An HE bomb that landed at the back of a house on Ouse Street near a baker's shop owned by T.K. Willson caused more injuries. Mr West, in his letter, describes how the bomb blasted a large hole in the wall big enough to drive a horse and cart through, adding: 'Floors are all down in the cellar, furniture just a pile of ruin, pictures hang akimbo.'

Passing over Chapel Street, Loewe dropped an incendiary on the roof of the local authority offices at the Exchange Buildings, where it did very little in the way of damage. However, the impact of an HE bomb on a quay wall facing the corner of Aire Street and Adam Street impressed the inquisitive Mr West.

> Stone blocks 2 feet thick, were splintered, and the solid masonry under them. Docks hydraulic pipes broken, log wood sent flying, railway wagons derailed and smashed to pieces – Lowther Hotel hasn't a window left, all blown out – woodwork included.

He noted that damage to windows extended to other neighbouring streets. Mr West then records a bomb falling on property owned by his employers, the Hamburg Shed at the docks, which smouldered for some hours before starting to burn at 6.00am the following morning. A bomb at the railway sidings at Bridge Street also caused West to marvel: 'A loaded coal truck, 14 tons, was shoved off the line, both rails broken thro and bent inward, aye and split lengthwise. An N.E.R. knocked into fragments and one of our butter vans smashed.'

A couple more HE bombs landed in a field near the Alum works and then L 9 turned away. She had been over the town for only about five minutes but her bombs claimed the lives of 16 and left two women with serious injuries, while two men, two women and five children suffered injuries of a lesser extent. Assessors estimated the damage caused to the town at about £7,000.

Loewe continued west to Snaith before turning back towards the coast. At 11.45pm he dropped three incendiaries in a field near Hotham, between Goole and Hull, without causing damage and went back out to sea near Hornsea at 12.12am. Loewe believed he had bombed the Hull docks and reported coming under heavy fire on his return to the coast, but there is no record of any AA guns engaging L 9 that night.[9]

The raid had a similar effect on the population of Goole as at Hull two months earlier. Many of the population made for the countryside, many out to Mount Pleasant north of the town. The exodus amazed Mr West:

> But you should have seen the fugitives fleeing. Mount Pleasant was swarming; swarming. The Harrison girls slept on the bare ground, there. See a barefoot woman, only nightdress on, a baby in her arms and two children pulling at her.
>
> Midnight – yes! twentieth century culture and all up to the knees in wet and field soil. We had had down pour all morning. Airmyn and Rawcliffe Roads were alive, all night.

The exodus was repeated the following night too, but the townsfolk went better prepared this time: 'Men and women, bairns and baskets, chairs and stools; aye and even beds were taken out to field and hedge side, road and lane, seeking safety.' But when the Zeppelins did not return the novelty quickly wore off and the residents slept in their own beds once more.

Three days later the local authority held an inquest on the deaths caused by the raid. The scene described in the local newspaper could equally be of any of the inquests held up and down the country in the wake of German air raids on unsuspecting British towns and cities:

> Large crowds of people gathered to watch the arrival of the jurymen and the various witnesses, most of whom were near relatives of those who had been so cruelly done to death by the murderous Huns. It was a quiet, orderly crowd, mostly composed of women, who desired in a mute way to convey to the suffering ones sympathy in their great trouble. The arrival of the mourning relatives, most of whom were women, was a pathetic sight. They came in groups, accompanied by friends, and most of the womenfolk were weeping. Those who had been ordered to give evidence passed quietly into the building.[10]

10 August 1915, 12.12am: Isle of Sheppey, Kent

While Zeppelin L 9 had been over Goole, the four Zeppelins heading for London enjoyed little success. In temporary command of L 10, Oblt-z-S Friedrich Wenke was leading a Zeppelin over England for the first time, like Loewe in L 9. Unlike Loewe he had the added pressure of flying with the leader of the Naval Airship Division, Peter Strasser, as his passenger. Wenke was off the Suffolk coast near Aldeburgh at 9.40pm and passed over Leiston 20 minutes later. Flying south-west across Suffolk, L 10 passed to the north of Ipswich, then steering across Essex to the west of Colchester before passing Maldon as she headed towards the Thames Estuary. Rain clouds were making observation difficult, so Wenke threw out a parachute flare north of Rochford at about 11.45pm, revealing the Thames just over four miles away.[11] But believing he was over East London, Wenke took L 10 out over the river and began dropping a number of bombs at the shipping below. He reported they landed among British warships, whereas they dropped among boats on the river close to the Nore Lightship moored off the mouth of the River Medway. British reports confirm the detonation of five or six bombs.[12] Wenke then took L 10 across the Isle of Sheppey where at 12.12am over Eastchurch he dropped 12 bombs, attracted by the landing flares burning at the RNAS airfield. Already warned of the Zeppelin's approach, two B.E.2c aircraft took off at 12.01am but were still climbing when the first small HE bomb landed about 600 yards from the airfield's hangars, followed by another four, each getting closer to the buildings. A sixth HE bomb, larger than the others and weighing in at 100kg, exploded close to the sheds but only smashed windows. L 10 also dropped six incendiary bombs, which all fell around the sheds, where an infantry detachment was able to extinguish them before the flames could take hold. Three minutes later, two HE bombs landed on Pump Hill, half a mile south of Eastchurch.[13] Crossing the River Swale, Wenke turned east and followed the coast towards Whitstable, where he headed out to sea at about 12.30am. Although the two pilots sent up to intercept L 10 (Flt Cdr R.J. Bone and Flt Cdr R.E.C. Peirse) were airborne for 90 minutes, they were flying blind because no searchlights had managed to locate her. Both, fortunately, managed to avoid the bomb craters that now pockmarked the airfield when they returned.[14]

9 August 1915, 10.19pm: Lowestoft, Suffolk

Zeppelin L 11 approached the Suffolk coast at the same time as L 10, just over four miles further north at Dunwich. But her commander, Oblt-z-S Horst von Buttlar, was way out in his navigation. Hindered by patches of dense fog, von Buttlar believed he was over Essex and, feeling that in the circumstances London was beyond reach, turned north and headed towards what he believed was the port of Harwich. He was in fact approaching Lowestoft, about 40 miles further north-east. Shortly before 10.15pm von Buttlar dropped an HE bomb on Leggett's Farm on the London Road at Pakefield, damaging fencing, a gatepost and windows.[15] Moments later he began dropping seven HE bombs on Lowestoft, which had suffered another air raid four months previously. The first bomb dropped near The Avenue on an area of land owned by Charles Day described as an open building plot used as a garden. It struck a 'lean-to' chicken house built against a 12-foot high wall, demolishing both and destroying two greenhouses. Half a mile on the second bomb struck a house and grocer's shop at 12 Lovewell Road, on the corner with Anchor Street. Although owned by Arthur Stebbings, Mrs Hammond occupied the premises with her two children and a niece, 18-year-old Kate Crawford. The bomb crushed the building and the house at No. 14 next door. Rescuers were able to pull Mrs Hammond and the children from the rubble with only minor injuries, but Kate Crawford, engaged to be married in October, was dead, 'crushed and suffocated' under the wreckage.

The next bomb landed about 150 yards further on, in the back garden of 29 Lorne Park Road, at the corner with St Leonard's Road. A police report states that the house, occupied by Henry Haws, was 'much damaged', while another report mentions damage to the party wall and outbuildings. Another 200 yards and von Buttlar's fourth bomb landed in Union Place on the west side of London Road, in the garden of florist William Sherwood where it smashed the glass and did other damage to his greenhouses. The fifth landed 150 yards on, in the back garden of 11 Wellington Esplanade, home to Miss Wood, causing considerable damage to the house and those adjoining, but there were no injuries. A few seconds later another HE bomb struck the roof of 2 Wellington Esplanade, occupied by a Miss Grindley, and 12 soldiers of 2/4th Norfolk Regiment who were billeted there. The bomb smashed the roof and destroyed a couple of rooms, causing injury to three of the men and their host. A final HE bomb fell on the pavement in Wellington Road on the sea front, about 60 yards further on, close to the Apsley Boarding House where more men of the 2/4th had their billets. Although the building suffered some damage there were no further casualties. Von Buttlar also dropped four incendiaries but these all landed in the sea.[16]

Poor visibility hampered attempts to oppose L 11's raid. A searchlight swept the sky after the first bomb fell on Lowestoft but the mist prevented it finding the raider. Two naval 6-pdr guns fired off 12 rounds without effect, but von Buttlar reported: 'The salvoes were relatively close to the airship and one shell burst close below the forward car.'[17] Von Buttlar did not need a second warning to turn for home. Meanwhile, word only reached RNAS Yarmouth of the presence of L 11 after the bombs began to fall on the town. Despite the poor conditions, Sqn Cdr Ireland took off in a B.E.2c at 10.31pm, six minutes after von Buttlar had gone back out to sea. Ireland searched in vain for an hour before returning to Yarmouth, where he found the airfield enveloped in thick fog. He landed badly: 'His undercarriage was wiped off and he landed on his bombs.' Fortunately they did not explode. An eyewitness describing the incident said: '... there was a terrific whistling and a crash, and out of the wreckage stepped Ireland, swearing because another machine had not been warmed up ready for him to take up.'[18]

The fourth Zeppelin of Strasser's attack force was Heinrich Mathy's new command, L 13, making its maiden voyage. Observers spotted her around 10.45pm off the north Kent coast at Reculver and again on the Essex side of the Thames Estuary at Shoeburyness 25 minutes later. But all was not well. Plagued with engine problems, Mathy turned back and at 11.55pm appeared off Foreness Point at the north-eastern corner of Kent, where he turned off the engines and drifted for about an hour while the crew attempted repairs. With his engines back on, Mathy released a large number of bombs over the sea in Sandwich Bay before limping back to Germany.[19]

10 August 1915, 12.28am: Dover, Kent

While Mathy had not fared well, Oblt-z-S Werner Peterson and Zeppelin L 12 had a far worse experience. Although he approached the north Kent coast in proximity to Mathy, Peterson turned back and appeared off Westgate at 10.48pm.[20] On a difficult night for navigation, Peterson now made a critical mistake. Under the impression that strong winds from the south had blown him northward, he decided that he must be off the coast of Norfolk between Haisborough and Winterton. Believing it was no longer possible to strike against London, Peterson decided to follow the coast and attack Harwich: 'On southerly course passed Yarmouth and Lowestoft, and finally Orfordness Lighthouse.'[21] In reality he was passing Margate, Ramsgate and Deal. It meant that when he saw lights that he thought were those of Harwich at 12.28am, he was actually approaching the well-defended port of Dover.[22]

As soon as the searchlights switched on a 3-inch gun, two 6-pdrs and five 1-pdr 'pom-poms' opened fire at L 12, estimated to be flying at a height of 5,000 feet, as she dropped her bombs over the harbour. Although carrying 22 HE bombs and 70 incendiaries, observers noted only 12 bombs falling. Three incendiaries landed on Admiralty Pier: two burnt out on the parapet while the third fell through a corrugated iron roof near the Transport Office, setting fire to the platform. An officer and some men quickly dealt with the blaze. All remaining bombs fell in the sea. One HE bomb exploded in the water close to the moored armed trawlers *Cleon* and *Equinox*. *Cleon* suffered some damage while bomb fragments riddled the sides and funnel of *Equinox*.

The blast caused mayhem below decks, where the crew were asleep: three suffered injuries from which one of them later died at Deal Infirmary. There had been another casualty that night too. When L 12 appeared at Westgate, a Sopwith Tabloid piloted by 23-year-old Flt sub-Lt Reginald Lord took off from the RNAS station there but he never saw the raider. With flares burning on the airfield for his return, Lord inexplicably hit the ground 50 yards before the first flare. His aircraft somersaulted twice, leaving it a total wreck. Willing hands dragged him clear of the wreckage but he suffered serious head and leg injuries. He died in hospital in the early hours of the morning.[23]

THE GUNS STRIKE BACK

As soon as the Dover guns opened fire, Peterson released water ballast as well as the bombs to make a rapid climb to 9,500 feet and turned away. But now he was in trouble. The second or third round fired from the 3-inch gun at Langdon Fort hit L 12, puncturing two of her 16 gas cells. The crew quickly assessed the damage at the rear of the airship and reported the bad news to Peterson:

> An examination showed several large holes in Cells 3 and 4, so that Cell 4 was completely empty thirty minutes later, while Cell 3, in spite of efforts to patch it, slowly ran out three-fourths empty. The ship began to sink slowly but steadily, in spite of being driven at an increasingly steep angle. Towards 2.40 [1.40am British time] all available spare parts, machine guns, provisions, etc., were thrown overboard. It was clear that the ship could stay in the air only a short time.[24]

Despite the desperate efforts of the crew, L 12 finally came down on the sea at about 2.40am. As she had been flying nose up it was clear that the rear gondola would hit the water first so Peterson ordered all but two men forward. These two were to manage the engines to the last from a precarious position outside the gondola standing on the handling rails. Then, when the gondola hit the surface they were to cut an opening in the envelope and find their way forward to join the rest of the crew, who made their way to the upper gun platform. But only one of the two men made it – there was no sign of Maschinistenmaat Richard Fankhänel. The only possible conclusion was that the impact had thrown the missing man off the gondola and he was now lost at sea. On a dark night on top of a floundering Zeppelin there was no chance of finding him. Fankhänel, however, did not give up:

> For the first few seconds he had been thrust under the water by the damaged stern of the ship. Moreover, he had great difficulty in swimming in his leather overalls ... He could see the ship through the darkness, a huge, amorphous, spectral mass slowly disappearing from view.[25]

With some difficulty, 33-year-old Fankhänel stripped off everything except his shirt and pants and began to swim after the drifting bulk of L 12, which a strong wind kept tantalisingly out of his reach. Eventually, however, his dogged determination paid off and he managed to grab the elevator at the rear and slowly crawled on all fours along the back of

L 12; his unexpected appearance 'greeted with loud and hearty cheers from his mates'.

Shortly after dawn, as the early morning mist melted away, a ship appeared coming towards them. Nervous moments followed for the crew of L 12 as they waited to see if it was German or British, then more cheers broke out when they recognized it as a German torpedo boat destroyer. The captain informed Peterson that it was not far to Ostend and that he would attempt to tow L 12 into port.

10 August, 8.15am: Dunkirk

At about 8.15am the news of a crippled Zeppelin under tow towards Ostend reached Eugene Gerrard, commanding No. 2 Wing RNAS at Dunkirk.[26] Ten minutes later Flt Cdr Joseph Smyth-Pigott took off in a B.E.2c for Ostend in very poor weather conditions to attack the downed Zeppelin.[27] As he swooped down on the target he noted there were now four destroyers surrounding L 12. At a height of 500 feet he released two 20lb bombs before climbing back up into cloud cover. Descending again to 500 feet and now under a heavy machine-gun fire from the destroyers as well as AA guns on the shore, Smyth-Pigott made a second attack. Bullets struck his propeller and fuselage as he dropped six grenades, but all missed the target. He landed safely back at Dunkirk 9.30am.

At 9.45am Flt sub-Lt Frank Besson headed for Ostend and found L 12 being towed in between the harbour piers. He straddled the target with four 20lb bombs, before dropping 12 grenades in his second attack. All missed their mark in the face of fierce anti-aircraft fire. Besson got away unharmed but another pilot was not so fortunate. Flt Lt David Keith-Johnston had taken off from Dunkirk ten minutes before Besson but never returned, shot down and killed over Ostend. Four other RNAS pilots tried their luck bombing L 12, now lodged up against the quayside in Ostend harbour, but without result, the last at about 1.30pm. Besson flew a high altitude reconnaissance over Ostend five hours later, reporting part of L 12 hidden by smoke generated 'by a big oil flare burning alongside'. Besson, however, was mistaken. The smoke was not from an oil flare – Zeppelin L 12 was on fire.

In between the attacks work had commenced salvaging parts of the wreck. Peterson had supervised the removal of the two gondolas and engines, but as they prepared to lift the undamaged front section of the frame from the water, disaster struck:

> The huge crane had just lowered its tackle on to the framework of the ship when she suddenly burst into flames ... Apparently one of the men engaged in securing the ship had not observed the requisite caution, but had left things in such a state that the escaping gas could easily ignite.[28]

When the flames died down L 12's career of just fifty days was over. Peterson and his crew, whose previous ship, L 7, had narrowly escaped destruction during the Friedrichshafen raid in November 1914, now had to wait another six weeks for a new ship, L 16, to be ready. For Strasser, this first concerted attempt on London had not turned out as he would have hoped, but the prize was great and two days later he tried again.

12 August 1915, 10.29pm: Woodbridge, Suffolk

The four Zeppelins that returned safely from the previous raid set out again on 12 August. This time the older L 9 was to target Hartlepool while L 10, L 11 and L 13 set course for London. After his raid on Goole, this time luck deserted Odo Loewe as one of the propeller shafts on L 9 became loose over the North Sea, forcing him to turn back. Similarly, Heinrich Mathy was having no luck with the new L 13. Engine problems recurred and he too had to abandon the mission. Friedrich Wenke, commanding L 10, did not reach London either, but at least he made landfall.

L 10 made the Suffolk coast at Pakefield, south of Lowestoft, at 9.25pm, but having encountered headwinds estimated at 40mph, Wenke considered it impossible to reach London so selected Harwich as a secondary target. On this, his second raid over England, Wenke demonstrated good navigational skills and followed a southward course, never passing too far away from the railway line to Ipswich. Three B.E.2c aircraft took off from RNAS Great Yarmouth between 8.30pm and 9.50pm but all returned with engine problems having seen no sign of the raider.[29] Five minutes after coming inland, L 10 came under fire from the maxim guns of the Shropshire Yeomanry at Benacre, and at 10.05pm, over Badingham, she jettisoned two petrol tanks, one landing in a meadow at Poplar Farm and the other in a crop field on Oaken Hill Farm.[30] Ten minutes later, over Wickham Market, Wenke released two parachute flares to check his position. Satisfied he was on course he continued towards Ipswich, dropping an incendiary bomb in a field owned by H. Sawyer at Pettistree, followed by another that landed on the Wickham Market to Woodbridge road at Melton. A policeman extinguished it. L 10 now approached the market town of Woodbridge. Although already in bed, 14-year-old Ruby Haywood lay awake; she was keen to see a Zeppelin for herself. Her father had been advised earlier that there was a possibility of a raid so when she heard her parents talking in the garden she leapt out of bed:

> You see I knew it meant there was a Zeppelin coming, and even then as I listened, I could hear a distant hum-m-m.
>
> Putting on my dressing gown and slippers and a big coat, I went out into the garden and soon saw the cause of the alarm against the stars. It appeared to be travelling very fast, for in a few minutes our guns commenced firing, but they shot short and we were obliged to go indoors, owing to the bullets which we could hear pattering around us like rain.[31]

The gun that had opened fire was a machine gun of the 2/12th battalion, The London Regiment. Second Lt Amsden, in command of the gun, noted the time as 10.29pm. Other battalions of the London Regiment then opened fire too with machine guns and rifles, a move that brought unintentional results in the form of a German response, as Rifleman Francis Pearson confirmed:

> No one ever discovered the idiot who originated the unofficial order, but down the line it came: *'Rapid independent fire!'* and immediately the air was filled with the crackle of musketry and stabbed with points of fire. I saw the Zeppelin turn slightly, and there was a series of dull thuds.[32]

In response to this attack, Wenke released four HE and 20 incendiary bombs on Woodbridge. The bullets had no effect on L 10 although one did strike an incendiary bomb as it fell. The bomb was later recovered.

The first bomb dropped may have been an incendiary that landed in Thoroughfare but it was the first HE bomb landing on the pavement outside No. 1 St John's Hill, just a short distance from the church, which proved the most deadly. The blast destroyed the house owned by Harry Welton, but his family escaped without injury. His daughter was particularly lucky; she had been looking out of an upstairs window when the bomb exploded, causing the floor to collapse beneath her. She managed to cling on to the windowsill until rescuers helped her down. The blast from the bomb also destroyed the house next door on the corner of New Street. Welton heard groans coming from the rubble and found 67-year-old Eliza Bunn alive, lying injured among the shattered debris that had once been her sitting room. With the help of some soldiers billeted nearby, Harry Welton carried Eliza clear of her house and also brought out the injured Jack Bunn, aged 12, but Eliza died shortly afterwards of her injuries. On the opposite side of the road to the bomb, a married couple, Roger[33] and Dora Tyler, were standing in their doorway at No. 4 St John's Hill. Dora died instantly while Roger, still conscious, was found lying on the kerb but he died soon after. Their three young children discovered cowering in the wrecked house were physically untouched by the effects of the bomb but it is impossible to believe they were not affected.

Another victim, a bricklayer Edward Turner, aged 50, served as a volunteer fireman and was on his way from his home in Beaconsfield Road to the Fire Engine House in Cumberland Street as the bomb exploded in St John's Hill. The blast killed him instantly, flinging his body some 20 yards through the air. Mr Turner's 20-year-old son Percy, who was walking alongside his father, suffered serious injuries from the explosion, which resulted in the amputation of a leg. Dennis Harris, aged 40, was crossing the road on his way home to St John's Street, the next street to St John's Hill, when fragments of the bomb cut him down. He later died of his injuries in Ipswich hospital. At 27 New Street, opposite St John's Hill, Charles Marshall and his family heard the approach of the Zeppelin and decided to leave their house to 'avoid danger', but while Charles, his wife and their daughter left, James, his 16-year-old son, remained behind to finish his cup of cocoa. He was still in the house when the bomb exploded. Damage from the blast rendered six of the houses in this section of New Street untenable, fatally wounding James and injuring Sarah Woods, aged 55, who lived next door at No. 25.

The damage caused by this bomb was extensive. Besides destroying five homes in St John's Hill, partly destroying 14 New Street and causing serious damage to those six houses in New Street, it also inflicted minor damage to eight other buildings in St John's Hill, as well as breaking windows and some doors and ceilings in about 30 other properties in New Street. St John's Church did not escape unscathed either. Bomb fragments struck the church's spire and stopped the clock at 10.30pm.

A young girl, Kathleen Chapman, lived 'five doors away', from the Tylers. She and her family had been watching from their front door.

'Our chief sensation was interest: we knew nothing then of the horrors of air raids.' As the sound of the Zeppelin's engines drew nearer, the family retreated inside but the bomb burst in the street moments later. Kathleen remembered 'being flung violently under the dining room table and lying there crying, "I am dead! I'm dead!"' The family took shelter in their cellar, 'gathering together in that damp retreat sobbing and clinging to each other'. When all seemed quiet again the Chapmans crept upstairs:

> A cold wind had arisen and was blowing through the house unhindered by doors or windows. A knot of terrified people, known and unknown, had crowded into the hall. Mother, mustering her courage, produced tea for them all from the debris in the kitchen, and at midnight we sat around the table trying to swallow it.[34]

No more than 100 yards on L 10 dropped a second HE bomb. This landed in the back garden of Mr Whitbread's house in Castle Street, where it excavated a great crater thirty feet in diameter and five or six feet deep and damaged the roof and windows of Edwards' Maltings in New Street. Also in Castle Street, bombs that dropped in the garden of William Steele destroyed eight glasshouses and set fire to a pigsty, killing three or four pigs and injuring others. Another HE bomb that caused much destruction landed at the Waggon and Horses public house at 1 Bredfield Street. The landlord, James Coleman, looked out of his window on to a scene of devastation. The bomb destroyed his stables, three pony traps, a loft and a cart shed as well as killing one of his ponies. The blast lifted slates from the roof of the inn, hurling them a considerable distance away, and smashed its windows and doors. Further damage from this bomb occurred to a house in Angel Lane and smashed the windows of two in Theatre Street. Other bombs landed in the grounds of the Buttrum's tower windmill in Burkitt Road, in Seckford Street and on the recreation ground south of Seckford Street, but none caused any damage. The last bomb landed on a house under construction on the outskirts of the town on the Ipswich Road.

Having passed over Woodbridge, Wenke continued towards Ipswich. Advised earlier of a possible raid, the RNAS mobile AA section had deployed seven guns. One crew took up a position on the golf course at Rushmere Heath, just outside Ipswich, from where it heard the hum of the approaching Zeppelin's engines. The gun was under the command of Lieutenant Phillips:

> Our driver, P.O. [Petty Officer] Dame, first saw her and we opened fire with the maxim, 2 Martini rifles with incendiary cartridges and 1 Martini with ordinary ammunition. After firing a few rounds the airship dropped 6 or 7 explosive bombs which fell all around the car but not near enough to do any damage.[35]

These bombs, three HE and three incendiary bombs, fell in fields owned by a Mr Dawson near Kesgrave and two HE bombs dropped in fields believed owned by a Mr Cooper at Rushmere, breaking some windows in the village. Lieutenant Phillips continued his report:

> I think that there was no doubt at all that our fire turned the Zeppelin, as when she was immediately over the car she turned in a very small circle and made off at a much faster speed in an easterly direction. We ceased fire at 10.42pm.

Whether the gunfire from the RNAS maxim was the reason for turning away from Ipswich or not, L 10 was now back on course for Harwich. She crossed the River Orwell near Chelmondiston at 10.55pm and, after a little confusion, approached Shotley, where she dropped an HE on the marshes, scooping out a great waterlogged hole in the soft soil.[36] Ahead lay the River Stour and Harwich.

Wenke approached the town and harbour from the west, dropping eight HE and four incendiary bombs on Parkeston village just west of Harwich. An HE bomb that detonated near Ray Hill cut the telephone wires to the AA gun positioned there. The lines also served a detachment of the 3rd Essex Regiment and Ray Farm. At the village, 300 yards south of Parkeston Quay, an HE bomb landed among houses on Tyler Street, destroying four and causing serious damage to ten others. Incredibly no one was killed, but two men, eight women, six children and a baby suffered painful but not life-threatening injuries; one man had a fractured leg but most of the others were treated for abrasions and burns. Two of the HE bombs and two of the incendiaries dropped in the river and one HE was swallowed up by the mud, but none struck the harbour, where a squadron of seven destroyers had docked about 40 minutes earlier.[37] A naval officer, Claude L.A. Woollard, looking on commented:

> Though even the splashes were much too close to be pleasant the only casualty was a mishap to the servant of the captain of one of

the destroyers: in his excitement he forgot that the guard rails on the deck were down, and walked overboard.[38]

When the first bombs dropped, Harwich's searchlights opened but the 6-pdr AA gun at Ray Hill only got off one round and the 'pom-pom' at Beacon Hill fired just two rounds before the crew lost sight of the target. Wenke crossed the mouth of the Stour and then the Orwell, heading north-east up the Suffolk coast, dropping a final incendiary bomb on Trimley marshes. Shortly after L 10 crossed the River Debden the RNAS mobile section at Shingle Street opened fire with two maxim guns, firing off about 60 rounds at 11.25pm. Wenke took L 10 out to sea to avoid the fire, then continued up the coast and came back inland at Orford about ten minutes later. Seemingly happy with his position, Wenke then went back out to sea and began his uneventful homeward journey. The same, however, could not be said for Horst von Buttlar and L 11.

13 August 1915, 1.00am: North Sea

Von Buttlar experienced significant engine problems as he approached the Suffolk coast and gave up the idea of coming inland. He turned south and reached Kent, where he followed a confused path without dropping any bombs before setting a course back across the North Sea. However, as L 11 approached the north-west coast of Holland the crew could see a huge storm brewing ahead as the headwind increased in strength. Von Buttlar descended to 4,500 feet and attempted to pass to the north of the storm but soon realized that his rapidly diminishing petrol stocks prevented that detour; instead he would have to fly through it. The concern now for Von Buttlar was to keep L 11 below pressure height. Hydrogen expands when atmospheric pressure decreases. The released hydrogen, now mixing with oxygen, becomes flammable, which is not the ideal scenario when passing through an electrical storm. Von Buttlar noted his pressure height was 12,000 feet so took L 11 down to 3,600 feet as he entered the storm. He called it 'a journey through hell':

> Suddenly the whole ship shook from the force of a violent vertical squall. We felt ourselves being forced down toward the sea. In the space of a few seconds the altimeter dropped 600, 900, 1500 feet.
>
> Then we were shot upward again, just as far as we had been driven down.

I had ordered a height of 3600 feet, but, as a matter of fact, we were flying far above 6000![39]

L 11 pushed on through the ever more violent storm, the clouds conjuring up 'gaunt spectres of a nightmare', while gigantic forks of lightning 'shot madly across the sky, followed by the roar and rattle of thunder like the firing of a thousand broadsides'. The vertical squalls continued to force L 11 down and then thrust her up again, while a new unearthly experience affected the crew. Von Buttlar received an odd message from the lookout on the gun platform on top of the envelope: 'The machine-gun sights are burning.' He sent his Executive Officer, Hans von Schiller, up to investigate:

> And the scene which met his eyes was such as he had never before beheld. The sights of the machine-gun were shooting out blue flames, while the sailors' caps all had a sort of halo round them.
>
> It was St Elmo's fire, burning on the machine-gun and attracted by the wire loops which are always to be found inside sailors' caps.
>
> I leant as far as I could out of the car and saw that we were flying through a violet cloud. It was traveling with us. We ourselves were radiating electricity, and the whole ship was, as it were, carrying a gigantic astral body along with it.[40]

Eventually L 11 passed through the storm and the crew gratefully reached safety back at Nordholz after their sobering experience. Zeppelin L 10 was to have a similar ordeal three weeks later with disastrous results (see page 159), but in the meantime she had a third chance of striking against London, and this time she made it count.

Chapter 13

'Gazing with Horror and Dread'

The new moon on the night of 10 August had been the catalyst for the recent sequence of raids by Strasser's Navy Zeppelins. Those that set out on 9 and 12 August had the advantage of the darkest skies, but favourable weather meant Strasser launched one more raid on the night of 17 August, after which increasingly brighter skies as the moon became full seven days later brought the flurry of raids to an end.

Determined to reach London after the two recent failed attempts, Strasser again named the city as the target for the raid and detailed four of his airships for the mission – L 10, L 11, L 13 and the newly delivered L 14.

Heinrich Mathy's run of bad luck with the new L 13 continued when mechanical problems forced him to turn back to Hage before he even sighted the English coastline. Kptlt-d-R Alois Böcker, who had previously commanded L 5, took L 14 out for the first time and remained off the coast of Norfolk for more than two hours trying to overcome engine problems. Having abandoned any attempt on London, Böcker's imaginative report claimed that he dropped his load of 50 incendiary and 20 HE bombs 'on the blast furnaces and factory premises in the vicinity of Ipswich and Woodbridge', industrial facilities associated with neither place. In fact Böcker's bombs landed in the sea south of the Cross Sand Lightship, about ten miles north-east of Great Yarmouth.[1]

17 August 1915, 9.55pm: Ashford, Kent

Von Buttlar, commanding L 11 again, also completed another fanciful report. He told of following the course of the Thames to the eastern outskirts of London, where he bombed Woolwich and came under heavy AA fire. In reality he never got within 40 miles of Woolwich.[2] Approaching Herne Bay on the north Kent coast at 9.30pm, von Buttlar was flying fairly low when he brought L 11 inland over the pier and attracted rifle fire from soldiers of the 42nd Provisional Battalion, forcing him to climb to about 7,000 feet.[3] From Herne Bay, von Buttlar headed south, passing over Canterbury, until reaching the railway running from Folkestone to Ashford, where he turned west towards the latter place. L 11 circled around Ashford at about 9.55pm then moved away before returning and flying over the south side of the town. Near the Canterbury Road she turned again and, flying from east to west, began releasing 19 incendiary and two HE bombs. Six incendiary bombs fell in gardens on the east side of the Canterbury Road, one landed in the cemetery and two in Queen's Road, also on the east side of the Canterbury Road. The only damage caused by these bombs was a partly burnt chicken run and two dead chickens. At Barrow Hill nine incendiaries and two HE bombs fell in cornfields owned by a Mr Bridge, resulting in the death of some of his sheep. The final bomb, an incendiary, landed in the grounds of a sanatorium on the Maidstone Road without causing any damage.

Von Buttlar then took L 11 north towards Faversham, but at 10.30pm, about two or three miles east of the town, he turned back and retraced his route southwards, passing over Selling to Molash, where reports show him circling as though looking for a target. Although there was an AA gun at Faversham, it was unable to fire. The managing director of the important gunpowder works there had previously pointed out to the authorities that when in action the searchlight attached to the gun illuminated his premises. When L 11 appeared, he was still awaiting the light's relocation, so he took matters into his own hands and cut its electric supply. His actions brought a terse comment in the report of the night's activity: 'The matter has been taken up.'

After searching for a target, at about 11.00pm von Buttlar clearly felt he had found one and began dropping 16 HE and 25 incendiary bombs. They fell between the villages of Badlesmere and Sheldwich. The bombs smashed windows in Badlesmere's church but most landed harmlessly in woodland at Sheldwich Lees and near the VAD hospital at Lees Court without causing any injuries.

Von Buttlar then took L 11 back to the coast north of Faversham, reaching the mouth of the Swale at about 11.30pm, but he came inland again near Whitstable and flew parallel to the coast until he reached Herne. Here 60 riflemen of the 57th (West Lancashire) Divisional Cyclist

Company opened fire, persuading von Buttlar to turn towards the coast and head out to sea over Herne Bay, where he had first arrived just over two hours earlier.

17 August 1915, 10.34pm: Walthamstow, London[4]

The remaining Zeppelin, L 10, again commanded by Friedrich Wenke, arrived over the Suffolk coast for the third time in eight days. During the month he held temporary command of L 10, Wenke had demonstrated good navigational skills, arriving over the same stretch of coastline each time.

Wenke came inland near Shingle Street at 8.56pm, coming under the now familiar fire from the maxim guns of two vehicles from the RNAS mobile section. British defences had received early warning of a possible raid and tried a new strategy this night. The Admiralty had purchased some steam trawlers, which they adapted to carry a seaplane. One of these, the *Kingfisher*, a former Lowestoft fishing boat, set sail early that evening hoping to find the approaching Zeppelins before the sky grew dark, but she was unsuccessful. Three aircraft also patrolled from RNAS Yarmouth, taking off at intervals between 7.15pm and 10.55pm, but none of the pilots observed any Zeppelin activity.[5]

Having bypassed the coastal defences, Wenke followed a well-worn path over the rivers Debden and Orwell. Keeping north of Harwich's guns, at 9.25pm he reached Manningtree in Essex, where he picked up the tracks of the GER that led to London (see Map 5).[6] Ten minutes later he observed a glow on the horizon to the south-west – the subdued lights of London. At about 9.40pm Wenke released an incendiary bomb or parachute flare over Ardleigh before passing Colchester and continuing to follow the railway to Chelmsford. The RNAS had an airfield at Broomfield on the outskirts of Chelmsford but, although L 10 passed close by at 10.05pm, two Caudron G.3s inexplicably did not take off until 40 minutes later. From Chelmsford, Wenke veered off to the west, reaching Chipping Ongar at 10.17pm, where he jettisoned a petrol tank and picked up a branch line of the GER leading towards Epping Forest. Just west of Epping stood the Royal Gunpowder Mills at Waltham Abbey, and as L 10 loomed towards it a 1-pdr 'pom-pom' fired off two rounds. Unwilling to test the accuracy of the gunners' fire, Wenke turned away to the south along the Lea Valley. Up until now the Zeppelin commander's navigational skills had been highly accurate but that was about to change. In his report Wenke described flying across the centre of London:

> Since it had turned into a clear, starry night, I steered for the west end of the city, in order to have the wind abaft the beam. At 11.30 p.m. [10.30pm British time] turned to an easterly course and crossed the centre of the city at 3,100 metres (10,200 feet), a little north of the Thames. Bomb dropping was ordered to begin between Blackfriars and London Bridges. Collapse of buildings and big fires could be observed.[7]

It is not clear whether the elation of being the first Navy Zeppelin to reach London distracted the crew or if L 10's liquid compass was faulty that night, but rather than taking a west to east course, Wenke flew north to south-east. And the body of water to starboard was not the Thames but the great line of reservoirs of the East London Water Works running down the Lea Valley from Waltham Abbey to Walthamstow. Perhaps the roads passing between the reservoirs added to the confusion, resembling the Thames bridges from a height of almost two miles. His first bomb did not land near Blackfriars as Wenke reported, instead two incendiaries fell at 10.34pm in Lloyd's Park, Walthamstow, where one failed to ignite. From there L 10 followed the line of Hoe Street with the next incendiary falling harmlessly at the back of houses in Orford Road and Third Avenue and one smashing through the roof of the Stratford Co-operative Buildings in Hoe Street. The bomb ignited on the shop floor but a nightwatchman extinguished it before it could set the premises on fire. However, it was with the dropping of the first HE bomb that matters took on a more serious nature.

17 August 1915, 10.36pm: Leyton, London[8]

That bomb landed in Bakers' Avenue and the sound of explosion was probably the first intimation for most residents of the area that a raid was under way. The blast demolished four houses let out as flats – 41, 43, 45 and 47 – and shattered practically every window in the street, but although nine people were injured, no one died in the blast. Seconds later three more HE bombs dropped in the grounds of Bakers' Almshouses on Lea Bridge Road. Built by the London Master Bakers' Pension and Almshouse Society in the middle of the nineteenth century, this fine Italianate building provided homes for respectable members of the baking trade who had fallen into poverty. Those respectable persons now received a rude awakening, the bombs 'considerably shaking about 20 of the houses and breaking windows'. Fortunately none of the bombs struck the buildings but one woman was seriously injured.

Wenke continued to release bombs as he crossed Lea Bridge Road. An HE exploded in the roadway between the Almshouses and the Leyton Tram Depot, ripping up tramlines and the road, striking the boundary wall and gate pillars of the Almshouses, as well as badly damaging the tram depot. The blast injured a man and shattered windows at the depot as well as in seven neighbouring shops and in numerous houses. Immediately afterwards three incendiaries struck the tram depot causing a fire, followed by an HE that landed in Dunton Road, just beyond the depot, badly damaging No. 28 as well as breaking windows and causing other minor damage to 70 houses in Dunton and Westerham Roads. Incredibly there were no personal injuries.

Wenke appears to have picked up the Tottenham & Forest Gate branch line of the Midland Railway at Lea Bridge Road. Following the tracks towards Leyton Station (now Leyton Midland Road Station) he dropped an HE bomb on 132 Farmer Road, badly damaging the house and breaking the windows in four others. Wenke then released a tight cluster of four more near the station. The first wrecked the station booking office and killed Moses Mayers, a 73-year-old nightwatchman sitting in his hut at roadworks taking place at the corner of Wesley and Midland Roads. The same bomb also caused considerable damage to a steamroller and smashed windows in 53 houses in Wesley Road. Another bomb badly damaged a house at 158 Leyton High Road, smashing windows in 31 houses in the street and those of a Wesleyan chapel. Lethal fragments from this bomb cut down and killed a 35-year-old woman, Edith Grace Lawrence, mother to a 20-month-old son, while David Reginald Smith suffered grievous injury and died within a few hours. The third bomb of this cluster dropped in Midland Road outside a railway arch where John Hamilton owned a billiard saloon, managed by his younger brother, 28-year-old Herbert.

Charles Nicolson had been playing billiards in the saloon with his father when the horror struck. Just as they were about to leave they heard the first of the HE bombs explode near the station:

> Most of the thirteen people in the place ran to the door. A second explosion occurred, nearer than the first.
>
> The front of the saloon was entirely of glass, with a coffee-bar just inside, at which the proprietor and his sister were serving. I do not

know what the others did in the few seconds before the third bomb dropped outside the saloon door. I ran to the nearest wall. The whole of the glass front was blown through the saloon, and my father, who flung himself under one of the tables, and I were both very badly cut about. We had an awful job to get out of the debris in the dark, and we dared not strike matches, as the place was full of escaping gas.[9]

Just before the bomb dropped, the manager, Herbert 'Bertie' Hamilton, shouted to his customers to get under the tables.[10] Everyone took cover, but Bertie was the unlucky one. He died in the wreckage of his saloon. Opposite the saloon, windows were shattered in 16 houses in Midland Road, adding another 12 injuries to the tally: six men, four women and two children, but only two were considered serious. Even before the glass had settled, another HE bomb exploded a few yards away in Moyers Road, where it inflicted slight damage to a number of houses, smashing windows in 27 of them.

Now south of Leyton station, Wenke dropped two incendiaries in Grosvenor Road but they had little impact, merely smashing windows in five houses, but the HE that followed, falling in Claude Road, had a shocking effect on the community.

PC Ede of 'J' Division, Metropolitan Police, was on duty nearby when the bomb exploded. He and Special Constable William Arthur Goodman ran towards the sound and on arriving in Claude Road found that the bomb had 'practically demolished' the house at No. 117 and smashed windows in 175 houses in Claude, Morley and Norlington roads. As the two men stared in disbelief at the wreckage, the cries of a child buried under the debris reached them. While they considered what to do, a neighbour came over to them with a ladder. They placed it against the front of the wrecked building and both men climbed up and into the wrecked house to search amongst the ruins:

> The child's cries continued and eventually, after crawling on their hands and knees beneath rafters, the officers found at the rear of the premises Thomas Pells, aged two years, pinned beneath a quantity of debris, consisting of pieces of timber and brickwork. The two Police Officers with great difficulty eventually succeeded in rescuing the child, and soon after they had done so that portion of the house collapsed with a great crash.[11]

Later that night rescuers pulled the bodies of the rest of his family from the wreckage. His father, a greengrocer, Thomas Howard Pells, his mother Amelia and his 3-year-old sister, Edith, were all dead. Little Thomas Pells survived his ordeal with only minor physical injuries, but who can tell how the experience scarred him mentally.

For his bravery during the rescue, PC Ede received a payment of £10 (the equivalent of about £1,000 today) from the Bow Street Police Court Reward Fund, but the fund was only to reward meritorious service by regular police officers and as such Special Constable Goodman was ineligible. The Commissioner of the Metropolitan Police, however, did not let the matter rest and applied to the trustees of the Carnegie Hero Trust Fund, who were happy to reward Goodman's brave conduct, matching the payment made to Ede, issuing him with a 'framed honorary certificate' and adding his name to the Trust's Roll of Honour.[12]

Two miles high over London, these details were unknown to the crew of L 10 as they continued on their bomb run over what they believed was the north bank of the Thames. An incendiary bomb broke windows at 181 Murchison Road, followed by another incendiary and two HE bombs which landed on the terraced houses in Albert Road. It appears that the HE bomb on 130 Albert Road failed to detonate although it still caused significant damage commensurate with a 50kg bomb smashing down through the house. Incendiaries at Nos. 57 and 78 may also have been faulty as only small fires broke out, but some damage occurred and a woman and child at the latter house received slight injuries. Two streets on and another incendiary dropped, falling on 62 Twickenham Road, where a small fire broke out.

An HE bomb next crashed down through a house at 78 Oakdale Road, but again it would appear it did not detonate, yet still caused much damage to the house and minor injury to a woman living there. Seconds later another HE bomb exploded in the street outside 84 Ashville Road. The concussion from the blast badly damaged 29 houses while breaking windows and inflicting minor damage to 123 others in Ashville, Pearcroft and Oakdale roads. Inevitably among destruction of this nature, there were casualties.

Joseph Edwin Hollington, a 34-year-old brewer's drayman, married to Edith for 12 years, was father to seven children with another due soon. He was standing behind his front door when the bomb exploded outside. The force of the blast smashed in the door, killing him, and it was only later when rescuers lifted it that they discovered his body underneath. (Edith, left to look after the large family on her own, struggled to cope and eventually had to put some of the children into an orphanage.[13]) On the opposite side of the road, at No. 75, the bomb cut down and killed James Frederick Ebbs, a 46-year-old butcher's salesman and father of five boys aged between eight and 19. The bomb also injured another 20 – four men, ten women and six children – but only in four cases were those injuries deemed serious.

Crossing over the GER line, Wenke released an incendiary bomb that landed harmlessly close to the tracks near Grove Green Road. The next four bombs fell in Leytonstone. Two fire bombs burst into St Augustine's Church in Lincoln Street. Flames gutted the church and it would be five years before it reopened for worship.[14] Another incendiary crashed through the roof of 93 Mayville Road, setting fire to the kitchen and badly damaging the contents of the room before the occupants could extinguish it. As the fire took hold, an HE bomb struck the ground at the back of Southwell Park Road, demolishing the rear of Nos. 63 and 65. At the first of these two houses, the bomb killed 67-year-old Philip Osborne, while three children at No. 65 lying in bed were buried under bricks from the chimney and roof, emerging unscathed despite almost suffocating from dust and soot. Minor damage extended to 132 houses in Lincoln Street and Mayville, Melford and Southwell Grove roads. Mr Osborne's son, 22-year-old Roland, was serving in the Royal Field Artillery when he received a telegram informing him of his father's death and granting him leave to return home:

> What a shock it was to me when I turned the corner of Southwell Grove Road and found I had also lost my home. I stood rooted to the ground, gazing with horror and dread. Where was my mother?
>
> A policeman came up, and when he knew who I was he did all he could for me. He knocked up a neighbour, who was very good to me and gave me a drink, trying to console me. Then I heard the terrible news. My Dad had been blown to pieces.
>
> Neighbours and police searched the ruins but could not find him. He was found early next morning lying in a neighbour's garden four houses away; but his hand was found in another street and a limb in a bedroom of another wrecked house. His trousers were hanging in an elm tree.[15]

There was, however, some good news for Roland Osborne. His mother was alive. She had gone to the cinema on the evening of the raid and stayed to watch the film twice through; it saved her life. Osborne was also surprised to discover that workmen who arrived four days after the raid to clear up the rubble found his pigeons alive, buried under the debris of the house.

Wenke dropped his last bombs on Wanstead Flats, a large open public space east of Leytonstone. Why he dropped two HE bombs and eight incendiaries there seems strange but in 1937 one author came up with an interesting theory. There are seven ponds and lakes on Wanstead Flats of varying size and Wenke, who believed he had followed the Thames, may have seen the reflections from these bodies of water and thought them to be the docks in London's East End. A reasonable assumption if you thought you were heading east along the north bank of the river. Ground navigation from two miles high on a dark and at times cloudy night had its difficulties.[16]

A HE bomb and two incendiaries landed close to the western edge of the Flats, where the blast seared across the open ground to streets nearby. Windows in 73 houses located in Harrow Road, Acacia Road and Montague Road were smashed. The other HE bomb exploded close to the model yacht lake at the junction of Lake House and Dames roads. The concussion from this blast smashed 162 panes of glass in 75 houses bordering the Flats, in Dames Road, Sydney Road, Knighton Road, Thorpe Road, Cann Hall Road and Capel Road. An incendiary bomb landed by Woodford Road, which crossed the Flats, followed by two that fell close to the bandstand – all three landing just yards from Angell's pond. Seconds later another incendiary fell on the Flats opposite the end of Tylney Road. The final two incendiaries dropped at the eastern end of the Flats after possibly being aimed at Alexandra Lake as one landed in the lake itself and the other in the garden of 4 Aldersbrook Road, where it set fire to a fence just a few yards from the lake.

Wenke now set a homeward course across Essex, apparently following the tracks of the GER towards Chelmsford, passing between Chipping Ongar and Brentwood at about 11.00pm. In his wake the shocked residents of Walthamstow, Leyton and Leytonstone discussed the losses in hushed tones: ten people were dead and another 48 injured, while estimates of material damage stood at £30,750.

There were other deaths too that could be attributed to the air raid but did not make the official statistics. Thomas Parkin, the Registrar of St Pancras, recalled one family in Leyton – a mother, father and two teenage daughters – scarred by the raid. They lived in a house close to where one of the bombs fell:

The younger daughter, who was having a warm bath at the time, hurriedly left the house inadequately clad, and in the chill night air contracted a cold which developed into pneumonia, from which she died a few days afterwards.[17]

Yet there was no indication in the newspapers the next day that the capital had come under attack. The press blackout was effective with only official announcements published; London was not even mentioned:

> Zeppelins visited the Eastern Counties last night and dropped bombs.
>
> Anti-aircraft guns were in action and it is believed that one Zeppelin was hit. Air patrols were active, but owing to the difficult atmospheric conditions the Zeppelins were able to escape.
>
> Some houses and other buildings, including a church, were damaged.[18]

Despite the claim in the announcement, L 10 had not been hit but air patrols were active, albeit without success. Although L 10 headed back towards Chelmsford, the two Caudron G.3s that took off from the RNAS station there at 10.45pm did not manage to intercept the returning Zeppelin and possibly did not see it. The information is hazy as both pilots crashed their aircraft when landing. One, Flt sub-Lt C.D. Morrison, suffered serious burns to his face and arms while also injuring a foot when three of his four bombs exploded as he hit the ground. The other pilot, Flt sub-Lt H.H. Square, patrolled for two and a half hours before he too crashed, putting him in hospital with serious injuries.[19] As for the anti-aircraft guns, besides the 1-pdr at Waltham Abbey, there is confirmation that the gun at Homerton in east London fired one round and a suggestion that a gun at Edmonton fired briefly too, but the searchlights had little success in finding the raider. Wenke confirmed this in his report when he wrote: 'The London searchlights cannot hold a ship at 3,100 metres in clear weather even if they have found her.'[20]

Over Chelmsford Wenke dropped two more HE bombs. The first detonated in a field at Admiral's Park to the west of the town, where it excavated a crater five feet deep and measuring 12 yards in circumference. The second bomb dropped about 900 yards further on, on a house at 7 Glebe Road. It penetrated the roof, passing through the bedroom and kitchen to the basement but fortunately for the occupants it failed to detonate.[21] Avoiding the guns of Harwich and Felixstowe once more and, with uncanny accuracy, Wenke flew over the RNAS mobile maxim guns at Shingle Street again before passing out over the coast at about 12.20am, exactly at the spot where he had come inland about three and a half hours earlier.

Wenke's period of temporary command of L 10 ended a week later, on 26 August, when it reverted to Klaus Hirsch.[22] Wenke's role at this time is unclear. He did not resume his previous role as Hirsch's executive officer nor was he reassigned to another Zeppelin crew for the next eight months. His absence from the control gondola of L 10, however, proved fortuitous for him. On 3 September, while on reconnaissance over the North Sea, Zeppelin L 10 flew through an electrical storm and exploded into a fireball with the loss of the entire crew.[23]

Summer 1915: London

The Zeppelin attacks in June and August had exposed the inability of home defence aircraft to engage the raiders. The author of the British official history of the air war wrote:

> Experience had made clear the difficulties which pilots had in finding an airship at night. Searchlights were few, and unless the Zeppelin was caught in a beam, which seemed at this time an unlikely event, or was betrayed by the bursting of her bombs, it was almost impossible for a pilot, once he was in the air, to locate her.
>
> Even if an aeroplane got in touch with a raider, the performance of the contemporary aircraft and their armament were such that there was small promise of an attack being successful.[24]

The Admiralty, who remained responsible for Britain's air defence, believed that as Zeppelins attacked at night, 'counter-attacks by the existing types of aeroplane were uncertain and precarious', and in consequence began to question, in view of the losses and damage to aircraft, whether they should prohibit night flying.[25]

The Army meanwhile did not miss an opportunity to criticize their service rivals. General L.E. Kiggell, Director of Home Defence at the War Office, received a minute from one of his officers, Lt Col R.H. James, in June 1915:

> Landing at night is difficult but not impossible with the system of illumination adopted by the Military Wing of the RFC. Of course the landing grounds must be sufficient in number and provided with the proper lighting facilities. As long as the navy are responsible for

the defence by aircraft we can do nothing in the matter, and they are not willing to do very much.

I would suggest that the attention of the Admiralty be drawn to the conspicuous lack of success attendant upon the efforts of their aircraft to fulfil the responsibilities they have undertaken.[26]

It is easy to be critical when ultimate responsibility lies with others, but that same month the Directorate of Military Aeronautics at the War Office demonstrated concerns of its own about night interceptions. Having confirmed that the RFC would offer some assistance to naval aircraft in opposing the Zeppelins, the instruction added: 'Military aircraft will co-operate whenever possible but at night it is not considered desirable to take to the air unless the airship can actually be seen or heard.'[27]

Any clarity that did exist in the Admiralty's Home Defence role became a little more obscure when Arthur Balfour replaced Churchill as First Lord of the Admiralty on 27 May 1915. Unlike his predecessor, Balfour had little enthusiasm for aviation and was keen to offload the obligation for Home Defence. Meetings followed in June and July between the Admiralty and the War Office, which resulted in the latter suggesting they could be in a position to assume responsibility by January 1916.

Changes at the top of the naval aviation hierarchy saw the arrival in September 1915 of a new senior officer, Rear-Admiral Charles Vaughan-Lee, a man with no aviation experience but now in position as Director of Air Services. This appointment made the role of Director of the Air Department, held by the able Murray Sueter, redundant. He found himself promoted to Commodore, First Class, but his involvement in naval aviation downgraded to Superintendent of Aircraft Construction. Vaughan-Lee quickly expressed the Admiralty's fading enthusiasm for the Home Defence role when he wrote on his first day in office:

> The many accidents resulting in considerable loss of life and material which have occurred to aircraft flying at night in Zeppelin raids raise the question as to whether the results obtained justify the continuation thereof ... At present most of our pilots who have been trained in night flying have gone abroad.'[28]

And what of the weapons these pilots of limited night flying experience had with which to engage the elusive raiding Zeppelins if they managed to find them? Since Reginald Warneford's bombs successfully brought down a Zeppelin in Belgium early in June 1915, this became the recommended tactic. But with the best quality aircraft destined for the Western Front many of those allocated to home defence were slow and lacked the climbing ability to get above their target to deploy their bombs – even if they did manage to locate it in the dark. Besides the Hales bomb, effectively used against the Düsseldorf Zeppelin shed in October 1914, defence aircraft could carry the 3.45-inch incendiary bomb. This device was released through a tube in the aircraft's cockpit floor, where it was ignited by electrical contact strips and came with two three-pointed hooks attached that would, hopefully, catch on to the airship's envelope.[29] The anti-Zeppelin arsenal also included petrol bombs and the fearsome-looking Fiery Grapnel. An RFC officer at Farnborough, L.V.S. Blacker, flying as observer had responsibility for one of these bizarre inventions:

> It consisted of a steel tube nearly five feet long filled with TNT. At one end of this tube were four arms with barbed hooks sharpened to razor edges. Outside it was lashed a portentous piece of pyrotechnics like a roman candle with a friction lighter. This awesome contraption was slung between the wheels of the poor little BE, which weighed less than 600lbs all up. To one end of it was shackled a couple of thousand feet of steel cable, which was wound on a drum located between the observer-gunner's knees. There was also a rope to pull, with which to ignite the friction lighter and detonate the bomb.[30]

Once a pilot caught sight of a Zeppelin his instructions told him to climb 1,000 feet above it and release the grapnel as the two aircraft closed. This action would pull a lanyard igniting the firework as the cable ran out:

> The pilot would then hook the sharp flukes of the grapnel into any suitable part of the airship. At that moment the observer-gunner, if he was not now mesmerized with fright, was to cut the cable with a pair of pliers (supplied by the management). With any luck, the roman candle would then burn down to the detonator of the TNT, which would blow the airship in half, while our little aeroplane might flap away unharmed.[31]

However, the Fiery Grapnel was untested in anger, like all the other devices available in 1915, because no defence aircraft ever managed to locate and climb above a raiding Zeppelin over England. In the case of the handful of pilots allocated the Fiery Grapnel, no doubt they were rather grateful none did.

After this latest raid on London, the cycle of the full moon meant there were no more attempts during August, but with the new moon set for 9 September those in authority had a good idea when to expect the Zeppelins' return if good weather coincided. It did.

8 September 1915, 1.30am: Monk Soham, Suffolk

With a Navy airship having equalled the Army's earlier raid on London, the pendulum now swung back to the Army. On 7 September three Army airships – two Zeppelins and a Schütte–Lanz – set out to resume the attacks on the capital for the first time since their losses of LZ 37 and LZ 38 in June. The two Zeppelins were new: LZ 74 became available in July and LZ 77 in the last week of August. The Schütte–Lanz – SL II – had entered service in May 1914 but a year later she was rebuilt, lengthening her by 39 feet. This increased her hydrogen capacity, and thereby her lifting ability, meaning she could fly higher and carry more bombs, but still less than the Zeppelins that she accompanied.

The first of the raiders, LZ 77, crossed the English coastline at Clacton in Essex at 10.40pm. Her commander, Hptmn Alfred Horn, was over England for the first time and perhaps he had a score to settle. He had been commander of Zeppelin Z IX, destroyed in its shed at Düsseldorf by Reggie Marix in October 1914.[32] He did not, however, find navigation over England easy. After following an erratic course for 95 minutes he reached the village of Hatfield Broad Oak at 12.15am – about 40 miles west of Clacton, with the centre of London lying 25 miles to the south-west. Although London would have been visible to Horn, and indeed there was searchlight activity over the city at the time, LZ 77 turned in the opposite direction, heading north-east into Suffolk and passing between Bury St Edmunds and Stowmarket at 1.05am.[33] Twenty-five minutes later, after almost three hours over England, Horn dropped his first bomb. The incendiary fell in a field on Church Farm in the small village of Monk Soham but was an anticlimax for the crew as it failed to ignite. A little under five miles further east, Horn dropped a second bomb at Framlingham. This HE bomb landed in a wheat stubble field at Pound Farm and, like the incendiary bomb, it failed to explode. The field lay close to a camp of the 1/3rd London Brigade, Royal Field Artillery, whose soldiers quickly formed a guard around the bomb, which had dug itself about three or four feet into the ground; their horses grazed unconcernedly in the field next to where the bomb dropped.

LZ 77 continued on an easterly course and five minutes later dropped her next bomb. This incendiary did ignite. It fell among buildings on the Earl of Cranbrook's Home Farm at Great Glemham, setting fire to farm machinery to the value of £7, this being the only material damage caused during the raid. Just south of Saxmundham, at the village of Benhall, Horn hovered for a while as though checking his position and released three more incendiaries but only two ignited. Two landed on Old Lodge Farm owned by George Bloss, one of these in a field of clover and the other in a wheat stubble field. The third also fell amongst wheat stubble, in a field on Green Farm, owned by T. Howard. Having dropped six bombs of which three had failed, Horn took LZ 77 north up the Suffolk coast before passing out to sea at Lowestoft at 2.20am. Just five minutes earlier a B.E.2c piloted by Flt Sub-Lt C.E. Wood took off from RNAS Yarmouth and patrolled for two hours but saw nothing of the departing raider.[34] Perhaps with recent episodes in mind, Wood jettisoned his bombs at sea before returning.

Horn did not cover himself in glory during his one and only raid over England, but the probing searchlights he must have seen over London around midnight told of a different story – his comrades had reached the city and were making their attacks.

Chapter 14

'An Absolute Feeling of Helplessness'

While Army Zeppelin LZ 77 had meandered ineffectively around Suffolk on the night of 7–8 September 1915, the other two raiders, Schütte–Lanz SL II and Zeppelin LZ 74, approached their mission to attack London with rather more determination. At 10.50pm, SL II crossed the coast at the mouth of the River Crouch and came under rifle fire from soldiers at Holliwell Point. Five minutes later LZ 74 came inland about nine miles further north, near Bradwell-on-Sea at the mouth of the River Blackwater. Both airships headed west on roughly parallel courses.

7 September 1915, 11.55pm: Cheshunt, Hertfordshire

The commander of LZ 74, Hptmn Friedrich George, had endured a difficult crossing as he struggled to gain the required altitude and had found it necessary to jettison his water ballast and 250 litres of fuel to lighten his ship.[1] Once inland he followed his orders to attack London from the north. His route took him past Maldon, Danbury and Chelmsford, which he passed at 11.25pm, then Ongar and North Weald Bassett before reaching Broxbourne in Hertfordshire 30 minutes later (see Map 5).[2] Of his route George reported:

> Only a few lights were visible on the ground and only a pale glow in the direction of the city of London when approaching at an altitude of about 3,200m: all the suburbs over which the airship passed were completely blacked out.[3]

Over Broxbourne, George turned LZ 74 southwards, believing he was actually over north-east London at the time, further south than his actual position. George now dropped a large number of bombs: 'The first bombs were released over Leyton railway station, in order to reduce LZ 74's flying weight rather than because of the interesting nature of the target.' LZ 74 was loaded with 72 bombs (40 HE bombs – 20 each of 58kg and 10kg – and 32 incendiaries).[4] At the point he released his bombs, rather than being over Leyton, he was at Cheshunt, eight or nine miles further north.

The police recorded the fall of 19 HE and 28 incendiaries (one HE failed to detonate) dropping between Windmill Lane in Cheshunt and the Turkey Street neighbourhood of Enfield. The area was renowned for the number of commercial horticultural nurseries. Lying close to the GER line and Theobald's Grove Station, Miles' Nursery and Metcalfe's Nursery were unfortunate in attracting 6 HE bombs and 14 of the incendiaries. Seven more HE bombs fell close by, causing serious damage to eight houses in Windmill Lane, Turner's Hill and Crossbrook Street, with another 36 properties suffering minor damage. The sound of the bombs now attracted the attention of the local anti-aircraft guns.

At 11.55pm a 3-inch gun and a 6-pdr at Waltham Abbey, as well as a 6-pdr at Cheshunt all opened fire, but the searchlight failed to hold LZ 74. Four minutes later a 3-inch gun at Enfield Lock joined in but all opened at a range of 6,000 feet, well below LZ 74, which had now gained height after dropping the bombs. The guns only got off six rounds between them, one of which failed to burst, and the Enfield Lock crew suffered a problem with their gun's breech. By the time they cleared it as the clock approached midnight, LZ 74 was gone, continuing on its journey to London with a reduced load of 21 HE bombs and just four incendiaries.[5]

7 September 1915, 11.35pm: Isle of Dogs, London

As LZ 74 continued south towards London, the city's previously sleeping skies were now alive with sweeping searchlights, gunfire and bombs. While George had made his wide approach to the city, Hptmn Richard von Wobeser, commanding SL II, had followed a more direct route, arriving over Leytonstone before turning south towards the major dock area of the Isle of Dogs. As von Wobeser approached the docks he prepared for action. Flying down the west side of the Isle of Dogs, he dropped eight incendiary bombs along the

'AN ABSOLUTE FEELING OF HELPLESSNESS'

line of the West Ferry Road, which led to and crossed over the gates of Millwall Dock. The bombs fell among the poor quality housing of the dockyard workers.[6]

The first of the incendiaries dropped in the back garden of 10 Havannah Street, digging a hole 18 inches deep but caused no further damage. The next fell on the pavement outside 2 Cheval Street, merely making a small indentation, followed by one that dropped at the back of E. Cracknell's home at 3 Malabar Street. The bomb broke a section of paving in the yard and scorched the corner of an outbuilding. The next struck J. Croker's house and grocery shop at 131 West Ferry Road. It fell through the house from the roof to the ground floor but did not ignite. More incendiaries fell as the unflappable Sergeant G. Hollis, on leave from No.21 Supernumerary Company attached to the 7th (City of London) Battalion, The London Regiment, was walking along West Ferry Road:

> An incendiary bomb was dropped in West Ferry Road about 10 yards east of the 'Tooke Arms' public house [165 West Ferry Road], followed in rapid succession by two more within a hundred yards or so of the first. A bomb dropped on the shop of a baker named Baldwin, in West Ferry Road [G.H. Baldwin, bakers and confectioners, 187 West Ferry Road], setting fire to the premises. I immediately rendered all possible assistance; first by getting the occupants out of the building, and secondly checking the fire until I could get at the bomb. When I reached it I immediately placed it in a bucket of water and removed it to a safe distance from the premises where I left it in the custody of a police constable. I then obtained the assistance of some civilians to help extinguish the fire which was raging in the top parlour and shop. The fire brigade were not available as they were engaged elsewhere. After doing everything possible, I assured the occupier of the shop that the place was safe as far as the shop was concerned.

When the fire brigade attended Baldwin's shop later, it reported that the shop and house of four rooms had suffered damage from 'fire, heat, smoke, water and breakage'. The third of the bombs mentioned by Sgt Hollis landed in the roadway near 195 West Ferry Road, where it made a small hole. The last of the incendiaries to fall along that road struck the premises of G. Robinson & Son Ltd., nut and bolt manufacturers, at No. 223. The bomb smashed through the roof, making a hole six feet by three feet but failed to ignite. So far the population of the Isle of Dogs had got off lightly with no injuries inflicted by any of the incendiary bombs, but that all changed as von Wobeser released his first HE bomb.

The bomb just missed the Millwall Dock gates. Travelling on for just a few yards more, it smashed into a four-roomed house at 9 Gaverick Street. Inside were two families: 32-year-old Sidney Boulton, his wife Anne, aged 29, and their 1-year-old daughter Doris lived in two rooms, with the other two occupied by lodgers, Elizabeth Cox, aged 27, and her two young children, Grace, just over two and 6-month-old William. The bomb demolished the house and those at 8 and 10 on either side. At No. 8, all four of the Bailey family sustained injuries: Thomas, 32, his wife May, aged 29, and sons Thomas (11) and John (7). At No. 10, John Charles Clear, aged 49, escaped from the rubble with just cuts to his legs. All 11 were taken to Poplar Hospital where nine were detained; only Thomas Bailey (senior) and John Clear were discharged that night after treatment. Besides the three demolished houses, Nos. 7 and 11 suffered serious damage and another 11 of the 27 houses in the street suffered smashed roofs, broken ceilings and shattered windows.

Von Wobeser was over the Thames when the last two bombs of this salvo landed. One sunk without trace below the river's murky depths, but the other bomb made its mark. Just south of the entrance to Millwall Dock, three sailing barges were riding at anchor. The *John Evelyn* and the *Louise* were side by side with the *Haste-Away* about 50 yards off. Ernest Frederick Gladwell, the 26-year-old master of the *John Evelyn*, was from Peldon, near Colchester, and knew the master of the *Louise*, Frederick Wright. The two men had spent part of the evening together on Wright's boat before Gladwell returned and joined the Mate, 37-year-old Edward John Bowles, on his own vessel.

An incendiary bomb dropped by SL II smashed with a resounding crash right into the after cabin where Gladwell and Bowles were sleeping. Loud and piercing cries awoke Wright on board the *Louise*, and as he rushed up on deck he saw the horrific sight of Gladwell and Bowles stumbling from their cabin screaming in agony as their clothes burnt fiercely. He managed to get both men on to the *Louise* and doused their burning clothes but it was clear they were both in a bad way. The Master of the *Haste-Away* called a fast motor launch, which arrived alongside the *Louise* ten minutes later and took the men ashore. They received treatment at Poplar Hospital but their injuries were too severe; Gladwell died on 10 September, followed two days later by Bowles.[7]

7 September 1915, 11.40pm: Deptford, London

Having crossed to the south bank of the Thames, von Wobeser now found himself over Deptford. His first two bombs on this side of the river, both incendiaries, landed in parts of the Deptford dockyard. The first fell on a wharf in the Royal Victualling Yard where it only succeeded in setting fire to some old sacks, while the heat generated by the burning bomb damaged four coils of steel hawser. Seconds later the second of these bombs landed in the Foreign Cattle Market, now occupied by the Army Service Corps' No. 1 Reserve Depot. The bomb burst through the skylight of J Shed, where it set fire to 20 wooden cases packed with tea and 12 large salt bags.

The next incendiary hurtled down from SL II towards Hughes Fields in Deptford, described as 'an obscure street ... consisting at that time of poor, rather dilapidated tenements'.[8] No. 34 was like most other houses in the street. It had five rooms, including a tiny attic, and provided a home for seven people, principally the Beechey family plus a friend of the family, 45-year-old Alice Peek. William James Beechey[9] was a 56-year-old coal merchant's crane driver. Married to Elizabeth, aged 49, they had four children living at home: William, 11, Elizabeth ('Lizzie'), 10, Margaret ('Maggie'), seven, and the youngest, Helena ('Nellie') aged three. The sleeping arrangements in the crowded house were that Lizzie shared the tiny attic bedroom with Alice Peek and the other children slept in with their parents. That night Lizzie was a little unsettled before bedtime and asked her mother if she could sleep with her but, as Lizzie later recalled: 'She told me to be a good girl, and then I should sleep with her the next night, but there never was a next night.'

The bomb smashed through the attic, passing through the 30-inch gap between the beds occupied by Lizzie and Alice Peek without harming either of them. Startled awake by the noise, a terrified Lizzie found the attic already full of smoke and ran downstairs:

> When I got down to my mother's bedroom, her room was on fire – I could hear the crackling of the flames inside, and my poor brother and two little sisters inside screaming. How I wish I had been given the strength to save them. Instead, I was paralysed with fright and ran out of the house.
>
> A neighbour picked me up and took me to her house. I was sitting by the window when I heard two people talking. They were saying my parents and brother and sisters were all dead and all lying on the pavement.[10]

The daunting task of identifying the bodies of her family fell to another daughter, 18-year-old Theresa, who then lived in Greenwich. Young Lizzie went to live at a Dr Barnardo's orphanage, later marrying and having three children of her own, but she never forgot the trauma of that night and the loss of her mother. In 1935, thinking of her own children she wrote: 'My silent prayer is that I may rear them and be able to give them all the mother-love I missed, and how I have missed it!'

7 September 1915, 11.45pm: Greenwich, London

Continuing on his easterly course, following the south bank of the Thames, von Wobeser now approached Greenwich. Two incendiaries dropped in Greenwich Road. One fell in the garden of S. Stidolph's house at No. 136 without damage, with the other one setting fire to a timber workshop and store at No. 161 owned by the brewers J. Lovibond & Sons. Another struck the roof of J. Monday's house at 20 Brand Street, causing some damage before falling harmlessly into the garden next door, and a fourth landed in the garden of a house occupied by W. Clark at 58 Royal Hill. SL II now passed over Greenwich Park dropping four or five more incendiary bombs but three failed to ignite. At least one landed close to the Royal Observatory but none caused any damage of note.

Beyond Greenwich Park, von Wobeser began releasing pairs of bombs about every half mile. The first pair fell in the Westcombe Park neighbourhood of Blackheath. An HE bomb exploded in the garden of 'Glenwood', a house in Mycenae Road owned by an eminent High Court judge, Sir Thomas Edward Scrutton. Seconds later an incendiary fell in the garden at 7 Glenluce Road, setting fire to a small patch of C.E. Williams' lawn. The second brace dropped on an open space known as Fossdene Fields in Charlton owned by the Drapers' Company, one of the City of London's ancient livery companies. One, an incendiary, landed near Wyndcliff Road where it burnt a patch of grass, but the HE dug a large crater when it exploded with the concussion from the blast smashing windows in 64 houses nearby.[11] A third pair, both incendiaries, then dropped in Charlton Lane as SL II neared Woolwich. One landed in the roadway but failed to ignite while the other set fire to 10 feet of garden fence at No. 44.

7 September 1915, 11.50pm: Woolwich, London

Another half a mile on and von Wobeser dropped an incendiary that landed in Pett Street, on the outskirts of Woolwich, but appears to have caused little or no damage. About 700 yards on and two more bombs fell in Kingsman Street right in the centre of Woolwich. Kingsman Street ran close to both the Dockyard Station and Dockyard entrance, and about a mile west of the main entrance to Royal Arsenal. One of the bombs, an incendiary, failed to ignite but the other, an HE bomb, exploded in the street, gouging a hole and smashing the gas and water mains. The shock wave from the explosion shattered the windows of 21 properties in Kingsman Street, including those of a public house called 'The Nelson', as well as 13 in Church Street, one in Short Street and four in Sun Street, one of which was the mortuary. Fortunately only three people suffered injuries from the storm of flying glass.

Much to the frustration of the commander of the Woolwich anti-aircraft defences, the first he knew of the imminent danger was when the bomb exploded in Kingsman Street, which he recorded at 11.50pm. A failure of the lights at his headquarters had resulted in a man arriving from the power station at 11.45pm to fix them. This man told the commander that the Arsenal was on standby and on checking this information he became aware of Zeppelin activity reported from the coast 50 minutes earlier. His frustration at the lack of information boiled over into his report:

> In fact had it not been for the accident of the light in my office failing, the first intimation I should have received that there was a Zeppelin nearer than Belgium would have been the dropping of a bomb within a mile of the Arsenal.[12]

The alarm now sounded and almost immediately the commander of a 6-pdr at the Arsenal sighted SL II overhead, held by the searchlight at Blackheath, and opened fire at 11.53pm. The gun fired off three rounds, while a 13-pdr across the Thames at the Royal Albert Dock fired a single shot – all burst short of the target. Observers reported that SL II 'was very high up, travelling very fast in a N.E. direction'. At three minutes past midnight an observer at the north-eastern end of Plumstead Marshes watched as the raider steered towards the east and disappeared from view. Captain Cook, an officer at the Royal Albert Docks, also reported the airship departing towards the north-east.

Interestingly, a report detailing the raid published in February 1918 by the Intelligence Section, General Headquarters, Home Forces, ignores these eyewitness statements regarding SL II heading away to the east. Instead it states that she turned back to the west, flew all the way back to a point south of the Tower of London, whereupon von Wobeser commenced a second bombing run across south-east London. At the same time the report claims that LZ 74, which had been approaching central London after jettisoning bombs over Cheshunt, arrived over the City with only one bomb left.[13] Joseph Morris adopted this summary when he wrote his detailed account of the raids in 1925 and it has been promulgated by every subsequent writer on the subject.[14] But the facts do not add up. No doubt the confusion arose as the two attacks were on the same general area of London. However, taking into account the usual single pass strategy employed by airship commanders over London, the time of the arrival of LZ 74 at the Thames, the recorded times of the bombs and Hptmn George's account of the number of bombs he carried and where he released the second batch, a different story emerges.[15]

8 September 1915, 12.10am: Bermondsey, London

After lightening his ship by dropping 19 HE and 28 of his 32 incendiaries around Cheshunt, George flew on a straight course to the south. He approached the unmistakable line of the Thames shortly after midnight, about ten minutes after the Woolwich guns ceased firing at SL II, but while searchlights continued to sweep the sky. George released a sighting incendiary bomb. It streaked down through the night sky to strike a bonded warehouse at 10 Cooper's Row in the shadow of Fenchurch Street Station, owned by Joseph Barber and Co. It was the first bomb to land in the 'square mile' of the City of London.

Striking the building, the bomb broke off about two feet of concrete before penetrating through several floors of the building, but most of the damage was confined to a back room on the first floor. Across the river now, George's report shows that he thought he could target the Surrey Docks but his first two HE bombs landed close together in Keeton's Road in Bermondsey, just over half a mile away. One landed on a building at No. 113 where S.H. Monk lived and ran his newsagent business. The blast severely damaged the building and No. 115 next door, as well as damaging a gas main in the street. Mrs J. Miller had moved from Sittingbourne in Kent to live with her aunt in Keeton's

Road when her husband went off to war. Shortly after midnight an unusual sound disturbed her, as she explained:

> I knew nothing of air raids, and failed to realize what all the noise was about.
>
> I ran out to see what was the matter, and as I reached the doorway there was a terrific crash: a bomb had fallen within a few yards of me ... bricks and debris were raining down, and as I felt myself falling I heard the screams of women and children.
>
> I remember no more until I 'came to' in Rotherhithe Hospital to which I had been taken with several other injured women.
>
> The thing I most vividly recall was my feeling of surprise at seeing my husband standing beside me – he had come home on 48 hours' leave.[16]

The second bomb in Keeton's Road exploded at the back of Nos. 51 and 53 but damage was limited to a fence, a chicken house, a classroom roof and a lavatory at the school.

8 September 1915, 12.15am: Rotherhithe, London

The line of Ilderton Road, Rotherhithe, ran almost a mile south of Keeton's Road. At No. 181, on the corner of Stockholm Road and just a few steps from the Surrey Canal that fed into the Surrey Docks, this large house of 15 rooms was let out as tenements.[17] The top floor was home to Thomas and Ellen Smith, both aged 35, and their five children. Thomas worked as a labourer at Cotton's Wharf. Dolly (aged 5) and Frederick (8) slept in the front room while the parents slept in an adjoining room. Along a short passage and in another room Minnie (11), Kitty (9) and Elsie (2) all shared a bed. Kitty and little Elsie were inseparable. That evening Mr and Mrs Smith had taken an excited Minnie out to buy a school uniform; she had won a scholarship and was starting a new school the next day. They had only arrived home again at 10.00pm and so as not to disturb her two sisters who were already asleep, Minnie slept right on the edge of the bed. LZ 74's next HE bomb dropped on the house, shaking a very brave young Frederick from his sleep:

> I was awakened by a terrible crash. I pulled Dolly out of bed and pushed her into the arms of my mother and father, who had just opened their door in alarm. As they left their bedroom a wall

> collapsed across the bed. I went dashing along the passage to call the other girls, closely followed by my mother. She pulled up in horror when I – vanished: where there had been a bedroom there was nothing, and I fell through three floors, landing on my feet among the ruins of the house. After what seemed like hours I was carried out by a neighbour, my legs torn and bleeding and my lungs full of gas.[18]

Such was the extent of the casualties at Ilderton Road that Frederick did not even make it on to the official list of those injured. The fire brigade pulled out Mr and Mrs Smith and Dolly from the front window on a fire escape, but there was terrible news to come for the family, as Frederick relates:

> The other three children were buried for hours under eighteen inches of concrete. Rescuers, talking to them, could hear them laughing one minute and saying their prayers the next. When they were finally reached, Elsie ... and Minnie ... were just alive: Kitty ... was dead. Minnie owes her life to her late night, because, being on the edge of the bed, she missed the crushing weight of the concrete that killed her sisters. Poor little Elsie, always with Kitty in life, joined her in death.

However, the deaths at Ilderton Road did not end with Elsie and Kitty Smith. The bomb claimed lives from the families living on the lower floors of the house too. The Scotten and Slade families were related; Eleanor Scotten and Emma Alice Slade were sisters. Eleanor Padbury had married William Scotten in 1886 and now lived at Ilderton Road with two daughters, Maud (22), Ethel (19) and a son, Ernest, aged 12. Emma Alice Padbury married George Slade two years later but he had died in 1907. Emma Slade now lived at the house in Ilderton Road with one of her daughters, Florence, aged 21. A son, Ernest (23), was a POW in Germany and another, 19-year-old Leonard, had joined the army just a month earlier and was stationed a few miles away at Catford. After Leonard joined the army, Emma Slade took in a lodger, 22-year-old Victor Daines, who served as a Special Constable, giving him Leonard's room.

The explosion that killed Elsie and Kitty Smith also killed Maud and fatally injured Ethel Scotten, as well as injuring their brother Ernest and their parents, William and Eleanor. The Slades suffered too. Florence worked as a telephonist/clerk for a book publisher in Fleet Street and was the sole provider for her widowed mother, Emma, but the bomb took her too and put her mother in hospital. Victor Daines also died. The following morning Leonard Slade was on the parade ground with the 11th Royal West Kents when an officer approached the new recruit saying: 'Private Slade, fall out. Here is a pass for you for a fortnight. Go home at once – you're needed.' He did not know what to expect:

> So off I went to Ilderton Road ... to find my home a complete wreck and barriers all round the tumbled-down house. A police inspector said I was trespassing telling me to 'hop it,' but I soon made known that I was the possessor of all this broken furniture, etc. He said, 'Come over the slipper baths; so over goes this full-blown soldier. 'Of course you're used to seeing sights, being a soldier,' he said. 'Will you tell me who this is?'
>
> He unrolled a bath towel in which was just a head of a poor chap who had been doing his bit as a Special Constable. He had slept the previous night in my bed, which was never found again.
>
> I was told my mother was in Guy's [Hospital] but before I could go to see her I had to borrow 5s. [shillings] from the police inspector. From her I learned that the ceiling of the bedroom had fallen on her head ...
>
> Next morning I had to identify three bodies, all of them relations of mine. Later on I came across the inspector, and he asked me for the 5s. but I was unable to pay him.[19]

It is clear that the bomb inflicted great trauma on Victor Daines' body. While the police recovered his head, an army officer reported finding a man's foot in the rubble.

Hptmn George and LZ 74 continued on their trail of destruction, dropping the next HE bomb in Sharratt Street, a turning off Ilderton Road. The bomb damaged No. 47, a house of six rooms let out as flats, leaving Frederick Beadon, aged 34, with a cut head and his 5-year-old son, John, and a woman, Mary Ann Connor, aged 62, both needing treatment for shock. The blast also smashed windows in seven other buildings in the street and those of a house in neighbouring Lovelinch Street. About 500 yards on an HE bomb exploded in the playground of a school at the corner of Monson and Hunsdon roads. The blast severely damaged the playground, smashed windows and damaged the roof, as well as impacting on the front gardens and fences of 38 and 40 Hunsdon Road.

8 September 1915, 12.20am: New Cross, London

George could now see that he was approaching a large railway junction and released another HE bomb over New Cross. It landed on a railway siding just outside New Cross Gate station on the London, Brighton & South Coast Railway, where it damaged about 20 feet of track as well as two railway trucks along with their contents. He may have aimed two more bombs at the railway too, but if he did they overshot a little. Instead one exploded on the roadway in Childeric Road, severely damaging it and shattering the water and gas mains, while the other smashed into a house at 32 Childeric Road, destroying it and severely damaging those at Nos. 30, 30A and 34. All four houses had seven rooms occupied as tenements. In addition, the blast smashed windows in 33 other houses in the street. The house the bomb struck, No. 32, was home to both the Suckling and the Pain families. Louisa Pain, aged 36, lived on the top floor with her three children, Cyril (6), Iris (5) and Winifred aged three. Her husband Cyril was away, serving in the Royal Navy. Louisa, who had been suffering with her nerves, heard the bomb explode on the railway siding and knew it must be an air raid. Moments later another bomb smashed right through her children's bedroom:

> I ran to the next room, where my three children were sleeping, but had only got as far as the door when the house collapsed like a pack of cards, burying us all. I had just been going off to sleep when the bomb exploded, and I felt the stuff loosen around me. I managed to get two of my children out, the boy and the younger girl, but God knows how I did it, for there was not a soul with me; people were afraid.
>
> All at once I seemed to get terrified, and instead of trying to save my other little girl of five I started to scream. Someone came and took the two children from me, who were injured, and I jumped over a wall and fell on someone else's house, where police found me. My little girl was brought out by the firemen at daybreak. I heard that they cried. She was just alive, but unconscious, suffering from concussion.[20]

Although Louisa and her children suffered injuries, they all survived. In the downstairs flat they were not so fortunate. Arthur and Emily Sucking and their 3-year-old daughter Doris all died. A horrified Louisa Pain later recalled: 'The bodies of two, husband and wife, were found on the next-door roof. Their child was shockingly maimed.'

This close concentration of HE bombs near the railway continued when the next one landed in the neighbouring road, Clifton Hill. It detonated on No. 66. The explosion demolished the six-roomed building, killing a married couple, Frederick and Emma Dann, leaving their 16-year-old daughter Janet injured, as well as a 71-year-old woman, Tamar Marchant. We must presume that Tamar's injuries were not serious as she lived to the grand old age of 91. The house next door, at No. 64, owned by E. Winnicott, suffered much damage, as did those at Nos. 68 and 70, which included a grocer's shop owned by A.S. Morris.

Hptmn George dropped just two more HE bombs. The first fell into the yard of a school in Edward Street, where it damaged part of the boundary wall, a toilet, the roof and smashed windows. The school backed on to Angus Street, where the blast also damaged a garden wall and outside toilet at No. 5 and smashed windows at No. 3. The last bomb landed behind Nos. 197 and 199 Edward Street, causing severe damage to the backs of both houses. Lesser damage extended to No. 203 while across the road, the houses at 194, 196 and 198 Edward Street all had windows smashed.

Having released his last bombs over New Cross at around 12.20am, George continued to follow a south-east course until he reached the area between Bromley and Chislehurst about 15 minutes later, where he turned north-east, heading back towards the Thames. At 12.50am LZ 74 neared the river at Purfleet, about seven miles east of Woolwich. The AA defences there, a 3-inch gun and a 'pom-pom', estimated LZ 74 flying at 10,000 feet and travelling at 40mph when they opened fire at her three minutes later. The 3-inch gun fired two rounds and the 'pom-pom' nine before the raider passed out of sight.[21] Without any more interference, LZ 74 continued on a north-east course across Essex and was recorded passing over the coast near Bradwell-on-Sea at 1.38am.

Von Wobeser and SL II, having followed a more northerly course back to the coast, were still overland when George passed out to sea. The report submitted by the crew of LZ 74 mentions sighting their comrades: 'While driving on eastwards they noticed the shape of a Schütte–Lanz and 15 minutes later the men realized the SL II was in the same situation.' Fifteen minutes later puts the time at about 1.55am; at that time British observations placed SL II approaching Walton-on-the-Naze as it neared Harwich, with LZ 74 apparently only six miles away.[22] At 2.10am Von Wobeser passed over Harwich, where the 'pom-pom' at Beacon Hill Fort fired off three rounds and a similar gun across the river at the Landguard Fort joined in, firing off six rounds. Passing over Felixstowe, SL II went out to sea at 2.20am. At the same time, a single B.E.2c took off from RNAS Felixstowe, piloted by Flt Cdr Ralph Hope-Vere, hoping to intercept the two home-bound raiders. Engine failure, however, brought the enterprise to a premature end, compelling the pilot into a forced landing near Trimley, wrecking his aircraft in the process, but Hope-Vere walked away without injury.[23] No other aircraft had attempted to oppose this two-airship raid over London that killed 18, injured 38 and caused damage estimated at £9,616.

However, what the British defences failed to achieve, the German raiders almost managed to inflict upon themselves. It appears that both SL II and LZ 74 lost their bearings on the return flight, with both finding themselves over neutral Holland and at least one appearing over Amsterdam. Coming under fire, they realized their navigational error and turned back towards Belgium. The crew of LZ 74 later discovered two strikes on the metal framework. Having lost one engine due to a mechanical fault, LZ 74 finally reached her home base at Namur just after 10.00am local time. SL II, however, had an even luckier escape. By the time she approached her base at Berchem St Agathe, only one of her four engines was still working and, unable to control the descent, von Wobeser came down outside the base. Terrifyingly for the crew, SL II landed on a house of which the chimney penetrated up inside the wooden framework. At the time there was a fire burning in the hearth but by an extraordinary stroke of good fortune the chimney forced its way up between two of the hydrogen cells and the heat vented away through a gas shaft.[24] After repairs, SL II continued to serve until January 1916 but she never raided England again.

8 September 1915, 9.30pm: Skinningrove, North Yorkshire

With the new moon rising on 9 September and good weather predicted, it was an ideal time for raiding. With two Army airships having reached London the previous evening, Peter Strasser did not intend to let the opportunity pass without striking against the capital with his naval Zeppelins. Accordingly, between 1.00pm and 2.20pm on 8 September, four Zeppelins left their bases in Germany to set a course for England. The older L 9 headed for the north of England while three 'p-class' Zeppelins – L 11, L 13 and L14 – targeted London. Engine problems, however, forced L 11 to turn back after about 30 minutes in the air. Shortly after the four airships had set out, British stations had intercepted the 'only H.V.B. on board' signals. The British authorities knew a raid was on, now the question was where would it strike?

Kptlt Odo Loewe commanded L 9 over England for the second time. He reached the coast near Whitby in North Yorkshire, between Sandsend and Kettleness, at 9.15pm.[25] After coming inland for a couple of miles he turned north, possibly following the railway, towards Hinderwell and Staithes, which he reached about five minutes later. Having circled above Staithes, Loewe steered west, passing over Easington as he scanned the ground below for Skinningrove where the Germans knew there was a large ironworks; they knew because German contractors had helped build it before the war. Just beyond Easington, observers reported that L 9 dropped an incendiary bomb in a field near Ings House, about 30 yards from the road. Later, closer inspection revealed this was in fact a jettisoned petrol tank. At Loftus Bank, Loewe dropped an HE that caused no damage, then over neighbouring Carlin How he released four incendiary bombs. Two landed in Scaifes Field and two in 'Watson's Garden', but none of them caused any damage.

Odo Loewe was now almost on top of Skinningrove but grew frustrated that he could not locate its Benzol plant. Benzol, a by-product of coal tar produced in the ironworks' blast furnaces, was used in the production of explosives. Advance warning of a possible raid had caused the extinguishing of the town's lights, and workers at the rolling mills had fled to seek shelter, much to the frustration of the managing director, T.C. Hutchinson, who lamented his machinery lying idle. Loewe released nine HE and 12 incendiary bombs over the industrial complex. Three of the HE bombs and four of the incendiaries spent their ferocity on smouldering slag heaps; others caused minor damage to a blast furnace. Then an HE bomb exploded on a railway line that ran between two buildings: one used for manufacturing the Benzol and the other for storing TNT.

Loewe could not have found a better target. Fortunately for the town and people of Skinningrove, the explosion only tore up part of the tracks, smashed water pipes, broke electric cables and smashed windows, but had a minimal effect on the buildings either side, with only two or three bricks damaged at the Benzol House. Another HE bomb dropped on the iron fence surrounding the TNT plant, merely damaging the railings, a barbed wire fence and the laboratory windows. It was a lucky escape, but there were more. An incendiary bomb landed directly on the Benzol House, but its concrete roof prevented any damage. In his report to the War Office, the commanding officer of the

Tees and Hartlepools Garrison gave a stark view of the outcome if an HE bomb had made a direct hit:

> If this bomb had hit the Benzol House or tanks (in which latter were stored 45,000 gallons of Benzol) in all probability the greater part if not all, of the Skinningrove Ironworks would have been destroyed.

An incendiary bomb caused minor damage to two railway trucks standing on a siding at the ironworks and damage further afield was listed in a report sent to the Home Office by J. Wright, the Acting Chief Constable at Northallerton. In it he detailed bomb fragments travelling about a quarter of a mile, damaging a door and smashing the windows of a house in Marine Terrace and the windows of the Co-operative Store in New Company Row. The final bombs dropped by L 9 all fell on the beach, three HE and an incendiary striking to the north of the jetty and two incendiaries on the south side. Having dropped his last bombs, Loewe retraced his route and flew out to sea at Sandsend at 9.45pm.

About seven miles away at RNAS Redcar, three aircraft were on standby but the first intimation they received that the enemy was in their midst was the sound of bombs exploding at Skinningrove. Shaken into action, the first aircraft, a Caudron flown by Flt sub-Lt A.J. Jacob, took off and laboured up into the sky, followed at five-minute intervals by Flt sub-Lt Johnston and Sqn Cdr Charles Rathborne, both flying B.E.2cs.[26] Of their search Rathborne wrote: 'The night was so dark that the Airship was not seen by any of the Aeroplanes, visibility being very bad and the atmosphere being rendered hazy in places by Middlesbrough smoke.'[27]

8 September 1915, 8.55pm: East Dereham, Norfolk

Further south, off the coast of Norfolk, other aircraft went up on receipt of the news of an impending raid. The early warning enabled the trawler *Kingfisher*, in position about 40 miles off Great Yarmouth, to launch her Sopwith Schneider seaplane but the pilot, Flt Lt Vincent Nicholl, did not manage to observe the incoming raiders. From RNAS Great Yarmouth, Sqn Cdr Ireland took off in a B.E.2c at 7.45pm, but just eight minutes later he was back, having made an impressive forced landing after a serious engine fault. Flt Lt John Cripps followed into the air five minutes after Ireland and had been searching for the incoming Zeppelins for 70 minutes. Engrossed in his mission or just forgetful,

Cripps failed to pump petrol into the gravity tank, causing his engine to stop when over Caister Marshes, north of Great Yarmouth.[28] Cripps prepared for an extraordinary forced landing, as revealed in the air station's Daily Report:

> Owing to complete darkness and mist on the ground, the pilot could see nothing but blackness underneath him, and as he was afraid of his bombs going off if he hit a house or a wall, he landed in the following manner. When his altimeter showed 100 feet he stepped out onto the planes, still holding his control lever. He held the machine down for about 6 seconds and then jumped off the machine, and fell on his shoulder on some soft mud and was unhurt. The machine landed by itself and sustained very little damage.[29]

At 8.12pm a third pilot, 30-year-old Flt sub-Lt Gerald Hilliard, set out to fly a two-hour patrol between Lowestoft and Cromer, searching for Zeppelins. At the end of his fruitless patrol he prepared to land at Bacton, a satellite landing field for Great Yarmouth, but he misjudged the distance and landed in an adjacent field. As he touched down on the rough ground the undercarriage of his B.E.2c collapsed and the bombs held in a frame under the aircraft exploded, killing Hilliard instantly. While current understanding was that bombs remained safe until they had fallen at least 200 feet, an investigation found that following a heavy impact the neck of the bomb close to the detonator could fracture, causing an explosion. As a result, night-flying pilots at Great Yarmouth received orders not to take bombs with them on patrol until engineers had found a solution.[30]

Hilliard's aircraft exploded at 10.12pm. By then two more Zeppelins were already making their presence felt over the British countryside hoping to reach London.

Two armed trawlers, *Conway* and *Manx Queen*, were cruising out towards the Happisburgh Lightship watching for Zeppelins. L 14, commanded by Kptlt-d-R Alois Böcker, first encountered *Conway*, which fired off eight rounds from her gun, at around 7.20pm, forcing L 14 to climb rapidly and head north. About 15 minutes later L 14 came under fire from the gun on the deck of *Manx Queen*, which fired nine rounds without effect.[31] She neared Cromer at 7.50pm and finally came inland a little further to the west, near Blakeney, 20 minutes later. But it was soon clear to Böcker that engine problems would prevent him reaching London. Instead he selected Norwich as his secondary target, but he never found it. At 8.35pm Böcker had reached Bawdeswell, about

15 miles north-west of Norwich, when he saw a concentration of lights close by. According to a police report, L 14 hovered over Bawdeswell for a few minutes, presumably trying to determine what the lights signified before heading towards them.[32] The lights were shining from a military camp of the 2/1st City of London Yeomanry at Bylaugh Hall, where rows of tents were laid out in the grounds about 400 yards from the main house.

At the sound of the Zeppelin's engines, quick orders ensured the extinguishing of all lights in the camp. Although unsure what he had seen, Böcker felt sure this was a worthwhile target and brought L 14 down a little lower before releasing an HE bomb that struck the ground about 150 yards from the camp and 400 yards from the hall. He then released between 14 and 17 incendiary bombs, which all fell in a neighbouring grass field and merely injured a cow.[33]

Böcker now steered a course that took L 14 to the market town of East Dereham, just over four miles to the south-west, which in his report he claimed was Norwich. Over the centre of the town he released 15 HE and 16 incendiary bombs. At 8.55pm an HE bomb struck the White Lion public house in Church Street, smashing the roof, blowing in the windows and severely injuring two customers, Harry and Sylvia Johnson. In White Lion Yard a house collapsed on Mr and Mrs Taylor but amazingly they were extracted from the rubble with only minor injuries. Elsewhere in Church Street other businesses suffered serious damage too: 'The entire place indeed, was in ruins and the walls of the buildings on the opposite side of the road were as full of holes as a pepperbox.' Lance Corporal Alfred Pomeroy, 2/1st City of London Yeomanry, was in Church Street when the bombs struck. They found his mangled body lying in the street and later discovered his left leg, ripped off by the blast, on the roof of a building next to the Corn Hall. The blast also cut down Harry Patterson, a 44-year-old jeweller. They discovered his body slumped in the entrance to the damaged headquarters office of the 5th (Territorial) Battalion, Norfolk Regiment, on the corner of Church and Quebec streets; a piece of the bomb had pierced the right side of his chest. An incendiary bomb set alight to an oil store at the rear of an ironmonger's shop in Market Place, causing a pall of smoke to hang over the town. The Corn Hall, the most notable commercial building in East Dereham, stood at a corner of Market Place. Although bombs fell all around, the structure of building itself was untouched, although concussion from one of the bombs shattered its impressive glass roof.

'AN ABSOLUTE FEELING OF HELPLESSNESS'

In Market Place a Mr Catton ran out of his house next to the Corn Hall when the bombs began to drop. At the same time a soldier, Private Thomas Frank McDonald of 2/1st City of London Yeomanry, was seeking shelter when an HE bomb struck Catton's house, destroying a large part of the upper storey. Buried under the debris, rescuers eventually dug McDonald out but he died in hospital three days later from a laceration of the brain.[34] The blast also killed 61-year-old James Taylor, a dealer in china and earthenware, who had just gone out to post a letter. They found his body in the street, his abdomen pierced by a fragment of the bomb. A bomb also injured another soldier of the City of London Yeomanry, Private Humphrey Parkinson[35], while Private A.W. Quinton of the 2nd London Mounted Brigade, Field Ambulance, received an injury during the raid while assisting the fire brigade.

Another bomb detonated on the road in St Withburga Lane where, as well as gouging a hole and bringing down a telegraph pole, 'it brought down part of the outbuildings of the Guildhall and played havoc with the roof of the infant's school on the other side of the road'. Seconds later a group of bombs dropped in the grounds of the vicarage off St Withburga Lane, which served as a VAD hospital. They fell near two marquees and a pair of bell tents erected in the grounds. While some patients attempted to smother incendiaries with blankets, the bombs caused much disruption to the hospital's orderly ways:

> As the bombs fell around the Red Cross Hospital the patients ran out and wounded soldiers, clad only in their nightshirts, were dodging the bombs amongst the trees in the Vicarage grounds. Some of them said it was more terrifying than the falling of shells at the front, for they had a chance of retaliating, but in this case there was an absolute feeling of helplessness.[36]

Heading south-west out of East Dereham, L 14 released another nine HE bombs over fields in the parish of Scarning, where they failed to cause any significant damage and where at least one, near Church Farm, failed to detonate. And there was also another rather strange discovery in a meadow at Scarning: a parachute attached to a packet containing 13 copies of various daily German newspapers, a leave pass issued to Bootsmannsmaat Hermann Wolff dated 7 September and a selection of four leaflets. Searchers also found a German naval officer's cap nearby. Although someone, possibly Wolff, deliberately dropped the papers overboard, there is no obvious reason why. Having off-loaded his bombs, and with troublesome engines to contend with, Böcker now turned to the north, towards Fakenham, and eventually crossed back over the north Norfolk coast at around 9.45pm.

An 8-year-old girl, Beryl Norton, lived on her uncle's farm at Scarning and in later years recalled her first trip into East Dereham after the raid:

> Next morning my uncle drove us in his horse and trap to Dereham station. Houses in Dereham had broken tiles and chimneys. Butchers in stripped blue and white aprons, bakers and grocers in white aprons were sweeping up broken glass all through the Market Place. Houses in Church Street had broken roofs and there was an odd smell in the air.[37]

Two of the three Navy Zeppelins that had come inland that night were now on their way back to Germany with disappointing results. Loewe's raid on Skinningrove had failed to strike the important ironworks there and Böcker's aborted attempt on London, which he believed he had redirected against Norwich, had instead struck the quiet market town of East Dereham. However, for the other Zeppelin commander, Heinrich Mathy, a momentous night awaited.

Chapter 15

'A Beautiful but Terrifying Sight'

Heinrich Mathy, the 32-year-old son of a banker, had from an early age shown a desire to join the Imperial Navy, an ambition he fulfilled in 1900 at the age of 17. He did well, serving on two cruisers, then transferring to destroyers before developing a fascination for airships in 1908. From 1912 to 1914 Mathy attended the *Marineakademie* (Imperial Naval Academy) at Kiel where they prepared promising officers for higher command. During term breaks he attended courses run by the Naval Airship Division, including the airship commander's course, making many flights on the L 1 and L 2. When L 1 crashed in September 1913, with the loss of Friedrich Metzing, the head of the fledgling Naval Airship Division, and other senior officers, Mathy thought command might be offered to him, but instead it passed to the more senior Peter Strasser.

In August 1914, at the outbreak of war, Mathy returned to the destroyer fleet but in January 1915 he transferred to the airship division. Strasser held Mathy in very high-esteem and the two developed a close bond. A German–American journalist, Karl von Wiegand, interviewing Mathy in September 1915, described him as 'a slender man … with closely cropped hair, which gives him the appearance of an entirely bald, smooth-faced person'.[1]

So far Mathy's raids had produced mixed results. In January 1915 Strasser gave him overall command of a four-Zeppelin attack on England, but bad weather forced him to abort. In April, when commanding L 9, he had scattered bombs over a wide area of Northumberland and then successfully bombed Hull in June. But when he took command of L 13 in July 1915, his first three forays the following month all turned back early due to problems with the new ship's engines. Inevitably, when he set out again in the early afternoon of 8 September, another failure must have been on his mind, but he need not have worried; this time his engines worked perfectly.

In his interview with Wiegand later that month, Mathy recounted aspects of the journey to England:

> As the sun sank in the west we were still a considerable distance out over the North Sea. Below us it was rapidly getting dark, but it was still light up where we were. One side of another Zeppelin [L 14] in grey war paint, like that of my own craft, was visible in the waning light against the clear sky as it glided majestically through the air. A low, mist-like fog hung over the spot in the distance where England was. The stars came out. It grew colder. We took another pull at our thermos bottles and ate something. As we neared the coast I set the elevating planes to go still higher, in order that our motors should not disclose our presence too soon.
>
> I cannot tell you exactly the time or place at which we crossed the coastline, as that might be of advantage to the enemy.[2]

In fact Mathy first appeared off Burrow Gap on the Norfolk coast near Holkham at 7.35pm. From his movements it seems clear that Mathy had chosen a route to London that started at The Wash. Just over an hour later he was off the coast near King's Lynn, where he finally came inland and picked up the Ouse River and railway south of the town. At 9.00pm L 13 reached Downham Market. From there Mathy seems to have lost his course for a while, following the man-made Old and New Bedford rivers as far as Mepal, west of Ely. Having dropped a parachute flare over the village of Sutton, Mathy regained his original course, passing Cambridge at 9.45pm from where he saw London's 'reflected glow in the sky'. Navigation was easy now. From Royston he followed the line of the old Roman road, Ermine Street (now the A10), to Ware and then, intending to attack London from the north-west, he headed towards Potters Bar, which he reached at 10.28pm.[3] From there he passed over High Barnet, then between Finchley and Mill Hill; the unmistakeable bends of the River Thames lay straight ahead in the distance (see Map 5). As Mathy commented:

> The Thames is an indestructible guidepost and a sure road to the great city. The English can darken London as much as they want, but they can never remove or cover up the Thames, from which we can always get our bearings.

8 September, 10.35pm: Golders Green, London

As he approached the London suburb of Golders Green at about 10.35pm, Mathy released an HE bomb that landed in a field owned by the Express Dairy at College Farm in Finchley. A local resident, Oswald Duchesne, noted that the blast shook the houses in the neighbourhood and, when he visited the crater the following morning, he observed the hole it had left was big enough to hold a horse and cart. Five incendiaries followed, landing harmlessly on fields at Decoy Farm then, as Mathy continued southwards, three more of the fire bombs dropped without effect, one at the corner of Leeside Crescent and Prince's Park Avenue, and two in a thin stretch of woodland through which Leeside Crescent passed. Moments later an incendiary smashed through the roof of an unoccupied house in Highfield Road, followed immediately by another in the back garden of 19 Alba Gardens. The final bomb of this salvo, an HE, exploded in a garden between Alba Gardens and Russell Gardens, the blast smashing a great number of windows in the area. Lightened by about 220kg, Mathy continued towards central London, which now lay only five miles ahead.[4]

Mathy's route brought L 13 in over Euston Station, where he reduced his speed to 37mph and gave the order to the crew to ready the bombs. At that moment, as Mathy recalled, the city's searchlights reached up to locate the raider:

> A large city seen at night from a great height is a fairylike picture. We are too high to see human beings on the streets below. There's no sign of life, except in the distance a moving light, probably from [railway] trains. All seems still. No noise ascends from below that can penetrate the sputtering motors and the whirring propellers.
>
> As if in the twinkling of an eye all this changes. A sudden flash and a narrow band of brilliant light reaches out from below and begins to feel around the sky. A second, third, fourth, and fifth come out, and soon there are more than a score of criss-crossing ribbons.

8 September, 10.45pm: Bloomsbury

At 10.45pm, as the lights found L 13, the 1-pdr 'pom-poms' based at Cannon Street and Gresham Street became the first of the London guns to open fire.[5] Over the next ten minutes many more joined in, as Mathy explained:

Now from below comes an ominous sound that penetrates the noise of the engines. There are little red flashes and short bursts of fire, which stand out prominently against the black background. From north, from south, from right, and from left they appear, and following the flashes there rolls up from below the sound of the guns. It is a beautiful, impressive but fleeting picture as seen from above, and probably no less interesting from below – the greyish dim outline of the Zeppelin gliding through the waving ribbons of light and the shrapnel cloudlets which hang thick about us. But we have no time to admire. Our eyes and minds must be concentrated on our work, for any moment, we may be plunged below, a shapeless mass of wreckage and unrecognisable human bodies.

Despite the excitement of the moment, Mathy's disciplined crew released their first bombs when over Bloomsbury in central London. The first two bombs, both incendiaries, landed at the same time, on the roofs of hotels at Nos. 8 and 22 Upper Bedford Place (now Bedford Way), where they caused some minor damage. A third incendiary landed at the edge of Russell Square, at the junction of Woburn Place and Southampton Row, with little effect. Even as that bomb landed, the first HE bomb was hurtling down. It landed in the central gardens of Queen's Square. As the bomb exploded it damaged a statue and flower pedestal while the blast shattered hundreds of windows in the surrounding buildings, which included hotels and a number of hospitals. Remarkably no one was injured.[6]

Around the corner at the Homeopathic Hospital in Great Ormond Street, John Stuart, an actor who went on to enjoy a long career in the film industry, was drifting off to sleep after undergoing a minor operation when the bomb exploded, waking him with a start. A few seconds later five incendiary bombs rained down on Ormond Yard, a neighbouring street. Now wide awake, Stuart heard 'a screeching, whining sound in the air, followed by a blinding flash', as the first incendiary bomb burst:

> We all lay in our beds waiting with our hearts in our mouths, wondering if another one would fall right on the hospital. I'll never forget those moments. Leaning out of my bed I saw through the window a red glow beneath which was a bright patch of light from which belched smoke and sparks and flames licking high up in the sky.
>
> The shouts and screams of people intermingled with police blowing whistles and the din of fire engine bells, while in the sky shrapnel from our guns was bursting.[7]

In Ormond Yard the bombs fell on a publisher's office, a cabinetmaker's workshop and stables owned by G. Bailey, as well as on homes. H. Hewitt, a 12-year-old schoolboy, lay asleep in bed. As the bombs struck, Hewitt and his family were 'awakened by terrific bangs and screams from neighbours in and around the building'. The sudden awakening left Hewitt with vivid images that stayed with him for the rest of his life:

> Looking through the window we saw flames leaping high into the air from the premises opposite, where a bomb had struck a gas main.
>
> We rushed for our clothes and ran for safety; but to our surprise we couldn't get any further than our landing, which was at the top of the building, for the stairs were absolutely packed with our neighbours. I shall never forget the sight. Some were in their night attire; some were praying.
>
> The guns were roaring and we could see lurid reflections from the fires which the bombs had caused.
>
> After an hour we heard the cry of 'All clear,' and the people began to make a move.
>
> Outside there was a terrible sight all round; the place was crowded with firemen and policemen. A bomb had fallen outside the stables of G. Bailey and Sons, transport contractors, where at least fifty horses were stabled. All of them had to be taken out and tied to posts, etc.[8]

Another incendiary dropped in East Street, at the junction with New North Street, before Mathy dropped his second HE bomb.

8 September, 10.49pm: Holborn

One resident of Ormond Yard who was not at home when the bombs struck was 23-year-old stable hand Henry Alfred Coombes, who lived at No. 26. He was drinking in The Dolphin public house at the corner of Lamb's Conduit Passage and Red Lion Street; it would have been better for him had he stayed at home that evening.

There is some discrepancy between the police and fire brigade reports as to exactly how many bombs fell near the junction of Theobald's Road, Red Lion Street and Lamb's Conduit Passage, as damage extended over a wide area, but it is clear that one HE bomb detonated in the street directly outside The Dolphin. It ripped up a twelve foot by ten foot section of footway, smashing a gas main running underneath and creating a fierce fire. The blast ripped through the National Penny Bank on the corner of Lamb's Conduit Passage and Theobald's Road and demolished the whole front of The Dolphin.[9] Unfortunately that was exactly where Henry Coombes was standing:[10]

> Outside it on Wednesday evening last after the place was closed a man and a woman were talking. The woman went off to buy some supper at a neighbouring shop; the man stood there to wait for her, and while he was waiting there fell at his feet the first of the explosive bombs. It killed the man outright; it blew pieces of paving stone on to the surrounding roofs, it blew in the front of the public house, reducing the stock to a mere mass of broken glass, over which still floats an indefinable odour of assorted forms of alcohol; it took off the top of a grand piano on the floor above, twisted the iron bedsteads, injured a woman who was sleeping there and reduced what had been the carefully kept living rooms of a small family to a mass of soot and dust and plaster and broken glass.[11]

Coombes' body lay buried and crushed beneath the rubble. The woman he was waiting for had gone to Privido's fried fish shop at No. 10 Lamb's Conduit Passage, where an incendiary bomb smashed through the roof setting the oil in the fish fryers alight. An HE bomb that exploded seconds later at No. 7 enabled the fire to spread quickly, endangering numerous lives in the close-packed buildings in this narrow thoroughfare. A schoolboy living nearby, Jack Marriage, had been woken by his mother with the less than comforting words, 'Don't be frighten the germans are here [sic]'. As he quickly got dressed he heard the explosion that killed Henry Coombes. Running outside barefoot, he saw people pointing to the sky and, following their gaze, saw two searchlights illuminating 'a silvery coloured thing in the shape of a cigar'. Having now put his boots on, the boy went with his family to see the small fire burning in East Street, but there were no firemen there. Having been told they were at a bigger fire, they carried on 'to see what this bigger fire was':

> It happened to be the National Penny Bank. The fire soon spread and three shops were alight before the firemen arrived. The flames were terrible and the [heat?] terrific and as soon as one fire was under control another burst out [and] undone all the firemens [sic] work which they worked hard to do … A fireman named Green

saved seventeen people. He went up again but their [sic] were no more people left and he was cut off from retreat. The poor man was at the top of the house. To save himself from being burnt to death he jumped to the ground.[12]

Nine men and seven women suffered injuries in the blaze. Fireman John Samuel Green, aged 30, had already assisted in the rescue of 18 people and was on the ground floor of another burning building when he heard that there were two people trapped on an upper floor. He did not hesitate to go to their rescue:

> Green thereupon ascended the staircase at imminent risk to his life. On reaching the upper floor he was enveloped in an outburst of flame, and being severely burned, he was compelled to throw himself out into the street. His fall was broken by a projecting lamp bracket, and he was not seriously injured by the fall, but the burns he had received proved fatal.[13]

After his fall, willing helpers took Green the short distance to the Homoeopathic Hospital in Great Ormond Street, but he never recovered from his burns and died on 17 September. Huge crowds lined the streets for Fireman Green's funeral procession in a public show of respect, and further recognition of his 'extraordinary bravery' followed with the posthumous award of the London Country Council's silver medal for bravery.[14]

High up above, Mathy and his crew, aboard the 'silvery coloured thing', turned on to an easterly course and continued to release their bombs. The next two landed amongst the solicitors' offices in Bedford Row. One only smashed windows, but the other struck No. 14, home to the offices of solicitors and architects as well as the Holborn Cycling Club. The blast caused serious damage to two floors of the building used by the club as well as damaging the roof of the building next door and that of a solicitor's office at 15 Jockey's Fields, which backed on to Bedford Row. In addition, it broke numerous windows at Raymond Buildings in Gray's Inn, where many barristers had their offices. Another bomb, an incendiary, just missed Raymond Buildings, landing on The Walks on its east side. Mathy followed a zig-zag course to distract the anti-aircraft fire aimed at L 13, with the police reporting the fall of his next two incendiary bombs at the junction of Gray's Inn Road and Little James Street, and near Holborn Town Hall at the junction of Clerkenwell Road and Gray's Inn Road.

The reports of all these bombs inundated the nearest police station, located on the corner of Theobald's Road and Gray's Inn Road. One of the men on duty, PC John Palmer, was a telegraphist and his role was to send this information on to police headquarters. As he continued to tap out the messages, news arrived at the police station that two incendiaries and an HE bomb had fallen on buildings on the Bourne Estate on Portpool Lane, a housing complex of five-storey blocks, built by the London County Council in the early years of the twentieth century. PC Palmer no doubt hesitated for a moment. The incendiaries had landed on Ledham and Redman Buildings, causing severe damage, and an HE had struck Laney's Buildings. Laney's was where PC Palmer lived with his wife and children.[15] In describing the building in *The Times*, a reporter commented: 'These buildings are strong, and the bomb did not penetrate far, you would hardly notice the damage to the roof if you pass it in the street.'[16] Outside the damage may not have been noticeable, but inside it was a different story.

The HE bomb struck the roof of Laney's Buildings. At flat No. 41 the blast damaged the walls and windows but the occupier, 46-year-old dressmaker Minnie Cheeseman, escaped and received hospital treatment for her injuries. The bomb wrecked three rooms at No. 44 occupied by Thomas and Kate Seyers, a couple in their thirties, and their 5-year-old daughter Cissie. All three suffered serious injury in the blast. The devastating explosion shattered four rooms at No. 42, home to the Couldrey family. Both John, 45, and Florrie Couldrey, 40, were severely injured, but worse was to come for the couple – their daughters, Hilda, aged 10, and 6-year-old Dolly both died. And there was one final tragedy too. At No. 58 the bomb spent its force on a bedroom at the rear of the flat. In the room were two children, 6-year-old Edward and his little sister, Winnie, just 6 months old. They were the children of PC Palmer. Palmer's wife, Mary, aged 30, was 'injured by shock', according to the report by the London Fire Brigade, but there was no hope for the two children, they were both dead.

Richard Haven was just leaving the Temple, one of London's four Inns of Court, where he worked, when a loud crash startled him:

> Looking up I saw that impossible London sight – a shell bursting in the air. Then another and another, while people appeared from nowhere and voices began to cry, 'They're here! They're here!' By this time the shafts of the searchlights were busy too, and I began to be aware of a glare in the sky over the city. Meanwhile the bangs and bursting shells went on. 'This is history, if you like,' I said to

myself, and possibly to others, for under the influence of such an outrage every one is one's friend. To think that I should have lived to see shells bursting over London. That is, however, all I could see, although 'There it is! There it is!' men were saying excitedly all round me, until, in Bouverie Street, one of those friendly strangers, whose eyes are always so much better than one's own, pointed out to me the Thing itself – a gleaming silvery grey body, about the size of a torpedo, moving stealthily away due north, far above the highest shell. There was something thrilling in the disdain of its progress; one could not withhold admiration from the commander of such an enterprise.[17]

Also peering incredulously into the sky that night was an American journalist, William G. Shepherd. The raid was in progress when he emerged into the street having enjoyed one of London's thriving shows:

> The curtain goes down. You file out of the theatre into a crowded street. Traffic is at a standstill. A million quiet cries make a subdued roar. Seven million people of the biggest city in the world stand gazing into the sky from the darkened streets …
>
> Among the autumn stars floats a long, gaunt Zeppelin. It is dull yellow – the colour of the harvest moon.
>
> The long fingers of searchlights, reaching up from the roofs of the city, are touching all sides of the death messenger with their white tips. Great booming sounds shake the city. They are Zeppelin bombs – falling – killing – burning.
>
> Lesser noises – of shooting – are nearer at hand, the noise of aerial guns sending shrapnel into the sky.[18]

Now passing over Hatton Garden and Farringdon Road, L 13 dropped incendiaries in St Cross Street and Kirby Street, and others in Farringdon Road. A six-storey building at 61 Farringdon Road suffered greatly when struck by an HE bomb. The building, occupied by the Brass Foundry & Lamp Co. Ltd., and a jewellery manufacturer, West and Price, shook as the bomb destroyed the three upper floors with other damage extending throughout the building. Every premises in the road between Nos. 29 and 79 endured damage to some extent, while tucked away behind No. 61, the drill hall of the 6th Battalion, The City of London Regiment, also suffered.[19]

Having crossed over Farringdon Road, Mathy steered L 13 towards the City. As he passed over the buildings of Smithfield Meat Market he released three incendiary bombs: two struck the roadway in West Smithfield, just south of the market's Central Avenue, while the third smashed through the roof of the Lock and Key public house at 62 West Smithfield, home to the landlady, Alice Jane Freeman, and her family. Hidden below Smithfield Meat Market lay a Great Western Railway (GWR) goods yard, which linked via the Metropolitan Railway with the company's London terminus at Paddington. A group of six GWR men were first to react. Seeing smoke emerging from the top of the pub, they dashed to the scene and forced their way in:

> The men groped their way up a staircase, which was quite dark, until a room with its blazing contents was reached. A large bomb, which had caused the fire, was observed at the foot of a bedstead. Hannon (an ex-soldier, who had seen active service) with great daring seized the missile, plunged it into a bucket of water and so rendered it harmless. The occupants of the house were rescued and tended by members of the staff. In some cases it became necessary to apply 'first aid' treatment, and Foreman Parry, an experienced ambulance worker, rendered the required assistance.[20]

By the time the fire brigade arrived, the fire was practically extinguished. For their prompt actions, the men received a commendation and gratuity from the GWR.[21]

8 September, 10.54pm: Bartholomew Close, London

Even before the GWR men had reached the Lock and Key, Mathy's next bombs were raining down on an open close on the edge of the City of London. The bombs narrowly missed the ancient church of St Bartholomew-the-Great in West Smithfield before incendiaries hit Nos. 23 and 69 Bartholomew Close. Flames quickly took hold. At the same moment an enormous 300kg HE bomb, the largest yet dropped from the air, landed in the close where, surrounded on all sides by tall buildings, the effect of the blast was seismic.

In 1897 a great fire had swept through the area surrounding Jewin Street, just east of Aldersgate Street. This had led to the installation of a number of small, duty fire-boxes, initially manned by a couple of watchmen provided with fire-fighting equipment. One of these stood in Bartholomew Close, but the demands of the war meant just one man, Charles Henley, was on duty that night. Standing at the door of the fire-box, Henley heard the noise of engines in the air and the distant thud of bombs. As he searched the sky, two men emerged from the Admiral Carter public house on the south side of the Close. He shouted across to the men, William Fenge, the landlady's husband, and Frederick Saunders, a transport driver from Bermondsey, asking if they could hear the noise. When they confirmed 'Yes', he replied, 'You had better run then'. But his advice came too late. At that moment the huge bomb crashed down onto an ornamental fountain, which it sliced apart, and ripped up a great section of roadway some 20 feet long by 15 feet wide. It shattered the fire-box and blew Henley off his feet. As the dazed watchman picked himself up he tried to take in the apocalyptic scene that surrounded him: 'I heard children calling "Fireman", from the windows of one of the buildings … I could see fire everywhere in the Close. At one place it was gas alight; in another it was a building on fire… I saw many houses much damaged and wrecked.'[22] Saunders and Fenge lay dead on the ground among the rubble. The force was felt within the Admiral Carter too with the landlady, Amy Maud Fenge, her son, 5-year-old Wilfred and Florence Leigh, aged 22, all suffering injuries that required hospital treatment.

At No. 21, in rooms above the Bartholomew Dairy on the east side of the close, Violet Buckthorpe, a girl aged 13, was being looked after by her grandmother while her parents were at the theatre. On the floor above, her sister Marjorie, just 2 years and 8 months old, was asleep in her cot. As the bomb detonated it shattered the front of the dairy, blew in every window in the building, dislodged bricks, ripped off part of the roof and devastated much of the interior. Terrified as she must have been, Violet's first thought was not to escape but to dash upstairs to rescue her baby sister. She scooped up Marjorie from where she lay covered in fallen plaster in the shattered room, but when she got back to the stairs they were showing signs of collapse. Clutching her sister as tightly as she could, Violet clambered down the rocking stairs, stepping over the gaps where some had fallen away and hanging on to the shaking banister for some support. When she emerged into the street she could find no one to help her so knelt down and prayed until a special constable appeared and took her to the shelter of a doorway. Violet now began to fear that her sister was hurt, so she removed her own dress, wrapped her sister in it and ran to the hospital. The doctors there pronounced Marjorie fit and well but, when asked about her own well-being, Violet told them she was fine. Looking at her bloodied head they thought differently and after examination removed a piece of glass from her ear. For her brave actions the Carnegie Hero Trust Fund added

Violet Buckthorpe's name to their Roll of Honour, and she received an inscribed watch and an educational grant of £30 for her bravery.[23]

High above, Mathy noted the effectiveness of the new bomb, presented to L 13 as a *Liebesgabe* – a love-gift – from the bomb factory:[24] 'The explosive effect of the 300kg bomb must be very great, since a whole cluster of lights vanished in its crater.'[25]

Bartholomew Close was an irregular shaped 'square' with four narrow roads leading in, all considered part of the close. Hardly a building in this whole area remained untouched by the effects of the huge bomb. More than a hundred yards away to the east, windows were smashed in Queen's Square (not the same Queen's Square where an earlier bomb dropped) and to the west the blast also smashed an estimated 1,200 windows at St Bartholomew's Hospital (St Bart's). Further damage occurred all along Little Britain and in Montague Court and Cox's Court, two narrow passageways off it.

A mechanic in the rear engine gondola of L 13, Pitt Klein, recalled his own experiences that night:

> Our bombs rained down; we raced to and fro on a zig-zag course over the capital. Enormous explosions rent the air. Huge columns of flame shot up into the sky. Debris flew. Fires broke out and spread.
>
> As if the city was crying out in pain, searchlight after searchlight sprang into life. In the space of a few seconds, in between carrying out orders, I counted twenty-two of the ghostly batteries of light. Occasionally we would be blinded by their intense beams ... Countless fires painted the sky blood red. The City quarter was lit up as bright as day.[26]

Richard Haven, who had watched Mathy's progress over Holborn from Bouverie Street, remained transfixed by the spectacle until he saw a glow developing over St Paul's. He boarded a bus in Fleet Street and alighted at the cathedral. Between there and the Guildhall he found the source of the glow; a huge fire was burning in Wood Street.

8 September, 10.56pm: Guildhall, London

Having released his 300kg HE bomb, with perfect timing Mathy released a salvo of about 15 incendiary bombs and at least one petrol tank. They landed on buildings in the narrow streets surrounding the Guildhall packed with textile warehouses. The first two set fire to a silk dealer's warehouse at 8 Staining Lane and a haberdashers based at 4 Fitchett's Court, with flames spreading to neighbouring premises. A massive blaze took hold at 84–89 Wood Street, the warehouse of wholesale hosiers Ward, Sturt & Sharp, and quickly spread along the street. An incendiary at 21–22 Silver Street set fire to another warehouse owned by the same company, destroying everything inside and leaving it a blackened shell. This fire spread into Addle Street, where another bomb gutted the warehouse of Glen & Co, woollen merchants and clothiers, and two more started major fires in other buildings in the road. Another bomb caused significant fire damage at three warehouses in Little Love Lane, off Wood Street. Mathy dropped a single HE bomb amongst the incendiaries, which struck an office building at 15–16 Aldermanbury, the blast affecting buildings all down that road. An incendiary also set fire to 60 Aldermanbury, occupied by manufacturing agents Chettle & Kinsey, from where the flames quickly spread to nine other buildings, including the church of St Mary the Virgin.[27] With great fortune for the City of London, L 13 passed just north of the historic Guildhall, before the next incendiary dropped on an office building at 36 Basinghall Street, followed by another in the roadway near the junction with Basinghall Avenue. An HE bomb that hit 61 Coleman Street, close to White's Alley, injured four women at No. 60, who all required hospital treatment. The one that landed next severely damaged the offices of the Provident Clerks' and General Mutual Life Assurance Association at 27–29 Moorgate Street, where two women, Jane Cumming and Emily Cox, both aged 40, required hospital treatment for their injuries.

Having travelled by bus to see the fire, Richard Haven, clearly a man who appreciated a good blaze, was not disappointed:

> I had seen many London fires, but none so fierce and vast as this ... Nor have I seen a fire so beautiful as this; the flames having a peculiar golden quality and raging with a joyousness that added to an excitement that was already almost too intense. One had also the knowledge that the buildings being warehouses in a non-residential district, no lives were in danger.[28]

While watching the fires burn, Haven bumped into a friend and they looked on together for 15 minutes before he set off for home, continuing to admire the fire, but then reality sunk in:

> But it was not until we were coming away ... that I knew how beautiful this fire really was; for then we saw its effect on St Paul's.

> It was indescribably lovely. You know what a snow mountain is like when it flushes at sunrise and sunset? Well St Paul's was like that, only instead of glowing with a gentle steadiness, the light rippled and danced on it. The stone may be said to have burst into flower. I shall never forget it. That will be my St Paul's evermore – a pulsating rose.
>
> I walked home, and then for the first time began to be aware of the other side of these raids. So far I had been among the sightseers and adventure-hunters; I was now conscious of the distress which such visitations can cause. I heard in dark doorways sobs and soothing words; I came on hysterical groups of women, many only partly dressed, and crying children, and all night, it seems, they walked the streets in fear or huddled together under cover.[29]

From Moorgate, and passing within 300 yards of the Bank of England, L 13 now crossed London Wall. Alfred Grosch, a night supervisor at the London Wall telephone exchange, heard the explosion from the HE bomb dropped in Moorgate:

> About 11.00 a fearful crash paralysed everyone, the lights all went out, and the shock caused many thousands of signals to glow on the switchboard. Pandemonium from guns (one was on Salisbury House, across the road) broke out.
>
> I strolled over to the window and looked out. A streak of fire was shooting down straight at me, it seemed, and I stared at it hardly comprehending. The bomb struck the coving of a restaurant a few yards ahead, then fell into London Wall and lay burning in the roadway. I looked up, and at that moment the searchlights caught the Zepp, full and clear, it was a beautiful but terrifying sight.[30]

Mathy dropped six incendiaries in London Wall, just east of the junction with Moorgate Street; three landed in the street and three on Salisbury House from where a searchlight operated, not a gun as Grosch recollected 20 years later. High above, Mathy had noted the gun firing from Tower Bridge then prepared to drop his final bombs:

> Manoeuvring and arriving directly over Liverpool Street Station, I shouted 'Rapid fire' through the [speaking] tube, and bombs rained down. There was a succession of detonations and bursts of fire, and I could see that I had hit well, and apparently done great damage. This has been confirmed by reliable reports we have since received. Flames burst forth in several places in that vicinity.

8 September, 10.58pm: Liverpool Street Station, London

An HE bomb struck London Wall Buildings in Blomfield Street, causing severe damage to No. 4 and lesser damage to the buildings either side. Then Mathy dropped another HE that fell at the junction of Blomfield Street and Liverpool Street. A soldier on leave, Hector Poole, was on a bus heading towards Liverpool Street from the other direction when the bomb exploded with horrifying effect:

> As we neared Liverpool Street Station the first bomb burst in the road, a few hundred yards in front, a direct hit on a bus of the 35A route. With a Special Constable, we rushed to the spot. The driver of the bus was standing in the road gazing at his hand, from which several fingers were missing. He seemed unaware of what had happened, and said, 'I think I've run over someone, mate. Help me get him out.' I looked under the bus and saw a man's head and shoulders. Much of the body had been blown to pieces.
>
> The bomb had apparently entered the bus over the driver's head, travelled through the floor, and burst beneath the platform of the conductor, who had been killed. The passengers were blown towards the front of the bus, shockingly injured and killed. The sole exception was a girl of about nine, who was seated on the remains of the floor and was crying. The lower part of both her legs was missing.[31]

The official records show three men killed on the bus, including 33-year-old Conductor Edward G. Harvey, but the exact number of those injured in the incident is unclear. The blast bored down almost three feet into the roadway, shattering the fronts of business premises down Blomfield Road and Liverpool Street and damaging windows at Broad Street Station. James Hossock, an army surgeon home on leave, was in London that night and had taken his son to the theatre. They were in a taxi approaching Liverpool Street Station when the bomb hit the bus. To Hossock it 'seemed as though the back of the cab were coming in'. The driver screeched to a halt and ran off, leaving Hassock and his 14-year-old son in the taxi:

> My boy and I got out to take shelter, and saw above us the Zepp lit up by searchlights and looking like a gigantic silver fish. The pavements were thick with boxes of chocolates, fish, jewellery, and every conceivable thing from shops whose windows had been blown out: my boy still thinks of the treasures he could have collected![32]

Sun Street Passage, a narrow thoroughfare passing between Broad Street and Liverpool Street stations, suffered the next bomb. The detonation ripped up a large section of roadway and damaged a railway arch by Pindar Street, used as a stables and store. A storm of flying metal bomb fragments and splintered wood flew down the passage, cutting down Thomas Minke, a 34-year-old policeman seeking shelter there. At St Bart's Hospital, itself recovering from damage caused by the Bartholomew Close bomb, doctors removed a bomb fragment from a 3-inch wound in his groin area, but infection took hold and he eventually died three weeks later.[33]

Meanwhile a No. 8 bus, driven by Frank Kreppel, was making its way from the East End to the City along Bethnal Green Road. Sitting on the top deck, Florence Williams was on her way home from work. As the bus approached the junction with Shoreditch High Street, Florence heard a loud bang and screams: 'Looking up at the sky, I saw the searchlights all meet upon a Zeppelin.' Another passenger on the bus, H.W. Player, saw the Zeppelin almost above them: 'As we got to the junction of these two roads the searchlight picked up a Zeppelin, and a beautiful sight it made. The driver of the bus opened out, towards the City, to get from under it and we had got as far as the old GER electric light station when a bomb fell.' The electricity generating station occupied premises at 233 Shoreditch High Street, at its junction with Norton Folgate and Worship Street. Initially the sight of the Zeppelin had held Florence spellbound, but as the bus turned into Shoreditch High Street and headed towards Norton Folgate she became frightened and began to cry. A woman on the seat opposite tried to comfort her and pulled her close:

> Something seemed to tell me to try to get off the bus, and I broke away from her, though she made a grab at me to pull me back. At that moment the bus stopped with a jerk and something dropped. There was an explosion and a blinding flash like lightning. The poor woman fell back with a terrible scream. I heard afterwards that she was dead.[34]

Having automatically covered her eyes with her hands, Florence stumbled to the back of the bus then experienced a sensation of falling. She fleetingly thought, 'is this death?', and wondered if she would go to heaven or hell. But Florence had fallen down the stairs at the back of the bus, her fall broken by a man on the bottom step, and together they landed sprawled in the roadway. Florence, shocked and dazed, crawled across the debris-sprawled road to the pavement, drawn by a red light marking a nightwatchman's hut. Peeping out, a scared old man saw her and pulled her inside. The nightwatchman settled her down, put his arm around her as her tears flowed, telling her 'not to cry, as the Germans up there would hear me'. Only then did Florence realize she was in pain. Later, doctors at the London Hospital discovered she was 'peppered with shrapnel'. They removed what they could but some remained to give her pain for the rest of her life.

The passenger inside the bus, H.W. Player, briefly knocked unconscious by the blast, had faint memories of being inside a burning bus and stumbling over a prostrate body on the floor. He next remembered hobbling along the road until two men sheltering in a shop doorway came to his assistance, taking him to a doctor in Spital Square, where it seemed he had entered a war zone:

> Inside the doctor's house the scene was terrible – wounded people lying all over the place. I was, of course, still dazed, but recollect the blood ... I had cuts over my hands and face. How long I had been in or about the bus after being hit, I cannot say, but I had nearly bled to death.[35]

This loss of blood flowed from six wounds in his left thigh. In one instance a bomb fragment had passed straight through. Taken to the London Hospital, Mr Player remained a patient there for three months.

Initial reports stated that the bomb killed six people on the bus and injured 12, but later the death toll increased to nine. Among them was the bus driver Frank Kreppel. Both his legs were shattered, which resulted in their amputation, but he died soon after.

All around the spot where the bomb exploded was chaos. The railway lighting station, workshops and stores suffered damage, and the force of the blast ripped up a large section of pavement, exposing broken electric cables and a smashed water main. Having bored down through the paving, the bomb also caused minor damage to railway tracks passing below. More than 40 premises in Shoreditch High Street suffered damaged to a greater or lesser degree, while 32 properties in Norton Folgate and 13 in Bishopsgate had their windows smashed.

Mathy had finished with London now and L 13 headed north prior to beginning the long journey back to Germany. He had held L 13's height at about 8,500 feet during the raid but, as they approached Edmonton, a shell fired from the gun on Parliament Hill burst so close to L 13 that she dumped a great cloud of water ballast and climbed immediately up to 11,500 feet. It was perhaps the only shot that really threatened her during the raid; an exasperated message sent from central control a few minutes earlier summed up the gun's performance that night: 'All firing too low. All shells bursting underneath. All bursting short.' The GHQ Intelligence Section's report succinctly summed up the defensive fire that night when it wrote: 'Ideas both as to the height and size of the airship appear to have been somewhat wild.'[36]

The American journalist, William G. Shepherd, who had emerged from the theatre with the raid in full swing stared skywards with countless others as that shell burst close to L 13:

> 'We've got it! It can't get away! There's shrapnel all around it!'
>
> 'Oh – my neck!' says a pretty girl in evening wraps. 'I can't look up a minute more!'
>
> But she does.
>
> All about you are beautifully garbed women and men in evening clothes. 'Oh's and Ah's!' long drawn out – exclamations of admiration like the sounds made by American crowds watching fireworks – greet the brilliantly white flashes of shrapnel …
>
> There are more cries.
>
> 'Good God! It's staggering!' as a shrapnel flash breaks, apparently near the great airship.
>
> But the Zeppelin moves on steadily.[37]

Mathy reached the coast of East Anglia between Great Yarmouth and Caister shortly before 2.00am and eventually arrived safely back at the airship base at Hage after a mission lasting 19 hours. Two weeks after the raid, the *New York World* published Karl Wiegand's interview with Heinrich Mathy. Reprinted in numerous newspapers, for the first time the British public knew the name of a Zeppelin commander responsible for bringing death and destruction to their streets.

Back in London, Shepherd reflected on how the war had changed those people around him:

> What a roar of joy would go up from the millions of this great city if they could suddenly see the yellow object transformed into the flash of one gigantic gas explosion … These men and women, flowers of the twentieth century culture, have become elemental … Killing has been put into the hearts of these crowds. If the men up

there in the sky think they are terrifying London they are wrong. They are only making England white-hot mad.

We are all brothers and sisters in the streets of London to-night – neither man nor woman, neither good nor bad – just human, outraged, mad, unwilling to die. This is a miracle the great gas bag in the air brings about.[38]

Mathy's passage over central London lasted no more than 15 minutes. Counting the casualties, the authorities revealed that the raid on the capital had cost the lives of 22 and left 87 people – men, women and children – bearing cruel injuries. Besides these losses, the London Fire Brigade estimated the capital suffered material damage to the value of £530,787, the greatest total of any single air raid on Britain throughout the war. 'Miracle' or not, after two raids on consecutive nights, with little or no effective response, those 'outraged' Londoners that Shepherd wrote about now began vociferously to demand action.

Chapter 16

'What Are You Going to do About These Airship Raids?'

September 1915: London

When Heinrich Mathy directed his Zeppelin across central London on the night of 8–9 September, he noted the threat of London's guns, as he revealed in his subsequent interview with Karl Wiegand. The experience left Mathy contemplating the dangers over London. He reported back: 'Within the range of the ... guns of London an airship can remain only a short time with a clear sky, in my opinion. Therefore in clear weather it will hardly be possible to aim at individual targets.'[1] One of Mathy's crew, Pitt Klein, also looked on apprehensively at the fire aimed at them, but admired its intensity:

> Shrapnel and shells howled and hissed up all around us; blast after blast rocked our ship; the accursed searchlight batteries held us fast. If we hadn't been up to our necks in it, we couldn't fail to have been impressed by this deadly firework display.[2]

Clearly, to a member of any Zeppelin crew flying over a city such as London, suspended beneath a million cubic feet of inflammable hydrogen, the fire of the anti-aircraft guns deserved respect. To them, each flash of gunfire could spell death, but they were unaware of the quality of the guns firing at them and many of the rounds in fact had no chance of reaching their target.

That night all of London's 26 guns had opened fire, sending a total of 299 rounds arching up towards L 13, but of those, 118 were fired by

1-pdr 'pom-poms' with the target well beyond their reach. In addition, eight of the guns that engaged were outside the main London area, part of the Woolwich AA gun sub-command, and their shells fell short of the target.[3] And this was another problem. Parts of shells fired by the AA guns landed in Bethnal Green, Stepney, Canning Town, East Ham, Poplar, Mile End, Dalston, Holloway, Highbury, Kentish Town, Highgate and Lambeth, damaging houses and resulting in minor injuries to two women and two children.[4]

While the effectiveness of the guns had been poor, not one aircraft took off to defend London that night. On the following morning large crowds of ordinary Londoners flocked to marvel at the damage inflicted on their city. In their hushed conversations one word was repeated – murder – an accusation echoed in the popular press. In the *Daily Mirror*, under the heading 'What We Realize Now', came a virulent response to the latest raids:

> For two nights in succession the enemy has been spreading death and destruction upon peaceful homes in or round about London and its neighbouring country. Suddenly from out of the sky the German has cast death in just as callous a spirit as ever common murderer slew his victim.[5]

The article went on to call for a 'great and lasting protest', but not a demand for revenge, instead 'a solemn outcry from the civilized peoples against the betrayal of all laws of honour, liberty and right by a renegade nation'. It concluded: 'There will be national peace, but there can never be domestic peace with the Germans for many generations. We cannot deal with murderers and infanticides.' While from the pulpit of St Paul's Cathedral, on the Sunday after this most recent raid, the Archdeacon of London, Ernest Holmes, began his sermon: 'I need not go further back than last Wednesday to tell you that battle has changed into murder.'[6]

Also on that day, in an article in the *Sunday Pictorial*, the editor of the staunchly patriotic *John Bull* magazine turned his influential voice to the question of the guns:

> And what about these Zeppelins? Can't we really hit them? Who was the Minister who said in the House of Commons some months ago that they could 'be sure of a warm welcome'? Was he wrong?'[7]

It was a question asked in the War Office and the Admiralty too.

Following the poor defensive showing after the first September raid on London, 'public feeling, already stirring from its lethargy, was instantaneous, for petitions and protests were set foot in all directions the next morning'.[8] With the second raid the following night, those same petitions and protests were ready for immediate use. On 9 September, 'citizens of all classes, from the Lord Mayor downwards, took steps to insure their participation in the general demonstration of dissatisfaction'.[9] As a military man observed:

> Such was the unanimity with which this course was adopted that the Government, in vulgar parlance, 'got the wind up' and 'got a move on' at once, which under other circumstances it would probably have taken them still many months to initiate.[10]

First to move was Lord Kitchener, the Secretary of State for War. On the morning after the second raid he summoned Major-General David Henderson, Director-General of Military Aeronautics and commander of the RFC, to the War Office. Kitchener peremptorily demanded: 'What are you going to do about these airship raids?' Somewhat taken aback, Henderson, pointed out that aerial defence was not the responsibility of the RFC, reminding him it lay with the Admiralty and the RNAS. Unmoved by his answer, Kitchener informed him, in no uncertain terms: 'If there are any more Zeppelin raids and the Royal Flying Corps do not interfere with them, I shall hold you responsible.'[11]

Later that same day, on Henderson's orders, a B.E.2c landed at Writtle, near Chelmsford, and another at Joyce Green, near Dartford, as the RFC prepared to take a more active role in London's defence. In addition, parties were dispatched to identify suitable sites to the east of London for the establishment of new airfields for the defence of the capital. Meanwhile, in the face of significant criticism, the Admiralty also wasted no time in making changes. It was not before time.

After a long and distinguished career in the Royal Navy, Admiral Sir Percy Scott officially retired in 1913 after 47 years' service. During this time he had specialized in gunnery, displaying an inventive genius and capacity for improvisation on numerous occasions, perhaps most famously during the Anglo–Boer War of 1899–1902. After retirement, the Admiralty retained the services of the outspoken admiral in an advisory role, but after he levelled serious criticism at the Admiralty's lack of preparedness in the face of the growing threat of submarines, this employment terminated on 30 December 1913. Six months later he again raised the subject in a letter to *The Times,* finding himself on the receiving end of a backlash from senior naval figures who were yet to grasp the impact submarines would have in the coming war. Despite offering his services to the Admiralty when war broke out in August 1914, it was only after the appointment of Lord Fisher as First Sea Lord in October 1914, that Winston Churchill, in his position as First Lord of the Admiralty, employed Scott as an adviser on gunnery efficiency and anti-submarine measures. Under these two powerful men, Scott's ideas made some progress, but when they both resigned in 1915 following the disastrous Gallipoli campaign, Scott lost much of his influence. He was therefore surprised when, two days after the Zeppelin raid on central London, a letter arrived from Arthur Balfour, Churchill's replacement, asking him to take over responsibility for London's gunnery defence. Sir Percy Scott accepted with alacrity.[12]

The appointment was well-received. In Parliament one MP, Sir Henry Dalziel, welcomed it 'with the greatest satisfaction', before raising pressing concerns regarding London's defence. In reply, Balfour explained that the defences were still in the process of development, but added that he believed it possible, within a reasonable time, to provide London with an adequate defence. He felt able to give this reassurance, 'in no small degree because I have a great belief in the organizing capacity and the energy and resource, the openness to new ideas, which has always characterized the distinguished Admiral who now has the defence of London immediately under his control'.[13] That 'energy and resource' immediately came to the fore.

On 11 September, Balfour met with Scott and introduced him to Alfred Rawlinson. Rawlinson had returned to England in May 1915 after suffering a wound on the Western Front while serving on the staff of IV Corps, commanded by his brother, Sir Henry Rawlinson. While in France, with the rank of colonel, Alfred Rawlinson had become involved in the aerial defence of Paris. Back in England, in June 1915, he received an appointment as Lt Cdr in the Royal Naval Volunteer Reserve (RNVR) to raise and train a squadron of armoured cars. Two months later, Rawlinson was flattered to receive a summons from the then Air Defence Commander, Murray Sueter, to advise on improving the effectiveness of London's guns and ammunition. Sueter no longer held that role, so Rawlinson now explained the inefficiency of the London guns to Balfour and Scott and discussed the arrangements in the French capital, which relied heavily on the excellent 75mm quick-firing guns that could fire a timed high-explosive shell up to a height of 14,000 feet.[14] When introduced in 1898 the gun was the first to feature a hydro-pneumatic recoil, making it the forerunner in modern artillery design.

> I was able to furnish exact particulars as to the Paris defences and as to the guns and ammunition there employed. It was then suggested that the First Lord should authorize me to proceed to Paris, and to endeavour to obtain immediately from General Gallieni, the Minister of War (whom I knew very well), samples of the most efficient anti-aircraft gun and ammunition then existing in the Paris defences.[15]

By bringing back an example of the mobile 75mm auto-cannon variant Scott hoped that engineers could produce a copy or perhaps improve on the French design. All agreed that it was important to action this as soon as possible and Balfour agreed to write an official request letter for Rawlinson to take to France.

Scott and Rawlinson hit it off at once. While awaiting Balfour's letter, Scott conducted an inventory of the London guns. Excluding those assigned to the Woolwich area, Scott recognized there were 18 protecting London, but dismissed the idea of the 1-pdr 'pom-poms' playing an effective role, which reduced this number to just 12 guns. From Rawlinson he knew that at the same time 127 guns defended Paris, with 80 more in the pipeline. While Scott and Rawlinson busied themselves devising improved ammunition for their British guns, which currently lacked a time-fuse capable of detonating a high-explosive shell, and pressing both the Navy and Army for more artillery, there was still no sign of Balfour's letter.

When Rawlinson drove to Scott's house on the morning of 16 September, the Admiral – a sworn enemy of red tape – had had enough. He immediately wrote a letter himself and handed it to Rawlinson, who set off for Folkestone at once, without even bothering to collect a change of clothes. Scott wired ahead to arrange for the passage of Rawlinson and his car to Boulogne and by that evening he had arrived in Paris. Using all his high-ranking contacts, Rawlinson secured a brand new mobile 75mm gun, had it tested, brought back to Boulogne, shipped to Britain and driven to London all within four days. As Scott put it: 'Owing to the promptitude of Commander Rawlinson, we had this gun on Horse Guard's Parade, under Mr. Balfour's window, before the official letter asking for it was written.'[16]

With the gun safely in London, Rawlinson selected a crew from those forming the armoured car squadron he had been training and set them to work to familiarize themselves with the new weapon. It was to form the nucleus of a Royal Navy Anti-Aircraft Mobile Brigade, initially based in West London, at the Talbot Car Works in Barlby Road, between Wormwood Scrubs and Ladbroke Grove.

11 September 1915, 11.50pm: Thornwood, Essex

The same day that Balfour, Scott and Rawlinson held their first meeting, Zeppelins returned. In keeping with the recent tit-for-tat nature of the raids, this time it was an Army Zeppelin, LZ 77, that appeared over England. Four days earlier, Hptmn Alfred Horn had brought LZ 77 inland and raided ineffectively across Essex and Suffolk; this latest attempt followed a similar course and resulted in a similar outcome.

With the defences on their toes after the two recent incursions over London, contradictory and confusing reports reached the Admiralty about the number of Zeppelins approaching the coast. In reality only one Zeppelin, LZ 77, offered a threat (see Map 6).

Flying low, at 3,500 feet, Hptmn Horn crossed the Essex coast less than a mile south of the Tillingham coastguard station, from where sentries manning a lookout post opened rifle fire, an action taken up by others on similar duty at Holliwell Point. LZ 77 climbed to 5,000 feet and passed south of Southminster, from where a 1-pdr fired off eight rounds. As LZ 77 neared Maldon at 11.20pm, observers reported a change of course to the south-west; it appeared she was heading for London.[17] At 11.37pm London received notification of an imminent raid. The GER halted all trains arriving in or leaving London to prevent their lights serving as a guide. In London, soldiers stood to and special constables reported for duty, while the munitions factories at Woolwich extinguished their lights for just over two hours, and for an hour at the gunpowder factories at Waltham Abbey and Faversham, bringing production to a halt.[18] Hptmn Horn, however, did not reach the capital.

Horn, who had struggled with navigation on his previous raid, now encountered fog over Essex, making his task even harder. From Ingatestone, LZ 77 headed westwards, passing south of both Chipping Ongar and North Weald Bassett, before reaching Thornwood, situated just to the north of Epping and some 18 miles north-east of central London. Down below, through the fog, something out of the ordinary attracted Horn's attention, prompting him to drop parachute flares. They revealed a large tented encampment. Circling around to the

237

east, LZ 77 passed over North Weald Bassett then back over Wintry Wood where, at 11.50pm, Horn began dropping eight HE bombs and 52 incendiaries. The camp, which stretched from Wintry Park Farm to Hayles Farm, was the temporary home of the Army's 2nd South Midland Division. Although four of the eight HE bombs landed within the camp lines of the 2/3rd (South Midland) Field Artillery Brigade, with incredible good fortune for the artillerymen, not one of them detonated. In fact none of the HE bombs detonated and an inspection later determined that this was due 'to their safety appliances not having been withdrawn'. Although a great number of incendiaries also dropped, they missed the artillery encampment completely, adding further to the good fortune of those below, as within the confines of the camp the artillery brigade had stored their entire ammunition supply. The only recorded damage happened when an incendiary bomb set fire to a mess tent in the camp of the 2nd Gloucester and Worcester Brigade.[19]

Having released his bombs, Horn began his homeward journey on a north-east course, taking him far to the north of the usual Army Zeppelin route across Essex. He passed Bury St Edmunds around 1.00am and, about 40 minutes later, the sound of his engines reached those in fog-shrouded Norwich. The coastguard station at Caister, north of Great Yarmouth, heard engine noise passing out over the coast at 2.05am. At that hour in September, however, Horn realized that if he encountered any delays on his return to his home base in Belgium, the sun would be rising before he reached safety. With the raw memories of the fate of LZ 37 caught in similar circumstances over Ghent three months earlier, Horn looked around for an alternative and secured a spare berth for LZ 77 at the Hage naval Zeppelin base on the German coast. Back in London meanwhile, with no sign of any threat to the capital materialising, the order for the troops and special constables to stand down finally came through at 2.50am.

The fog also made life difficult for the aircraft allocated to the defence of London that night. Two Caudron G.3s only took off from RNAS Chelmsford when LZ 77 was already approaching Norwich on her way home and, no doubt with some relief on the part of Henderson following his fiery meeting with Lord Kitchener two days earlier, the RFC's B.E.2c based at Writtle also took to the air. The pilot, Lt Morison, patrolled for an hour but saw nothing of LZ 77. When he landed, he reported despondently that unless searchlights illuminated raiding Zeppelins, a pilot could only find them by pure chance.[20]

12 September 1915, 11.30pm: Dedham, Essex–Suffolk border

That evening, 12 September, while Horn and his crew carried out the numerous necessary routine checks on LZ 77 in preparation for her journey from Hage back to Belgium, the Army launched another solo Zeppelin raid, this time sending Hptmn Friedrich George and LZ 74 to attack London. As on the previous night, fog over the south-east hindered the raid (see Map 6).

The British authorities received a report of a Zeppelin passing out to sea over Nieuport in Belgium at 7.50pm, but at that point no one had any idea where it was heading. It was just before 10.30pm, when a Zeppelin passed over the Kentish Knock Lightship anchored north of Margate, that observers could report she was heading towards the Essex coast. She came inland at about 10.50pm, between Walton-on-the-Naze and Frinton-on-Sea, appearing to follow the railway line westwards to Wivenhoe and then Colchester, which she passed over at 11.08pm.[21] London, alerted now to a possible raid, issued orders to halt train traffic in and out of the capital. From Colchester, where the railway turns south-west towards London, LZ 74 appears to have lost the line in the fog and proceeded to the north-west, dropping two HE bombs in a field at Wormingford at 11.05pm, followed by another at Mount Bures about a mile and a half further on. All three failed to cause any damage other than digging craters in the soil.

At Mount Bures, George appears to have picked up railway tracks again, turning south and following them to the village of Wakes Colne, over which he arrived at 11.15pm. At this point his manoeuvring appears to confirm George was experiencing navigation problems because he then steered to the east. Passing Boxted and entering Suffolk, he then turned to the north-west at Dedham, from where a RNAS mobile maxim gun on Gun Hill opened fire, followed by another positioned near the church at Stratford St Mary.[22] The gun on Gun Hill was actually travelling along the road when two special constables stopped it and informed the nonplussed commander, sub-Lt. Guy Pollock, RNVR, that the Zeppelin was directly overhead: 'It was difficult to accept this astounding information, as we could hear nothing and see nothing … However, I pulled up in a suitable position and prepared for action with the redoubtable Maxim gun.' Pollock then grabbed the crew's Martini–Henry rifle, a weapon he described as being 'of respectable ancestry … firing a luminous – and perhaps incendiary – bullet with a maximum range of five hundred yards':

> Eventually I fired a shot with this in the supposed direction of the Zeppelin alleged to be hovering over us, in the hope of showing it up. But my direction was wrong.
>
> 'No, you fool!' said the special constable standing by my side. 'Too much to the right!'
>
> I fired again.
>
> 'You blanked and blithering idiot!' murmured the special constable. 'Too much to the left!'
>
> Meanwhile the gun crew had no target, and our supposed airship was still silent and invisible.
>
> So, 'Look here,' I said, 'suppose you take a shot.' And he did so. And in the light of this wretched bullet, which looked like a miniature star shell, burst and all, the Zeppelin became instantly visible, a sharply defined black pencil straight above our heads in a clear and starlit sky.
>
> So we let go. We loosed two belts of maxim ammunition into her, – she was so low and so good a target that it would be no surprise to find that her envelope was holed by a few stray bullets, – and I snatched back the honorable Martini–Henry to have some private but ineffectual rifle practice of my own.[23]

Flying at a height between 5,000 and 6,000 feet, observers on the ground considered LZ 74 'at no very great height, and presented a splendid mark'. Even so, the maxims made no real impact on her as she twisted around to the east as though searching for the guns. Watching her movements, Pollock realized his actions had stirred the Zeppelin into action as: '… our bird woke up and her engines roared, and a shower of bombs dropped all around and about the village of Stratford St Mary, lying just below us.' The time was now about 11.30pm. The bombs, five incendiaries and 11 HE, all landed on fields at Hills Farm. Although the Suffolk Police painstakingly recorded three of the HE bombs exploding 15, 25 and 70 yards from houses, the only damage they recorded was smashed glass in a greenhouse and a skylight, plus some broken fences and telegraph wires. Continuing eastward, LZ 74 dropped eight more bombs at East Bergholt, the four HE and four incendiary bombs all landing harmlessly in fields.[24]

George now resumed a north-east course, which took him over Ipswich, but presumably the fog shrouded the town as he dropped no bombs there. At 11.45pm, however, over Rushmere on the eastern side of the town, another RNAS mobile maxim gun car opened an optimistic fire on LZ 74. She retaliated by dropping four HE bombs, which landed near St Andrew's Church and at 'no great distance from the car'. One failed to detonate but, although the others exploded, they caused no damage.

Adopting a defensive zig-zag course, George continued towards the north-east, passing Woodbridge at 11.50pm from where another RNAS mobile maxim gun lay in wait.[25] This time however the crew was unable to locate the target, although one of the men armed with a Martini–Henry rifle defiantly fired off a few of the old incendiary rounds that back in May the War Office had informed the RFC were 'useless against Zeppelins'.[26] Continuing on the same course, LZ 74 approached the coast at Aldeburgh at 12.05am, from where the crew of a fifth mobile maxim car reported her 'rather high, but distinctly seen' and opened fire. Untroubled by this, LZ 74, however, was now experiencing engine problems and George ordered them switched off as she drifted northwards along the coast for a short while. Having corrected the problem, LZ 74 eventually left the coast between Southwold and Sizewell at 12.18am and safely reached Belgium.

As well as the gunfire LZ 74 encountered over Essex and Suffolk, one home defence aircraft managed to get airborne following the initial report of a Zeppelin passing over the Kentish Knock. Armed with this minimal information, a B.E.2c flown by Flt sub-Lt F.T. Digby rose from RNAS Eastchurch on the Isle of Sheppey in Kent, to patrol an empty sky for a little over an hour.[27] Once in the air, pilots had no radios so were unable to receive new information. While Digby completed his fruitless patrol, LZ 74 was operating about 40 miles away to the north. Although untroubled that night, LZ 74's career was nearing its end. Just over three weeks later, on 8 October 1915, she crashed into a foggy hillside in the forested Eifel region between Germany and Belgium. The crew survived this hair-raising experience but extensive damage resulted in the scrapping of their airship.

13 September 1915, 5.40pm: Margate, Kent

In the meantime, however, raiding continued. The ever-opportunistic seaplane flyers of *See Flieger Abteilung 1* saw a chance on the afternoon of 13 September and grabbed it, sending a single, unidentified aircraft, across the sea from the Belgian coast to Kent in a typical raid (see Map 2). The town of Margate received no warning of danger and so, when the aircraft approached at high speed at 5.40pm, many out enjoying a late afternoon walk looked up admiringly, presuming the 'bright speck hovering high in the sky on a sunny, cloudless day' to be British.[28] Only when the first two bombs exploded on the beach, sending great clouds of sand up into the air, did those same people realize the pilot was intent on bringing the war to Margate.[29] The next bomb landed in the Newgate Gap, close to the bridge that spanned the 60-feet deep chasm leading down to the beach. Then, coming inland over the Cliftonville district, the pilot released his fourth bomb as he approached the Queen's Highcliffe Hotel. The bomb exploded in the hotel gardens. Across the street at 1 Eastern Esplanade, a boy scout, John Dyde, was helping out at the VAD hospital established at Wanstead House, formerly a convalescent home for the Infant Orphan Asylum at Wanstead on London's north-eastern outskirts. Dyde looked on as the bomb destroyed the calm of the hospital:

> I shall never forget how a room full of nurses talking and drinking afternoon tea changed into a terror-stricken crowd at the deafening crash of a bomb that fell into the garden of the Queen's Hotel, opposite. The matron, by her calm, cool manner, brought everybody to sanity again.[30]

Seconds later another bomb detonated close by, in shrubs by the entrance to The Oval, where a bandstand stood. A sixth immediately followed, landing in the back garden of 4 Eastern Esplanade, no doubt further traumatising the nurses at the hospital.

From the beach, where the first bombs landed, to the start of Godwin Road was a distance of just 300 yards. Surprised by the unusual noises, some people in that road came out into their gardens to see what had caused them just as the next bombs landed. They had no time to react. The first of three bombs exploded in the road opposite No. 2 Godwin Road, shattering the front windows in all the houses from Nos. 1 to 8. At that moment 34-year-old Alice Jessie Wilson was standing with her mother on the path by the front door of No. 2. Razor-sharp bomb splinters flashed towards them, slashing at Alice's thighs and cutting open a finger and a foot. The next bomb, at No. 14, wrecked the roof and rooms at the top of the house. Sitting in the front room on the top floor, 31-year-old Miss Gladys Hazlitt, visiting from Hammersmith in London, and Mrs Florence Meager, aged 51, were taking tea when the bomb struck. They were both lucky to escape with just thigh injuries inflicted by fragments of the bomb. The third bomb in Godwin Road landed in the garden of Malabar House, close to No. 26 where Agnes

Robins, aged 40, kept a lodging house. Agnes was by her front door and tried to get back inside when fragments of the bomb cut into her, causing a serious puncture wound in her back between the shoulders. She died two days later, earning the unwanted distinction of being the first person in Britain killed by a bomb dropped from an aeroplane.

The pilot of the German seaplane had one more bomb to drop, his tenth. It fell in the street in Albion Road close to a house called Brooklyn Lodge. Walter May, driving his horse-drawn cab along Albion Road, had an extraordinary escape. According to the police report, May was 'driving a fare which he was about to set down in Albion Road when a bomb exploded under his horse and riddled it with bomb splinters'. May escaped with just an injury to the big toe on his left foot while his passenger also sustained just a minor injury. The bomb killed May's horse, and another in the street 'died of fright'. But they were not the only casualties caused by the bomb.

Dora Andrews, a 51-year-old nursemaid, was in the garden of a bungalow called 'The Nook' in Albion Road, holding a child in her arms when a bomb fragment injured her as it dug into her left shoulder. Then tragedy stuck at Brooklyn Lodge. Kate Bonny, aged 37, was standing by the garden gate, watching out for her parents who were due back from London, when the bomb exploded. Her parents arrived a few minutes later to the horrific discovery of their daughter 'pitifully mangled by shell splinters'. A police report went into more detail: 'Sustained several punctured wounds on chest; lacerated wound left thigh; punctured wound right heel; cut on back and left arm.' But as the police noted, her chest wounds were serious, ending their report with 'Recovery doubtful'. Kate Bonny died in hospital on 17 September and was buried in Ramsgate's Jewish cemetery. On her gravestone are the words, 'Killed by a German bomb on the eve of the Day of Atonement'.

Having now dropped his last bomb, the pilot of the seaplane made off to the east. Lt Col Bryan, commanding the 45th Provisional Battalion of the Manchester Regiment, ran outside his headquarters in Eastern Esplanade when he heard the first explosions. He saw the seaplane and immediately phoned the RNAS base just along the coast at Westgate, who informed him one aircraft was just starting up and a second would follow. The two B.E.2c aircraft saw the raider as he headed out to sea and gave chase, but gradually he pulled away from his pursuers and they returned at 7.30pm.[31] Back in Margate, Lt Col Bryan reported large crowds beginning to form after the raid and that the police appeared powerless. He took matters into his own hands, collected together as many of his men that he could find and cleared Godwin and Albion roads so ambulances could collect the injured. His men remained in position until the police and special constables were able to take over. The lone raider had claimed two lives, injured six others and escaped unmolested; there seemed no answer to this type of lightning raid.

Later that day the Navy Zeppelins attempted one more strike against London as the moon approached the end of its latest 'dark' cycle.

14 September 1915, 12.10am: Bucklesham, Suffolk

This final raid of the month, which set out on 13 September, was unusual in that the Army's LZ 77 joined the Navy Zeppelins. The Army Zeppelin, temporarily berthed at Hage, was due to fly back to Belgium later that day, but Hptmn Horn received permission to take part in the raid before completing the journey. Pitt Klein, one of the mechanics on L 13 reported Horn, 'thrilled to be able to participate in a raid against England with us'.[32] Four Zeppelins set out, L 11 and L 14 from Nordholz, L 13 and LZ 77 from Hage.

Once out over the North Sea, the four airships took their own course, but the weather quickly began to deteriorate. Initially a light mist appeared, which gradually thickened. L 13 attempted to fly below it but found it extended down to 1,500 metres, a height Mathy would not go below for fear of attack from the guns of ships or submarines, while his heavy bombload prevented climbing above it. Pitt Klein found it anything but an enjoyable experience:

> We were freezing our backsides off. Our lungs seared from breathing in the cold moist air. It was a most unpleasant feeling flying on for hour after hour like this, not being able to see a thing beyond the airship.

> Night fell; the murk thickened.

> Tired out and in a daze we sat staring at the engines.

> Next moment the engine telegraphs rang with a great sense of urgency.

> 'All engines full ahead!'

> Immediately the order was repeated, and was followed up by a third repetition in the form of a personal visit.

> 'We're in real trouble! Get every ounce of power you can out of the engines!

'WHAT ARE YOU GOING TO DO ABOUT THESE AIRSHIP RAIDS?'

> In a split second we had opened the carburettor levers up to full. Groaning and juddering along its entire length, the ship tore upwards at an angle we had previously not thought possible.
>
> What was happening?

Klein and his comrades in the rear engine gondola peering out into the gloom were suddenly 'rooted to the spot with fear' – another Zeppelin was heading straight towards them on the starboard side. The men expected the two to collide at any second, but the elevator helmsman pushed forward at the crucial moment and the tail of L 13 lifted as the other Zeppelin, whose helmsman had chosen the opposite course, passed under L 13 with, as Klein dramatically relates, 'millimetres to spare'. It later transpired the other Zeppelin had been LZ 77. Due to the appalling weather, Horn had aborted the mission and turned for home when LZ 77 found itself on a collision course with L 13. The two other Navy Zeppelins, L 11 and L 14, also wisely abandoned the mission, but Heinrich Mathy in L 13 continued.

When a gap finally appeared in the thick cloud, Mathy was able to identify the Suffolk coast at Orfordness (see Map 6). British observers reported the sound of engines out over the sea at 11.15pm. Mathy headed south as the clouds closed in again. Although they gave the crew a feeling of isolation, about 15 minutes later searchlights reaching up from Harwich caused an eerie, diffused glow all around L 13. Alerted by the sound of her engines, then catching a brief glimpse of L 13, a 6-pdr AA gun fired 12 rounds in her general direction. Hearing a strange ripping sound, they believed they may have scored a hit.[33] As a bewildered Pitt Klein recounts, a new crisis now engulfed L 13:

> Suddenly the ship gave a huge shudder. I was knocked off my feet and caught hold of the engine to steady myself.
>
> What was that?
>
> A direct hit? Were we on fire? Our hearts were in our mouths; our pulses raced, our temples pounded.

In the control gondola, Mathy shouted to the helmsman controlling the elevators to 'Climb! Climb! Climb!', but Obersteuermannsmaat Friedrich Peters informed him he could not – L 13 was losing height. Then Klein's engine stopped. Mathy sent his executive officer, Kurt Friemel, to discover what had happened and, together with Segelmachersmaat Ernst Kaiser (responsible, among other things, for maintenance of the gas cells) and Maschinistenmaat Friedrich Rohr (in control of fuel) they found the answer. Klein had also gone up to the narrow catwalk to investigate why the flow of fuel to his engine had ceased; the others told him what had happened: 'The shell had cut the gangway in two and had gone off inside a gas bag, but had immediately been snuffed out by the pure hydrogen.' He also discovered Rohr holding together two ends of a broken fuel pipe that had been severed and learned that the power cable serving the radio was cut too. In fact the shell had slashed open two of the gas cells and it proved impossible to stem the flow of escaping hydrogen, losing 80% from one and 85% from the other.

While the crew were doing all they could to cobble together repairs, L 13 appeared to circle, first northwards towards the River Debden, then west, passing over Trimley and Shotley, before twisting back to the north-east and crossing the River Orwell near Levington. To add to L 13's woes, at 12.10am a RNAS mobile maxim gun commanded by sub-Lt F.E. Slee of the RNVR, described as 'an entirely elderly barrister', opened fire from Levington Heath just as Mathy had decided to begin dropping his bombs to lighten the ailing L 13.[34]

The first of L 13's bombs (an HE) landed, as the Suffolk police meticulously recorded, in a field 56 yards from a lodge at the entrance to Bucklesham Hall. They reported: 'A fragment went through the door, broke some cups and saucers, dislodged a few bricks in the chimney, and other fragments damaged glass.' Four more HE bombs and two incendiaries landed harmlessly in fields around Bucklesham Hall, and a HE and three incendiary bombs fell in a meadow at Newbourne Hall followed by a single HE bomb in a marsh on Street Farm at Newbourne. On the eastern edge of the same farm, towards the village of Hemley, two HE and two incendiaries landed in a field planted with mangelwurzels. Fields surrounding Hemley Hall received two HE bombs and the same number of incendiaries; one of the HE bombs cut right through the trunk of an ash tree with a diameter measuring 12 inches. Then, where the fields of Hemley Hall neared the River Debden, four more HE bombs dug themselves into the marshy ground before L 13 crossed the river and rained down two HE and 20 incendiaries on marshy land at Well Hall Farm, between the villages of Sutton and Shottisham.[35]

14 September 1915: Hage and London

Freed of the weight of the bombs, L 13 rapidly gained height and Mathy set a direct course back to Germany. He crossed the coast near Orfordness at 12.25am and, once over the North Sea, the crew jettisoned 'all the engine spares, most of the machine guns and most of the ammunition'. Mathy also dumped 800 kilos of fuel as he approached the Dutch coast and prepared to take the risk of flying the shorter route back to Hage over neutral Holland. The Dutch never hesitated to defend their air space, but L 13 got through. Although Mathy released another 500 kilos of oil, spare parts and water prior to landing, L 13 came down heavy. Pitt Klein was back in the rear engine gondola when she hit the ground:

> The two air bumpers on the bottom of the gondolas were smashed to pieces, and dug up the ground like ploughs. The rear gondola was pushed up into the hull. We would have been quite badly injured if we hadn't thrown ourselves flat on the floor just in time.

In his report, Mathy added that girders were broken over the control gondola and the impact had bent the gondola struts and some of the propeller shafts.[36] Taking part in a raid that departed on 13 September, in an airship numbered L 13 may have been tempting fate for some. Narrowly avoiding a mid-air collision, being hit by anti-aircraft fire over England and running the gauntlet of the Dutch defences were certainly not regular occurrences. Pitt Klein, however, did not put their survival down to good fortune:

> We were especially thankful that the people who had designed and built her [L 13], had made her strong enough not to break in half despite the loss of two gas cells, and yet still be able to complete the long, long flight back from England under her own power.

Repairs to L 13 began on 14 September and, despite her traumatic trip, she was ready for service again four days later. The increasing brightness of the moon, however, brought the current raiding cycle to an end.

There was, however, a rather strange postscript to the September raids, one reported in the British newspapers on 14 September.

While L 13 had conducted its raid over London on 8 September, one of her crew had planned a little prank. While north of the capital he threw overboard a cloth bag attached to small parachute. The bag eventually came to earth in the grounds of Wrotham Park, between Potters Bar and Barnet. When discovered, the bag was found to contain a well-scraped shoulder blade of a pig or ox – sources do not agree – on which was painted inscriptions and a rather crude depiction of a worried looking Sir Edward Grey, the Foreign Secretary, with a Zeppelin bomb about to drop on his head. Alongside the drawing were the words '*Was fang ich, armer Teufel, an?*' (What shall I, poor devil, do?). On the other side the German humour continued with reference to the naval blockade of Germany: '*Zum Andenken an das ausgehungerte Deutschland*' (A memento from starved-out Germany).[37]

The reports of the incident no doubt raised a smile or two, but otherwise the situation looked bleak. Zeppelins appeared able to cruise over Britain largely unmolested whenever they chose, killing civilians and destroying property at will. The appointment of Admiral Scott was a visible sign that, for London at least, there was a new attitude towards aerial defence. Whether he would receive the support he needed to make a difference remained to be seen.

Chapter 17

London Surrounded

After the raids of September 1915, the need for improvements to the existing Home Defence arrangements was clear if Zeppelin raiders were to encounter any significant opposition. British metrological experts advised that with the new moon rising on 8 October and a decent period of weather predicted from 8 to 12 October, the next window of opportunity for the raiders seemed clear. In a rush to offer a more substantial opposition, the War Office informed the Admiralty it would do what it could to help defend London, and made plans for temporary defensive arrangements.

The Admiralty, meanwhile, had formed a sub-committee to consider the aeroplane defence of the capital. On 16 September it recommended that London needed 40 aeroplanes for its defence, with 24 pilots and four new airfields in addition to those at Hendon and Chingford. But before adopting these recommendations, the committee sent one of its number, Sqn Cdr John Babington, to Paris to study the French capital's air defences.[1] When Babington submitted his report on 27 September, the sub-committee completely revised its recommendations. While Paris utilized a blackout, guns, searchlights, listening posts, and had 60 pilots and 30 aircraft available, those aircraft played a minor part: 'French opinion seemed unanimous that aeroplane pilots had the greatest difficulty in finding an airship in the dark.'[2]

In response, the Director of Air Services, Rear Admiral Vaughan-Lee, rejected the plan to increase the number of aircraft assigned to the defence of London. Instead, on 28 September, the Admiralty merely agreed to improve existing airfields and train more pilots for night-flying, but with the proviso that overseas units had first call on these newly trained men. The Admiralty's airborne contribution to London's defence remained the four night-flying trained pilots based at Hendon

249

and Chingford. Elsewhere, Admiral Sir Percy Scott ploughed his own furrow, begging and borrowing guns from wherever he could.

After Kitchener had threatened Henderson with holding him personally responsible if the RFC did not oppose future Zeppelin raids, he had responded by securing land in Essex at Sutton's Farm near Hornchurch and at Hainault Farm, a few miles from Romford, where he established airfields and allocated two B.E.2c aircraft to each. With only the most basic facilities, they were operational by 3 October. The War Office instigated its temporary three-tier defence plan on 5 October to run until 12 October in anticipation of a raid during the darkest period of the new moon. The first tier involved cordons of ground observers, positioned on the coast with others forming three rings, 80 miles, 60 miles and 13 miles out from the centre of London. These men, drawn from local military commands, were connected by telephone to Home Defence headquarters in London. In addition, the observers had rockets of different colours to indicate to the crews of searchlights and guns, as well as pilots, the direction a Zeppelin was taking. Reports from these fixed points could also give an idea of the raider's speed. The second tier utilized mobile 13-pdr guns, drawn from those mobilising at Woolwich, distributed at various points on the north-eastern approaches to London. The third tier saw six night-flying pilots posted to the airfields at Joyce Green, near Dartford, and to the two new ones at Hainault Farm and Sutton's Farm. There were also pilots standing by at Northolt, to the west of London.[3]

Frustratingly, by 12 October, the day when these temporary arrangements were due to expire, there had been no sign of the anticipated Zeppelin raid. The War Office became concerned that the Germans had gained knowledge of their plan so kept it in operation, issuing a false order for the 13-pdr guns to prepare for a return to Woolwich. Later, secret orders redeployed six guns to pre-selected positions at Hatfield and Broxbourne in Hertfordshire, and Loughton, Romford, Hainault Farm and Sutton's Farm in Essex, while two remained in position at Royal Albert Dock and Plumstead near Woolwich. Replacement pilots also arrived at the two new airfields on the morning of 13 October.[4]

In Germany, Peter Strasser received orders on 5 October to select the port of Liverpool on the north-west coast of England as his next target. The port served as a major destination for American goods coming into Britain. Strasser hoped to launch a raid the next day but unexpected bad weather coincided and it was another week before he could unleash his Zeppelins. The weather, however, precluded a long-range attack on Liverpool, so Strasser authorized London as the target instead. At Nordholz and Hage five Zeppelins prepared for action: L 11, L 14 and L 15 at the former, and L 13 and L 16 at the latter.[5]

13 October 1915, 8.45pm: Horstead, Norfolk

Oblt-z-S Horst von Buttlar was first in the air in L 11, departing from Nordholz at 12.22pm local time. Although Strasser appeared to have a carefully planned strategy for his Zeppelins to surround London, von Buttlar appears to have had other ideas. Although the first to leave Germany, L 11 was the last to come inland around two hours after the other four raiders. Von Buttlar later reported he had made his attack by flying up the Thames, dropping his bombs on West Ham, the London docks and at Woolwich. He described the effectiveness of his attack: 'On dropping the fourth bomb an especially heavy explosion was seen, and three big fires were started which a half hour later still glowed through the light cloud layer.'[6] A dramatic outcome indeed, but like other reports filed by von Buttlar, it did not rely heavily on facts.

Von Buttlar brought L 11 inland over Bacton on the north-eastern coast of Norfolk at 8.25pm.[7] An RNAS mobile maxim gun on the coast opened fire but failed to distract von Buttlar, neither did a machine gun manned by men of the 1/6th Norfolk Cyclists that opened fire from North Walsham ten minutes later. His south-west course was leading L 11 towards Norwich but, about eight miles north of the city, something caught his eye as he approached the villages of Horstead and Coltishall. Circling now, at 8.45pm von Buttlar dropped four HE and three incendiary bombs on the parish of Horstead, where all landed in open fields and only succeeded in smashing seven panes of glass in cottages nearby. Nine more HE bombs dropped on fields between Coltishall and Great Hautbois, near to Coltishall railway station. Two failed to detonate and the other seven broke a few more windows as well as partly wrecking a tin shed. Seven incendiary bombs released at the same time landed close to a small cluster of three cottages, but before any fires took hold, the occupants effectively doused the burning bombs with buckets of water.

Possibly picking up the railway at Coltishall, von Buttlar passed near Wroxham and, now heading south, approached the eastern outskirts of Norwich just before 9.00pm. At Mousehold Heath, however, a 15-pdr field gun of a Territorial unit, the 1/1st Leicestershire Royal Horse Artillery – not intended for an anti-aircraft role – optimistically fired two rounds at the oncoming Zeppelin. Those two rounds were enough to convince von Buttlar to head back towards the coast. He reached Great Yarmouth 20 minutes later and set a course from there back to Nordholz, where he submitted the report on his success over 'London'. The Norfolk villages he actually bombed lay about 100 miles north of Woolwich.

The other four Zeppelins crossed the North Sea individually but made a pre-arranged rendezvous near the Happisburgh Lightship, off the north-east Norfolk coast. With L 13 leading, all four came inland between 6.15pm and 6.40pm on a narrow stretch of coast between Bacton and Happisburgh. Alerted by the passage of Mathy's leading Zeppelin, the RNAS mobile maxim gun at Bacton fired off a number of rounds at L 14, L 15 and L 16 as each passed. All four followed a similar course to the west of Norwich as far as the Thetford area, which they all reached between 7.25pm and 8.10pm before diverging. L 13 and L 14 were to pass to the west and east of London respectively and make their attacks from south-west and south-east, while the two latest Zeppelins, L 15 and L 16, would have the shorter journey and approach from the north.[8]

13 October 1915, 9.02pm: Hatfield, Hertfordshire

Kptlt Heinrich Mathy, in the control gondola of L 13, followed a course to the south-west, intent on passing around to the west of London. He planned an initial attack on the Hampton waterworks, south-west of London, before gaining height and pressing on for the city. L 13 passed Newmarket and Saffron Walden then, when north of Harlow at 8.45pm, she turned west, crossing into Hertfordshire on a course that took her past Hertford and Hatfield (see Map 7).

At Hatfield, one of the 13-pdr mobile AA guns that had relocated earlier that day stood silently in a field at Birchwood Farm, about a mile north of the town. Annoyingly for Lt Sturgeon of the Royal Garrison Artillery and his gun crew, their telephone was out of operation and they were receiving information by dispatch riders from Hatfield Police Station. At 8.50pm a police sergeant, William Olding, arrived at Birchwood Farm with news of a Zeppelin reported from Hertford. He could have saved himself a journey as the searchlight was already shining towards Hertford and 'the engines of a Zeppelin could be heard quite plainly'. Within five minutes of Olding's arrival, Sturgeon saw L 13 and at 9.02pm gave the order to open fire.[9] The gun fired two rounds. In the rear gondola of L 13 the mechanic Pitt Klein observed: 'One particular anti-aircraft battery whose gun barrels were synchronized with searchlights, was trying especially hard to get us.'[10] Mathy immediately ordered the release of two HE bombs. Sturgeon reported that one landed 220 yards from his gun, the other 175 yards away, adding: 'When the ship appeared directly overhead they again dropped two bombs. One of these landed 70 yards N.W. of gun, and the other about 100 yards due North of gun.' The latter bomb failed to detonate.

Sturgeon fired a third round, which he believed had struck a propeller, but L 13 was unharmed. At the same time Pitt Klein felt the bombs had done their work: 'They hit home, for as soon as the terrible explosions went off, the searchlights went out and the gun barrels fell silent.'[11] But Klein was mistaken. As L 13 passed broadside on, the crew attempted to fire a fourth round but at the critical moment the gun's main spring broke, putting it out of action. As L 13 disappeared in the direction of St Albans, calm returned to Birchwood Farm and Sergeant Olding took the opportunity to inspect some nearby cottages for damage. He reported that three, those occupied by Elizabeth Horsey, David Rumney and William Wilds, had all their windows smashed.

After his brush with the gun at Hatfield, Mathy resumed his course, skirting to the west of London, passing Watford and Rickmansworth (9.30pm) then Uxbridge and Staines, where he passed close to the Hampton waterworks, but did not see it. Continuing on the same heading, L 13 crossed the Thames at Weybridge at 9.50pm before reaching Effingham. At Gomshall, between Dorking and Guildford, Mathy seemed to realize he had missed his target and turned to the west. Trying to identify his position, Mathy dropped a flare over Clandon at 10.00pm and five minutes later passed over Newlands Corner on the North Downs.

13 October 1915, 10.25pm: Guildford, Surrey

In a valley south-west of Newlands Corner stood the village of Chilworth, home to a gunpowder mill. A 1-pdr 'pom-pom' stood guard over the mill, manned by a crew from the Sussex Royal Garrison Artillery, commanded by Lt Young, supported by No. 3 Supernumerary Company, 2/5th Battalion, Royal West Surrey Regiment. At the sound of approaching engines, the officer commanding the garrison ordered lights out and work at the mill ceased. Approaching from the east, L 13 now passed over the darkened gunpowder mills but then, after travelling on for about a quarter of a mile, dropped a parachute flare that bathed the surrounding countryside in light before circling back over the western boundary of the gunpowder mills. The 1-pdr opened fire but L 13 turned away and, passing over Guildford, continued for about three miles to the village of Wood Street, where she circled around once more and headed back towards Guildford, the crew preparing to commence bombing.[12] Mathy believed he had finally found Hampton and its elusive waterworks. Contemporary maps show a complex water system south-east of Guildford where the River Wey and River Wey Navigation wind serpentine-like around flood plains. His bombs fell across the southern part of the town, from the St Catherine's district to Shalford, across this river system.

At 10.25pm Mathy dropped a parachute flare, followed immediately by his first bomb, which landed in Guildown Road. The bomb exploded in the garden of a house named Little Croft, where it gouged a large crater, broke 146 panes of glass in the house, damaged the roof, walls and ceilings, broke furniture and ripped doors off their hinges but harmed none of the occupants of the house.[13] The next bomb detonated in a field on Braboeuf Farm, quickly followed by the first of two that exploded in Chestnut Avenue. One of these dug a hole in the road, knocking down 21 feet of stone wall and causing damage to greenhouses and other buildings, while the other landed 60 yards further along the road, destroying 30 yards of garden fence and smashing a number of windows. Another bomb broke windows and damaged ceilings and the roof at St Catherine's Cottage, close to the Portsmouth Road, and also damaged the neighbouring property, Montague House. Across the Portsmouth Road the same bomb caused further damage, breaking windows at Langton Priory Lodge, many more at Langton Priory and smashing 105 panes of glass at the Hope & Anchor public house, which also suffered other minor damage.

Over the railway line now, which ran from Portsmouth to London, Mathy's next bomb dug a deep hole in the embankment and damaged the exposed northbound track as it ran between two tunnels, while also smashing roof tiles and windows in two cottages close by. George Parson and family lived in one of the cottages in The Valley, a narrow road running towards the railway. At the sound of the bombs, the family took shelter under the stairs, which collapsed, but there were no injuries. Mr Parsons kept a small piece of railway track with a fragment of the bomb embedded in it on his mantelpiece for many years afterwards.[14] Seconds later a bomb landed in an extensive chicken run in the garden of a house called The Beacon, killing seventeen of the birds. A second bomb also landed in the grounds, destroying 20 feet of a stone and brick wall adjoining the River Wey. Mathy's ninth and tenth bombs landed on the far bank of the river. The first of this brace brought down telephone wires and damaged the riverbank while the second, landing 60 yards on, broke more telephone wires and killed a swan. The final two bombs landed on the golf course at Shalford Park, excavating an unwelcome bunker on the seventh green.

Satisfied he had hit his initial target, Mathy reported: '... twelve 50kg explosive bombs were now dropped on the pumping and power stations; the hits were well placed.'[15] Mathy took L 13 away on an easterly course, passing over the gunpowder mill at Chilworth once more. The 1-pdr opened fire again. In his report, 2nd Lt E. Milton concluded: 'After a lapse of a few minutes she returned flying much lower ... Rapid fire was continued until she was obscured ... No damage was done to the Powder Factory.' The gun fired 77 rounds at L 13, but Milton bemoaned the fact that they had no tracer shells or searchlights, making their already difficult task nigh on impossible. Some of the Royal West Surreys had added to this futile gesture by opening up with their rifles at L 13, at a range recognized as too great by their commanding officer.

After flying on a path across Surrey, at about 11.05pm L 13 approached Tandridge near Oxted, where she passed close to another Zeppelin, Kptlt-d-R Alois Böcker's L 14, which had approached London around the eastern side of the city. Although Mathy's navigation had been out, Böcker had been even further off course.

13 October 1915, 9.05pm: Otterpool Camp, Kent

After Thetford, Böcker took L 14 on a southerly course, intending to swing around the east side of London, but a heavy mist all down the eastern side of England played havoc with his navigation. He crossed the mouths of the rivers Blackwater and Crouch in Essex without seeing them and, even more confusing for his navigation, crossed the mist-shrouded seven-mile-wide stretch of the Thames estuary between Shoeburyness and the Isle of Sheppey at 8.40pm without realising. Böcker continued on his southward course, now heading across Kent, no doubt growing increasingly concerned that he had not yet found the Thames.

After passing to the east of Ashford, Böcker changed course towards the south-east and shortly afterwards he saw water through the clouds and a large military camp straight ahead. He concluded that he had finally found the Thames, and Woolwich.[16] The body of water he saw off to starboard was, however, not the Thames, it was the English Channel, and the vast camp below was that at Otterpool, one of the many outlying military camps in the Folkestone area. The 'neat rows of well-lighted bell tents' were home to the men of 5th Brigade, Canadian Field Artillery, and the Canadian 8th Howitzer Brigade.[17]

At 9.05pm the sound of L 14's engines approaching from the west reached the Otterpool Camp. Lt Col William King, commanding the 8th Howitzer Brigade, looked towards the sound and 'saw a cigar shaped aircraft ... I should judge it to be about 6000 feet up'. He immediately ordered his trumpeter to sound 'Lights Out'. In one of the tents Cpl William O'Brien had been writing a letter home when the order came down the line: 'We had learned to do things on the jump and this prompt action probably saved our lives. As it was, the tent where I lived was punctured by some of the shrapnel.'[18] Just a minute or so after the first sighting a bomb dropped. Lt Col King reported: 'I heard the explosion of a bomb ... I saw the flash and heard the report. Half a minute later I heard four or five more reports being followed by a cloud of black smoke.'

Böcker dropped four bombs along a line about 250 yards in length. A road running north–south separated the Howitzer Brigade camp from that of the 5th Brigade and all fell to the east of the road on the side occupied by the latter. The first fell in a meadow empty of troops but shrapnel flew across the road to the Howitzer Brigade camp, killing two men of 29th Battery: Gunner Charles Peterkin and Sgt Edward Harris. Sgt Frederick Conway had been in his tent with Harris when they heard the 'Lights Out' call. Both men went to the tent's entrance and Conway stepped out to make sure his men had followed the order. He then heard the Zeppelin: 'About a minute after that an explosive shell dropped and Sgt Harris immediately fell, he groaned once and expired.'

The second bomb destroyed the Guard Tent of 5th Brigade, then the third bomb exploded in the brigade's horse lines, followed by the fourth that fell among the men's tents and obliterated three. Inevitably in such a closely packed encampment there were casualties. A Canadian officer from the Howitzer Brigade looked on:

> Then we could hear the hum of the engines and all that was left to see were five pillars of black smoke standing ghostlike in the yellow fog. I stood about 120 yards from where the bomb fell. I heard it sing as it fell through the air.

> The officer than rounded up some men and went to the camp of 5th Brigade to see if he could help.
>
> It was awful. One bomb struck the guard tent, and one fell in the horse lines. Thirteen men were killed almost instantly ... They were literally blown into fragments.[19]

On the following morning the commanding officer of 5th Brigade admitted the outcome remained unclear: 'It is difficult at present however to separate the killed from the wounded, as the wounded were taken away very quickly by ambulances and those killed were mutilated to such an extent that they could not be identified.' Eventually 5th Brigade was able to report the loss of 13 men. The bomb in the horse lines claimed victims too; the final tally showed 15 horses dead and another three wounded.[20]

Böcker now steered to the north-east where another military camp was laid out a short distance away at Westenhanger. He released two bombs but they fell a little early and exploded on a racecourse, where the blast broke a few windows. Passing over Sandling, Böcker reached the sea at Hythe and must now have realized his navigation error because he followed the coastline to the south-west for more than 20 miles until he reached Pett, between Winchelsea and Hastings. There he turned inland on a north-west course. The mist hid his progress until he loomed over the village of Frant in East Sussex at 10.30pm and dropped seven incendiary bombs. One failed to ignite and the others burnt themselves out without causing any damage.[21] Fifteen minutes later L 14 reached Tunbridge Wells (see Map 7).

Lady Annette Amelia Matthews, wife of Sir John Bromhead Matthews, KC, lived in the town and kept a diary:

> War has come to our doors at length. Last night at 10.45pm a violent explosion occurred close by, followed immediately by two more. There was a faint burring, purring sound, but nothing further. I was still up & dressed, & so was J. The children slept peacefully on; the rest of the house, very trim and neat in dressing gowns, came down from their rooms & we waited & we did not go to the cellars because all the noise had ceased.
>
> J. went out & discovered that it was indeed a Zeppelin & that bombs had been seen to drop somewhere not that far off.[22]

The three bombs had dropped on open ground in Calverley Park, about three quarters of a mile from the Matthews' home in Hurstwood Lane, and not far from the railway station. They caused slight damage to one house and broke many windows. As the sound of L 14's 'purring' passed over the centre of the town she continued on her great detour towards London and, at about 11.05pm, near Oxted, she passed within close range of Mathy and L 13. From Oxted, Böcker headed north-west while Mathy departed to the north-east.

13 October 1915, 11.20pm: East Croydon, Surrey[23]

About 15 minutes later Böcker approached the railway junction at East Croydon and decided to attack.[24] His first bomb fell in a narrow passage between 45 and 47 Edridge Road. The explosion blew out the fronts of both buildings, causing the bedroom floors to collapse. A newspaper report described the scene:

> In one of the upper bedrooms a mother and daughter were sleeping. They were thrown out on to the street through the place where the ground-floor window should have been, both escaping with their lives. In the next house a little boy lying in his cot was buried under the debris of the wrecked roof of the house, and in order to release him the whole roof had to be lifted up, so securely was the cot pinned down. There was not a stick of furniture nor a piece of china left whole in either of these two houses – only two small pictures remained with the glass unbroken.[25]

W.C. Coles was on his way back to East Croydon station through darkened streets after visiting friends in South Croydon when he heard a whirr and a crash followed by a blinding flash:

> I was sent staggering and then, the next second, a deafening explosion laid me out and I knew no more.
>
> I came round to find myself lying in the gutter with a stream of water pouring over me from a smashed water main. Remembering that a friend lived close by, I groped my way to his front door. I found him amongst a scene of wreckage in his dining room: french windows destroyed, dining-table driven to the far end of the room against the sideboard, and furniture just anyhow.[26]

Standing, dazed, amongst the wreckage of his friend's dining-room, Mr Coles still took some comfort from the situation: 'Fortunately the whisky was inside the sideboard.'

Crossing over Park Lane, the next two bombs dropped in gardens between Woodstock Road and Beech House Road, then two more fell in Beech House Road. One exploded in the rear garden of No. 10 digging a huge crater, but the other dropped with devastating effect on No. 12, home to John Currie, his three sons, Gordon (aged 15), Roy (14), Brian (10) and their housekeeper. Everyone in the house was asleep when the bomb exploded. The housekeeper gave evidence at the subsequent inquest:

> I was fast asleep when I heard an awful explosion which awoke me. I seemed to spring from the top of the bed to the bottom. Then I groped my way to the door which I found was on the floor. I stayed there because the side wall had fallen in on the stairs and landing. I called out to the father asking if he was all right. He replied 'I'm all right but I can't move.' Then next I called for the boys, only the elder one answered, he said, 'Do get help'. I shouted to the lady next door ... the wall was out and I could see into her house ... I said, 'Our staircase is cut off, will you get help'.[27]

Neighbours quickly rallied round and extricated John Currie first, then the fire brigade arrived and rescued the housekeeper before starting the delicate work to recover the boys. But as the local newspaper reported in gory detail, it was too late:

> Medical evidence showed that the second boy [Roy] was dead when he reached the hospital. He had a very severe scalp wound, his right foot was torn half away and he had a large wound on his left foot. The eldest boy [Gordon] was suffering from many wounds on the back and left hip, and on the right thigh were two large wounds. A piece of blanket or mattress had been driven through one wound and a piece of shrapnel was found in the body. He had wounds on both arms and his chest and was suffering from shock and collapse. The youngest boy [Brian], who was dead when the rescuers reached him, had the back of his head smashed, the bones being in small pieces. On the right side of the body was a wound over a foot long through which the ribs protruded. Another large wound was on the right thigh which was fractured. The right leg below the knee was smashed and the left foot was fractured. There were numerous wounds and cuts all over the body and face.[28]

While under treatment in hospital, where he received the news of the death of all three of his sons, John Currie 'suffered mental collapse from his terrible loss'.[29]

The next three bombs straddled the main railway line south of East Croydon Station, between Chatsworth Road and Park Hill recreation ground, where they caused some damage to the track and cracked a water main that crossed it. L 14 then passed over the factory of Creed, Bille & Co., engaged in war work. If Böcker saw it as a target, the three bombs he now released were dropped a second or two late. Instead of striking the factory they smashed into Oval Road about 200 yards beyond it.

A 19-year-old electrician, Robert Arthur Thompson, heard the bombs and dashed out of No. 57 into the street, where a bomb fragment struck him with terrific force. Dazed when the ambulance men found him, he could not say where he was injured, but his injury was clear, the blast had torn off an arm. He died in hospital. Another young man, 21-year-old grocer, Percy John Brookes, ran out into the road from No. 62. As he did so a fragment of the bomb struck him in the stomach, leaving him slumped against a wall. He died the following day.[30] Damage in the street was extensive, with six houses wrecked, four damaged and a water main burst. Dressmaker's assistant Jane Miller, aged 50, lived at 51 Oval Road, one of those wrecked. She had rushed towards the cellar at the sound of the first bomb. Her stepfather had fought his way through the debris to find her, but when he eventually discovered her she was already dead.[31]

A short distance further on Böcker released two more bombs; one exploded in the garden of 42 Leslie Park Road, the force of the blast slicing off the back of the house, while the other exploded behind Nos. 33 and 34, gouging out a huge crater and causing extensive damage to both properties. The next bomb struck 'Glendalough', a house owned by Dr J.H. Thompson, on the corner of Morland Road and Lower Addiscombe Road. Although the bomb shattered the roof and caused other significant damage, no one in the house sustained injury. There is also a report of another bomb digging a crater five feet deep on a tennis lawn in Morland Road. This is not confirmed elsewhere, but at 39 Morland Road, Jesse Wilmot Jones, a 61-year-old surveyor died of shock. A widowed Belgium refugee, also 61, died of similar causes in St James Road.[32]

Böcker now dropped another bomb that claimed lives. It smashed into the 73 Stretton Road home of the Walter family, wrecking it and damaging three others. The husband and elder son were both away in the Army, but Eliza, aged 52, Daisy (23) and Sidney (15) were at home asleep. All three died in the rubble. The bomb awoke a sailor home on leave from the Royal Navy:

I was awakened by a terrible bang, and screaming. I rushed downstairs, and found my mother and sister down in the basement, frightened so much that I could not get a word out of them. Just then – 'Bang!' again.

I ran out into the street, and saw lights up the road. Up I went – I guessed help was needed – but I was late. Police and firemen were just fetching a man and women out dead. What a sight! And the noise of the wounded was heart-rending.[33]

Böcker had one more bomb to drop; it fell in Howard Road but failed to explode. He now steered away from East Croydon, heading north-east. The fifteen HE bombs had dropped in about two minutes.

While Böcker had bombed East Croydon, Mathy and L 13 had progressed slowly to the north-east and had reached Bromley when L 14 reappeared at about 11.30pm. The two now headed towards Bickley, where it appears they came dangerously close to one another when Mathy crossed the path of Böcker's L 14. The British authorities were unaware of this at the time and it appears that neither officer recorded the incident in their logs, but the details emerged 11 months later. In September 1916, members of the crew of L 14, who were then manning L 33, were captured and questioned by naval intelligence. They revealed that L 14 had narrowly avoided a collision over south London in October 1915 and that Böcker had lodged a protest over the handling of the other Zeppelin.[34] For now though, having dropped all her bombs, L 14 set course for home. She crossed the Thames at 11.50pm between Erith and Purfleet, with guns at the latter place opening fire on her. She continued on a north-east course across Essex, over the mouth of the Blackwater at about 12.35am, and the Stour about 25 minutes later, then proceeded across Suffolk towards Saxmundham, where she turned east and left the English coast near Aldeburgh at about 1.45am. As she progressed, she attracted fire from two maxim guns of the 3rd Battalion, Essex Regiment, at Wrabness and a RNAS mobile maxim gun at Melton, near Woodbridge, but none inflicted any damage. L 14 arrived back at Nordholz at 10.30am local time, but so bad was the fog that she was unable to land and reach the safety of her shed for almost another five hours. When she finally landed, L 14 had been in the air for close to 27 hours.

13 October 1915, 11.45pm: Woolwich, London

After his close encounter with L 14, Mathy took L 13 northwards, approaching the River Thames at Woolwich, and believed he made a bomb run over the Royal Albert and Royal Victoria Docks on the north bank of the river.[35] Instead, and without realising, his bombs struck Woolwich, one of Germany's prime targets, home to the Royal Artillery and the Woolwich Arsenal. As she closed on the target the searchlight at Blackheath caught L 13 and the nearby 3-inch 20 cwt gun opened fire at 11.45pm, firing eight rounds at her. A gun of the same type at Honor Oak also engaged, firing nine rounds. A minute later and two 6-pdrs at the Arsenal opened fire, getting off 37 rounds, joined by a single 6-pdr at Abbey Wood firing three, and from Plumstead two 'pom-poms', two mobile 13-pdrs and a 3-inch 20 cwt added to the defensive fire. Yet despite this concentration of gunfire, it did little to disrupt L 13's progress.[36]

Pitt Klein, from one of L 13's engine gondolas, reported:

> At 00.40 [11.40pm] our 300 kg bombs rained down. An enormous bang and blastwave rent the air, as if the whole world had just been put out of joint. The blood red glare of flames lit up the London sky. The chains of incendiary bombs sent up great plumes of smoke. Blocks of houses fell to earth with a crash. The noise of the explosions mingled with that of the defences' guns, adding to the chaos, din and sounds of destruction.[37]

Mathy dropped three HE bombs and 14 incendiaries on the Royal Artillery barracks.[38] The first HE bomb exploded in the middle of the front parade ground, damaging the mess. An eyewitness recalled that it 'broke all the windows in front, the poor mess hasn't a pane of glass left'. The second HE smashed into an empty barrack room in the East Square, standing in as a mess room. The room was therefore empty when the bomb exploded, destroying it and a stable directly below where four men suffered slight injuries: Arthur Mazefield (aged 26), Embra Samuel (33), James Penfold (38) and Victor Gray (15), while one horse died and nine others sustained injuries. Five incendiaries also landed in East Square where they were dealt with swiftly. The third HE bomb landed at the western end of the Grand Depot barrack complex. The blast smashed down the end wall of the clothing store and damaged the boundary walls between the barracks and St John's Passage, and one between the barracks and St John's Church, smashing windows at the church and damaging its roof and doors. In Wellington Street, outside the barracks, twenty properties suffered broken windows and two others experienced more significant damage. At the time the bomb exploded, Mrs E. Talbot was hurrying to a friend's house, which had a cellar, carrying her 2-year-old son in her arms: 'I was almost there: bombs came nearer and nearer; one hit a house on the opposite side of the street. Something whizzed past my face and my baby screamed.' A fragment from the bomb, flying across the road, had hit her son and resulted in him losing his right arm.[39]

Nine incendiaries then fell in a line across the Grand Depot barracks where they caused little damage, and an eyewitness considered that the soldiers appeared to see the incident as great entertainment: '… the fires were put out at once and the men worked splendidly and thought the whole thing as good as a cinema.' At the same time other incendiaries fell outside the confines of the barracks. One in St John's churchyard had no effect, but another caused slight damage to the adjacent school. Three more dropped on properties in Wellington Street, in rear gardens or yards, without inflicting any damage of note. Two incendiaries in Thomas Street, outside the eastern end of the Grand Depot barracks, burnt out Percy Long & Co.'s furniture showroom and store at No. 8, and one nearby at York House, New Road, dropped harmlessly in the garden. At 5 Cross Street a property occupied by J. Murray, used as a dwelling, office and store, suffered serious damage when an incendiary set fire to the ground floor. The last two incendiaries that fell on civilian property in the town landed at Beresford Square. One at No. 15, occupied by corn dealers Sanders Brothers, smashed through a roof and ceiling before setting fire to a storeroom on the second floor, while the other landed without damage in a garden at the rear of the Capital and Counties Bank at 20 Greens End on the edge of Beresford Square. Having passed over the town, the great complex of the Woolwich Arsenal now lay dead ahead between the town and the Thames, but Mathy only had two HE bombs and five incendiaries left on board.

For Maude, one of the girls working in a Cartridge Shed at the Arsenal, listening to the bombs exploding over the town and barracks was terrifying. With lights out the 22 girls, two women and two men in the shed huddled together 'trembling in fear and horror':

> Crashes outside told us bombs were dropping very near, though so far none had exploded actually in the Arsenal. We began to breathe more freely. But … Crash! … Crash! They had found their mark. Bombs were falling in the Arsenal now.
>
> God! The horror, the terror! We poor creatures were only human beings after all, and little more than kids at that: I don't think there was a girl of more than seventeen.

We started to scream. Some fainted, others became hysterical, others again moaned and groaned in sheer, but pardonable funk ...

It seemed to me that the whole earth blew up... and a rain of debris fell around us.

Though it was only a few moments it seemed ages before lights were turned on again. By a miracle none of us in that shed was killed ...[40]

An HE bomb had exploded on the Carriage Works, near to the Cartridge Sheds where Maude was cowering. It struck the roof of the Main Machine Shop, smashing the roof and windows, wrecking a crane and damaging other machinery. Nine people were hurt in the Arsenal, one of whom later died of his injuries. Of Mathy's five incendiary bombs, three dropped near the surgery, one landed on the roof of a new machine shop on Avenue 'G' causing minor damage to the roof and floor below, and one in '5th' Street. Leaving the Arsenal now, L 13 dropped one more HE bomb, which landed on Plumstead Marshes close to a magazine. As she made off, the guns at West Ham and Clapton Orient football ground had opened fire, but by 11.54pm all local gunfire had ceased.

Mathy crossed the Thames opposite Dagenham at about 11.55pm, brushing off fire from the mobile 13-pdrs at Sutton's Farm and Beacontree Heath, near Romford, and at rather longer range by the guns at Erith and Purfleet. As L 13 approached Colchester from the west, a mobile RNAS maxim gun fired 150 rounds at her from a position at Marks Tey, followed ten minutes later by a mobile 1-pdr at Colchester that fired 42 rounds, while other members of the crew took more than 20 pot-shots, firing outranged incendiary bullets from Martini–Henry rifles. Untroubled, L 13 continued on her course, passing Ipswich, Wickham Market, Saxmundham and out to sea at Dunwich in Suffolk at 2.00am.

13 October 1915, 10.00pm: Hertford, Hertfordshire

While Mathy and Böcker had been busy south of London, Oblt-z-S Werner Peterson and Kptlt Joachim Breithaupt approached the capital from the north.

Peterson had taken command of the Navy's latest Zeppelin, L 16, just 20 days earlier, on 24 September. This first foray across the North Sea did not pass without incident. L 16 started to fly nose-heavy and to correct this Peterson ordered the release of water ballast from the front of the ship. Unfortunately, such was the angle that most of the water hit the top of the control gondola and a stream of it poured down the radio transmitter's ventilator, putting it out of action and requiring the operators to take it apart, dry the components and reassemble them.[41]

Having come inland towards Thetford with L 13, L 14 and L 15, Peterson initially headed south from there. At 9.05pm, as he approached Chelmsford, a RNAS mobile maxim gun opened fire at L 16, the gun crew estimating her height at just 4,000 feet. From there, Peterson changed his heading to the south-west, passing Ingatestone and on to Kelvedon Hatch from where a 1-pdr 'pom-pom' fired off six rounds at 9.35pm. Deterred from continuing on this course, Peterson took L 16 away to the north-west, reaching Sawbridgeworth ten minutes later, from where he saw lights glowing about ten miles distant, and a river.[42] The lights convinced Peterson it was London and, logically, that the river was the Thames (see Map 7). Swinging around to the north, Peterson prepared to make his attack, on what he concluded in his report were factories and railway yards in Stratford, East Ham and West Ham.[43] The lights that were attracting Peterson, however, were not in London, instead they were shining from the hospital and the factory of millers, G. Garratt and Sons, in Hertford, the county town of Hertfordshire, and the river was not the Thames but the River Lea.[44]

At around 10.00pm L 16 dropped a cluster of seven incendiaries on the Hartsham recreation ground in the north-east of the town, at the junction of the rivers Lea and Beane and close to the swimming baths. Two HE bombs followed, one landing on allotments on The Folly, an island between two arms of the Lea, and the other in Norris's Yard, Priory Street. Damage occurred to windows and the roofs of houses on The Folly, and wrecked a house at 1 Frampton Street. A third HE bomb then streaked down to explode in the roadway at Bull Plain. Four men – James Gregory, an organist and professor of music, John Henry Jevons, Borough Surveyor, Ernest Thomas Jolly, a bank cashier and George Cartledge, a draper – were standing at the front door of the Conservative Club at Lombard House when the bomb exploded. All four died. A labourer, Charles Spicer, was also killed as he walked past and four other men suffered injury. The blast from the bomb demolished 37 Bull Plain, killing a 3-year-old child, George Stephen Game; wrecked Nos. 25, 27 and 29, injuring three women; and caused lesser damage to a number of other properties in the street. Another man, Frederick Castle, working in Morris's Warehouse on Bull Plain, had the main artery in his left leg cut but he recovered in hospital. A man, who signed himself as 'G', later ventured into the town to see the damage:

On Bull Plain there was a scene of desolation and destruction, with a cavernous hole in the road outside the Conservative Club, and wrecked buildings all around. A little group of the members had been watching the Zeppelin when a bomb fell. Four men were killed instantly, whilst another lost an arm. All trace of one man was lost: the only article belonging to him found was a cuff with a link on it. The spectacle inside the club lobby was gruesome in the extreme. There was much blood, and remnants of clothing of the men lay about.[45]

Before the debris had settled in Bull Plain, Peterson released a salvo of 12 incendiaries and two more HE bombs. They struck the area around Old Cross. The HE bombs fell at the junction of Maidenhead Yard, The Wash and Mill Bridge, with one on McMullen's Buildings and the other on Illot's Flour Mill. Damage extended across all the surrounding roads, leaving two men and a woman in Maidenhead Yard needing hospital treatment. Two soldiers in the area, Walter Kemp and Alfred Humphrey, both of the East Anglian Brigade, Royal Field Artillery, were also detained in hospital. The incendiaries landed in the streets and yards near the library, which suffered slight damage, as did a number of other business premises and shops.

Peterson now followed St Andrew's Street, dropping his sixth HE bomb together with another cluster of seven incendiaries in the garden of Dr James Burnett-Smith's home, North House, on North Road. Another HE bomb also landed in North Road. Two soldiers of 2/1st Norfolk Battery, Royal Field Artillery were passing when it exploded. One, named Macnamee, suffered three wounds in his back and a lacerated leg but he survived, however, his comrade, 21-year-old Bombardier Arthur John Cox, was killed. The bombs also wrecked a public house, The Cold Bath, and Bates Motor Works, as well as smashing a great number of windows, doors and ceilings in North Road, Hertingfordbury Road and St Andrew's Street.

Continuing to follow North Road, Peterson dropped an eighth HE bomb in the garden of a house opposite the junction with Cross Lane. Fortunately for the occupier, Mr Perkins, it failed to explode. Three incendiaries dropped at the same time, with one landing in the garden of his neighbour, Mr McDonald, and two in the next garden at the home of Mr Wilson. The ninth HE bomb also fell in North Road, with deadly effect. The bomb landed in the roadway near the gates of Hertford Hospital. Opposite, in the yard of Garratt's Mill, fragments of the bomb struck two labourers, Arthur Hart (aged 51) and Charles Waller (43), killing them both. The bomb also damaged a wall and railings at the hospital and smashed many windows. At the neighbouring property, the rectory of St Andrew's Church, the Reverend Gardner's home also had windows smashed and damage to a wall and the roof, with similar damage inflicted on an outbuilding. Other properties nearby also lost their windows from the concussion of the blast.

Peterson's final incendiary bomb, fell in a garden at Sele Mill before he released a final salvo of five HE bombs. They just missed the hospital, two landing in a field adjoining the hospital grounds and three in Welch's Meadow, which inflicted some damage on Sele House and at dwellings at Sele Grange, but no one was injured.

Having released all 14 HE and 30 incendiaries, Peterson's mission was over and he steered L 16 away on a course heading north-east. At 10.15pm he passed over Little Hadham then, as they approached Newmarket 30 minutes later, an RNAS mobile maxim gun opened fire, but it was the only opposition L 16 encountered before she reached the Norfolk coast at Mundesley about five minutes after midnight.[46]

Around midnight, as L 16 passed out to sea, L 11 was already over two hours into her return flight across the North Sea, L 13 was starting her homeward journey after bombing Woolwich, and L 14 had crossed the Thames and was making her way homeward across Essex. At about the same time another of the raiders, L 15, was over Suffolk going out to sea near Aldeburgh.

Earlier in the evening, the crews of both L 13 and L 16 reported sighting a Zeppelin in action over the centre of London. Pitt Klein, looking out from L 13, later recalled: '... one of our colleagues was hard at work, under constant fire like us... Across the City columns of smoke and flame rose up. Our colleagues were doing well.'[47] From his viewpoint, about 18 miles away, Klein was watching the devastating attack made on central London by Joachim Breithaupt's L 15, an attack that was to become known as the 'Theatreland Raid'.

Chapter 18

'The Earth Shook and Trembled'

Born in January 1883, Joachim Breithaupt joined the Navy aged 20. After training, and with the rank of Fähnrich-zur-See, he served on the battleship SMS *Kaiser Karl der Grosse* from 1905 to 1908, was promoted to Oberleutnant-zur-See later that year, and went on to fulfil a number of varied naval appointments before joining the battleship SMS *Kaiserin* in October 1913. Yet for some time Breithaupt's fascination lay with airships: 'Even before the war I had repeatedly applied for airship duty, but my applications were always turned down because the number of available airships was small and there was a superfluity of personnel.'[1]

Once the war commenced, however, he received an enquiry asking if he still wished to join the Naval Airship Division. Breithaupt welcomed the opportunity and transferred in October 1914, with the rank of Kapitänleutnant. After six months' training he qualified as an airship commander and in April 1915 took over command of Zeppelin L 6. He remained with her until August, when he and his crew transferred to the latest 'p-class' Zeppelin, L 15, the first of this class to have more powerful engines: four 240hp Maybach engines instead of the 210hp. They took delivery of L 15 in September 1915 and flew her from the new factory at Löwenthal to her base at Nordholz, relegating L 6 to the role of training ship.

On 13 October, both L 15 and her crew were raiding England for the first time. In the plan, L 15 was to attack London from the north. Encountering thick fog over the North Sea, she climbed above the gloom, where the sky opened up dramatically, as Breithaupt described:

> What a marvellous picture. Below all dense cloud and above brilliant sunshine. The airship steered a safe course between the

cloud masses of various altitudes, from which the golden sun was reflected … We seemed to be flying over a glacier, and between the clouds other aircraft were visible from time to time.[2]

13 October 1915, 8.40pm: Broxbourne, Hertfordshire

As L 15 crossed the Norfolk coast near Bacton, she encountered fire from the RNAS mobile maxim gun there, but she passed on towards Thetford without hindrance. From there she continued southwards until, when just south of Braintree in Essex at 8.10pm, she changed course to the west (see Map 7). Breithaupt now had London in his sights:

> As we flew over the land we guided ourselves from time to time by discharging [parachute flares]. About [8.30] the Thames was well marked out below us with its characteristic windings. All water ballast was now thrown out in order to obtain the greatest possible height. All hands took their stations for action. London lay darkly under us, only a few lights showing.
>
> Suddenly, from all sides, searchlights leaped out toward us, and as we flew over Tottenham a wild cannonade from the anti-aircraft stations began. The shells burst at a good height right in our course. I therefore rose, after letting off three explosive bombs, and endeavoured to make an attack from another quarter.[3]

Breithaupt's observation of only a few lights showing in North London was inaccurate. The lack of lights was more to do with the fact that he was not over London at all, rather he was at Broxbourne in Hertfordshire, about ten miles north of Tottenham. The 'wild cannonade' he described was the eight rounds fired at L 15 by the mobile 13-pdr moved to Broxbourne earlier that day.

Positioned in Church Fields, the gun, commanded by Lt Gonne, also had a supporting searchlight. First, Gonne heard L 15's engines then, at 8.40pm, he saw her and opened fire:

> I engaged him and after the first two rounds, three bombs were dropped in the field within one hundred yards of the gun. The gun detachment was blown down by the concussion, but as soon as possible we continued to engage the Zeppelin until it was out of sight … The Zeppelin passed over at a height of about five to six thousand feet … One 30cwt lorry belonging to No. 50 Coy. Royal Engineers was completely put out of action by a bomb and also the motor car belonging to the section under my command.[4]

Happily, Gonne was also able to report that his section had escaped injury barring a few bruises. Deterred by the fire of Lt Gonne's 13-pdr, Breithaupt decided to continue around the north-west London suburbs to try his luck further on. Observers at Potters Bar, High Barnet, Elstree and Edgware all reported his progress, but after that last sighting, at 9.03pm, L 15 disappeared for a while.[5] She reappeared passing Hyde Park and steering for the centre of London.

13 October 1915, 9.20pm: Covent Garden, London

At the same time the House of Commons was sitting, but the sound of artillery fire from outside brought forward a murmured response from those present: 'Zeppelins! Zeppelins!' A reporter, Michael MacDonagh, described a rush by Members and journalists out into the gloom of New Palace Yard, lit only by a handful of shaded lampposts:

> We all scattered about the Yard and looked upwards, trying to locate the Zeppelin. 'There she is,' someone cries. 'Where?' 'There!' In a southerly direction, over the Thames, I could see a long, black object so high up that it seemed to be moving among the stars. For a few minutes the airship, crossing the Thames in a north-easterly course and passing almost directly over New Palace Yard, was then played upon by two searchlights, and in their radiance she looked a thing of silvery beauty sailing serenely through the night, indifferent to the big gun roaring at her from the Green Park, whose shells seemed to burst just below her.[6]

The 3-inch, 20cwt gun in Green Park fired five rounds at L 15 at a height estimated at 9,000 feet, but she sailed on unchecked this time. Breithaupt was determined to drop his bombs on London.

After passing over the Houses of Parliament, L 15 headed towards Charing Cross Station and the Strand.[7] At the same time, an army officer on leave from the Western Front, Major T.A. Lowe, was driving along the Strand in a taxi when it stopped suddenly and the driver ran off. Puzzled by the driver's actions, Lowe too got out. Looking upwards, all suddenly became clear.

> Right overhead was an enormous Zeppelin. It was lighted up by searchlights, and cruised along slowly and majestically, a marvellous sight. I stood gaping in the middle of the Strand, too fascinated to move.

> Then there was a terrific explosion, followed by another and another. The earth shook and trembled: so did I.[8]

This thing of beauty that held MacDonagh, Lowe and countless others entranced that evening, now transformed into a harbinger of death.

A number of London's famous theatres were located between the Strand and Covent Garden. At the Aldwych Theatre the packed audience was enjoying *The Prodigal Son*; at the Strand they thrilled to the adventures of *The Scarlet Pimpernel*; while at the Lyceum they came to see the powerful drama *Between Two Women*; and at the Gaiety no one appeared concerned by the musical comedy's prescient title, *Tonight's the Night*.

At the Lyceum, on the corner of Wellington and Exeter streets, the play had reached the second interval and many of the audience went outside to buy refreshments from fruit sellers in the street or from The Old Bell, a public house across the road. The area was dark as required by the lighting regulations. Those in the street could see searchlights criss-crossing in the sky, but that was not unusual. They may have cast an occasional wary eye upwards but otherwise they carried on going about their business. Newspaper sellers shouted out the headlines, street vendors called out their wares, their stalls barely lit by the feeble light cast from their oil lamps, and some listened as a barrel organ fumbled with the melody of the moment, 'Keep the Home Fires Burning'.[9]

Into this scene of urban normality the first of Breithaupt's HE bombs hurtled down and struck the rear of the Lyceum. Pandemonium broke out in the theatre. Lilian Grundy was waiting for her brother to return from getting a drink when the bomb hit. She pressed herself up against a wall as other bombs exploded in the street: 'In absolute silence, it seemed we waited for death – or life. Everyone seemed just turned to stone.'[10] Another theatregoer, G. Hannam, was there with a friend and recalled the confusion:

> How we got out I can never remember. Men were carrying their women-folk out over their shoulders; children were being helped; people were calling for each other. I helped a poor old gentleman up who had fallen, and blood was running down his face where somebody had knocked him down.[11]

Outside the theatre, in Exeter Street, the bomb had also seriously damaged Nos. 36 and 37, killing 23-year-old Arthur Giles while injuring both Amy Spink and Catherine Myers.[12]

Immediately after that first bomb, another exploded in the middle of Wellington Street, right in front of the Lyceum. The blast dug up a large section of the roadway, broke open two gas mains, destroyed a long stretch of electrical cable as well as shattering windows and damaging buildings all around, including the offices of *The Morning Post* newspaper. It exploded where those who had left the theatre during the interval were buying their refreshments. When the first bomb detonated a number of people dived into The Old Bell for shelter, but it did them no good. Charles Davies, aged 48, and his son were among them. The son threw himself behind the counter, which protected him from the vicious flying glass, but the explosion caught his father, who had stooped down below the window. As they carried Charles out, he said to his son: 'I think they have done me; they have smashed my legs.' Closer inspection revealed that the blast had blown off his left kneecap. He died from blood poisoning caused by fragments of clothing carried into the wound. Others in the pub died too and a number suffered injury. A 16-year-old girl who worked for a theatrical costumier made a dash for the pub but was struck on the thigh by a bomb fragment before she could reach it. She too died from blood poisoning after pieces of cloth entered her wound.[13] A woman serving at a fruit stall opposite The Old Bell was selling some apples when she glanced up:

> ... it seemed to me that the sky opened and a ball of fire came down. I did not hear a sound: I was stunned ... the scale was blown out of my hand and was picked up with a big hole through it. The woman I was serving was instantly killed. If it had not been for her, standing in front of me, and being a big woman, I think I should have been killed ... I got off with shrapnel wounds in my head and legs.[14]

Those who now emerged from the Lyceum took in the scene of carnage that confronted them. One of them was Lilian Grundy, now looking for her brother:

> I got to the street, and a dreadful sight it was. A broken gas-main was flaring up from a huge crater, and ambulance men were carrying stretchers of dead and wounded ... I heard someone say: 'Six men killed in a public house at the corner.' Imagine the fever of impatience with which I waited for my dearly-loved brother to come to me. Presently, thank God, he came. Never were brother and sister more glad to see each other![15]

Others were not so lucky. The London Fire Brigade listed 17 people killed and 21 injured by the Wellington Street bomb. A journalist reporting the statement made by a police surgeon at the inquest described some of the injuries encountered at The Old Bell:

> ... he saw the body of a man. Both thighs were smashed, and there had been a good deal of haemorrhage. Another dead man he saw had a cut right through the neck, produced apparently by a piece of glass which had severed both carotid arteries. There was also injury to the spine. A third case was that of a woman who had been wounded in the face. The lower part of her spine had been smashed, and there was a perforated wound in the chest.[16]

A few minutes before the first bomb struck the Lyceum, the stage manager at the Gaiety handed the call-boy, 18-year-old James Wickham, some letters to post in Catherine Street. As he left he bumped into 'Billy', a young lad aged 13, who ran errands at the theatre. The two of them crossed over Aldwych and started to walk up Catherine Street along the side of the Strand Theatre. Wickham stopped for a moment to light a cigarette and as he did so he heard the noise:

> ... a dreadful sound that London knew only too well – a sound like no other on earth. It was the mournful wail created by the velocity of a descending bomb ...
>
> It exploded three yards from where we were standing. It flung me against the wall next the pit entrance to the Strand Theatre. It sucked me back again. It dashed me to the ground. Masonry fell. Glass rained. I felt unhurt; only dazed. Yet I had twenty-two lumps of shrapnel embedded in me. They carried me downstairs to the bar of the Strand Theatre ... I asked for Billy, but he had been blown to pieces. I could hear screams in the street outside.[17]

Those inside the Strand Theatre were a little more fortunate. Miss A.A. Birch and her two sisters were enjoying the performances of Julia Neilson and Fred Terry in *The Scarlett Pimpernel* when they heard the first two bombs explode:

> Everyone jumped to their feet. The Zepps were here! For a moment we were all petrified wondering whether there was to be a third bomb, and, if so, whether it would be on top of us. The moment passed.
>
> Then – Swish! – and a deafening crash. A third bomb had arrived, and had missed us by a few yards. The glass of the windows

splintered to fragments, which flew in all directions; window-frames were forced from their settings, and woodwork was torn from the ceilings. Many people hurriedly left.[18]

Yet among the confusion there was also calm. Even in adversity, the show must go on, as Miss Birch explained:

> Soon all the performers were on the stage, and Mr Terry was addressing the audience, advising them to remain in the comparative safety of the theatre.
>
> Then he turned to the members of the cast and said, 'We will continue'. A scarcely perceptible pause, a sign of assent from the players, and Lady Blakeney and Chauvelin resumed their dialogue. It was strange to hear the sound of traffic through the gaping windows.

After the bomb outside the Strand Theatre, L 15 dropped four more in Aldwych: one landed in the roadway close to the junction with Drury Lane; another near the junction with Kingsway; and remaining two fell to the east of Houghton Street on the former Aldwych Roller Skating Rink, now occupied by the War Refugee Committee for Belgians. These last two caused serious damage to the corrugated iron and wood building, but there was no one on the premises at night. One witness, David Taylor, writing to his sister described how the bomb 'made a mess of it' and that 'the explosion ripped the whole thing from end to end, leaving just the roof trusses bare'.[19]

Edwin Austin and his wife were on the upper deck of a No. 68 bus that turned into Aldwych from the Strand just as the bombs fell. The bomb at the junction with Drury Lane bomb exploded near to the Aldwych theatre and close to the bus, driven by Charles James Tarrant with Charles Rogers as the conductor. They found Rogers, aged 45, lying dead in the street by the bus with a wound on the left side of his chest where a jagged fragment of the bomb had penetrated into his lung. Tarrant, the 30-year-old driver, was dying from a large wound in the back of his neck. A passenger on the bus, Thomas Joseph Pinchon, a special constable on his way to report for duty, also died.[20]

Mrs Austin saw some people rush off the bus but she and her husband did not follow:

> We were in the front seat, and my husband said 'Stay here, where we are!' We crouched down by the name board, and this saved our lives; we felt the concussion of the bombs pass over our heads.

> A piece of shrapnel did hit us, and both of us were injured; my husband was in Charing Cross Hospital for five weeks.[21]

The bomb cut down others in the street too and killed a 74-year-old newspaper seller, William Breeze. Between the Lyceum and the Aldwych theatres, a distance of only 190 yards, the death toll had now grown to 21 dead with at least 46 injured. Among those killed were Thomas Hawley, a 61-year-old bootmaker, whose daughter could only identify his body by his clothes, and 45-year-old David Patton, a house painter. He had been looking for work when hit by bomb fragments, but insisted those helping attend another man first. Mary Louise Shore, the 44-year-old wife of a soldier, died the next day from her injuries; her husband identified the body. Others included a 23-year-old waiter and Edwin Robey, a soft goods manufacturer, who was out for the night with his wife.[22]

Lilian Grundy, who eventually found her brother in the aftermath of the explosions at the Lyceum, had one final trauma to face that night as the siblings turned into Aldwych:

> It was impossible to get a bus or a cab, so we walked home to King's Cross, over window glass which shone like frosted glass on the pavements. As we passed a windowless, forsaken bus, I stepped into an ominous red pool, from which I hastily withdrew. 'Bloke killed there.' Said the solitary man in charge.[23]

Everyone who could tried to help the injured, even a troop of Boy Scouts based near the Strand rushed to the scene. One of the troop, however, was missing. The errand boy from the Gaiety Theatre, who was one of their number, was now fighting for his life. Scout Leader Frank Hutton led his boys into action:

> In semi-darkness the dead and injured lay about on road and pavement in all directions.
>
> We picked up at the bottom of Kingsway a bus driver [Charles Tarrant] whose bus had been hit and wrecked. He was terribly injured, and died in hospital soon after we got him there. At the back of the Lyceum the roadway was alight, and the fire brigade at work on it.
>
> Shutters taken down from shop windows we used as stretchers, carrying the injured one at a time, placed lengthways, in our Scouts' trek cart to Charing Cross Hospital.[24]

Hutton commented that the average age of his troop exposed to this trauma was 14. But while the scouts were helping with the injured, L 15 continued dropping bombs and Breithaupt found a brief moment to take in the scene.

> The picture we saw was indescribably beautiful – shrapnel bursting all around (though rather uncomfortably near us), our own bombs bursting, and the flashes from the anti-aircraft batteries below …
>
> And over us the starlit sky! Still, at such a moment one is inclined to be a little insensitive to the beauties of Nature and to the feelings of the people below. It is only afterward that all this comes to one's consciousness. At the moment it is necessary to concentrate one's attention.[25]

13 October 1915: Lincoln's Inn, London

Breithaupt remained focused and continued releasing bombs. An HE bomb that dropped outside the Bankruptcy Court in Carey Street caused some damage to the building as well as to the pavement and railings. Two incendiaries followed, falling on the Royal Courts of Justice, where they set fire to the roof of a new extension, slightly damaged the west side of the main building and started a fire in a paint store at the rear. Next to feel the force of L 15's bombs was Lincoln's Inn, one of London's Inns of Court. An HE bomb struck the five-storey buildings at 8 and 9 New Square, where a number of barristers had their chambers. The explosion shattered the two upper floors while lesser damage extended through the other rooms of the two buildings. Another bomb immediately followed, landing outside the northern wall of the Chapel in Old Square.[26] The blast pockmarked the stone of the Chapel and destroyed two of its historic seventeenth century stained glass windows.[27] It also caused damage to the surrounding buildings in Old Square. One more bomb, an incendiary, fell within Lincoln's Inn, setting fire to the roof of 8 Stone Buildings.

Chancery Lane runs along the east side of Lincoln's Inn, linking High Holborn and the Strand. Those in the street heard the bombs and started to run. One of them, 53-year-old George Percy Brown, a caterer, had spent the evening at his masonic lodge before dropping in to see a friend on his way home. As they chatted, the sound of exploding bombs reached them, whereupon Brown exclaimed: 'My God, here they are, I must go home.' He dashed out of the house and ran down Chancery Lane.[28]

Breithaupt's next bomb, an HE, exploded in Chancery Lane, between Stone Buildings on one side and a range of shops, offices and homes from Nos. 53 to 73 on the other side, including the Chancery Lane Safe Deposit. The blast caught John Silburn and Winnie Williams, causing injury, but killed the running figure of George Percy Brown. Back at the Strand, Brown's son was with the Boy Scout troop helping the injured. The force of the explosion shattered gas and water mains running under Chancery Lane, pitted the walls of Stone Buildings and caused damage to all the properties across the road. David Taylor, who had seen the bomb damage at the former Aldwych Roller Skating Rink, also went to Chancery Lane, where he noticed a curious effect caused by the burst water main: 'The water got under the wood block paving [in the road] and lifted it for about 100 yards, leaving it in graceful waves.'[29]

At Clifford's Inn, just off Fleet Street, the flamboyant, bohemian artist, Nina Hamnett, was having dinner with a friend. She was about to leave to catch the No. 68 bus from Aldwych to take her home, but her friend persuaded her to stay for another drink. They heard the bombs. Finishing her drink, Nina walked along Fleet Street and crossed over Chancery Lane, but she was not happy: 'When I got to Chancery Lane it was about six inches deep in water ... the water was rushing down the street. I was annoyed as I had a pair of new shoes on and got them wet.' She trudged along the Strand through broken glass until she reached the junction with Wellington Street and Aldwych. The gas main in Wellington Street outside the Lyceum was burning and on seeing the huge green flame she thought another bomb had just landed and sat down on the doorstep of a bank, 'thinking that death was rapidly approaching'. It was from there that she saw the No. 68 bus: 'The people in the 'bus that I should have taken, if I had not had another cigarette and a drink, were sitting in the 'bus with their heads blown off.'[30]

13 October 1915: Gray's Inn, London

From Chancery Lane, L 15 crossed over High Holborn and dropped her next bombs over Gray's Inn, another of the Inns of Court. An HE bomb detonated in the gardens just ten feet from the west wall of 4 Gray's Inn Square. The blast smashed a breach in the wall about ten feet wide and eight feet high, smashing the contents of the room on the ground floor and wrecking the barristers' chambers and offices on the ground and first floors of 3 and 5 Gray's Inn Square.

In one of the rooms was a priest, Philip Sidney. He served at the Church of St Alban-the-Martyr on the other side of Gray's Inn Road, but had rooms at Gray's Inn Square. He had just climbed the stairs and sat down to take his boots off when he heard the bomb explode in Chancery Lane. Thinking it safer to be downstairs, he only got as far as the landing before the bomb detonated just outside:

> All I remember is the loudest explosion I ever heard, accompanied by a strong, incessant singing noise in my ears.
>
> Then I saw a great oak door suddenly lift itself off its hinges and fly past me at great speed, just missing my head. There was a noise of falling brickwork and flying glass all round me. A terrific tornado of wind took me off my feet and, like the man on the flying trapeze in the popular song, I found myself flying through the air with the greatest of ease; and then everything seemed suddenly to go out: complete blank and blackness.[31]

The blast sent Sidney flying down two flights of stairs to land in the front doorway buried under fallen rubble with his clothes torn to shreds. The next thing he remembered was a bright light shining into his eyes and two policemen standing over him. 'I heard one say to the other: "He's dead. I'm afraid to get him out of this." On hearing this I woke up with a start and said: "No I'm not. I've been blown up by a Zepp bomb."' Incredibly, Philip Sidney only suffered bruises and a deep cut to his left hand.

L 15 dropped some incendiary bombs over Gray's Inn too. One smashed through the roof of 14 South Square but failed to ignite. Two landed in Gray's Inn Square, one of them damaging an electricity distribution box and breaking a section of pavement, while another crashed through the roof of the Benchers' Robing-room attached to the ancient Great Hall. As one eyewitness recounted, flames quickly engulfed the single-storey, flat-roofed building: 'A few seconds sufficed to make this room a furnace. The open door showed nothing but one white sheet of rolling flame.' Determined to prevent the fire spreading to the Great Hall, the housekeeper at Gray's Inn, Charles Sansom, quickly gathered willing hands and together they succeeded in dousing the fierce fire by pouring water through the hole the bomb had made in the roof.[32]

After Gray's Inn, Breithaupt turned to the east, dropping an incendiary that caused a large fire in a five-storied business premises at 58–62 Leather Lane, occupied by an optician, a diamond setter and a china merchant, followed by three incendiaries in Hatton Garden, causing fires at Nos. 49, 66 and 67. The next incendiary landed in Farringdon Road. During Heinrich Mathy's raid over the area on 8–9 September, all buildings from Nos. 29 to 79 suffered damage to a greater or lesser extent, but No. 81 had escaped untouched. This time, however, No. 81 was not so lucky, the bomb setting fire to the roof and two upper floors of the five-storied building occupied by wholesale jewellers H. Williamson Ltd. All the time L 15 progressed over central London the anti-aircraft guns kept up a steady if inaccurate fire. Unfortunately one of these shells also landed in Farringdon Road, killing 26-year-old William Henry Clayton.

13 October 1915, 9.25pm: Moorgate, London

While the anti-aircraft fire continued to be largely ineffective, London did now have the new French 75mm mobile gun acquired by Lt Cdr Rawlinson from Paris in September. Rawlinson had spent the day training his men at their base at the Talbot Works near Ladbroke Grove and had dismissed them to their billets at 6.00pm, with orders for them to reassemble three hours later. A little before 7.00pm, however, he received a phone call informing him Zeppelins had crossed the coast and could reach London at around 9.00pm. Rawlinson sent out orders to the men's billets and those that were there began to 'dribble in' while he supervised the preparation of the gun and ammunition caisson for action. At 8.25pm Rawlinson received orders to proceed with the gun to a position selected for it in the City, at the Honourable Artillery Company (HAC) ground, which lay between City Road, Bunhill Row and Chiswell Street. But he still did not have enough men to guarantee the efficient working of the gun, 'so was forced to await their arrival in an absolute agony of impatience'. Finally, at five minutes past 9 o'clock, all was ready and Rawlinson, in his own car, led the gun and caisson out on to the road with all headlights lit and sirens on. The problem now was to make their way right across London through the traffic in the shortest time possible:[33]

> Everyone understood at once, in the light of their experience during the previous month, the moment they saw us coming, that an air raid was imminent. They did not, however, know 'where to go' or 'what to do,' though none of them had any doubt at all that the *most pressing* and *most vital* thing they had to do was TO GET OUT OF OUR WAY.

Rawlinson's convoy made good progress until it reached Oxford Street, the major shopping thoroughfare in the West End:

> After passing Marble Arch the traffic in Oxford Street became much thicker. The noise of our 'sirens' being as 'deafening' as the glare of our lights was 'dazzling,' the omnibuses in every direction were seeking safety on the pavement. I also observed, out of the corner of my eye, several instances of people flattening themselves against shop windows, the public being at that time infinitely more fearful of a gun moving at such a terrific speed than they were of any German bombs.

The excitement of Rawlinson's journey, however, did not end there. From Oxford Street he continued along Holborn, noting as he did so that his speed was 56mph – possibly the fastest any one has ever driven down this extremely busy London thoroughfare either before or since! But in Holborn, disaster threatened when Rawlinson realized there were roadworks directly ahead and that the traffic formed a solid mass in the only open path. Considering it too late to break, Rawlinson made the immediate decision to smash straight through the road works, noticing that they appeared almost complete beyond the trestles and pole that blocked his passage. Satisfied that the road ahead offered minimal threat, without slowing down he headed straight for the pole:

> The infernal 'pole' itself, however, I did not like the look of at all, as, being in a very low car, I was in painful uncertainty what would happen, not whether or not it would *hit* me, but *where* I should catch it, whether in the face or lower down.

Rawlinson was lucky. His car tyres hit the pole and split it in two, the sections flying up into the air and away to each side, with the car only suffering minor damage to the radiator. A similar pole blocked the exit from the roadworks but help was at hand this time:

> I observed a member of that most gallant and reliable force, the London Police, moving a great deal quicker and less sedately than he was accustomed to move. He was actually rushing, without his helmet and at top speed, towards the other pole ... This he succeeded in removing in the very nick of time, being just able to push it over on the ground before we reached it.

After Holborn, Rawlinson encountered no more delays, but as the 75mm anti-aircraft gun swung into position at the HAC grounds, he looked up and saw L 15 heading straight towards them at a height he estimated from 8,000 to 10,000 feet. He could hear the 'insistent roar of its engines' punctuated by the sound of exploding bombs. To speed up the process of preparing the gun for firing, the bullish Rawlinson let his car headlights illuminate it, aware that this could also draw the attention of the Zeppelin: 'This fact, however, did not worry us at all, as the nearer they came to *us* the better chance we had of *hitting them.*'

With no time to use any instruments to judge the range, Rawlinson made a quick mental calculation of the Zeppelin's speed, height and range, passed this on to the crew, who immediately fired their first shot at 9.25pm:

> We then all watched anxiously, during the interminable seconds of the 'time of flight' of the shell, to observe the 'burst'. When it finally came it was 'short', but it must have very considerably surprised the enemy who had been informed, with what had been great accuracy a fortnight or so previously that there were no anti-aircraft *high-explosive* shells in the London defences.[34]

Rawlinson reported that L 15 kept on coming straight towards their position, and then his gun-layer called out, 'Gun no longer bears, sir'. The 75mm gun's maximum elevation was 83 degrees, giving it a 'dead circle' directly over the gun. All they could do now was realign the gun for when L15 became a target again in a few seconds. Meanwhile, Rawlinson waited for the Zeppelin's bombs to fall on them:

> They fell all right, I don't know how many of them but they made the devil of a noise, and brought down several of the houses on the Moorgate Street side of the ground, with a roar of falling masonry.

Rawlinson was pleased, it meant the Zeppelin had passed them and would not come back. He fired a second shot; this time they saw the shell burst 'above and quite close' to the target, then heard more bombs dropping to the east of his position. He also saw L 15 release a great cloud of water ballast as it began to climb out of range of his gun as quickly as possible. In an official report released by the German authorities, it stated: 'A German airship was the object of unusually hot fire, but was not damaged.'[35]

Up above, commenting on the anti-aircraft fire, Breithaupt noted:

> The shells exploded for the most part too high. From all sides blazed the flashes of the guns. We had only one thing to do – carry on and trust in our star. What effect the bombs had at the places where flames were observed I cannot say, but I believe it was pretty warm in the City.[36]

Since Breithaupt dropped his bomb on Farringdon Road, he had travelled about three quarters of a mile without releasing more, until he dropped the two that fell 400 yards south of Rawlinson's gun. They exploded in Finsbury Pavement, a road running between Finsbury Square and London Wall. The bombs smashed gas and water mains, damaged buildings let out as offices, shops and homes and smashed countless windows, with the damage extending from Finsbury Pavement to South Place, Moorfields and Ropemaker Street. But they also claimed lives; as in 'Theatreland', just ordinary people in the wrong place at the wrong time.

Henry William Cansbrook, a 37-year-old solicitor's clerk, special constable and father of four from Carshalton, Surrey, was getting off a bus when a fragment of the bomb struck him. He was still alive when he reached hospital, informing nursing staff, 'They caught me in the back'. The fragment opened a wound measuring about an inch, fractured the eighth left-side rib and penetrated his lung. Cansbrook died the following day.[37] A gunner of the Royal Field Artillery, 19-year-old Henry Absolom from Bethnal Green in East London, had a few hours leave on 13 October and used it to visit his family. The bomb cut him down while on his way back to barracks; he died from 'syncope brought about by a wound in the back'.[38] Absolom's mother was dead and his father an invalid, so it fell to his 15-year-old sister, Susan, to identify the body:

> About midnight I was awakened. Two policemen had come to tell us my brother had been killed ... I was taken through the City, and shown the spot where the bomb was dropped just outside Moorgate-street station, where they found my brother.
>
> From there I was taken to Golden-lane Mortuary to identify him. Imagine the shock! Not only did I see my brother, but many of the victims of the night's raid – a most horrible sight I shall never forget.[39]

Margaret Whelan, a 25-year-old waitress, had gone to a Young Women's Guild meeting after work. When it finished she had some shopping to do. It was then that she fell victim to one of the bombs in Finsbury Pavement, the fatal wound being in her neck. Nearby another body lay slumped in the street. A bomb fragment had killed tobacconist's assistant, Henry Vinson, aged 25, passing down through his body from his head, damaging his heart and stomach. A fifth victim, 50-year-old office cleaner Caroline Louisa Hill, when told there was a Zeppelin about said, 'It's best to go home early', but two minutes later she staggered into a shop badly injured.[40] A bomb fragment, about one inch by a quarter of an inch, had struck her back and smashed a rib, before damaging the liver and lodging in the right pleural cavity surrounding the lung. She died in hospital a week later. The last person killed by these bombs clung on to life for 22 days. A tiny fragment of the bomb had struck George Alwyn Ruse, aged 18, another tobacconist's assistant, as he was about to go down the steps leading to Moorgate Street Underground station. Weighing only three grams, the fragment pierced his back, fractured his spine and crushed his spinal cord. While undergoing treatment he suffered serious kidney and bladder infections in hospital and eventually died on 4 November.[41] In addition to those killed, the bomb injured eight.

13 October 1915, 9.30pm: Aldgate, London

Breithaupt and L 15 passed Liverpool Street Station on their port side as they prepared to release their final bombs on London. The first crashed down on 1 Minories, a large building standing on the corner of Aldgate High Street and Minories. The explosion partly demolished the building, which housed the London & South Western Bank on the ground floor and Trubilsky and Harris' hotel on the upper floors. The buildings on either side – John Pearce's restaurant at 2 Minories and the Rose and Crown public house at 79 Aldgate High Street – also suffered badly. At the Rose & Crown, Jacob Shilofsky, a tailor from Mile End, was having a drink with his wife, Hettie, when the sound of gun fire reached them. The Belgian landlord shouted for everyone to get down to the cellar and about 30 of his customers reached safety as the bomb exploded, but Hettie and Jacob did not. The blast collapsed the ceiling above them before they could reach the cellar steps. Although injured, Jacob managed to extricate himself, but when he called for his wife, she answered from below the rubble, 'I am killed; I can't come out'.[42] He managed to pull his wife free but her pain must have been excruciating as a fragment of the bomb had buried itself deep in her left thigh, shattering her femur into a great number of pieces, leaving muscle and tendons exposed. The fragment extracted from the wound measured two and a quarter inches by an inch wide and weighed 17 grams. Hettie, a mother of six, died in hospital the following day.[43] Seven other people close by were also injured by the bomb and a horse in the street was killed. The blast shattered shop fronts and windows in 14 other premises in Minories, caused varying amounts of damage to 30 properties in Aldgate High Street, smashing windows in 20 buildings in Houndsditch and three in Church Row.

Beyond Minories, Breithaupt may have noticed the concentration of railway tracks east of Fenchurch Street Station, because his next two bombs landed in close proximity to them. The first exploded at the rear of 92 Chamber Street, which ran parallel to the line, and less than 300 yards from the Royal Mint. The blast dug a crater in the ground and caused havoc in the house, which was let out as tenements. Four people inside sustained injuries: Frederick Coster, John Wilshan, Reuben Pizer and Mary Hearn. Along both sides of Chamber Street other dwellings suffered lesser damage, with this extending to properties in Great Prescot Street that backed on to Chamber Street, and smashed windows in Leman Street. Seconds later another HE bomb exploded on the east side of Leman Street, in Mill Yard. It caused severe damage at 10 and 11 Mill Yard, two houses of five rooms each let out as tenements, and injured two of the occupants, Sarah Hose and Kelvos Cohen. The effects of the bomb were also felt in Leman Street, where it damaged the Black Bear public house and a tobacconist shop next door at No. 141, while also knocking down a large brick wall and breaking windows at Leman Street Station.

Breithaupt now had one final bomb for London. It fell on Prince's Square, between Cable Street and the London Western Dock. The bomb struck No. 54, occupied by J. Smith & Co., tarpaulin manufacturers, wrecking the building and killing a horse. The bomb also damaged the building next door, which comprised cow sheds and a dairy belonging to W. Jones, injuring a cow. The crash of broken glass from 12 other buildings in the square was the final sound of the raid as L 15 departed. The AA guns ceased firing at 9.35pm as L 15 disappeared from view – the raid itself had only lasted ten minutes. They had not hit L 15 but a number of their shells caused damage on the ground. As well as the shell that landed in Farringdon Road, the London Fire Brigade recorded the fall of ten in East London, another in Clifton Street, not far from where Rawlinson's 75mm gun opened fire, one on the Dempsey

Arms public house on Oxford Street and two in Westminster, one of which smashed through the roof of the Westminster Public Library in Great Smith Street, just 250 yards from Westminster Abbey. In London a total of 38 people died as a result of the raid with another 87 injured.

13 October 1915, 9.40pm: Sutton's Farm, Essex

Generally the anti-aircraft guns had not had a great night, and it had also been another night of frustration for the aircraft. Shortly before 8.00pm, advised of Zeppelins in the Thetford area, the War Office ordered the airfields at Northolt, Hainault Farm, Sutton's Farm and Joyce Green to each send up one B.E.2c if weather permitted. There was much ground fog about. Northolt was declared unfit for flying, but at 8.00pm 2nd Lt F.H. Jenkins took off from Hainault Farm. Having seen nothing he returned to base at 9.30pm, five minutes before Breithaupt ended his bombing run over London. With fog shrouding the airfield, he landed a little short of the runway, striking a hedge and barbed wire fence, which broke the propeller and slashed at the fabric covering the lower wing. Lt R.J. Tipton took off from Joyce Green at 8.20pm, cleared the layer of mist and climbed to 8,000 feet, but at about 9.25pm be began to lose engine pressure, forcing him to return. Capt. Leslie da Costa Penn-Gaskell took the second patrol from Joyce Green, taking off at 9.40pm, but engine problems forced him to turn back before he reached the patrol height of 8,000 feet.[44]

John Slessor, an 18-year-old 2nd Lieutenant, had only reported for duty at Sutton's Farm that morning. He had only one night flight under his belt so, with fog building up, he gratefully received instructions to delay his take-off until he could see the airfield's landing flares through the gloom. At 9.40pm he took his chance. He had only climbed his B.E.2c to 2,500 feet when he saw a searchlight fix on the homebound L 15. At 9.50pm, L 15 had flown close to the airfield at Hainault Farm and 2nd Lt C.E. Wardle took off from there in pursuit, but never saw L 15 again once he was airborne. He lost his flare path in the fog as he returned and damaged his B.E.2c on landing. Meanwhile, Slessor urged his slow-climbing aircraft upwards, keeping his eye on L 15 for three or four minutes before he ran into a layer of cloud. When he emerged L 15 had gone. Slessor kept up an unsuccessful search before eventually abandoning the hunt and returning to Sutton's Farm at 11.15pm. As he came in to land through the low-lying fog, a searchlight operator turned on his light thinking to assist his approach, but it only succeeded in blinding the young pilot. His B.E.2c came down in a vegetable field, tipped up on to its nose, broke its undercarriage and damaged a wingtip, but a much relieved Slessor walked away unharmed.[45]

Confirming the Admiralty's dim view of night-flying Zeppelin patrols, none of the RNAS pilots left the ground that night but, although the RFC pilots had no luck, their efforts did not go unnoticed. Nor did the efforts of the mobile 13-pdrs placed at Loughton and Hainault Farm, as both had opened fire on L 15 as she passed, getting off ten rounds between them. Breithaupt, although he thought he was nearer Leyton than Loughton, recognized that London's defences were showing a marked improvement over what he had been told to expect:

> We breathed more freely as about [9.45pm] we left the City behind us. Then suddenly, as we were about over Leyton, from a direction in which we had not expected it, a new and murderous fire began. At the same time, through the rays of the searchlights a shower of enemy airplanes flashed.[46]

For Breithaupt, it was now time to reflect on their mission.

> Now that the airship was out of the chief danger zone and there was time to take note, it was possible for the crew to enjoy the whole drama and with their comrades to feel the pride of being employed in the service of the Fatherland.[47]

Heading out on a north-east course, L 15 received 'pom-pom' fire at about 9.55pm from the gun at Kelvedon Heath, then continued on the same course towards Ipswich. On the east side of the town, sub-Lt F.E. Slee of the RNVR was in position with another mobile 'pom-pom' on Rushmere Heath. Seeing the approach of L 15, he gave the order to open fire. After 50 rounds the crew reloaded with another belt and, after firing 20 of these, L 15 circled back towards the gun and dropped four HE bombs. They landed about 400 yards south of the target, one on a golf course, one in a field of potatoes and two in a turnip field. L 15 then resumed a north-east course, while the 'pom-pom' fired off a third and final belt as the target melted into the night sky. Without any of the technical instruments necessary for accurate fire or searchlights, the gun had been no more than a minor irritation to Breithaupt and his crew rather than a threat. A mobile maxim gun at Woodbridge opened fire on L 15 at about 11.30pm but she continued on her course, reaching the coast at Aldeburgh at a few minutes before midnight. There was, however, an unceremonious end to the mission ahead.

Breithaupt reached the vicinity of a fog-blanketed Nordholz at around 10.00am local time, with only two hours of fuel left. He waited, hoping the fog would lift, but it remained stubbornly in place. At about 11.40am, he could wait no longer and made the first of a number of landing attempts, but each time he descended into the fog he failed to see the ground and, fearing he might strike one of the airship sheds, or even the gasometer, climbed up again. Two of his engines were now dead and the other two only working intermittently. At noon, with time running out, Breithaupt descended again. At 250 feet he threw out the landing ropes in the hope that someone on the ground would see them, but it was to no avail, and then the last two engines finally gave out. Rather than be carried out to sea by the wind, Breithaupt released hydrogen and the front of L 15 crumpled into moorland about three miles from Nordholz. Seven days later, however, with repairs made, L 15 transferred to her new berth at Hage.[48] It had been quite an eventful first raid for Joachim Breithaupt and the crew of L 15, an eventful foray that proved to be the last German air raid of 1915.

Chapter 19

The Home Front Line

The October 1915 raid on Britain came close to fulfilling Germany's great hope for the Zeppelins – a multi-airship raid on London, the financial heart of the country and the hub of the British Empire. The difficulties of navigation over England, however, had meant that only one actually reached the central part of the city. In an aid to navigation, German airships were now able to send radio messages back to Germany to request a position check. Two ground stations in Germany would respond, giving the airship's bearing by wireless telegraphy. With the two bearings transferred to a map, the point where they met indicated the airship's position. Certainly at this early stage the accuracy of these findings left a lot to be desired, as the general proximity of the ground stations – Nordholz and Borkum being only 80 miles apart – coupled with the distance the signals had to travel, meant the angle of interception remained narrow and therefore limited accuracy. The signals also had the added disadvantage that British direction-finding stations could pick them up too. On that October night, no Zeppelin sent location requests until they were about to embark on the return flight over the North Sea. By the end of the raid the British had recognized the individual call signs for each Zeppelin, with L 13 using U.N., L 15 transmitting as U.O., L 14 was U.U., L 16 sent out the signal U.L. and L 11 used U.J.. It was the first time Zeppelins had sent such messages while over Britain. The accuracy of the location system did improve in time as new ground stations were established, but Zeppelin commanders kept its use to a minimum to conceal their position from the British.[1]

Compiled by Lt Col R.H. James of the Directorate of Home Defence and distributed on 23 October, the report that commented on the Zeppelin radio signals also presented a wide-ranging analysis of the response delivered by the War Office's temporary defence arrangements. The strategy of deploying three lines of observers had worked well, prompting the report to conclude:

> The satisfactory working of the 'Observer' Cordons, however, gave ample warning both to the aeroplanes and to the guns and lights. It is, therefore, open to question whether it would not be better to rely entirely upon reports from pre-arranged observer stations and so avoid crowding telephone lines with reports from other sources, which are often vague and unreliable. The success of the cordon system on its first trial seems to point to the desirability of its extension West and South of London.

The sheer number of telephone messages received at Home Defence headquarters from the observers, however, severely tested its resources. There were four dedicated telephone lines at the War Office switchboard for these incoming reports, and a ten-line switchbox from which another telephone could contact directly any or all of ten specified important 'stations', but those on duty soon recognized the limitations of the arrangements:[2]

> Extreme difficulty was experienced in taking in long distance messages owing to the unavoidable babel of five simultaneous telephone conversations in one room.
>
> The urgent need of a room equipped with the necessary sound proof telephone compartments was demonstrated in a manner which leaves no room for doubt.

The report recommended a room with six incoming telephone lines and a separate room with three lines for outgoing calls.

The military were also generally pleased with the role of the mobile 13-pdr guns, which took up their new positions on the morning of the raid, noting that all came into action. The report attributed this success to the careful logging of Zeppelin routes on previous raids, although the efficiency of the guns came into question, a consequence of 'the lack of experience and training of the personnel'. In his analysis, Lt Col James felt sure that the unexpected positions of these mobile AA guns had served to confuse the raiders, who received briefings on known gun positions prior to an attack. This conclusion appears to be borne out by German reports on the night's raid. The mechanical failures experienced by some guns though led James to recommend that, where possible, guns be sited in supporting pairs, 'so that in the event of the failure of one gun the fleeting opportunities presented for attacking the raiders may not be wholly lost'.

The role of the aeroplanes during this October raid also received attention, and while the observer cordon passed on information regarding approaching Zeppelins in time for aircraft to get airborne and reach patrol height, the poor weather conditions had hampered the response by the RFC, and the RNAS had sent up no aircraft at all. There was a call for more well-illuminated landing grounds as well as an increase in searchlights to help locate raiding Zeppelins, but the experiment in sending different coloured rockets up as a means of advising pilots of the direction taken by the raiders failed, the rockets being more visible from the ground than in the air.

All these defensive arrangements highlighted by the report, were those put in place by the War Office against an anticipated October attack, yet responsibility still officially lay with the Admiralty. After the raids on London in September, the Admiralty had appointed Admiral Sir Percy Scott to direct London's gunnery defence. Having accepted the appointment and reviewed the limited guns available, Scott had requested more through the proper channels. The Admiralty, however, worked at its own pace. As Scott put it: 'Nothing could put any life into their movements.' When, two days after the October raid, he enquired about his order for more guns, the First Lord, Arthur Balfour, discovered that the paperwork was still awaiting attention. Scott immediately responded by placing an order for the guns himself, but when the factories contacted the Admiralty for confirmation the whole process bogged down again. On 18 October he had had enough and put pen to paper, presenting Balfour with what amounted to an ultimatum:

> If I am to be responsible for the gunnery defence of London, I must be allowed to do things in my own way, and not be interfered with by the Admiralty. If the Admiralty are to settle what guns are to be used for the defence of London, and how they are to be obtained, then they become responsible for the gunnery defence of London and I resign.
>
> If I am to remain in charge of the gunnery defence of London I must have a free hand to procure what is wanted, how best I can, and not to be handicapped by Admiralty red-tapism.[3]

The resignation of Admiral Sir Percy Scott would have raised some awkward questions after the Admiralty had heralded his appointment just five weeks earlier, so Balfour stepped in and the logjam began to clear. Still doubting the speed of the Admiralty departments under Balfour though, Scott wrote direct to Sir John Jellicoe, commander of the Grand Fleet, in his quest for guns:

> He promptly wired back that I could have twenty.
>
> We extracted out of the Admiralty with difficulty another fourteen guns; Lord Kitchener [Secretary of State for War] very promptly gave me some; and with others that we picked up I found that in a very short time we had increased our number of guns from twelve to one hundred and eighteen.[4]

The sheer variety of guns involved led the Prime Minister, Herbert Asquith, to describe them as 'a menagerie', but Scott reasoned that 'any guns were better than no guns'. Having the guns, however, was not the same as being able to use them. All these guns needed high-angle mountings fitted before deployment in an AA role, but these would take a considerable time to manufacture. Frustrated by this delay, Scott looked to France again, this time securing 34 of the excellent 75mm guns along with 20,000 rounds of high-explosive ammunition. Scott envisaged a plan involving two gun rings around London requiring the installation of 104 guns supported by 50 searchlights, in addition to those guns directly defending the capital. By the end of November 1915, he had earmarked 152 guns, but the delays in constructing the mountings meant they only became available piecemeal.[5] By mid-November, Scott had 24 guns ready for service, double the number available on his appointment two months earlier. Among those 24 defending London in November were Rawlinson's mobile guns. Besides the original 75mm gun, Rawlinson acquired three more of the same type from France, and in addition had mounted eight Vickers 3-pdr guns on Lancia motor lorries, a 3-inch, 20cwt gun on a Daimler lorry and another of this type on a trailer hauled by another Daimler. Nine of these were included in the mid-November tally. The mobile brigade had found a new home too, in the grand stables at Kenwood House in Hampstead, North London, offered to them by the house's occupier, the exiled Grand Duke Michael of Russia.[6]

While Rawlinson had been busy organising his mobile AA brigade, he also found time to make a significant improvement to the ammunition these guns were firing. When Admiral Scott took control he discovered there was no time fuse considered 'safe' for use with high-explosive shells and that the problem had remained unsolved for a number of years. Instead, most of the available guns fired common shells that, 'had so small a bursting charge that they could do no harm to a Zeppelin, and they returned to earth almost as intact as when they were put into the guns'.[7] Aware that much of Rawlinson's previous work had involved testing high-explosives and manufacturing fuses, he passed on the problem to his able deputy. Rawlinson claims that an hour later he presented Scott with a drawing showing a modification to an existing fuse that rendered it 'absolutely safe' for use with HE.[8]

Rawlinson next turned his attention to investigating the shells themselves. On the principal of what goes up must come down, shells fired into the air will ideally break up into small pieces, reducing the risk to life and property on the ground. The standard shell at the time, however, required a base much thicker than the sides to cope with the force exerted on it by the propellant charge. Although the sides of the shell would break into small pieces when it exploded, inevitably the more solid base remained intact and in itself became a dangerous missile to those below. Rawlinson redesigned the shells, removing the need for thicker metal at the base by changing its shape from flat to domed. This offered similar resistance to the propellant but allowed it to fragment into small pieces when detonated, creating a greater potential for inflicting damage on the target, while offering a reduced risk to those below.[9] With the new design to hand, Scott now needed to get them manufactured. Fully aware of the unhurried nature of the Admiralty's administration system, Scott decided, 'The Admiralty had to be avoided', and looked to France once more:

> So I took the designs over to Paris and placed the order with a motor-car manufacturer, who executed the work well and quickly. In a very short time I saw my way to providing most of the guns used for the defence of London with satisfactory time-fuses and high-explosive shells.[10]

The danger to the population that Scott hoped these new shells would reduce was very real. The novelty of these early air raids meant many people chose to be out in the open, for the urge to see one of the enemy's hated airships far outweighed fears of personal injury. Nothing like this had ever happened before and people wanted to see it for themselves, to share in a unique experience. Words like terror, beauty, fascination, excitement, horror and fear appear equally in contemporary eyewitness accounts. There is no doubt that the sight of a lone Zeppelin high in the sky, caught by searchlights and illuminated to a silvery glow, had a terrible beauty of its own. And, importantly, if that Zeppelin was not directly over you, it became a sight to excite and thrill and not one to fear. To those out in the street, mesmerized by these remarkable inventions of the new century, the unseen threat presented by falling shrapnel seemed a small price to pay.

The subject of public air raid warnings regularly echoed in the corridors of power, but they resulted in a decision that warnings were inappropriate for London, but permitted towns and cities elsewhere in the country to follow their own paths. In response to questions on the subject in the House of Commons, the Home Secretary, Sir John Simon, gave an extensive answer on 21 October 1915.[11] He first explained that although the authorities received notification of the presence of Zeppelins over the North Sea, in many cases they were on scouting missions and did not come inland. The authorities also received news when Zeppelins crossed the coast, but at this point there was no way of knowing if London was a target. To advise the whole of London to the possibility of a raid, he explained, when more often than not one did not materialize would be counter-productive and frustrating for the population. Continuing, Sir John disclosed that even if a threat to London did appear, it was not possible to predict where the attack would strike. As he pointed out, this was 'for the best of all reasons, that the Zeppelin itself had not the remotest idea, and there were strong reasons for believing that it had not only no idea in advance but a very hazy idea after the event'. The Home Secretary added that a London-wide warning could even assist the raiders in finding their target:

> A better guide could not be imagined for a Zeppelin wandering about the flats in Essex or about Epping Forest than suddenly hearing the unanimous chorus of all the church bells and steam whistles of the Metropolis.

He then questioned what Londoners would do if advised that a raid may take place in an hour or two. His conclusion, based on evidence from previous raids, was that they would congregate in the streets to watch, thus endangering themselves. Figures of air raid casualties so far showed that more injuries occurred in the street than in houses, and these at times when the majority of people would normally be indoors. This, he felt, 'went to show that the probable consequence of telling everybody that there might be a Zeppelin to-night would not reduce the number of people suffering injury'. He also explained that he had considered the problem presented by places of entertainment. If the patrons of theatres and cinemas were warned, he feared large numbers would find 'the alternative attraction too good to be missed' and run out into the street. And if the audiences attempted to go home, they would find train services from the main London stations suspended when air raids threatened, forcing crowds to gather at these prime targets. Sir John informed the Commons that the Government believed, 'that, on the whole, it was better not to attempt to warn people of the suggested approach of the Zeppelins'. He then concluded that the decision was not made 'to conceal from the people of England the truth,' rather, 'It was a deliberate policy adopted as a practical decision after most carefully weighing the pros and cons of the matter'. It would, in fact, be another 21 months before London adopted a public air raid warning system.

There was also another important subject under discussion in the late autumn of 1915 – when would the War Office assume responsibility for home air defence? Since Winston Churchill originally accepted responsibility on behalf of the Admiralty in September 1914, when the RFC was fully committed to support the British Expeditionary Force in Europe, it had always been with the understanding that it was a temporary arrangement. Although unable to take on the task, many within the Army remained critical of the Admiralty's handling of the situation in the intervening period. Then, following Arthur Balfour's appointment as First Lord of the Admiralty in May 1915, he formally asked the War Office to relieve the Admiralty of the role. Two conferences followed in the summer of 1915, which resulted in the War Office stating that 'if no fresh calls were made on the Royal Flying Corps the army might be in a position to meet home defence air requirements about January 1916'.[12] Yet no one pressed this to a conclusion, until the War Office raised the question again in September 1915, following the Admiralty's appointment of Sir Percy Scott to command the capital's anti-aircraft guns. The Admiralty was still absorbing the report on the Paris defences at the time so proposed another conference in mid-December, however, the War Office refused to delay further and insisted on bringing it forward to 10 November.[13]

At the conference, representatives of the Admiralty proposed that the Army assume responsibility for the air defence of the whole of Britain from a line drawn about 20 miles inland from the coast, while the Navy pilots defended that 20-mile sector and out to sea. Although the Director-General of Military Aeronautics, Sir David Henderson, agreed to this arrangement, he still needed War Office approval, but that was not forthcoming. Instead, the War Office counter-proposed that the Navy deal with all enemy aircraft approaching the British coast, while the Army would confront any that came inland. The Admiralty agreed, and on 29 November presented details of the proposed transfer of responsibility for approval to the Cabinet's War Committee. Frustratingly for all concerned, approval remained on hold. Lord Kitchener was away in the Dardanelles and in his absence and without his views, the committee was reluctant to rubber stamp the agreement. In the meantime, the Army and Navy, assuming approval was only a matter of time, began a gradual process of transferring London's guns and searchlights.[14] Yet there were many twists and turns ahead before the official handover of responsibility would finally take place in February 1916.

While this indecision prevented much genuine progress in developing an effective aerial defence through the late autumn of 1915, Britain was fortunate in that wintery weather blew in after the October raid and prevented any more air attacks that year. From that first air raid in December 1914, when a single aeroplane dropped a bomb in a garden in Dover, German aircraft had made 25 incursions over England, 20 of these raids made by airships and five by aeroplane. These 20 airship raids were carried out by 35 airships (33 Zeppelin and two Schütte–Lanz), with two of the Zeppelins – the Navy's L 10 and the Army's LZ 38 – each taking part in five raids.[15]

The effectiveness of these raids, however, led to differing opinions. British reporting dismissed the raids as largely ineffective, but in Germany the press rejected the idea of limited damage on mainly civilian targets, believing them an attempt to cover up the real impact their raids were having. As one writer, a former naval officer, Ernst Graf zu Reventlow, cynically commented in a German newspaper after the September 1915 raids:

> People in Germany will continue as before to pass over with a cool and intelligent smile the reports which may be expected in the next few days in the English newspapers and the news sent to neutral countries. The world will learn once more that no material damage has been done, but that an old man and a young girl have been seriously injured, and that some babies have been burnt in their cradles. We shall also hear of the bomb in the girls' school, and of the person of middle age whose arm has been torn from his body.[16]

The reports filed by Zeppelin commanders, telling of raging fires in the docks and huge warehouses collapsing under the weight of their bombs, were exactly what the German people expected of their iconic airships. They saw the British stories of their venerated Zeppelins bombing tiny villages and ploughing up farmers' fields as just that, stories, providing clear evidence to them that the campaign was taking its toll on the British people. But generally, the reports published in the British press rang true. While restrictions placed on reporting in June 1915 prevented newspapers naming where the bombs had fallen, they could still intimate the region and describe the damage inflicted.

While the early raids of 1915 were largely experimental, by the autumn the Zeppelin crews were gaining in confidence and experience, and the raids had begun to have a real impact on the prime target of London. More Zeppelins were on the way too to keep up the pressure. Between the October 1915 raid and the end of the year, seven new Zeppelins rolled off the production line. The Army and Navy both received three of these 'p-class' models, but the Navy also received Zeppelin L 20 in December 1915, the first of a new 'q-class'. It was a timely addition because on 17 November, eleven days after the Navy took possession of L 18, an accidental fire destroyed her in her shed at Tondern in Schleswig-Holstein.

The commander of the Naval Airship Division, Peter Strasser, maintained a total belief in the ability of Zeppelins to carry the war effectively to Britain and constantly pushed the airship's designers for improved models. Even before the first 'p-class' was completed in May 1915, the demand for a larger model had been made, with the proviso that it must be housed within the constraints of the sheds then available. The Navy, however, rejected the subsequent designs and in July 1915 revised its request, asking instead for a significantly larger model, measuring around 650 feet in length and driven by six engines instead of the standard four. This new model, designated the 'r-class', promised a dramatic overall increase in performance. To accommodate it, orders instructed engineers to lengthen some existing sheds and change the specification of those under construction. In the meantime, alterations were authorized to improve the existing 'p-class' design, lengthening the framework to allow the insertion of two more gas cells. This became the 'q-class'. The alterations extended the model from 536 feet in length to 585 feet, still within the dimensions of the standard Zeppelin sheds, while increasing its hydrogen volume by 137,700 cubic feet, boosting it up to 1,264,100. The extra lift generated by the hydrogen increased its official ceiling by about 1300 feet and allowed it to carry an extra 1,400kg (about 3,000lb) of crew, fuel or weapons.[17] The Navy would add five 'q-class' Zeppelins to its fleet between December 1915 and May 1916, in which latter month it would also take delivery of L 30, the first of the new 'r-class' Zeppelins. Its performance, as anticipated, was far superior to any of the previous types. The British dubbed it the 'Super Zeppelin' and Strasser felt convinced that this weapon could give him the decisive edge in the aerial war over Britain in 1916. Meanwhile, the Army would trail in its acquisitions, receiving seven 'q-class' Zeppelins over the coming 12 months, and no 'r-class' until 1917, by which time its airships were no longer targeting Britain.

Zeppelin's rival firm, Schütte–Lanz, continued to deliver its wooden-framed airships. The Navy had lost two of her Schütte–Lanzs, from the base at Seddin on the Baltic, towards the end of the year: in November, SL 6 exploded just after take-off, killing all on board; and a month later a storm destroyed SL 4 in its shed. At the end of 1915 just three Schütte–Lanz airships were still flying – SL II, SL 3 and SL 7 – but plans were well-advanced for a new model, the E-type, of which eight would appear in 1916, numbered from SL 8 to SL 15. One of them, the Army's SL 11, would have a lasting impact on the air war over Britain.

In Britain defence against air raids in 1915 had been poor. Behind the scenes though there was a glimmer of hope for the future. The armaments available to home defence pilots in 1915 to combat airships were inadequate, but throughout the year three men were independently working on a solution. John Pomeroy, a New Zealand inventor, Flt Lt Frank Brock,[18] now of the intelligence section of the Admiralty Air Department, and an engineer from Coventry, John Buckingham, had all been experimenting with either explosive or incendiary bullets, weapons that targeted the Zeppelin's Achilles heel – its highly inflammable hydrogen. Trials took place through 1915 and all three bullets went into production in 1916. Although none appeared to be completely reliable on its own, when used in combination they offered a promise of success. There was a new tracer bullet on its way too. Messrs Aerators, the makers of the Sparklet soda syphon, were involved in war production, making bullets for the French, but they would deliver the new tracer to Britain's pilots in 1916; it quickly became known as the 'Sparklet'.

When Britain declared war on Germany in August 1914, the country had no organized system of air defence. Only very slowly did that improve, forcing the British public to accept that the Home Front was also an extension of the front line – a home front line – with civilians liable to be killed in their homes by enemy fire just as soldiers were on the Western Front. The 20 airship raids in 1915 claimed the lives of 207 people while injuring 533; the five raids by aeroplanes killed two and injured six.[19] Casualties occurred the length of England, from Tyneside in the industrial north, to Kent, the 'Garden of England', in the south (see Map 8). As well as the human cost, these raids carried a destructive threat to property too, with material damage caused by German airships estimated at £815,406, and the irritant raids by aeroplanes amounting to £570. It should be noted, however, that of the damage attributable to airships, two-thirds was as a result of Heinrich Mathy's raid on London in Zeppelin L 13 on the night of 8–9 September. These figures may also be an underestimate though, as local fire brigades and the police often compiled them within a few hours of the raid to satisfy the urgent demands of the home defence authorities. It is also difficult to offer a modern financial evaluation of this damage. A simple inflation calculation on the figure of £815,406 returns a figure of about £75million, and £570 equates to £53,000 today, but most of this damage was inflicted on buildings, and property prices have risen way beyond the bounds of inflation in the intervening 100 years.

As early as summer 1914, Konteradmiral Paul Behncke, Germany's Deputy Chief of Naval Staff, had expressed his belief that airship raids in or near London could 'cause panic in the population which may possibly render it doubtful that the war can be continued'. After a year of raids and over 700 civilian casualties, the British public did not panic in the face of this new type of warfare, but there was anger and frustration at the lack of an obvious response to the Zeppelin raiders, who appeared to come and go at will. Now a growing voice began to be heard, common among ordinary people for some time, but now spreading to businessmen and MPs – a demand for reprisals, air raids on German towns. It provoked many a letter to the editor of *The Times* – including one from Sir Arthur Conan Doyle, the creator of Sherlock Holmes, suggesting a 'small avenging squadron of swift British aeroplanes'[20] – but this mood failed to gain the support of the government. As 1915 drew to a close, for the civilian population of Britain, little appeared to have changed. Change, however, lay just around the corner.

At the dawn of 1916, Britain's overland aerial defence was about to come under new management, and new weapons were on their way - explosive and incendiary bullets. Could they provide the long-awaited antidote to the Zeppelin ascendancy? Meanwhile, Germany was also making big strides forward, with the new 'Super Zeppelins' ready to roll off the production line in a few months' time. Just nine years had passed since Lord Northcliffe dramatically announced 'England is no longer an island', following Alberto Santos-Dumont's record-breaking flight of just 722 feet. Since then progress in aviation had been astonishing. Now, the lessons learned were about to be put to the test as the air war over Britain entered a new highly destructive and deadly phase.

APPENDICES

The gutted remains of 165 West Road, Southend-on-Sea, home to Herbert Pensam, his wife, three daughters and a maid. An incendiary dropped by Zeppelin *LZ 38* in the early hours of 10 May 1915 set fire to the house. All five of the family jumped from the two upper front windows. (Author's Collection)

The wrecked frontage of the Bull and George Hotel in High Street, Ramsgate. Two high-explosive bombs dropped by Zeppelin *LZ 38* passed through the building and detonated on the ground floor at around 2.00am on 17 May 1915, killing two guests. (Author's Collection)

German Army Zeppelin *LZ 38*, commanded by *Hauptmann* Erich Linnarz, had been responsible for the raids on Ipswich, Bury St. Edmunds, Southend and Ramsgate then, on 31 May 1915, became the first Zeppelin to bomb London. (Author's Collection)

Extensive bomb damage in Walter's Terrace, off Waller Street, Hull, looking towards Southcoates railway station. The bomb dropped here by Zeppelin *L 9* at around midnight on the night of 6/7 June 1915 caused extensive damage and killed four people living in the street. (Historic Military Press)

Holy Trinity Church in Hull looms steadfastly above a mountain of smouldering rubble, all that is left of the popular Edwin Davis' draper store after Zeppelin *L 9* bombed the town at around midnight on the night of 6/7 June 1915. (David Marks Collection)

Zeppelin *L 12* towed into Ostend harbour by a German ship after anti-aircraft guns damaged two of her gas cells during a raid on Dover harbour during the night of 9/10 August 1915. (Author's Collection)

The X marks the door of 4 St. John's Hill in Woodbridge, where Mr and Mrs Tyler were standing when a bomb from Zeppelin *L 10* exploded in the street at around 10.30pm on 12 August 1915. The explosion killed them both, but their three children asleep in the house survived. (David Marks Collection)

The damaged headquarters office of the 5th (Territorial) Battalion, Norfolk Regiment, on the corner of Church and Quebec streets in East Dereham, Norfolk, blasted by a bomb dropped from Zeppelin *L 14* on the evening of 8 September 1915. The body of one of those killed in the raid, jeweller Harry Patterson, was found slumped in the doorway. (David Marks Collection)

The raid on London on the night of 8 September 1915 caused the most material damage of any raid on Britain throughout the war. Incendiary bombs dropped by Zeppelin *L 13* caused serious fires in textile warehouses in the tightly packed streets around London's Guildhall. This photograph shows the gutted Addle Street warehouse of woollen merchants Glen and Co. (Author's Collection)

This No.8 bus was heading south along Norton Folgate in London on the evening of 8 September 1915 when a bomb dropped by Zeppelin *L 13* exploded in the street. Amongst those who died was the driver, Frank Kreppel. (Author's Collection)

A group of two incendiary and one high-explosive bomb of the types used by German Army Zeppelins and dropped by *LZ 77* near Thornwood in Essex on the night of 11/12 September 1915. The spherical HE bomb (which failed to detonate) is of the A.P.K. type. (David Marks Collection)

The wreckage of 73 Stretton Road, East Croydon, caused by a bomb dropped from Zeppelin *L 14* on the night of 13 October 1915. The bomb killed the three occupants, Eliza Walter and two of her children, Daisy and Sidney. (Historic Military Press)

The scene outside the Lyceum in London's Covent Garden, the morning after the raid by Zeppelin *L 15*. The photograph, taken from Wellington Street, is looking down Exeter Street with the Lyceum on the left and The Old Bell public house on the right. The area was extremely busy when a bomb exploded here shortly before 9.30pm on 13 October 1915. (Author's Collection)

The extraordinary effect of the bomb blast in Chancery Lane, London, on the night of 13 October 1915. A bomb dropped by Zeppelin *L 15* burst a water main and, as an eyewitness observed, 'The water got under the wood block paving and lifted it for about 100 yards, leaving it in graceful waves'. (Author's Collection)

The bomb that exploded outside the Strand Theatre in Catherine Street, Covent Garden, mortally wounded Edward Howard (age 13) and seriously injured his friend James Wickham (18). Wickham had stopped to light a cigarette; they were just three yards away when the bomb detonated. (Author's Collection)

Damage caused by the last bomb dropped on London in 1915. The bomb released by Zeppelin *L 15* on the night of 13 October struck 54 Prince's Square, between Cable Street and London Western Dock, wrecking the premises occupied by tarpaulin manufacturers, J. Smith & Co., and killing a horse. (Author's Collection)

Appendix I

German Airship Numbering Systems

The identification numbers of German Zeppelins can appear quite confusing as each airship had two numbers: a manufacturer's number (the sequential number given it by the Zeppelin Company) and a service number, designated by the Navy or the Army. In most cases these two numbers differed, but for a while the Army service number was the same as the manufacturer's number, one of three different systems the Army used.

Navy Zeppelins

The Navy system was the simpler of the two services. The Navy named its first Zeppelin L 1 (Luftschiff 1 = Airship 1). As it was the fourteenth airship made by the Zeppelin Company it also had a manufacturer's number: LZ 14 (Luftshiff Zeppelin 14). Throughout this book I have only used service numbers. The Navy continued with this system throughout the war. So the Navy's fifteenth Zeppelin was L 15, but as it was the forty-eighth airship built by Zeppelin it also had a manufacturer's number of LZ 48. Navy Zeppelin service numbers were painted on near the airship's nose.

Army Zeppelins

Army numbering was more complex. The Army first used Roman numerals to denote service numbers. The Army designated its first Zeppelin as Z I (Zeppelin I). It was the third Zeppelin built by the

Zeppelin Company so had manufacturer's number LZ 3. The Army continued in this way sequentially until Z XII (twelve), then it appears there was an uneasiness about giving the next Zeppelin the number Z XIII (thirteen). Instead, the Army chose to adopt the manufacturer's number as the service number. This meant its next Zeppelins were numbered LZ 34, LZ 35, LZ 37, LZ 38 and LZ 39. The Army did not have LZ 36 as the Zeppelin with this manufacturer's number went to the Navy, becoming L 9.

After taking delivery of LZ 39, the Army changed to a third system. Although still based on the manufacturer's number, the new system added 30 to it. When the Zeppelin Company handed over LZ 42, the Army gave it the service number LZ 72. It seems the idea was an attempt to confuse the Allies as to just how many Zeppelins there were. The Army painted these numbers on near the nose, although in some cases it just applied LZ.

Schütte–Lanz airships

The wooden-framed Schütte–Lanz airships had a sequential numbering system, which served as both a manufacturer's number and service number for both services, with one small change. The first two airships were numbered using Roman numerals – SL I and SL II. From the third airship, numbering changed to SL 3, SL 4, etc. As with Zeppelins, these numbers were also painted close to the nose, but from SL 10 onwards only the letters SL were added. The fact that SL II (two) showed the number on its nose and SL 11 (eleven) did not has led to some photos of the earlier airship being mistaken for SL 11, the first German airship shot down over mainland Britain (3 September 1916).

Appendix II

Airship Raids 1915

Date	Airships over England	Material Damage (£)	Casualties (Killed)	Casualties (Injured)
19 Jan.	L 3 and L 4	7,740	4	16
14 Apr.	L 9	55	0	2
15–16 Apr.	L 5 and L 6	6,498	0	1
29–30 Apr.	LZ 38	9,010	0	0
10 May	LZ 38	5,301	1	2
17 May	LZ 38	1,600	2	1
26 May	LZ 38	987	3	3
31 May	LZ 38	18,596	7	35
4–5 Jun.	L 10 and SL 3	8,740	0	8
6–7 Jun.	L 9	44,795	24	40
15 Jun.	L 10	41,760	18	72
9–10 Aug.	L 9, L 10, L 11 and L 12	11,992	17	21
12 Aug.	L 10	3,649	6	24
17 Aug.	L 10 and L 11	30,750	10	48
7–8 Sep.	LZ 74, LZ 77 and SL II	9,616	18	38
8–9 Sep.	L 9, L 13 and L 14	534,287	26	94
11–12 Sep.	LZ 77	0	0	0
12–13 Sep.	LZ 74	8	0	0

13–14 Sep.	L 13	2	0	0
13–14 Oct.	L 11, L 13, L 14, L 15 and L 16	80,020	71	128
	TOTALS	815,406	207	533

Appendix III

Individuals Killed in Air Raids – 1915

One of the questions I am often asked is 'Where can I find a National Register of those killed in air raids during the First World War'. The simple answer is, there isn't one.

The official Government returns for 1915 state that 207 people were killed in Zeppelin raids in 1915, a further two in aeroplane raids. These returns, however, do not list names. During the research for this book I have made a note of the details of those killed as I found them and, surprisingly, by the end of the project I was only short by fourteen names. Information on those who are missing would be welcomed.

While the official lists give 207 killed it seems clear that cases of those who died of 'shock' during raids are not always included so the real total is likely to be more but can now never be fully ascertained.

Ian Castle
www.IanCastleZeppelin.co.uk

Abbreviations

PC	Police Constable
SC	Special Constable
F/man	Fireman
Pte	Private
L/Cpl	Lance Corporal
Gnr	Gunner
Dvr	Driver
Bbr	Bombardier
Sgt	Sergeant

Deaths During Zeppelin Raids

Date	Name	Age	Place
19 January	Samuel Smith	53	Gt. Yarmouth
	Martha Mary Taylor	72	Gt. Yarmouth
	Alice Gazley	26	King's Lynn
	Percy Goate	14	King's Lynn
10 May	Agnes Whitwell	60	Southend-on-Sea
17 May	Florence Lamont	43	Ramsgate
	John Herbert Smith	42	Ramsgate
26 May	Marion Pateman	7	Southend-on-Sea
	May Fairs	35	Westcliff-on-Sea
	Florence Smith	25	Westcliff-on-Sea
31 May	Caroline Good	46	London
	Henry Good	49	London
	Elizabeth May Leggett	11	London
	Elsie Leggett	3	London
	Leah Lehrman	16	London
	Samuel Reuben	8	London
	Eleanor Willis	67 (or 74)	London
6/7 June	Georgina Cunningham	27	Hull
	Elizabeth P. Foreman	39	Hull
	Joanna Harman	67	Hull
	George Hill	48	Hull
	Jane Hill	45	Hull
	Edward Jordan	10	Hull
	Hannah Mitchell	42	Hull
	Alfred Matthews	50	Hull
	George Mullins	15	Hull
	Norman Mullins	10	Hull
	Emma Pickering	68	Hull
	Maurice Richardson	11	Hull

APPENDIX III

	Violet Richardson	8	Hull
	Sarah Ann Scott	36	Hull
	Eliza Slade	54	Hull
	Tom Stamford	46	Hull
	Ellen Temple	50	Hull
	Alice P. Walker	30	Hull
	Millicent Walker	17	Hull
	William Walker	62	Hull
	Annie Watson	58	Hull
	William Watson	67	Hull
	Florence White	30	Hull
	George Isaac White	3	Hull
15 June	Albert Bramley	54	Jarrow
	Matthew Carter	55	Jarrow
	John Cuthbert Davison	31	Jarrow
	Karl Kalnin	22	Jarrow
	Joseph Lane	67	Jarrow
	Ann Isabella Laughlin	62	Jarrow
	Robert Thomas Nixon	32	Jarrow
	Frederick Pinnock	31	Jarrow
	Lawrence Frazer Sanderson	16	Jarrow
	Thomas Henry Smith	23	Jarrow
	Ralph Snaith	48	Jarrow
	William Stamford	40	Jarrow
	Joseph Thornicroft	31	Jarrow
	William Grieves Turner	20	Jarrow
	George Ward	18	Jarrow
	John George Windle	27	Jarrow
	William Erskine Cook Young	16	Jarrow
	PC Robert Telford	22	Willington Quay
9 August	Kezia Acaster	32	Goole
	Sarah Acaster	65	Goole

	Sarah Ann Acaster	34	Goole
	Alice Carrol	4	Goole
	Gladys May Carrol	3	Goole
	James Carrol	31	Goole
	May Carrol	30	Goole
	Hannah Goodall	74	Goole
	Beatrice Alice Harrison	6	Goole
	Florence Harrison	4	Goole
	Agnes Pratt	36	Goole
	Margaret Pratt	9 months	Goole
	Alice Smith	17	Goole
	Violet Stainton	18	Goole
	Annie Elizabeth Woodall	3	Goole
	Grace Woodall	31	Goole
	Kate Crawford	18	Lowestoft
12 August	Eliza Bunn	67	Woodbridge
	Dennis Harris	40	Woodbridge
	James Marshall	16	Woodbridge
	Edward Turner	50	Woodbridge
	Dora Tyler	40	Woodbridge
	Roger Tyler	31	Woodbridge
17 August	James Frederick Ebbs	46	London
	Herbert Hamilton	28	London
	Joseph Edwin Hollington	34	London
	Edith Grace Lawrence	35	London
	Moses Mayers	73	London
	Philip Osborne	67	London
	Amelia Pells	24	London
	Edith Pells	3	London
	Thomas Howard Pells	26	London
	David Reginald Smith	25	London
7/8 September	Elizabeth Beechey	49	London
	Helena Beechey	3	London

APPENDIX III

	Margaret Beechey	7	London
	William Beechey	11	London
	William James Beechey	56	London
	Edward John Bowles	37	London
	SC Victor Daines	22	London
	Emma Dann	45	London
	Frederick Dann	44	London
	Ernest Frederick Gladwell	26	London
	Ethel Scotten	19	London
	Maud Scotten	22	London
	Florence Slade	21	London
	Elsie Smith	2	London
	Kitty Smith	9	London
	Arthur Suckling	30	London
	Doris Suckling	3	London
	Emily Suckling	29	London
8/9 September	Harry Patterson	44	East Dereham
	James Taylor	61	East Dereham
	2/1st City of London Yeomanry		
	Pte Thomas Frank MacDonald	21	East Dereham
	L/Cpl Alfred Pomeroy	28	East Dereham
	Henry Alfred Coombes	23	London
	Dorothy Couldrey	6	London
	Hilda Couldrey	12	London
	Frederick John Elgar	42	London
	William Fenge	36	London
	F/man John Samuel Green	30	London
	Edward G. Harvey	33	London
	Frank Kreppel	26	London
	PC Thomas Minke	34	London

311

	Adolphe Alfred Newman	36	London
	James W. E. Palmer	5	London
	Winifred M. Palmer	6 months	London
	Frederick Saunders	50	London
	William Stoltz	28	London
	8 unknown		London
13 October	Percy John Brookes	21	East Croydon
	Brian Currie	10	East Croydon
	Gordon Currie	15	East Croydon
	Roy Currie	14	East Croydon
	Jane Miller	50	East Croydon
	Robert Arthur Thompson	19	East Croydon
	Daisy Walter	23	East Croydon
	Eliza Walter	52	East Croydon
	Sidney Walter	15	East Croydon
	George Cartledge	56	Hertford
	George Stephen Game	3	Hertford
	James Gregory	55	Hertford
	Arthur Hart	51	Hertford
	John Henry Jevons	57	Hertford
	Ernest Thomas Jolly	29	Hertford
	Charles Spicer	32	Hertford
	Charles Waller	43	Hertford

2/1st Norfolk Battery, Royal Field Artillery

	Bbr Arthur John Cox	21	Hertford
	George Alexander	23	London
	Elizabeth M. Baldwin	16	London
	Amelia Baxter	68	London
	William Breeze	74	London
	George Percy Brown	53	London
	SC Henry William Cansbrook	37	London
	William Henry Clayton	26	London

312

APPENDIX III

Elizabeth Coker	55	London
Charles Davies	48	London
Frederick James Eagles	47	London
Ellen Francis	55	London
Arthur Giles	23	London
Thomas Edward Hawley	61	London
Caroline Louisa Hill	50	London
Edward Arthur Howard	13	London
Kate A. Jones	23	London
George Kirby	50	London
John Frederick Manton	88	London
David Patton	45	London
SC Thomas Joseph Pinchon	24	London
Edwin J.B. Robey	27	London
Charles Rogers	45	London
George Alwyn Ruse	18	London
Hetti Shilofsky	38	London
Mary Louise Shore	44	London
Mary Ann Simpson	62	London
Alice Lillian Smith	16	London
Charles James Tarrant	30	London
Henry Vinson	25	London
Margaret Whelan	25	London
William Wilkins	34	London
5 unknown		London

Royal Field Artillery

Gnr Henry Absolom	19	London

17th Battery, 5th Brigade, Canadian Field Artillery

Gnr Ernest Bayes	23	Otterpool Camp
Dvr Charles Boeyckens	27	Otterpool Camp
Gnr Pringle Borthwick	27	Otterpool Camp

313

Gnr Douglas R. Johnston	25		Otterpool Camp
Gnr Sydney George Lane	23		Otterpool Camp
Dvr Samuel McKay	21		Otterpool Camp
Bbr David J. Phillips	24		Otterpool Camp
Gnr Richard D Simpson	32		Otterpool Camp
Gnr Richard Stewart Truscott	20		Otterpool Camp

18th Battery, 5th Brigade, Canadian Field Artillery

Dvr Thomas Dickson	32		Otterpool Camp
Gnr Wilfred G. Harris	28		Otterpool Camp
Gnr Henry A. Horn	19		Otterpool Camp
Gnr Harry Rixon	24		Otterpool Camp

8th (Howitzer) Brigade, Canadian Field Artillery

Sgt Edward C. Harris	33		Otterpool Camp
Gnr Charles G. Peterkin	26		Otterpool Camp
Unknown man	?		Woolwich Arsenal
Total Deaths		**207**	

Deaths During Aeroplane Raids

Date	Name	Age	Place
13 September	Kate Bonny	37	Margate
	Agnes Robins	40	Margate
	Total Deaths	**2**	

References and Notes

Chapter 1: 'No Longer an Island'

1. Wallace, *Flying Witness*, p.24.
2. ibid, p.52.
3. Raleigh, *The War In The Air*, Vol.1, pp.109–10.
4. Gollin, *The Impact of Air Power on the British People and Their Government, 1909–1914*, p.218.
5. Details of mission, ibid, pp.217–8.
6. Count Zeppelin launched his first airship in July 1900 and began operating commercial airships in 1909. That same year the German military purchased its first Zeppelins.

Chapter 2: Something Out of Nothing

1. Jones, *The War In The Air*, Vol.3, pp.72-3.
2. ibid, p.71.
3. Raleigh, *The War In The Air*, Vol.1, p.411.
4. See Appendix 1 for explanation of German airship numbering systems.
5. *The Times* Digital Archive (TDA), *The Times*, 18 March 1913, p.7.
6. Lehmann and Mingos, *The Zeppelins*, p.11.
7. ibid, p.12.
8. ibid.
9. ibid, p.13.
10. TDA: *The Times*, 27 August 1914, p.7.
11. Although it has become common in English to refer to the Army Airship Service as the commanding authority that oversaw the use and deployment of Army airships, it is not technically correct as there is no Army equivalent to the Navy's *Marine-Luftschiff-Abteilung*. Although Army airships officially came under the direction of the OHL (Oberste Heeresleitung – Army High Command), often the individual Army to which the airships were attached exerted control over their use.

12. Jones, *The War In The Air*, Vol.3, p.72.
13. ibid, p.81.
14. Churchill, *The World Crisis*, Vol.1, pp.220–1.
15. Raleigh, *The War In The Air*, Vol.1, p.272.
16. The National Archives (TNA), AIR1/2543, *Commodore Murray F Sueter's Papers*.
17. Sueter, *Airmen or Noahs*, p.181.
18. TNA: AIR1/724/76/5, *Reminiscences of Group Captain C R Samson Aug 1914–Sep 1915*.
19. ibid.
20. ibid.
21. Jones, *The War In The Air*, Vol.3, pp.78–9.
22. Raleigh, *The War In The Air*, Vol.1, pp.375–6.

Chapter 3: Attack is the Best Form of Defence

1. Jones, *The War In The Air*, Vol.3, pp.80–1.
2. Churchill, *The World Crisis*, Vol.1, p.341.
3. On the creation of the Royal Flying Corps in 1912, there was a Military Wing administered by the War Office, a Naval Wing administered by the Admiralty, and a Central Flying School at Upavon in Wiltshire, equally financed by both bodies to provide advanced training for qualified pilots.
4. TNA: AIR1/2543.
5. For a detailed account of the Cologne and Düsseldorf raids see, Castle, *The Zeppelin Base Raids – Germany 1914*.
6. TNA: AIR1/2099/207/20/2 *Reports of reconnaissances carried out by naval aeroplanes, etc.*
7. TNA: AIR1/724/76/5.
8. Szigeti, *WW1 Aero No.128*.
9. Lea, *Reggie*, p.27.
10. Grey's report in TNA, CAB37/121/127, *Air raid on Düsseldorf and Cologne*.
11. Szigeti, *WW1 Aero No.128*.
12. From diary of Louis Cesar Duhaut, courtesy of his great grandson, Benoit Dubus.
13. Lea, *Reggie*, p.27.
14. From diary of Louis Cesar Duhaut, see note 12.
15. Lea, *Reggie*, p.28.
16. ibid, p.30.
17. Jones, *The War In The Air*, Vol.3, pp.82–3.
18. ibid, p.83.
19. ibid, p.84.
20. Stoney, *Twentieth Century Maverick*, pp.66–71.

REFERENCES AND NOTES

21. Chadwick, 27 years later, designed the Avro Lancaster bomber of WWII fame.
22. For papers relating to the raid and the pilot's reports see, TNA, AIR1/361/15/228/37 *Reports and papers concerning the raid carried out by the RFC [sic] on Friedrichshafen*; TNA, Air1/2099/207/20/2 *Reports of reconnaissance and operations and attacks of Zeppelin airship factory at Friedrichshafen*. For a detailed account of the raid see Castle, *The Zeppelin Base Raids – Germany 1914*.
23. Forder, *The Friedrichshafen Raid* at www.verdon-roe.co.uk.
24. Bleibler, Wissenschaftliches Jahrbuch 2001, pp.9–16.

Chapter 4: 'Forcing England to Her Knees'

1. Robinson, *The Zeppelin In Combat*, p.78.
2. ibid, p.79.
3. ibid.
4. ibid, pp.79-80.
5. White, *The Gotha Summer*, pp.32–4.
6. Robinson, *The Zeppelin In Combat*, pp.80–1.
7. ibid, p.81.
8. Cole & Cheesman, *The Air Defence of Britain 1914–1918*, p.18; Dover Express, *Dover and the European War*, p.13; TNA: WO 158/975, *Aeroplane and Seaplane Raids Dec 1914–Nov 1916*.
9. Cole & Cheesman, *Air Defence*, pp.19–20.
10. Details of Dover raid compiled from papers in TNA: AIR1/568/16/15/128, *Air raids on England 24 Dec–25 Dec 1914*.
11. Cole & Cheesman, *Air Defence*, p.20.
12. Cole & Cheesman, *Air Defence*, pp.20–1.
13. ibid.
14. Details of raid compiled from papers in TNA: AIR1/568/16/15/128. Quote taken from eyewitness account in this file printed in *The Times*, 26 December 1914.
15. TNA: AIR1/2417/303/42, *Cuttings from London Evening News*, 12 March 1935.
16. For a detailed account of the 'Cuxhaven' raid see, Castle, *The Zeppelin Base Raids – Germany 1914*.
17. Account of raid compiled from TNA: ADM 186/567, *Seaplane Operations against Cuxhaven 25 Dec 1914*; Robinson, *The Zeppelin In Combat*, pp.69-74; Buttlar-Brandenfels, *Zeppelins Over England*, pp.38–47.
18. Buttlar-Brandenfels, *Zeppelins Over England*, pp.40-6.
19. Jones, *The War In The Air*, Vol.3, p.85.
20. ibid, pp.87–8.

21. Robinson, *The Zeppelin In Combat*, p.81.
22. ibid, pp.81–2.

Chapter 5: 'Oh, Good God, What is It?'

1. Zeppelin L 7 remained at Leipzig in eastern Germany until 23 January when it transferred to Nordholz.
2. Robinson, *The Zeppelin In Combat*, pp.83–4.
3. ibid, p.87.
4. ibid, p.87.
5. ibid, p.84.
6. TNA: WO 158/935, *Airship Raids Jan–Jun 1915*, p.4.
7. Wyatt, *Death From The Skies*, p.11.
8. *Manchester Guardian*, 21 Jan 1915, p.7.
9. Account of raid compiled from Wyatt, *Death From The Skies*, pp.11–17; *The Times*, 20 Jan 1915 p.8 & 21 Jan 1915, p.9; *Manchester Guardian*, 21 Jan 1915, p.7, TNA: WO 158/935, p.4.
10. In 2012 a plaque was placed on St Peter's Villa recording the damage caused to it by the bomb and also the deaths of Samuel Smith and Martha Taylor.
11. Wyatt, *Death From The Skies*, p.48.
12. ibid, pp.46–8.
13. ibid, p.14.
14. TDA: *The Times*, 26 Dec 1914, p.8.
15. *Manchester Guardian*, 21 Jan 1915, p.7.
16. ibid.
17. TDA: *The Times*, Jan 20 1915, p.8.
18. Wyatt, *Death From The Skies*, p.16.
19. A plaque on the building claims this to be the first bomb dropped on Britain in WW1. That 'honour' actually belongs to Dover where the first bomb landed on 24 Dec. 1914. The bomb on Sheringham is not the first Zeppelin bomb either, that landed a few minutes earlier at Ormesby St Michael, dropped by L 3.
20. Storey, *Zeppelin Blitz*, pp.37–8.
21. Robinson, *The Zeppelin In Combat*, p.86.
22. Wyatt, *Death From The Skies*, p.21.
23. ibid, p.22.
24. TDA: *The Times*, Jan 22 1915, p.34.
25. Account of raid compiled from Wyatt, *Death From The Skies*, pp.24–30; *The Times*, 20 Jan 1915 p.8, 21 Jan 1915, p.10 and 22 Jan 1915, p.34; *Manchester Guardian*, 21 Jan 1915, p.7, TNA: WO 158/935, p.5.
26. Wyatt, *Death From The Skies*, p.30.
27. Robinson, *The Zeppelin In Combat*, p.86.

28. TDA: *The Times*, 25 Jan 1915, p.6.
29. ibid, 9 Feb 1915, p.7.
30. The fate of L 3 and L 4 in, Robinson, *The Zeppelin In Combat*, pp.100–1.

Chapter 6: 'Discovering a New Country'

1. Jones, *The War In The Air*, Vol.3, pp.91–2.
2. ibid, pp.92-3.
3. Lehmann and Mingos, *The Zeppelins*, p.104.
4. Cole & Cheesman, *Air Defence*, p.28. There may have been a fifth bomb but this is unclear.
5. Account of raid on Essex compiled from TNA: AIR1/568/16/15/130 *Air Raids on England 21 Feb. 1915;* TNA: WO 158/975; British Newspaper Archive (BNA): *Essex County Chronicle*, 26 Feb. 1915, p.3. All eyewitness quotes are from *Essex County Chronicle* unless otherwise stated.
6. BNA: *Daily Record and Mail*, 22 Feb. 1915, p.5.
7. BNA: *Diss Express*, 5 Mar. 1915, p.6.
8. BNA: *Cambridge Independent Press*, 26 Feb. 1915, p.5.
9. Robinson, *The Zeppelin In Combat*, p.90.
10. After the naval Battle of Dogger Bank, on 4 Feb. 1915, von Pohl replaced von Ingenohl as commander of the High Seas Fleet.
11. Robinson, *The Zeppelin In Combat*, pp.90–2.
12. Lehmann and Mingos, *The Zeppelins*, p.48.
13. ibid, *The Zeppelins*, p.52–6.
14. Robinson, *The Zeppelin In Combat*, pp.92–3.
15. BNA: *Newcastle Daily Journal*, 16 Apr. 1915, p.5.
16. Robinson, *The Zeppelin In Combat*, p.93.
17. Account of raid compiled from TNA: AIR1/568/16/15/133, *Air Raids on England 14 Apr. 1915*; TNA: WO 158/935, pp.7–8; BNA: *Newcastle Daily Journal*, 15 Apr. 1915, p.10 & 16 Apr. 1915, p.5; BNA: *Morpeth Herald*, 16 Apr. 1915, p.7. Eyewitness quotes from *Newcastle Daily Journal* unless otherwise specified.
18. TNA: AIR1/568/16/15/133.
19. BNA: *Morpeth Herald*, 16 Apr. 1915, p.7.
20. ibid.
21. *Manchester Guardian*, 16 Apr. 1915.
22. BNA: *Morpeth Herald*, 16 Apr. 1915, p.7.
23. *Manchester Guardian*, 16 Apr. 1915.
24. BNA: *Morpeth Herald*, 16 Apr. 1915, p.7.
25. Interview originally printed in *New York World* on 23 September 1915 and reprinted widely. See note 1, Chapter 15.
26. Jones, *The War In The Air*, Vol.3, p.95.

Chapter 7: 'Only H.V.B. on Board'

1. WO 158/935, p.9. This report by the Intelligence Section, General Headquarters, incorrectly identified L 5 as Zeppelin L 9, which was refitting after the raid on Northumberland the previous day.
2. TDA: *The Times*, 17 Apr. 1915, p.5.
3. TNA: AIR1/568/16/15/134, *Air Raids on England 15-16 Apr. 1915*; *Dundee Courier*, 17 Apr. 1915, p.3.
4. TNA: AIR1/568/16/15/134.
5. ibid and TNA: WO 158/935, p.9–10.
6. Account of Lowestoft raid compiled from TNA: AIR1/568/16/15/134; TNA: WO 158/935; BNA: *Dundee Courier*, 17 Apr. 1915, BNA: *Gloucester Journal*, 17 Apr. 1915, BNA: *Liverpool Echo*, 16 Apr. 1915.
7. BNA: *Dundee Courier*, p.3.
8. BNA: *Gloucester Journal*, p.8.
9. BNA: *Liverpool Echo*, p.8.
10. BNA: *Dundee Courier*, p.3.
11. BNA: *Gloucester Journal*, p.8.
12. BNA: *Liverpool Echo*, p.8.
13. *Illustrated War News*, 21 Apr. 1915, pp.20–1.
14. TDA: *The Times*, 17 Apr. 1915, p.5.
15. Robinson, The Zeppelin In Combat, pp.93–4.
16. Buttlar-Brandenfels, *Zeppelins Over England*, p.52.
17. Account of Maldon raid mainly compiled from TNA: AIR1/568/16/15/134; TNA: WO 158/935; BNA: *Essex Newsman*, 17 Apr. 1915
18. Buttlar-Brandenfels, *Zeppelins Over England*, p.53.
19. BNA: *Liverpool Echo*, 16 Apr. 1915, p.8.
20. www.facebook.com/8thworcesters100/843843095685897 – see post dated 16 April 2015.
21. TNA: AIR1/568/16/15/134.
22. Morris, *German Air Raids on Britain 1914–1918*, pp.22–3.
23. Buttlar-Brandenfels, *Zeppelins Over England*, p.57.
24. ibid, pp.59-60.
25. Cole & Cheesman, *Air Defence*, pp.49–50.
26. ibid, p.32, Robinson, *The Zeppelin In Combat*, p.83.
27. Cole & Cheesman, *Air Defence*, p.50.
28. TNA: AIR1/569/16/15/135 *Air Raids on England 16 Apr. 1915*.
29. Account of Kent raid mainly compiled from TNA: AIR1/568/16/15/135; TNA: WO 158/975; BNA: *Dundee Courier*, 17 Apr. 1915; *South Eastern Gazette*, 20 April 1915.
30. www.yesterdayremembered.co.uk/memory/1543/.
31. See Appendix I.

REFERENCES AND NOTES

Chapter 8: 'The Devils Have Come!'

1. Robinson, *The Zeppelin In Combat*, p.385.
2. Kollman, *Das Zeppelinluftschiff*, Tabell II.
3. Account of Ipswich raid compiled from TNA: AIR1/569/16/15/136 *Air Raids on England 29–30 Apr. 1915*; TNA: WO 158/935; BNA: *Coventry Evening Telegraph*, 30 Apr. 1915, p.3; *Manchester Guardian*, 1 May 1915.
4. A newspaper report states that the girl was Goodwin's daughter, but another source says that Elsie was a niece.
5. TNA: *The Times*, 1 May 1915, p.5.
6. Account of Bury St Edmunds raid compiled from TNA: AIR1/569/16/15/136; TNA: WO 158/935, BNA: *Bury Free Press, 1 May 1915, p.5; Bury Free Press, 8 May 1915*, pp.6–7; BNA: *Coventry Evening Telegraph*, 30 Apr. 1915, p.3.
7. TDA: *The Times*, 1 May 1915, p.5.
8. TNA: AIR1/569/16/15/136; TNA: WO 158/935.
9. BNA: *Bury Free Press, 8 May 1915*, p.6.
10. Robinson, *The Zeppelin In Combat*, p.92.
11. Account of Southend raid compiled from TNA: AIR1/569/16/15/137 *Air Raids on England 9-10 May 1915*; TNA: WO 158/935; *Southend Standard Air Raid Supplement 13 May 1915*.
12. TDA: *The Times*, 11 May 1915, p.9.
13. At the time, Army Zeppelins used the spherical A.P.K. (Artillerie-Prüfungs-Kommission) (Artillery Test Commission) HE bombs while the Navy used the tear-drop shaped Carbonit HE bombs.
14. *Southend Standard Air Raid Supplement* 13 May 1915.
15. TDA: *The Times*, 14 May 1915, p.9.
16. TDA: *The Times*, 13 May 1915, p.10.
17. Robinson, *The Zeppelin In Combat*, p.94.

Chapter 9: A Glimmer of Hope

1. Oak-Rhind, *The North Foreland Lookout Post*, p.4.
2. BNA: *Portsmouth Evening News*, 17 May 1915, p.6.
3. Account of Ramsgate raid compiled from TNA: AIR1/569/16/15/138 *Air Raids on England 16–17 May 1915*; TNA: WO 158/935; TDA: *The Times*, 18 May 1915, p.5; BNA: *Dover Express*, 21 May 1915, p.5; BNA: *Portsmouth Evening News*, 17 May 1915, p.6; *Thanet Advertiser*, Thanet's Raid History, pp.3–4.
4. Details from the Death Certificates of John Smith and Florence Lamont, and information contained in the 1911 Census.
5. BNA: *Edinburgh Evening News*, 19 May 1915, p.6.

6. BNA: *Manchester Evening News*, 20 May 1915, p.5. There appears to be some confusion in the reporting of the deaths of Florence Lamont and John Smith, with some newspapers stating that both lived in Thornton Heath (this is not substantiated by their Death Certificates) and confusing Mrs Lamont with Smith's wife.
7. Easdown, *A Glint in the Sky*, p.25.
8. Cole & Cheesman, *Air Defence*, p.54.
9. Dover Express, *Dover and the European War*, p.16. In recognition of this achievement by the Dover AA Corp, those on duty that night were entitled to wear a silver brassard on their uniform. The men were: Sub Lieutenant J.R.P. Clarke, RNVR, Chief Petty Officer F. Rigden, Leading Seaman E. Gandy, Searchlight Workers J.B. Holyman, A.R. Smith, A.E. Winn, S.D. Percival and Leading Seaman H. Summers, RN.
10. BNA: *Dover Express*, 21 May 1915, p.5.
11. Details of attack on Zeppelin LZ 39 from TNA: AIR1/569/16/15/138.
12. Spenser Grey took part in the raid on the Zeppelin shed at Cologne in October 1914. See Chapter 3.
13. John Babington took part in the raid on the Zeppelin works at Friedrichshafen in November 1914. See Chapter 3.
14. TNA: AIR1/569/16/15/138.
15. Account of Southend raid compiled from TNA: AIR1/569/16/15/139 *Air Raids on England 26–27 May 1915*; TNA: WO 158/935; TDA: *The Times*, 28 May 1015, p.8;BNA: *Essex County Chronicle*, 28 May 1915, p.10; BNA: *Newcastle Daily Journal*, 28 May 1915, p.5.
16. BNA: *Essex County Chronicle*, 28 May 1915, p.10.
17. BNA: *Nottingham Evening Post*, 28 May 1915, p.4.
18. BNA: *Portsmouth Evening News*, 17 May 1915, p.6.
19. BNA: *Essex County Chronicle*, 28 May 1915, p.10.
20. In the five months since the first aeroplane raid on Dover these aerial attacks had killed ten people and injured 25 with material damage estimated at the time in the region of £32,000.
21. TNA: AIR1/569/16/15/137.

Chapter 10: London's Burning

1. Robinson, *The Zeppelin In Combat*, p.92.
2. Linnarz, *The Great War... I Was There!*, Part 11, pp.448–9.
3. TNA: WO 158/935, p.17.
4. Linnarz, *The Great War ... I Was There!*, Part 11, p.450.
5. Morison, *War on Great Cities*, pp.40–41. In May 2015 Hackney Council erected a plaque on the house to commemorate it as the first in London to be bombed in WW1.

REFERENCES AND NOTES

6. Account of London raid compiled from TNA: AIR1/569/16/15/140 *Air Raids on England 31 May–1 Jun. 1915* (including London Fire Brigade report); TNA: WO 158/935; TNA: MEPO 2/1650 *Zeppelin Raid 31 May [Met. Police] Divisional Reports*; TDA: *The Times*, 3 & 4 Jun. 1915; *Hackney & Stoke Newington Recorder*, 2 May 1919; Morison, *War on Great Cities*.
7. TNA: AIR1/2417/303/42, 20 February 1935.
8. *Hackney & Stoke Newington Recorder*, 2 May 1919, p.3; Morison, *War on Great Cities*, pp.42–4.
9. TDA: *The Times*, 3 Jun. 1915, p.3; Morison, *War on Great Cities*, pp.44–7.
10. TNA: AIR1/2417/303/42, 16 February 1935.
11. BNA: *Newcastle Daily Journal*, 5 Jun. 1915, p.3.
12. Linnarz, *The Great War … I Was There!*, Part 11, p.450.
13. TDA: *The Times*, 4 Jun. 1915, p.5; Morison, *War on Great Cities*, pp.48–9.
14. Linnarz, *The Great War … I Was There!*, Part 11, p.451.
15. Cole & Cheesman, *Air Defence*, pp.56–9.
16. Travers, *Vale of Laughter*, pp.76–7.
17. TNA, MEPO 2/1650 *Zeppelin Raid 31 May [Met. Police] Divisional Reports*.
18. Pankhurst, *The Great War … I Was There!*, Part 11, p.447.
19. *Hackney & Stoke Newington Recorder*, 2 May 1919, p.3.
20. Pankhurst, *The Great War … I Was There!*, Part 11, pp.447–8.
21. Jones, *The War In The Air*, Vol.3, p.100.
22. *Neueste Nachrichten*, quoted in Poolman, *Zeppelins Over England*, p.42.
23. Longmore, *From Sea to Sky*, p.46.
24. TNA: AIR1/672/17/134/36 *Report on Destruction of Two Zeppelins*.
25. ibid.
26. Gibson, *Warneford, VC*, p.55.
27. Travers, *Vale of Laughter*, p.80.
28. Gibson, *Warneford, VC*, p.60.
29. Longmore, *From Sea to Sky*, p.46.
30. ibid, p.47.
31. TNA: AIR1/672/17/134/36.
32. Gibson, *Warneford, VC*, p.87.
33. ibid, p.89.
34. ibid, p.95.
35. TDA: *The Times*, 8 Jun. 1915, p.9.
36. Gibson, *Warneford, VC*, p.117.

Chapter 11: The 'Experiment' is Over

1. *Hackney & Stoke Newington Recorder*, 2 May 1919, p.3.
2. TDA: *The Times*, 2 Jun. 1915, p.6.
3. Robinson, *The Zeppelin In Combat*, p.96.

4. TNA: WO 158/935.
5. Robinson, *The Zeppelin In Combat*, p.96.
6. BNA: *Yorkshire Post*, 21 Dec. 1918, p.9.
7. TNA: WO 158/935.
8. Robinson, *The Zeppelin In Combat*, p.96.
9. Sittingbourne Remembers, *Zeppelins Over Milton*, at www.pigstrough.co.uk.
10. Easdown, *A Glint in the Sky*, p.27.
11. Mansfield, *History of Gravesend in the County of Kent*, p.154.
12. ibid, pp.154–5.
13. TNA: AIR1/2417/303/42, 5 Mar. 1935.
14. Mansfield, *History of Gravesend*, pp.155–6.
15. TNA: AIR1/2417/303/42, 15 Feb. 1935.
16. Cole & Cheesman, *Air Defence*, p.59.
17. Robinson, *The Zeppelin In Combat*, p.97.
18. TNA: WO 158/935.
19. Robinson, *The Zeppelin In Combat*, p.97.
20. TNA: AIR1/569/16/15/142 *Reports and correspondence concerning the Zeppelin raid on Hull.*
21. Details of the Hull raid are compiled from: TNA: AIR1/569/16/15/142; TNA: WO 158/935; BNA: *Yorkshire Post*, 21 Dec. 1918, Credland, *The Hull Zeppelin Raids 1915–1918.*
22. BNA: *Yorkshire Post*, 21 Dec. 1918, p.9.
23. ibid.
24. Credland, *The Hull Zeppelin Raids*, p.123.
25. ibid, p.27.
26. BNA: *Yorkshire Post*, 21 Dec. 1918, p.9.
27. Jones, *The War In The Air*, Vol.3, pp. 180–1.
28. TNA: WO 158/935.
29. Imperial War Museum, Documents Cat. No. 12358, *Diary of Jeanne Berman* in Papers of H. Miller.
30. The owner of Edwin Davis & Co later claimed the store's losses alone amounted to £100,000. See *Yorkshire Post*, 21 Dec. 1918, p.9.
31. TDA: The *Times*, 7 Jun. 1915, p.8.
32. TDA: The *Times*, 17 Jun. 1915, p.8.
33. Credland, *The Hull Zeppelin Raids,* pp.48–9.
34. ibid, p.58.
35. TNA: AIR1/570/16/15/143 *Air Raids on England 15–16 June 1915.*
36. Morris, *German Air Raids on Britain*, p.38 and TNA: WO 158/935, p.26.
37. TNA: WO 158/935, p.27.
38. Details of the Tyne raid compiled from TNA: AIR1/570/16/15/143.
39. BNA: *Yorkshire Post*, 21 Dec. 1918, p.9.

REFERENCES AND NOTES

40. Many personal details of the raid can be found on Philip Strong's excellent website which explores his family history, www.strong-family.org/lane/chapter_7.
41. Morris, *German Air Raids on Britain*, p.39.
42. Cole & Cheesman, *Air Defence*, pp.62-3.
43. Robinson, *The Zeppelin In Combat*, p.98. The new stations were on the island of Sylt and at Bruges, over 300 miles apart.
44. Robinson, *The Zeppelin In Combat*, p.125.
45. See Endnote 30.

Chapter 12: The Guns Strike Back

1. Robinson, *The Zeppelin In Combat*, pp.115–7.
2. For the route of L 9 see, TNA: WO 158/936 *Airship Raids 9 Aug. –14 Sep. 1915*, p.6. This official report produced in Feb. 1918 incorrectly assigns the command of L 9 to Hptmn August Stelling.
3. Cole & Cheesman, *Air Defence*, pp.64–6.
4. Robinson, *The Zeppelin In Combat*, pp.117–8.
5. *Goole Times*, 20 Dec. 1918.
6. TNA: AIR1/570/16/15/144 *Air Raids on England 9–10 Aug. 1915*.
7. Details of Goole raid complied from TNA: AIR1/570/16/15/144, *Goole Times*, 20 Dec. 1918.
8. Mr West's letter is available in the World War One section of www.thegooleexperience.weebly.com.
9. TNA: WO 158/936, p.6.
10. *Goole Times*, 20 Dec. 1918.
11. For L 10's route see, TNA: WO 158/936, p.7.
12. ibid.
13. TNA: AIR1/570/16/15/144.
14. Cole & Cheesman, *Air Defence*, pp.64–6.
15. Details of Lowestoft raid compiled from TNA: AIR1/570/16/15/144; TNA: WO 158/936.
16. The accounts by the military and Suffolk Police in TNA: AIR1/570/16/15/144 differ as to when the four incendiaries were dropped. The military say near the beginning of the raid but the police say they were dropped at the end.
17. Morris, *German Air Raids on Britain*, p.45.
18. Snowden Gamble, *The Story of a North Sea Air Station*, p.134.
19. TNA: WO 158/936, *p.8*; Robinson, *The Zeppelin In Combat*, p.118.
20. TNA: WO 158/936, p.7.
21. Robinson, *The Zeppelin In Combat*, p.118.

22. Details of Dover raid compiled from TNA: AIR1/570/16/15/144; TNA: WO 158/936; Dover Express, *Dover and the European War*, p.16–7.
23. TNA: AIR1/570/16/15/144.
24. Robinson, *The Zeppelin In Combat*, pp.118–21.
25. Buttlar-Brandenfels, *Zeppelins Over England*, pp.129–32.
26. Gerrard had planned the 1914 raids against the Zeppelin sheds at Cologne and Düsseldorf. See Chapter 3.
27. Details of aeroplane attack on Zeppelin L 12 from TNA: AIR1/629/17/122/15 *No.2 Aeroplane Wing RNAS*.
28. Buttlar-Brandenfels, *Zeppelins Over England*, pp.135–6.
29. Cole & Cheesman, *Air Defence*, p.67.
30. Details of Woodbridge raid complied from TNA: AIR1/570/16/15/145 *Air Raids on England 12–13 Aug. 1915*; Woodbridge Reporter & Wickham Market Gazette, 9 Sep. 1919.
31. Ruby Hayward's account can be found on the University of Suffolk's blog at www.uoshistory.wordpress.com/2015/09/23/.
32. TNA: AIR1/2417/303/42, 23 Feb. 1935.
33. The *Woodbridge Reporter* article gives Mr Tyler's name as Robert Samuel, however the only male Tyler who died in Woodbridge in the Jul–Sep quarter of 1915 given on the General Register Office (GRO) Index is Roger H. Tyler, aged 31.
34. TNA: AIR1/2417/303/42, 8 Mar. 1935.
35. TNA: AIR1/570/16/15/145.
36. TNA: WO 158/936, p.12.
37. TNA: AIR1/570/16/15/145.
38. TNA: AIR1/2417/303/42, 20 Feb. 1935.
39. Buttlar-Brandenfels, *Zeppelins Over England*, p.64.
40. ibid, pp.65–6.

Chapter 13: 'Gazing With Horror and Dread'

1. Jones, *The War In The Air*, Vol.3, p.114.
2. Robinson, *The Zeppelin In Combat*, p.124.
3. Details of the raid on Kent compiled from TNA: AIR1/570/16/15/146 *Air Raids on England 17–18 Aug. 1915*; TNA: WO 158/936.
4. Although historically considered part of Essex, London's urban expansion first raised the question of Walthamstow 'moving' to the County of London in 1907. After numerous delays, it became a municipal borough in 1929. Throughout this time, the Post Office and Metropolitan Police considered it a London district.
5. Cole & Cheesman, *Air Defence*, pp.68–9.

REFERENCES AND NOTES

6. Details of the raid on London compiled from TNA: AIR1/570/16/15/146; TNA: WO 158/936.
7. Robinson, *The Zeppelin In Combat*, p.124.
8. Originally a part of Essex, Leyton followed a similar path to Walthamstow in officially becoming a part of London. See note 4.
9. TNA: AIR1/2417/303/42, 8 Feb. 1935.
10. For background information on those killed see *By Evil Chance, The Air Raid on Leyton* at www.petenichol.me.uk/page51.
11. TNA: MEPO 2/1586 *Metropolitan Police, Commendations 1915–1916*.
12. ibid.
13. Simpson, *Air Raids on South-West Essex in the Great War*, p.93.
14. ibid, note 6, p.200.
15. TNA: AIR1/2417/303/42, 1 Mar. 1935.
16. Morison, *War on Great Cities*, p.56.
17. TNA: AIR1/2417/303/42, 1 Feb. 1935.
18. TDA: *The Times*, 19 Aug. 1915, p.6.
19. Cole & Cheesman, *Air Defence*, p.69.
20. Robinson, *The Zeppelin In Combat*, p.124.
21. TNA, AIR1/570/16/15/146.
22. Robinson, *The Zeppelin In Combat*, p.388.
23. See Chapter 11.
24. Jones, *The War In The Air*, Vol.3, p.106.
25. ibid.
26. Cole & Cheesman, *Air Defence*, pp.33–4.
27. ibid, p.36.
28. ibid, pp.36-7.
29. MacBean & Hogben, *Bombs Gone*, pp.26 and 28.
30. Blacker, *The Adventures and Inventions of Stewart Blacker*, pp.46–7.
31. ibid, p.47.
32. See Chapter 3.
33. Details of the raid on Suffolk compiled from TNA: AIR1/571/16/15/147 *Air Raids on England 7–8 Sep. 1915*; TNA: WO 158/936.
34. Cole & Cheesman, *Air Defence*, pp.69–70.

Chapter 14: 'An Absolute Feeling of Helplessness'

1. George's account in Griehl & Dressel, *Zeppelin! The German Airship Story*, p.82.
2. TNA: WO 158/936.
3. Griehl & Dressel, *Zeppelin! The German Airship Story*, p.82.
4. ibid.
5. TNA: AIR1/571/16/15/147.

6. Details of the raid on London compiled from TNA: AIR1/571/16/15/147; TNA: WO 158/936.
7. Morison, *War on Great Cities*, pp.57–62. Both men are named on the Tower Hill Memorial in Trinity Square Gardens, which commemorates those of the Merchant Navy and fishing fleets who lost their lives in the two World Wars.
8. ibid, p.63–4.
9. On the 1911 Census, Beechey's name is given as James William.
10. TNA: AIR1/2417/303/42, 8 Feb. 1935.
11. The blast smashed windows in 40 houses in Victoria Road, 12 in Inverine Road, eight in Wellington Road and four in Swallowfield Road.
12. TNA: AIR1/571/16/15/147.
13. TNA: WO 158/936.
14. Morris, *German Air Raids on Britain 1914-1918*, pp.54–5.
15. Griehl & Dressel, *Zeppelin! The German Airship Story*, pp.82–5.
16. TNA: AIR1/2417/303/42, 7 Mar. 1935.
17. For personal details of the families living at Ilderton Road see, www.LewishamWarMemorials.wikidot.com/incident:7-September-1915.
18. TNA: AIR1/2417/303/42, 9 Feb. 1935.
19. ibid, 9 Mar. 1935.
20. ibid, 8 Feb. 1935.
21. TNA: AIR1/571/16/15/147.
22. Griehl & Dressel, *Zeppelin! The German Airship Story*, p.85.
23. Cole & Cheesman, *Air Defence*, pp.69–70.
24. Robinson, *The Zeppelin In Combat*, note 2 on p.125.
25. Details of the raid on Skinningrove compiled from TNA: AIR1/571/16/15/148 *Air Raids on England 8–9 Sep. 1915*; TNA: WO 158/936.
26. Cole & Cheesman, *Air Defence*, pp.70–1.
27. TNA: AIR1/571/16/15/148.
28. Cole & Cheesman, *Air Defence*, pp.70–1
29. Snowden Gamble, *The Story of a North Sea Air Station*, p.137.
30. ibid, p.138.
31. Jones, *The War In The Air*, Vol.3, pp.119–20.
32. TNA: WO 158/936, pp.29–30.
33. Details of the raid on East Dereham compiled from TNA: AIR1/571/16/15/148; TNA: WO 158/936; *Eastern Daily Press*, 30 Dec. 1918.
34. It has long been understood that McDonald's given names were Leslie Frank, and as such they appeared on the Commonwealth War Graves Commission (CWGC) search facility, the memorial screen at Hammersmith Old Cemetery and on the regiment's memorial at St. Bartholomew-The-

Great, West Smithfield. I have recently been contacted by McDonald's great nephew, Brian Jeffreys, who, however, has been able to confirm that he was actually Thomas Frank. The CWGC have subsequently corrected their search facility and it is hoped in time that amendments can also be made to the memorial screen and regiment memorial.
35. The article in the *Eastern Daily Press*, published three years later, states that Parkinson died of his wounds. I have, however, found no evidence to support this. He does not appear alongside Pomeroy and McDonald on the regiment's memorial in the Church of St Bartholomew-The-Great in West Smithfield, London, or in the Commonwealth War Graves Commissions records. The regimental museum also has no record of Parkinson's death.
36. *Eastern Daily Press*, 30 Dec. 1918.
37. Beryl Norton's memories at www.mattishall-village.co.uk/Beryl%20Norton-1.htm.

Chapter 15: 'A Beautiful but Terrible Sight'

1. All quotes from Mathy's interview *How I bombed London: Zeppelin Captain's Story* can be accessed at www.trove.nla.gov.au/newspaper/article/131506731.
2. ibid.
3. TNA: WO 158/936.
4. Details of raid on Golders Green compiled from TNA: AIR1/571/16/15/148.
5. Details of raid on London compiled from TNA: AIR1/571/16/15/148; London Metropolitan Archives (LMA), LCC/FB/WAR/03/001-002, *London Fire Brigade Daily Report 8–9 Sep. 1915*; eyewitness accounts as indicated.
6. Amongst the buildings on Queen's Square were: The Alexandra Hospital for Children, The Home for Working Boys, the Examination Hall of The Royal College of Physicians and Surgeons and The National Hospital for the Paralysed and Epileptic. A small plaque surrounded by paving in the central gardens of Queen's Square commemorates the bomb: 'On the night of the eighth of September 1915 a Zeppelin bomb fell and exploded on this spot. Although nearly 1000 people slept in the surrounding buildings no person was injured.'
7. TNA: AIR1/2417/303/42, 1 Mar. 1935.
8. ibid, 6 Mar. 1935.
9. At The Dolphin, a clock that stopped when the bomb exploded still hangs on the wall. Originally showing 10.49pm, over the intervening century the hands have 'dropped' a little.

10. Coombs death certificate gives his occupation as 'Horsekeeper', which is the equivalent of a stable hand. As he lived in Ormond Yard where G. Bailey had stables, it is possible that he worked there. In 1937, Morison, in *War on Great Cities*, stated that Coombs was an employee of the London Gas Light and Coke Company. It appears Morison took this information incorrectly from the London Fire Brigade Daily Return report, which actually gave the details of the Gas Light Company as owners of the gas main destroyed by the same bomb, and which lists Coombs death separately.
11. TDA: *The Times*, 18 Sep. 1915, p.7.
12. British Library, Add MS 39257–39258, *Essays by pupils of Princeton Street Elementary School, Holborn.*
13. Minutes of the Fire Brigade Committee of the London County Council, 14 Oct. 1915.
14. ibid. The Fire Brigade gave a pension of £30 per year to Fireman Green's wife and a 'compassionate allowance' of £5 per year for his son until the age of 15. The trustees of the Carnegie Hero Trust Fund later matched both payments and also paid the rent on Mrs Green's home.
15. Morison, *War on Great Cities*, pp.73–4.
16. TDA: *The Times*, 18 Sep. 1915, p.7.
17. Lucas, *Mixed Vintages*, pp.69–70.
18. TDA: *The Times*, 25 Sep. 1915, p.6.
19. There is a plaque on No. 61 commemorating its destruction in 1915 and subsequent rebuilding in 1917. It is now known as the Zeppelin Building.
20. *Great Western Railway Magazine*, Nov. 1915, pp.278–9.
21. The men were: F.R. Tackley, G.R. Yarnall, A.W. Strahan, J. Hannon, Bailey and a foreman, A.H. Parry, who administered first aid. Bailey, however, did not appear on the list of those commended when reported in the *GWR Magazine*, Jan. 1916, p.31.
22. Morison, *War on Great Cities*, pp.74–5.
23. Mee, *Arthur Mee's Hero Book*, p.221; The Carnegie Hero Trust Fund.
24. TNA: WO 158/936, p.29.
25. Robinson, *The Zeppelin In Combat*, p.127.
26. Klein, *Bombs Away! Zeppelins at War*, p.39.
27. The church was gutted during the Blitz in 1940, and in 1966 the building was dismantled and the church rebuilt in Fulton, Missouri, USA, as a memorial to Winston Churchill, who had died the previous year.
28. Lucas, *Mixed Vintages*, p.71.
29. ibid, pp.72–3.
30. TNA: AIR1/2417/303/42, 1 Feb. 1935.

31. ibid, 4 Feb. 1935.
32. ibid, 21 Feb. 1935.
33. St Bartholomew's Hospital Catalogue (SBH), SBHB/PA/2/33, *Surgical post mortem register 1915*.
34. TNA: AIR1/2417/303/42, 13 Feb. 1935.
35. ibid, 26 Feb. 1935.
36. TNA: WO 158/936, p.28.
37. TDA: *The Times*, 25 Sep. 1915, p.6.
38. ibid.

Chapter 16: 'What Are You Going to do About These Airship Raids?'

1. Robinson, *The Zeppelin In Combat*, p.127.
2. Klein, *Bombs Away! Zeppelins at War*, p.39.
3. TNA: WO 158/936, p.32.
4. TNA: AIR1/571/16/15/148.
5. BNA: *Daily Mirror*, 10 Sep. 1915, p.5.
6. TDA: *The Times*, 13 Sep. 1915, p.8.
7. BNA: *Sunday Pictorial*, 12 Sep. 1915, p.6.
8. Rawlinson, *The Defence of London 1915–1918*, p.8.
9. ibid, p.9.
10. ibid.
11. Jones, *The War In The Air*, Vol.3, p.161.
12. Scott, *Fifty Years in the Royal Navy*, p.304.
13. TDA: *The Times*, 16 Sep. 1915, p.10.
14. Rawlinson, *Defence of London*, p.266.
15. ibid, p.10.
16. Scott, *Fifty Years in the Royal Navy*, p.311.
17. TNA: WO 158/936, p.33.
18. TNA: AIR1/571/16/15/149, *Air Raids on England 11–12 Sep. 1915*.
19. ibid; TNA: WO 158/936; Chance, *Subaltern's* Saga, accessed at www.worcestershireregiment.com/wr.php?main=inc/whs_chance_2.
20. Cole & Cheesman, *Air Defence*, p.72.
21. TNA: WO 158/936 *Airship Raids*, p.35.
22. TNA: AIR1/572/16/15/150 *Air Raids on England 12–13 Sep. 1915*.
23. Pollock, *How We Bluffed the Germans*, Living Age, 15 Jan. 1928, pp.173–4.
24. TNA: AIR1/572/16/15/150.
25. ibid.
26. Cole & Cheesman, *Air Defence*, p.32.
27. ibid, p.72.

28. *Thanet Advertiser*, Thanet's Raid History, p.4.
29. Details of raid on Margate compiled from TNA: AIR1/572/16/15/151 *Air Raids on England 13 Sep. 1915*; *Thanet Advertiser*, Thanet's Raid History, pp.4-5.
30. TNA: AIR1/2417/303/42, 5 Mar. 1935.
31. Cole & Cheesman, *Air Defence*, p.72.
32. Klein, *Bombs Away! Zeppelins at War*, all quotes in this chapter pp.41–5.
33. TNA: AIR1/572/16/15/152 *Air Raids on England 13–14 Sep. 1915*.
34. Pollock, *How We Bluffed the Germans*, Living Age, 15 Jan. 1928, p.173.
35. TNA: AIR1/572/16/15/152 *Air Raids on England 13–14 Sep. 1915*.
36. Robinson, *The Zeppelin In Combat*, pp.128–9.
37. TNA: WO 158/936, p.29.

Chapter 17: London Surrounded

1. Squadron Commander John Tremayne Babington took part in the Friedrichshafen Raid in November 1914. See Chapter 3.
2. Jones, *The War In The Air*, Vol.3, pp.123–4.
3. ibid, pp.127–8.
4. ibid, p.128.
5. Robinson, *The Zeppelin In Combat*, pp.129–30.
6. ibid, p.130.
7. Details of von Buttlar's raid compiled from TNA: AIR1/572/16/15/153 Parts 1 and 2 *Air Raids on England 13–14 Oct. 1915*; TNA: WO 158/937 *Airship Raid 13–14 Oct. 1915*.
8. TNA: WO158/937.
9. TNA: AIR1/572/16/15/153 Parts 1 and 2.
10. Klein, *Bombs Away! Zeppelins at War*, p.47.
11. ibid.
12. Details of raid on Guildford area compiled from TNA: AIR1/572/16/15/153 Parts 1 and 2.
13. The house was designed by the architect Edwin Lutyens, whose later work included many of the memorials erected after the war, including the Cenotaph in London.
14. Information from conversation with Richard Dunning, a former local resident.
15. Robinson, *The Zeppelin In Combat*, p.135.
16. ibid, p.136.
17. Grout, *Thunder in the Skies: A Canadian Gunner in the Great War*, p.133.
18. Ibid.
19. *New York Times*, 7 Nov. 1915, p.2.
20. Details of raid on Otterpool Camp compiled from TNA: AIR1/572/16/15/153 Parts 1 and 2.

21. TNA: WO 158/937, p.5.
22. Cunningham and Castle, *Tunbridge Wells Civic Society Newsletter*, Autumn 2015, p.10.
23. Although part of the County of Surrey at the time, it was a London Metropolitan Police district.
24. Details of raid on East Croydon compiled from TNA: AIR1/572/16/15/153 Parts 1 and 2 and other sources as indicated.
25. BNA: *Surrey Mirror and County Post*, 19 Oct 1915, p.4.
26. TNA: AIR1/2417/303/42, 6 Feb. 1935.
27. *Croydon Advertiser and Surrey County Reporter*, 23 Oct. 1915.
28. ibid.
29. Moore and Sayers (eds.), *Croydon and the Great War*, p.29.
30. TDA: *The Times*, 18 Oct. 1915, p.5.
31. ibid.
32. ibid.
33. TNA: AIR1/2417/303/42, 6 Feb. 1935.
34. TNA: WO 158/937, p.4.
35. Robinson, *The Zeppelin In Combat*, pp.135–6.
36. TNA: WO 158/937, pp.13–4.
37. Klein, *Bombs Away! Zeppelins at War*, p.47.
38. Details of raid on Woolwich compiled from TNA: AIR1/572/16/15/153 Parts 1 and 2; TNA: WO 158/937; LMA: LCC/FB/WAR/03/001–002, *London Fire Brigade Daily Report 13–14 Oct. 1915*.
39. TNA: AIR1/2417/303/42, 9 Mar. 1935.
40. ibid, 6 Feb. 1935.
41. Robinson, *The Zeppelin In Combat*, p.136.
42. TNA: WO 158/937, p.8.
43. Robinson, *The Zeppelin In Combat*, p.136.
44. Details of raid on Hertford compiled from TNA: AIR1/572/16/15/153 Parts 1 and 2; TNA: WO 158/937.
45. TNA: AIR1/2417/303/42, 15 Feb. 1935.
46. TNA: WO 158/937, p.8.
47. Klein, *Bombs Away! Zeppelins at War*, pp.46–7.

Chapter 18: 'The Earth Shook and Trembled'

1. TNA: AIR1/2397/267/1 *Articles by Kptlt Breithaupt – Some of my Experiences During the War*.
2. ibid.
3. Breithaupt, *How We Bombed London*, Living Age, 15 Jan. 1928, pp.170–3.
4. TNA: AIR1/572/16/15/153 Parts 1 and 2.
5. TNA: WO 158/937, p.8.

6. MacDonagh, *In London During the Great War – The Diary of a Journalist*, pp.82–3.
7. Details of raid on London compiled from TNA: AIR1/572/16/15/153 Parts 1 and 2; TNA: WO 158/937; LMA: LCC/FB/WAR/03/001–002, *London Fire Brigade Daily Report 13–14 Oct. 1915*; eyewitness accounts as indicated.
8. TNA: AIR1/2417/303/42, 6 Feb. 1935.
9. Wickham, *The Great War … I Was There!*, Part 11, p.452.
10. TNA: AIR1/2417/303/42, 15 Feb. 1935.
11. ibid.
12. LMA: LCC/FB/WAR/03/001-002, *London Fire Brigade Daily Report 13–14 Oct. 1915*.
13. TDA: *The Times*, 26 Oct. 1015, p.15.
14. TNA: AIR1/2417/303/42, 27 Feb. 1935.
15. ibid, 15 Feb. 1935.
16. *The Times*, 18 Oct. 1915, p.5.
17. Wickham, *The Great War … I Was There!*, Part 11, pp.452-454. Wickham wrote his account thirty-three years after the event and his memories of 'Billy' may have become blurred by time or by his own trauma, or 'Billy' may have been a nickname. Wickham gives the boy's age as 15 but the inquest gave the age of the unnamed boy messenger as 13 (*The Times*, 18 Oct. 1915, p.5). The only victim of the raid in that area aged either 13 or 15 on the GRO Death Index was 13-year-old Edward Howard. He was not blown to pieces but died of his wounds the following day.
18. TNA: AIR1/2417/303/42, 6 Feb. 1935.
19. Taylor's letter of 4 Nov. 1915 can be accessed at www.ww1-letters.com/letters/london-1915-16/page/5/.
20. TDA: *The Times*, 18 Oct. 1915, p.5. The report on the inquest gives the age of the special constable killed as 34, however the General Register Office index gives his age as 24, as does the entry on www.policerollofhonour.org.uk.
21. TNA: AIR1/2417/303/42, 19 Feb. 1935.
22. TDA: *The Times*, 18 Oct. 1915, p.5. Details of the victims are a result of taking names from the London Fire Brigade Daily Report, searching for their deaths on genealogy websites to ascertain their ages, then linking them with the inquest reports, which were only able to publish ages and occupations. By linking the three sources, I have been able to give names, ages and occupations of some victims.
23. TNA: AIR1/2417/303/42, 15 Feb. 1935.
24. ibid, 6 Feb. 1935.
25. Breithaupt, *How We Bombed London*, pp.170–3.
26. LMA, LCC/FB/WAR/03/001-002, *London Fire Brigade Daily Report 13–14 Oct. 1915*.

REFERENCES AND NOTES

27. Damage to the outer stonework of the chapel is still visible, as is also damage inflicted on the undercroft. There is a plaque on the wall and a small white disc in the road showing where the bomb landed.
28. TDA: *The Times*, 18 Oct. 1915, p.5.
29. www.ww1-letters.com/letters/london-1915-16/page/5/.
30. Hamnett, *Laughing Torso*, pp.85–6.
31. TNA: AIR1/2417/303/42, 9 Feb. 1935.
32. Gray's Inn, *The War Book of Gray's Inn*, pp. xxi–xxiii.
33. Rawlinson, *Defence of London*, pp.22–6.
34. ibid, pp.27-8.
35. TDA: The Times, 8 Nov. 1915, p.7.
36. Breithaupt, *How We Bombed London*, pp.170–3.
37. SBH: SBHB/PA/2/33, *Surgical post mortem register 1915*.
38. TDA: *The Times*, 18 Oct. 1915, p.5.
39. TNA: AIR1/2417/303/42, 7 Feb. 1935.
40. TDA: *The Times*, 27 Oct. 1915, p.5.
41. SBH: SBHB/PA/2/33, *Surgical post mortem register 1915*.
42. *TDA: The Times*, 18 Oct. 1915, p.5.
43. SBH: SBHB/PA/2/33, *Surgical post mortem register 1915*.
44. Cole & Cheesman, *Air Defence*, pp.73–5.
45. Sutton, *Raider's Approach*, pp.14–17. Slessor enjoyed a long career, becoming Marshal of the Royal Air Force in 1950.
46. Breithaupt, *How We Bombed London*, pp.170–3.
47. TNA: AIR1/2397/267/1 *Articles by Kptlt Breithaupt – Airships and the Airship Service During the Great War.*
48. Robinson, *The Zeppelin In Combat*, p.137.

Chapter 19: The Home Front Line

1. *A Report on the Zeppelin Raid of 13/14th* in TNA: AIR1/572/16/15/153 Parts 1 and 2.
2. These ten 'stations' were: Buckingham Palace, AA Admiralty, London District Command, Eastern Command, Central Force, Sandringham, Admiralty Duty Captain, Admiralty Director of Intelligence Division, Directorate of Military Aeronautics, and Military Assistant at Woolwich Arsenal.
3. Scott, *Fifty Years in the Royal Navy*, pp.313–4.
4. ibid, p.309.
5. Scott, *Fifty Years in the Royal Navy*, p.315. Scott listed the 152 guns in his 'menagerie' as follows:
    10 - 4.7 guns
    7 - 4-inch guns

- 35 - French 75mm guns
- 4 - 4-inch Greek guns
- 20 - 15-pdr B.L.G
- 12 - 2.95 Russian guns
- 34 - 6-pdr guns
- 19 - 3-inch guns
- 11 - 3-pdr guns

6. Rawlinson, *Defence of London*, p.46.
7. Scott, *Fifty Years in the Royal Navy*, p.305.
8. Rawlinson, *Defence of London*, pp.34–5.
9. ibid, pp.38–9.
10. Scott, *Fifty Years in the Royal Navy*, p.308.
11. TDA: *The Times*, 22 Oct. 1915, p.12.
12. Jones, *The War In The Air*, Vol.3, p.154.
13. ibid, pp.154–5.
14. ibid, pp.155–6.
15. See Appendix 2.
16. TDA: *The Times*, 14 Sep. 1915, p.3.
17. Figures from Kollman, *Das Zeppelinluftschiff*, Tabell II; Robinson, *The Zeppelin In Combat*, p.385.
18. Frank Brock had assisted Noel Pemberton Billing in planning the Friedrichshafen Raid in November 1914. See Chapter 3.
19. Airship raid casualties, killed: 207 – 110 men (19 in armed forces), 61 women and 36 children. Injured: 533 – 277 men (33 in armed forces), 148 women and 75 children. Aeroplane raid casualties, killed: 2 women. Injured: 6 – 2 men and 4 women. See Appendix 2.
20. TDA: *The Times*, 15 Oct. 1915, p.8.

Bibliography

Ash, Lieutenant Colonel Eric: *Sir Frederick Sykes and the Air Revolution 1912–18* (London 1999).

Ashmore, Major General E.B.: *Air Defence* (London 1929).

Austen, Chas. A.F.: *Ramsgate Raid Records 1915–1918* (Originally published around 1919, reprint Ramsgate 2006).

Blacker, Barnaby: *The Adventures and Inventions of Stewart Blacker: Soldier, Aviator, Weapons Inventor* (Barnsley 2006).

Buttlar-Brandenfels, Freiherr Treusch von: *Zeppelins Over England* (London 1931).

Castle, H.G.: *Fire Over England – The German Air Raids in World War 1* (London 1982).

Castle, Ian: *London 1915–17 – The Zeppelin Menace* (Oxford 2008).

_____: *The First Blitz – Bombing London in the First World War* (Oxford 2015).

_____: *The Zeppelin Base Raids – Germany 1914* (Oxford 2011).

Charlton, L.E.O.: *War Over England* (London 1936).

Churchill, Rt. Hon. Winston S.: *The World Crisis*, Vol. I (London 1923).

Cole, Christopher & Cheesman, E.F.: *The Air Defence of Britain 1914–1918* (London 1984).

Credland, Arthur G.: *The Hull Zeppelin Raids 1915–1918* (Stroud 2014).

Dover Express: *Dover and the European War 1914–18* (Dover 1919).

Easdown, Martin, with Genth, Thomas: *A Glint in the Sky* (Barnsley 2004).

Fegan, Thomas: *The 'Baby Killers' – German Air Raids on Britain in the First World War* (Barnsley 2002).

Gardiner, Ian: *The Flatpack Bombers – The Royal Navy and the Zeppelin Menace* (Barnsley 2009).

Gibson, Mary: *Warneford, VC* (Yeovilton 1979).

Gollin, Alfred M.: *The Impact of Air Power on the British People and Their Government, 1909–1914* (Stanford, CA 1989).

Gray's Inn: *The War Book of Gray's Inn* (London 1921).

Grayzel, Susan R.: *At Home and Under Fire – Air Raids and Culture in Britain from the Great War to the Blitz* (Cambridge 2012).

Griehl, Manfred, & Dressel, Joachim: *Zeppelin! The German Airship Story* (London 1990).

Grout, Derek: *Thunder in the Skies: A Canadian Gunner in the Great War* (Toronto 2015).

Hall, Ian: *Zeppelins Over the North East* (Alnwick 2014).

Hammerton, Sir John (Ed.): *The Great War … I Was There! – Undying Memories of 1914–1918*, Part 11 (London 1938).

Hamnett, Nina: *Laughing Torso* (New York 1932).

Jenkins, Gareth: *Zeppelins Over Bury* (Revised edition, Needham Market 2016).

Jones, H.A.: *The War in the Air – Being the Story of the Part Played in the Great War by the Royal Air Force*, Vol. III (Oxford 1931).

Klein, Pitt (trans. Reid, Alastair): *Bombs Away! Zeppelins at War*, (Privately Printed 2016). Originally published as Klein, Pitt: *Achtung! Bomben Fallen* (Leipzig 1934).

Kollman, Franz: *Das Zeppelinluftschiff – seine Entwicklung, Tätigkeit und Leistungen* (Berlin 1924).

Layman, R.D.: *The Cuxhaven Raid – The World's First Carrier Air Strike* (London, 1985).

Lea, John: *Reggie – The Life of Air Vice Marshal R.L.G. Marix CB DSO* (Bishop Auckland 1994).

Lehmann, Capt. E.A. and Mingos, H.: *The Zeppelins* (London 1927).

Longmore, Sir Arthur: *From Sea to Sky* (London, 1946).

Lucas, E.V. (Ed.): *Mixed Vintages* (London 1919).

MacBean, Wing Commander John A. & Hogben, Major Arthur S.: *Bombs Gone – The Development and Use of British Air-Dropped Weapons from 1912 to the Present Day* (Wellingborough 1990).

MacDonagh, Michael: *In London During the Great War – The Diary of a Journalist* (London 1935).

Macmillan, Norman: *Sir Sefton Brancker* (London 1935).

Mansfield, F.A.: *History of Gravesend in the County of Kent* (Gravesend 1922, reprinted as *History of Gravesend*, 1981).

BIBLIOGRAPHY

Marben, Rolf: *Zeppelin Adventures* (London 1931).

Marks, David: *Let The Zeppelins Come* (Stroud 2017).

Mee, Arthur: *Arthur Mee's Hero Book* (London 1921).

Moore, H. Keatley and Sayers, W.C. Berwick (Eds.): *Croydon and the Great War – The Official History of the War Work of the Borough and its Citizens from 1914 to 1919* (Croydon 1920).

Morison, Frank: *War on Great Cities – A Study of the Facts* (London 1937).

Morris, Joseph: *German Air Raids on Britain 1914–1918* (Originally published 1925, reprinted Dallington 1993).

Neumann, Major Georg Paul (trans. Gurdon, J.E.): *The German Air Force in the Great War* (Originally published 1921, reprinted Bath 1969).

Oak-Rhind, Edwin Scoby: *The North Foreland Lookout Post in the Great War 1915–1917* (Ramsgate 2005).

Parker, Nigel J.: *Gott Strafe England – The German Air Assault Against Great Britain 1914–1918*, Vol.1 (Solihull 2015).

Poolman, Kenneth: *Zeppelins Over England* (London 1960).

Powers, Barry D.: *Strategy Without Slide-Rule* (London 1976).

Raleigh, Walter: *The War in the Air, Vol.1* (Oxford 1922).

Rawlinson, A.: *The Defence of London 1915–1918* (London 1923).

Rimell, Raymond L.: *Zeppelin! A Battle for Air Supremacy in World War I* (London 1984).

_____: *Zeppelins at War 1914–1915* (Berkhamsted 2014).

_____: *Zeppelin*, Vol. 1 (Berkhamsted 2006).

Robinson, Douglas H.: *The Zeppelin In Combat – A History of the German Naval Airship Division, 1912–1918* (Atglen, PA 1994).

Scott, Admiral Sir Percy: *Fifty Years in the Royal Navy* (London 1919).

Simpson, Alan: *Air Raids on South-West Essex in the Great War* (Barnsley 2015).

Snowden Gamble, C.F.: *The Story of a North Sea Air Station* (Originally published 1928, reprinted London 1967).

Stoney, Barbara: *Twentieth Century Maverick – The Life of Noel Pemberton Billing* (East Grinstead 2004).

Storey, Neil R.: *Zeppelin Blitz – The German Air Raids on Great Britain During the First World War* (Stroud 2015).

Sueter, Rear Admiral Murray F.: *Airmen or Noahs; Fair Play for Our Airmen; the Great 'Neon' Air Myth Exposed* (London 1928).

Sutton, Squadron Leader H.T.: *Raider's Approach* (Aldershot 1956).

Thanet Advertiser: *Thanet's Raid History* (Originally published Ramsgate 1919, reprinted Ramsgate 2006).

Travers, Ben: *Vale of Laughter – An Autobiography* (London 1957).

Urban, Heinz: *Zeppeline – der Kaiserlichen Marine 1914 bis 1918* (Meersburg, 2008).

Wallace, Graham: *Flying Witness – Harry Harper and the Golden Age of Aviation* (London 1958).

White, C.M.: *The Gotha Summer – The German Daytime Air Raids on England, May–August 1917* (London 1986).

Wyatt, R.J.: *Death From The Skies – The Zeppelin Raids over Norfolk 19 January 1915* (Norwich, 1990).

Magazines and Journals

Bleibler, Jürgen: 'Luftkreig über Friedrichshafen 1914-1918', *Wissenschaftliches Jahrbuch 2001 – Zeppelin Museum Friedrichshafen.*

Breithaupt, Kapitänleutnant: 'How We Bombed London', *The Living Age*, Vol. 334, No. 4322, 15 Jan. 1928.

Cunningham, John and Castle, Ian: 'The Night the Zeppelin Came', *Royal Tunbridge Wells Civic Society Newsletter*, Autumn 2015.

'During a recent Zeppelin raid …', *Great Western Railway Magazine*, Vol. XXVII, No.11, Nov. 1915.

Linnarz, Major Erich: 'I Was London's First Zepp Raider', *The Great War… I Was There! – Undying memories of 1914–1918*, Part 11, 13 Dec. 1938.

Pankhurst, Sylvia: 'I Was In London's First Air Raid', *The Great War… I Was There! – Undying memories of 1914–1918*, Part 11, 13 Dec. 1938.

Pollock, Guy C.: 'How We Bluffed the Germans', *The Living Age*, Vol. 334, No. 4322, 15 Jan. 1928.

'Staff Commendations', *Great Western Railway Magazine*, Vol. XXVIII, No.1, Jan. 1916.

Szigeti, Marton: 'Archiv: Marton Szigeti', *WW1 Aero*, No.128, May 1990.

Wickham, James: 'Grisly Death Over The Gaiety', *The Great War… I Was There! – Undying memories of 1914–1918*, Part 11, 13 Dec. 1938.

Archival Sources

The National Archives (TNA), Kew, London
AIR 1   Air Ministry: Air Historical Branch: Papers (Series 1)
WO 158   War Office: Military Headquarters: Correspondence and Papers, First World War
CAB 37   Cabinet Office: Photographic Copies of Cabinet Papers
MEPO 2   Metropolitan Police: Office of the Commissioner: Correspondence and Papers

The British Library, King's Cross, London
Archives and Manuscripts – Add MS 39257–39258 – Impressions of the airship raids over London

Imperial War Museum, Lambeth, London (Department of Documents)
No.12358, Private papers of H. Miller (inc. diary of Jeanne Berman)

London Metropolitan Archives (LMA), Clerkenwell, London
LCC/FB/WAR/03 – London County Council: Fire Brigade Department: Wartime Measures: Returns of Air Raid Fire calls

Hackney Archives, Hackney, London
Hackney & Stoke Newington Recorder

The Times Digital Archive (TDA)
The Times

The British Newspaper Archive (BNA)
Bury Free Press
Cambridge Independent Press
Coventry Evening Telegraph
Daily Mirror
Daily Record and Mail
Diss Express
Dover Express
Dundee Courier
Edinburgh Evening News
Essex County Chronicle
Essex Newsman

Gloucester Journal
Liverpool Echo
Manchester Evening News
Morpeth Herald
Newcastle Daily Journal
Nottingham Evening Post
Portsmouth Evening News
Sunday Pictorial
Surrey Mirror and County Post
Yorkshire Post

Index

Admiralty, 3, 5, 6, 11, 12, 14, 15, 17, 24-26, 29-32, 43, 51, 63, 88-90, 116, 118, 134, 138, 144, 180, 188-189, 233-235, 237, 249, 286, 290-292, 294-295, 297, 317 (note 3), 336 (note 2)
Aircraft,
   British,
      Avro 504, 6, 115, 117
      B.E.2b, 17, 18, 20, 23
      B.E.2c, 158, 165, 167, 170-171, 192, 206, 208-209, 234, 238, 241, 243, 250, 285-286
      Blériot XI, 161
      Blériot Parasol, 134
      Bristol T.B.8, 35, 37, 39, 78, 161,
      Caudron G.3, 180, 187, 208, 238
      Henri Farman HF27, 138
      Morane-Saulnier L, 138-141
      Nieuport, 116-117
      Short Folder, 41
      Short Type 74, 41
      Short Type 135, 41
      Sopwith 80hp Tractor, 17
      Sopwith Gunbus, 134
      Sopwith Schneider, 208,
      Sopwith Seaplane 880, 89
      Sopwith Sociable, 18
      Sopwith Tabloid, 18, 20, 21, 22, 23, 168
      Sopwith Two-seater Scout, 89
      Vickers FB5 'Gunbus', 37-39
      Voisin, 116,
      Wight seaplane, 37
   German,
      Albatros, 33, 90
      Albatros BII, 90-91
      Aviatik, 33
      Friedrichshafen FF 19, 41
      Friedrichshafen FF 29, 35, 37-39, 41, 64
Aircraft Crew,
   British,
      Babington, Flight Commander (Flt Cdr) John, RNAS, 26, 29, 117, 249
      Barnes, Flight Lieutenant (Flt Lt) Douglas, RNAS, 134-135
      Besson, Flight sub-Lieutenant (Flt sub-Lt) Frank, RNAS, 170
      Bigsworth, Flt Cdr Arthur Wellesley, RNAS, 117-118

Bone, Flt Cdr R.J., RNAS, 166
Briggs, Squadron Commander (Sqn Cdr) Edward, RNAS, 26-29
Buss, Flt Lt Harold, RNAS, 37, 39
Cannon, Flt sub-Lt Roland, RNAS, 26-27
Chidson, 2nd Lieutenant (2nd Lt) Montagu, RFC, 38-40
Collet, Lieutenant (Lt) Charles, RNAS, 17-19
Cripps, Flt Lt John, RNAS, 208-209
Digby, Flt sub-Lt F.T., RNAS, 241
Draper, Flt Cdr Chris, RNAS, 161
Grey, Lieutenant Commander (Lt-Cdr) Spenser, RNAS, 18, 20-21, 23
Hilliard, Flt sub-Lt Gerald, RNAS, 209
Hinkler, Leading Mechanic (LM) Bert, RNAS, 78, 158
Hope-Vere, Flt Cdr Ralph, RNAS, 206
Ireland, Flt Cdr de Courcy Wynder Plunkett, RNAS, 89, 167, 208
Jacob, Flt sub-Lt A.J., RNAS, 208
Jenkins, 2nd Lt F.H., RFC, 285
Johnston, Flt sub-Lt, RNAS, 208

Keith-Johnston, Flt Lt David, RNAS, 170
Kilner, Flt sub-Lt B.D., RNAS, 116
Leigh, Flt sub-Lt Peter, RNAS, 78
Lord, Flt sub-Lt Reginald, RNAS, 168
Mack, Flt sub-Lt R.G., RNAS, 161
Marix, Lt Reginald, RNAS, 18, 20-23, 191
Martin, Corporal (Cpl), RFC, 38-40
Meddis, LM G.E., RNAS, 116-117
Mills, Flt sub-Lt John, RNAS, 138-139, 153
Morison, Lt, RFC, 238
Morrison, Flt sub-Lt C.D., RNAS, 187
Mulock, Flt sub-Lt Redford Henry, RNAS, 115-116
Nicholl, Flt Lt Vincent, RNAS, 208
Notley, LM C., RNAS, 89
Peirse, Flt Cdr R.E.C., RNAS, 166
Penn-Gaskell, Capt. Leslie da Costa, RFC, 285
Rathborne, Sqn Cdr Charles, RNAS, 208
Robertson, Flt sub-Lt A.W., RNAS, 134
Robinson, Flt Cdr C.E., RNAS, 158
Rose, Flt sub-Lieutenant John, RNAS, 138-139
Shepherd, Sqn Cdr Philip, RNAS, 26-27

INDEX

Sippe, Lt Sydney, RNAS, 20-21, 23, 26, 28-29
Slessor, 2nd Lt John, RFC, 285-286, 336 (note 45)
Smyth-Pigott, Flt Cdr Joseph, RNAS, 170
Square, Flt sub-Lt H.H., RNAS, 187
Tipton, Lt R.J., RFC, 285
Travers, Flt sub-Lt Ben, RNAS, 134-135, 140
Wardle, 2nd Lt C.E., RFC, 285
Warneford, Flt sub-Lt Reginald, RNAS, 116-117, 138-143, 153, 189
Wilson, Flt Lt John, RNAS, 138-139, 153
Wood, Flt Sub-Lt C.E., RNAS, 192

German,
v. Arnauld de la Pérriere, Oberleutnant-zur-See (Oblt-z-S) Friedrich, 35
v. Frankenberg, Fähnrich-zur-See (Fähn-z-S) Ludwig, 37-39
Heym, Fähn-z-S Thomas, 64, 66-67, 69-70
v. Kanne, Oberleutnant (Oblt) Freiherr Dietrich, 90-92
Moll, Oblt-z-S Hermann, 35
Prondzynski, Oblt-z-S Stephen, 35, 37-39, 64-67, 69, 70
Ritter, Offizierstellvertreter Karl, 90-93

Aircraft units (German),
Brieftauben Abteilung Ostende, 33
Feldflieger Abteilung Nr. 41, 90
Fliegerkorps der OHL, 33
Seeflieger Abteilung 1, 35, 37, 241

Airfields,
RNAS,
Atwick, 161
Chelmsford (Broomfield), 180, 187, 238
Chingford, 134, 249-250
Dover (Guston Road), 35, 37, 134
Eastchurch, 5- 6, 11-13, 35-37, 39, 90, 92, 121, 134, 140, 149, 165, 241
Felixstowe, 5, 11, 206
Furnes, 116, 138, 139
Hendon , 11, 134, 140, 249
Isle of Grain, 11, 37, 121, 149
Killingholme, 153
Redcar, 208
Rochford, 134
St. Pol, 116, 138, 142
Westgate, 92, 115-116, 134, 243
Whitley Bay, 78, 158
Yarmouth, 5, 46, 62, 89, 95, 167, 171, 180, 192, 208-209
RFC,
Brooklands, 37
Chelmsford (Writtle), 234, 238
Farnborough, 37, 190
Hainault Farm, 250, 285-286
Joyce Green, 38, 40, 62, 149, 234, 250, 285
Northolt, 149, 250, 285
Sutton's Farm, 250, 264, 285

Air raid warnings, 70, 109, 120, 126, 152, 154-155, 162, 207, 289, 293-294
Airships,
  Schütte-Lanz, 7, 160, 295, 297, 304 (Appendix I)
  German Army,
    SL II, 7, 196, 198-200, 206, 297, 304-305 (Appendix II)
    SL 7, 297
    SL 11, 297, 304 (Appendix I)
  German Navy,
    SL 3, 45, 304 (Appendix I), 305 (Appendix II)
    SL 4, 297, 304 (Appendix I)
    SL 6, 297
  Zeppelins, 3, 7, 8, 15, 31, 43, 44, 45, 46, 48, 61, 64, 72, 89, 93, 160, 297, 303-4 (Appendix I)
    Hansa, 7
    Sachsen, 7, 8, 10, 33-34
    Viktoria Luise, 3, 7
  German Army,
    Z II, 7
    Z III, 7
    Z IV, 7, 94
    Z V, 9
    Z VI, 8
    Z VII, 7, 9
    Z VIII, 7, 9
    Z IX, 7, 10, 18-19, 22-23, 41, 191
    Z X, 93
    Z XII, 71, 72, 303 (Appendix I)
    LZ 35, 93, 304 (Appendix I)
    LZ 37, 137-138, 141, 149, 153, 191, 238, 304 (Appendix I)
    LZ 38, 94, 110, 149, 295, 302 (Appendix 1) 303 (Appendix II), (29/30 Apr 1915) 95, 97-98, 102, (10 May 1915) 103-105, 109, (17 May 1915) 112, 114-115, 116, (26 May 1915) 119, 121, (31 May 1915) 125-128, 130-134, (7 Jun 1915) 137-139, 153, 191
    LZ 39, 116-118, 137-138, 304 (Appendix I)
    LZ 74, 191, 193-194, 200-201, 203, 205-206, 239-241, 305 (Appendix II)
    LZ 77, 191-193, 237-239, 244-245, 305 (Appendix II)
    LZ 86, 139
    LZ 97, 139
  German Navy,
    L 1, 213, 303 (Appendix I)
    L 2, 34, 213
    L 3, 7, 10, 32, 45-49, 53-54, 60- 62, 305 (Appendix II)
    L 4, 10, 45-47, 54-62, 305 (Appendix II)
    L 5, 40-43, 45-46, 79-81, 83, 87, 89, 110-111, 178, 305 (Appendix II)
    L 6, 40-42, 45, 47, 79, 84, 87-89, 154, 268, 305 (Appendix II)
    L 7, 27-28, 30, 41, 79, 83, 171
    L 8, 45, 71
    L 9, 46, 71-77, 79, 145, 149-150, 152-153, 160-162, 164-165, 171, 206-208, 213, 304 (Appendix I), 305 (Appendix II)

INDEX

L 10, 111, 145-149, 154-160, 165-166, 171-172, 174-178, 180-181, 184, 187-188, 295, 305 (Appendix II)
L 11, 145, 154, 166-167, 171, 176-179, 206, 244-245, 251, 267, 288, 305-306 (Appendix II)
L 12, 145, 168-171, 305 (Appendix II)
L 13, 160, 167, 171, 178, 305-306 (Appendix II) (8 Sep 1915) 206, 213-215, 219, 221, 224-226, 229-230, 232, (14 Sep 1915) 244-247, 298, (13 Oct 1915) 251-255, 258, 261-262, 264-265, 267, 288,
L 14, 178, 206, 209-211, 214, 244-245, 251-252, 255-258, 260-261, 265, 267, 288, 305-306 (Appendix II)
L 15, 251-252, 265, 267-270, 274, 276-279, 281, 283-288, 303 (Appendix I), 306 (Appendix II)
L 16, 171, 251-252, 264-267, 288, 306 (Appendix II)
L 18, 296
L 20, 296
L 30, 297
Airship Commanders,
  German Army,
    George, Hauptman (Hptmn) Friedrich, 193-194, 200, 203-205, 239-241
    v. d. Haegen, Oberleutnant (Oblt) Otto, 141

Horn, Hptmn Alfred, 19, 191-192, 237-239, 244-245
Lehmann, Hptmn Ernst, 8, 9, 64, 71
Linnarz, Hptmn Erich, 94-95, 97-98, 102-104, 109, 111-112, 114-115, 118-121, 124-128, 130-131, 133-134, 137, 139
Masius, Hptmn Hans, 116, 118
v. Wobeser, Hptmn Richard, 194, 196-200, 205-206
German Navy,
  Beelitz, Kapitänleutnant (Kptlt) Helmut, 71
  Böcker, Kapitänleutnant der Reserve (Kptlt-d-R) Alois, 79-81, 83, 88, 110-111, 178, 209-212, 255-258, 260-1
  Boemack, Kptlt Fritz, 145-146
  Breithaupt, Kptlt Joachim, 264, 267-271, 276-278, 282-287
  v. Buttlar-Brandenfels, Oberleutnant-zur-See (Oblt-z-S) Horst Julius Ludwig Otto, Freiherr Treusch, 40-42, 47, 84, 86-88, 122, 154, 166-167, 176-180, 251-252
  Fritz, Kptlt Hans, 47-49, 54, 61
  Hirsch, Kptlt Klaus, 41, 111, 145-148, 154-159, 188
  Loewe, Kptlt Odo, 161-165, 171, 207-208, 212

347

Mathy, Kptlt Heinrich, 45-46, 155, 171, 178, (14 Apr 1915) 71-79, (6 Jun 1915) 149-150, 152-154, (9 Aug 1915) 167-168, (8 Sep 1915) 213-217, 219, 221-222, 224-227, 229-232, 279, 298 (14 Sep 1915) 244-247, (13 Oct 1915) 252-255, 258, 261-264,

Peterson, Oblt-z-S Werner, 28, 30, 79, 83-84, 168-171, 264-267

v. Platen-Hallermund, Kptlt Zdenko Magnus Karl Friedrich, Graf, 47, 54-57, 59-61

Wenke, Oblt-z-S Friedrich, 165-166, 171-172, 174-176, 180-183, 185-188

Airship Organisation,
    Naval Airship Division, 10, 33-34, 40, 42-43, 62, 90, 110-111, 143, 145, 149, 159, 213, 268
    Army airship service, 10, 139, 143, 316 (note 11)

Airship Sheds,
    Ahlhorn, 160
    Berchem St. Agathe (Brussels), 71, 138, 206
    Bickendorf (Cologne), 21
    Etterbeek (Brussels), 71
    Evere (Brussels), 71, 95, 102-103, 116, 118, 124, 137-139
    Friedrichshafen, 25-28, 30, 41, 79, 111, 171
    Fuhlsbüttel (Hamburg), 45-47, 61, 79, 87
    Golzheim (Düsseldorf), 18-19, 21-22
    Gontrode (Ghent), 71
    Lohausen (Düsseldorf), 19, 21-22
    Maubeuge, 71
    Namur, 111, 206
    Nordholz (Cuxhaven), 25, 30, 40-42, 45-47, 87, 110-111, 158-159, 177, 244, 251-252, 261, 268, 287-288
    Tondern, 296

Anti-Aircraft artillery, 10, 16, 24, 36-40, 43, 87, 91-92, 112, 115, 125, 133-134, 137, 147, 149, 155, 187, 194, 199, 205, 219, 232-233, 236-237, 247, 251, 253, 276, 281-282, 284-285, 291, 294,

Anti-Aircraft artillery (mobile), 63, 66, 101, 125, 134, 174, 176, 180, 188, 236-237, 239, 241, 246, 250-252, 261-262, 264-265, 267, 269, 279, 286, 289, 291

Anti-Aircraft gun positions,
    Abbey Wood, 262
    Admiralty Arch, 11
    Blackfriars, 24
    Blackheath, 137
    Cannon Street Hotel, 24, 215
    Carville, 155
    Cheshunt, 194
    Chilworth, 253, 255
    Clapton Orient Football Ground, 43, 134, 264
    Cleadon, 158
    Cliffe, 104
    Crown Agents Office, 11
    Dover,
        Langdon Battery, 115, 169
        Drop Redoubt, 115
    Edmonton, 187
    Enfield Lock, 194

INDEX

Erith, 43, 264
Faversham, 90, 91, 179
Felixstowe, 87, 187
Finsbury Park, 137
Foreign Office, 11
Green Park, 24, 270
Gresham Collage, 24, 215
Harwich,
    Beacon Hill, 176, 206,
    Landguard Fort, 87, 206
    Ray Hill, 175, 176
Homerton, 187
Honor Oak, 43, 262
Immingham, 152
Kelvedon Hatch, 265, 286
Low Walker, 155
Nine Elms, 24
Pelaw, 155
Plumstead, 250, 262
Purfleet, 10, 38, 40, 261, 264
Parliament Hill, 43, 229
Royal Albert Dock, 199, 250
St. Helen's Court, 24
St. James's Street, 24
Shoeburyness, 98, 119, 121, 125
Southminster, 119, 134, 237
South Shields, 158
Stallinborough, 152
Stowmarket, 97
Sunk Island, 152
Temple, 24
Thames Haven, 104
Tilbury, 147
Tower Bridge, 24, 226
Waltham Abbey, 10, 43, 180, 187, 194,
Waterloo, 24
West Ham, 137, 264
Woolwich Arsenal, 199, 262
Antwerp, 10, 17-23, 26

'Baby killers', 137
Bachmann, Vizeadmiral Gustav, 71, 160, 161
Balfour, Arthur (First Lord of the Admiralty), 189, 235-237, 290, 291, 294
Behncke, Konteradmiral Paul, 31, 32, 44, 298
Belfort, 25-26, 29
Berlin, 31, 43, 61, 124, 160
v. Bethmann-Hollweg, Theobald, (German Chancellor), 160
Bidon, General (Dunkirk garrison), 14
Blériot, Louis (Aviation pioneer), 2
Bombed places,
    Ashford, 179
    Badingham, 171
    Badlesmere, 179
    Bedlington, 73-74
    Belstead, 95
    Benhall, 192
    Benton, 75
    Borden, 91
    Braintree, 65-66
    Bradfield St. George, 97
    Bredfield, 102
    Bromeswell, 102
    Broxbourne, 269-270
    Bucklesham Hall, 246
    Bury St. Edmunds, 97-98, 101-102, 122
    Bylaugh Hall, 210
    Carlin How, 207
    Chelmsford, 187
    Cheshunt, 194, 200
    Chilworth, 253-254
    Choppington, 73-74
    Cliffe, 39
    Coggeshall, 66-67

Colchester, 68-69
Coltishall, 251
Cramlington, 74-75
Creeting St. Mary, 102
Dover, 35-36, 115, 168-169
Driffield, 145
Dudley, 75
East Bergholt, 240
Eastchurch, 165-166
East Croydon, 258-261
East Dereham, 210-212
East Howdon, 157
Easton Bavents, 81
Faversham, 91-92
Framlingham, 191
Frant, 257
Goole, 162-164
Gosforth Park, 75
Gravesend, 146-148
Great Glemham, 192
Great Hautbois, 251
Great Yarmouth, 48-54
Grimsby, 152-153
Grovehurst, 91
Guildford, 253-254
Hatfield, 252-253
Hazlerigg, 75
Heacham, 55-56
Hebburn, 77, 156
Hemley Hall, 246
Henham Hall, 80
Hertford, 265-267
Heybridge, 86-87
Horstead, 251
Hotham, 164
Hull, 149-154
Hunstanton, 55
Ipswich, 95-97, 102
Jarrow, 156-157
King's Lynn, 57-60

Leigh-on-Sea, 103-104
Loftus Bank, 207
London,
    Aldgate, 283-284
    Bartholomew Close, 222-224
    Bermondsey, 200
    Bloomsbury, 216-217
    Charlton, 198
    Covent Garden, 270-276
    Dalston, 128-129
    Deptford, 197-198
    Golders Green, 215
    Gray's Inn, 219, 277-278
    Greenwich, 198
    Guildhall, 224-225
    Holborn, 217-219
    Hoxton, 130-131
    Isle of Dogs, 194-196
    Leyton, 181-185
    Leytonstone, 133, 185
    Lincoln's Inn, 276
    Liverpool Street Station,
        226-228
    Moorgate, 225-226, 281-283
    New Cross, 204-205
    Rotherhithe, 201-203
    Shoreditch, 131, 228-229
    Stoke Newington, 125-128, 133
    Stratford, 133
    Walthamstow, 180-181, 186
    Wanstead, 186
    Whitechapel, 132-133
    Woolwich, 199, 261-264
Lowestoft, 81-83, 89, 166-167
Maldon, 84-86, 88
Margate, 241-244
Marks Tey, 67
Melton, 102, 172
Milton Regis, 146

INDEX

Monk Soham, 191
Mount Bures, 239
Nettlestead, 97
Newbourne, 246
Ormesby St. Michael (Little Ormesby), 48
Otley, 102
Otterpool Camp, 255-257
Oxney, 115-116
Pakefield, 166
Parkeston, 175
Pettistree, 172
Rainham, 146-147
Ramsgate, 112-115, 122
Reydon, 80-81
Rushmere, 174-175, 240, 286
Scarning, 211
Seaton Burn, 75
Sheldwich, 179
Sheringham, 54-55
Shotley, 175
Shottisham, 246
Sittingbourne, 91-92, 146
Skinningrove, 207-208
Snettisham, 56
Southend-on-Sea, 103-109, 119-121
South Shields, 157-158
Southwold, 80
Stratford St. Mary, 239-240
Thornham, 55
Thornwood, 237-238
Thundersley, 104
Trimley marshes, 176
Tunbridge Wells, 257-258
Wallsend, 76-77, 155-156
Westcliff, 103-104
Westenhanger, 257
West Sleekburn, 73
Whitton, 97

Willisham, 97
Wilmington Quay, 157
Woodbridge, 172-174
Woolpit, 102
Wormingford, 239
Bowhill, Lieutenant Frederick, RN, 41
British Army,
  Brigades,
    2nd Gloucester and Worcester Brigade, 238
    1/3rd London Brigade, Royal Field Artillery, 191
    2/3rd (South Midland) Field Artillery Brigade, 238
  Units,
    57th (West Lancashire) Divisional Cyclist Company, 179
    City of London Yeomanry, 210-211
    Essex Regiment, 52, 100, 120-121, 175, 261
    Leicestershire Royal Horse Artillery, 251
    London Regiment, 195, 221
    Loyal North Lancashire Regiment (42nd Provisional Battalion), 179
    National Guard, 53, 60
    National Reserve, 50
    Norfolk Cyclists, 251
    Norfolk Regiment, 167, 210
    Northern Cyclist Battalion, 73
    Notts and Derby Regiment (The Sherwood Foresters), 65-66

Royal Dublin Fusiliers, 91
Royal Engineers, 2, 87, 90, 270
Royal West Surrey Regiment, 253, 255
Shropshire Yeomanry, 171
Suffolk Regiment, 98
Sussex Cyclists, 81
Sussex Royal Garrison Artillery, 253
Brock, Frank, sub-Lt, RNVR (later Flt Lt, RNAS), 26, 297
Buckingham, John, 297

Calais, 13, 33, 72, 112, 116
Canadian Army,
    5th Brigade, Field Artillery, 256-257
    8th Howitzer Brigade, 256-257
Carnegie Hero Trust Fund, ix, 184, 223-224, 331 (note 14)
Central Flying School, 6, 17, 140, 317 (note 3)
Chadwick, Roy, 26, 318 (note 21)
Chatham, 15-16, 37, 39, 43, 146-148
Chattenden, 10
Churchill, Winston S. (First Lord of the Admiralty), 11-12, 15-17, 19-20, 24, 29-30, 40, 118, 137, 189, 235, 294, 331 (note 27)
Cody, Samuel Franklin, 2
Cologne, 8, 10, 17-18, 21, 23
Committee of Imperial Defence (CID), 3-4
Cuxhaven, 25, 30, 40, 159

Deal, 36-37, 92, 112, 115, 168
Duhaut, Louis Cesar (French POW), 22

Dover, 16, 32, 35-37, 39, 43, 64, 91, 115, 168, 169
Dunkirk, 13-15, 17, 19, 34, 92
Düsseldorf, 10, 17-18, 21-23, 25, 32, 41, 71

v. Falkenhayn, General Erich, 32-34, 160
Flamborough Head, 145-146, 149, 154-155
Friedrichshafen, Raid, 25, 27-30
    Zeppelin Works, 25, 26, 30

Gerrard, Maj Eugene, RMLI and RNAS, 17-19, 170
Grand Fleet (British), 40
Great Yarmouth, 45, 46, 48-49, 54, 60, 84, 178, 208-209, 230, 252
Gunpowder mills, 179-180, 237, 253-255

Handelsschiffsverkehrsbuch (H.V.B.), 90
Happisburgh, 48, 84, 252
Heligoland, 30, 40-41
Henderson, Major-General David, RFC, (Director-General of Military Aeronautics), 234, 238, 250, 295
High Seas Fleet (German), 10, 30, 32, 40, 43-45

Immingham, 12, 32, 152
v. Ingenohl, Vizeadmiral Friedrich, 32, 35, 44-45
Ingham, 48
Journalists,
    MacDonagh, Michael, 270-271

INDEX

Needham, Henry Beach, 142-143
zu Reventlow, Ernst Graf, 295
Shepherd, William G., 221, 230-231
v. Wiegand, Karl, 61, 213-214, 230, 232

Kiggell, General L.E., Director of Home Defence (War Office), 188
King's Lynn, 46, 56-57, 60, 63, 214
Kitchener, Lord, Secretary of State for War, 15, 234, 238, 250, 291, 295
Klein, Pitt (Zeppelin crewman), 224, 232, 244-247, 253, 262, 267

Lea Valley, 180, 181
Légion d'honneur, 142
Liège, 8
Lighting restrictions, 24-25, 64, 84, 97, 271
Lightships,
    Cross Sand, 178
    Galloper, 95
    Happisburgh, 209, 252
    Nore, 165
    North Goodwin, 116
    Sunk, 146
    Tongue, 112
Liverpool, 32, 43, 109, 250-251
Lodge Hill, 10
London, 19, 109, 110, 135, 136, 137, 143-144
    For air raids on, see *Bombed places - London*
    As bombing target, 31-33, 37-38, 47, 71, 118-119, 145, 149, 159, 161, 171, 178, 180, 191
    Defences of, 11, 15-16, 24-25, 43, 62, 250, 281, 286, 288-289, 290, 292, 294-295
    Restrictions on bombing of, 31, 35, 44, 45, 70, 72, 102, 103, 124, 160, 161
London Fire Brigade, 127, 129, 137, 195, 202, 220, 222, 231, 273, 275, 331 (note 14)
Longmore, Wing Commander Arthur, RNAS, 138-140
Lusitania, 109-110

Manchester, 32
Metzing, Korvettenkapitän Friedrich, 34, 213
Mühler, Alfred (Zeppelin crewman), 141-142

Northcliffe, Alfred Harmsworth Lord, 1, 2, 299

Observers (ground defences), 84, 112, 146, 167, 168, 199, 207, 237, 239, 240, 245, 250, 270, 289, 290
O'Gorman, Mervyn, (Royal Aircraft Factory), 3
Ostend, 12-14, 17, 19, 23, 33, 71, 90, 116-118, 170

Pankhurst, Sylvia, 135-136
Pemberton Billing, Noel, RNVR, 25-27, 29
Philipp, Konteradmiral Otto, 32-33, 44
v. Pohl, Admiral Hugo, 31-34, 44, 71
Pollock, sub-Lt. Guy, RNVR, 239-240
Pomeroy, John, 297
Portsmouth, 10, 15-16, 32, 43, 78

353

Press restrictions (D. notices), 122-123
Purfleet, 10, 38, 40, 205, 261, 264

Railways,
- Brighton & South Coast, 204
- Great Eastern (GER), 57, 81, 83, 131, 180, 185-186, 228, 237
- Great Western (GWR), ix, 222
- Lancashire & Yorkshire, 163
- Midland, 182
- North Eastern, ix, 76, 162

Rawlinson, Alfred, Lieutenant-Commander, RNVR, 235-237, 279, 280-282, 291-292

Riots, anti-German, 109-110, 136-137, 154

Rivers,
- Aisne, 19
- Blackwater, 84, 119, 121, 193, 255, 261
- Chelmer, 86
- Crouch, 104, 193, 255
- Debden, 95, 176, 180, 246
- Elbe, 40, 42
- Humber, 12, 32, 43, 45, 47, 54-55, 60, 79, 149-150, 152, 161-162
- Jade, 42
- Marne, 19
- Medway, 10, 12, 16, 37, 39, 43, 165
- Meuse, 18
- Orwell, 95, 175-176, 180, 246
- Ouse, 46, 162, 214
- Rhine, 21, 27, 33
- Roer, 18
- Stour, 175-176, 261
- Swale, 90-91, 166, 179
- Thames, 12, 24, 32, 37-38, 40, 43-45, 47, 64, 104, 125, 146, 165, 167, 178, 181, 196-198, 200, 205, 214, 253, 255, 261-264, 267, 269-270
- Tyne, 32, 43, 45, 60, 72, 76-78, 154-159
- Weser, 42
- Wey, 254-255

Royal Flying Corps (RFC), 6-7, 11, 37, 62, 149, 188-190, 234, 238, 241, 250, 286, 290, 294

Royal Naval Air Service (RNAS), 6-7, 10-12, 32, 35, 63, 90, 115-116, 121, 125, 134, 138, 140, 170, 234, 286, 290
- No. 1 Squadron, 140, 142

Royal Naval Volunteer Reserve (RNVR), 24, 26, 235, 239, 246, 286

Royal Navy (ships),
- HMS *Adventure*, 149
- HMS *Arethusa*, 40-42
- HMS *Empress*, 40-42
- HMS *Engadine*, 40
- HMS *Fearless*, 40
- HMS *Marshal Ney*, 156
- HMS *Patrol*, 155
- HMS *Riviera*, 40
- HMS *Undaunted*, 40-42
- HMT *Cleon* (armed trawler), 168
- HMT *Conway*, 209
- HMT *Equinox*, 168
- HMT *Kingfisher*, 180, 208
- HMT *Manx Queen*, 209
- E11 (submarine), 42

Samson, Commander Charles, RNAS, 6, 12-15, 17, 19, 20-21, 24
Santos-Dumont, Alberto (Aviation pioneer), 1, 2, 299

INDEX

Sarell, Philip (British vice-consul), 14, 15
Scarborough, 137
Scott, Admiral Sir Percy, RN, 234-237, 248, 250, 290-292, 294
Searchlights, 43, 63, 118, 158, 162, 166-168, 179, 188, 194, 238, 249-250, 252-253, 255, 269, 285-286, 290, 293
    London, 16, 24, 43, 133, 187, 191-192, 194, 199-200, 215, 218, 220-221, 224, 226-228, 232, 262, 270-271, 286, 291, 295
    Harwich/Felixstowe, 87, 176, 245
    Dover, 115, 118
Seely, Colonel J.E.B., (Under Secretary of State for War), 3
Sheerness, 37, 39, 146
Shepherd, Squadron Commander Philip, RNAS, 26-27
Siegert, Major Wilhelm, 33
Southampton, 26, 32
Special Constables, 24, 74, 100, 105, 107-108, 116, 119-120, 126, 135, 147, 152, 183-184, 202-203, 223, 227, 237-240, 244, 274, 282
Sueter, Capt Murray, RN, 3, 6, 12, 15, 24-26, 63, 118, 189, 235
Staaken, 160
Strasser, Korvettenkapitän Peter, 33-34, 44-48, 57, 79, 83, 87, 89, 110-111, 143, 145, 154, 158-159, 161, 165, 167, 171, 178, 206, 213, 250-251, 296, 297

Terschelling, 47
Tilbury, 37, 38, 147

v. Tirpitz, Großadmiral Alfred, (Navy Minister), 32, 34
Tudor, Rear Admiral Frederick, (Third Sea Lord), 16, 43
Turner, Thomas Charles (photographer), 150
Tyrwhitt, Commodore Reginald, 40-41

Vaughan-Lee, Rear-Admiral Charles, 189, 249
Victoria Cross, 142
Vlieland, 54, 61
Voluntary Aid Detachment (VAD), 100, 113, 148, 179, 211, 242

Waltham Abbey, 10, 43, 180-181, 187, 194, 237
War Office, 6-7, 11, 189, 233, 249-250, 289, 294
Weapons,
    Artillery,
        75mm 'auto-cannon', 235-236, 279, 281, 285, 291, 336-337 (note 5)
        1-pdr 'pom-pom', 10-11, 16, 24, 43, 63, 87, 104, 115, 119, 134, 152-153, 158, 168, 176, 180, 187, 205, 215, 233, 236-237, 253-255, 262, 264-265, 286
        3-inch, 20cwt, 10, 16, 24, 78, 90, 104, 119, 125, 155, 168, 169, 194, 205, 262, 270, 291, 336-337 (note 5)
        3-pdrs, 16, 43, 291, 336-337 (note 5)
        4-inch, 10, 149, 3336-337 (note 5)

355

6-pdr Hotchkiss, 16, 24, 43, 97, 104, 115, 155, 167-168, 176, 194, 199, 245, 262, 336-337 (note 5)
12-pdrs, 42
13-pdrs, 155, 199, 250, 252, 262, 264, 269, 270, 286, 289
Bombs,
   3.45-inch incendiary, 190
   Hales, 11, 22, 28, 41, 117, 190
Bullets,
   Explosive, 297-298
   Incendiary, 78, 117-118, 175, 239, 241, 264, 297, 299
Fiery Grapnel, 190-191
Grenades, 11, 115, 117, 120, 170
Lewis gun, 117, 140

Maxim gun, 37-39, 125, 152, 171, 175-176, 180, 188, 239-241, 246, 251-252, 261, 264-265, 267, 269, 286
Wilhelm II, Kaiser, 31-32, 34-35, 44, 70-72, 102, 119, 124, 131, 160-161
Winterton, 48, 168
Wireless telegraphy, 55, 89, 158-159, 288
Woolwich, 32, 43, 178-179, 198-199, 233, 236-237, 250, 261-262, 267
Woolwich Arsenal, 32, 199, 262-264

Zeebrugge, 23, 35, 39, 64, 116-117
Zeesen, 160